The Disorder of Political Inquiry

The Disorder of Political Inquiry

Keith Topper

Harvard University Press

Cambridge, Massachusetts

London, England • 2005

Library of Congress Cataloging-in-Publication Data

Topper, Keith Lewis, 1958–
The disorder of political inquiry / Keith Topper.
p. cm.
Includes bibliographical references and index.
ISBN 0–674–01678–5 (alk. paper)
1. Social sciences—Methodology.   2. Social sciences—Philosophy.
3. Political science—Methodology.   4. Political science—Philosophy.
5. Naturalism.   6. Power (Social sciences) 1. Title.

H61.T63   2005
300'.72—dc22   2004060692

For Lyle and Sam

Contents

Acknowledgments

For those who devote themselves to the life of the mind, the most pre-
cious gift of all is provided by spouses, friends, colleagues, and anonymous readers who, without any expectation of reward or recognition,
direct their extraordinary intellects to the projects of others. Having been
the beneficiary of an embarrassingly large number of such gifts, it is a
delight to express publicly my deepest gratitude to those who have lent
their time and energy to the task of clarifying, refining, rethinking, and
challenging what often seemed like a baggy monster of a project. Indeed,
these persons have been so thoroughly integral to the development of
this book that I am tempted to retract the standard disclaimer releasing
them of any responsibility for the ideas contained herein. Unfortunately,
my obstinance has occasionally exceeded my appreciation of their wise
counsel and consequently they cannot in fairness be implicated in whatever deficiencies this study may contain.

I am especially grateful to Carole Pateman, Bert Dreyfus, and the late
Richard Ashcraft, who in very different ways and over many years have
been exemplary critics and steadfast supporters of this project. All of them
have been part of it from its inception, and have provided invaluable
guidance and commentary. It is difficult to imagine what this book would
look like in the absence of their intellectual and personal friendship. I am
also deeply appreciative of Tom McCarthy and Stephen White, who provided a meticulous reading of the manuscript and many of the most
insightful criticisms of it. I am equally indebted to Roxanne Euben, who
not only read the full manuscript with great care, but also incurred in-
ordinately large phone bills discussing it. My former colleague, Dan Sabia,
provided exceptionally thoughtful commentary on virtually the entire

manuscript. Finally, I am deeply grateful to the late Pierre Bourdieu, who met with me several times while I was living in Paris, and to Richard Rorty, who has generously given his time for personal interviews.

I have also benefited considerably from friends and colleagues who regularly took time out of their busy schedules to read portions of the manuscript, to discuss in detail important aspects of the project, and/or to provide the conversation and intellectual stimulation that have sustained me over the past several years. Foremost among them are Jim Bohman, Peter Euben, Jill Frank, Bob Gooding-Williams, Clifford Geertz, Susan Herbst, Bonnie Honig, George Kateb, Cristina Lafont, Orville Lee, Rob Lipton, Brad Macdonald, Eric Massey, John Medearis, Sara Monoson, Bill Niemi, Ruth O'Brian, Dan O'Connor, Terry Pinkard, Gary Remer, Ron Rogowski, Paul Roth, John Sanbonmatsu, Charles Taylor, Miguel Vatter, Michael Wintroub, and Norton Wise. As a graduate student at UCLA, I had the rare opportunity to be a founding member of the *Strategies* reading group and editorial board, whose members provided multiple perspectives and lively debate during a formative period of intellectual development. David Case provided thoughtful and refreshingly ironic commentary on the manuscript, as well as superb assistance in editing it. Crina Archer, Matt Halling, Jeff Lordi, Brett Ommen, and Christella Roederer all provided extremely valuable research assistance. Finally, I would like to thank my colleagues in the Department of Communication Studies and Department of Political Science for their warm collegiality and exceptional support.

It has been a pleasure to work with Michael Aronson, my editor at Harvard University Press. Michael has provided several helpful suggestions regarding this project and unwavering support of it.

Progress on this book was aided by the generous financial support of several institutions and endowments. Many of the ideas in this book first took form during a year spent in Paris as part of the UCLA Paris Program in Critical Theory. The program's director, Sam Weber, should be commended for providing me and many others with the encouragement to pursue freely our ideas. At a later stage, I also benefited considerably from a National Endowment for the Humanities Summer Institute Fellowship. I am particularly grateful to the institute's co-directors, Jim Bohman and Paul Roth, for providing an ideal opportunity to think and rethink almost all of the important issues in the philosophy of the social sciences. I also want to thank Northwestern University's University Research and Grants

Committee, as well as the Alice Berline Kaplan Center for the Humanities, for grants that facilitated the completion of this project.

Portions of three previously published articles, in revised form, are used with permission: "Richard Rorty, Liberalism, and the Politics of Redescription," *American Political Science Review* 89 (December 1995): 954–965, © 1995 by the American Political Science Association; "In Defense of Disunity: Pragmatism, Hermeneutics, and the Social Sciences," *Political Theory* 26 (August 2000): 509–539, © 2000 Sage Publications, Inc.; and "Not So Trifling Nuances: Pierre Bourdieu, Symbolic Violence, and the Perversions of Democracy," *Constellations* 8 (March 2001): 30–56, © 2001 Blackwell Publishers Ltd.

Without a doubt, my greatest debts are to those members of my family who have supported and lived with this project for as long as I have. My parents, Bev Friedman and Gene Topper, have graciously supported my educational and intellectual pursuits for many years, and have had the extraordinary decency to do so even when they clearly worried about the employment prospects of anyone who used the word "epistemology" as frequently as I did. My parents-in-law, Barbara and Eric Massey, impassioned conversationalists par excellence, have also been models of kindness and generosity. An altogether different order of gratitude and thanks goes to the two people who live with me (and, by extension, this project) on a daily basis. This, I realize all too well, is not always an easy thing to do. Lyle Massey, whose love and friendship sustained this project from its earliest stages, has read every word of the book (at least once) and has commented on it with remarkable intelligence, sympathy, and imagination. Even more, her daily conduct, moral passion, and insistence that ideas be given worldly form have inspired me from the moment we became more than mere acquaintances. Without her love, patience, and generosity, this book never would have been completed. Although a more recent arrival on the scene, Sam Topper has changed my life profoundly. His unbounded imagination and sheer exuberance for life, as well as his sense of humor, encyclopedic knowledge of the Bob Dylan songbook, and willingness to engage anyone, constantly remind me of the pure visceral joys of human life itself. It is to them that I dedicate this book.

The distinctive characteristic of practical activity, one that is so inherent that it cannot be eliminated, is the uncertainty which attends it.

—JOHN DEWEY, *The Quest for Certainty*

Impossible, as one turns these pages, not to think of Maurice Merleau-Ponty's teaching and of what was for him the essential philosophical task: never to consent to being completely comfortable with one's own presuppositions. Never to let them fall peacefully asleep, but also never to believe that a new fact will suffice to overturn them; never to imagine that one can change them like arbitrary axioms, remembering that in order to give them the necessary mobility one must have a distant view, but also look at what is nearby and all around oneself. To be very mindful that everything one perceives is evident only against a familiar and little-known horizon, that every certainty is sure only through the support of a ground that is always unexplored. The most fragile instant has its roots. In that lesson, there is a whole ethic of sleepless evidence that does not rule out, far from it, a rigorous economy of the True and False; but that is not the whole story.

—MICHEL FOUCAULT, "For an Ethic of Discomfort"

Introduction: The Social Science Wars

It is a rare moment when academic controversies migrate from the class-rooms and courtyards of college and university campuses to the front pages of the *New York Times, London Observer,* and *Le Monde.* And yet in the past several years two such disputes have attracted the attention of a wider public: Alan Sokal's "hoax," published in the journal *Social Text,* and the self-named "Perestroika" movement that recently emerged within the discipline of political science. These two incidents have provoked wide interest and response precisely because each has radically disrupted the intellectual status quo, raising questions about the nature of objectivity, truth, and meaningful inquiry in the social sciences. Apart from the general disruption caused by these twin interventions, what is perhaps most striking about them is the de facto alliance forged between an otherwise unlikely pair of principals. That is, starting from what might appear to be diametrically opposed analytical perspectives and advancing sharply different proposals for reform and renewal, Sokal and the author of the Perestroika memo, identified (perhaps erroneously) as Mr. Perestroika, are nonetheless joined in their conviction that scholarship in the social sciences is presently in a state of deep crisis. Like two competing versions of the Fall, they converge on what they identify as disciplinary degeneration, even as they disagree vehemently about its causes and the road to salvation. In short, these two events describe the stakes and delimit the boundaries of a sustained conflict best described as the "social science wars."

This book analyzes and clarifies these recent controversies about competing modes and models of political and social inquiry, the nature of political and social knowledge, and the present and future state of political

1

and social science—what it is and might be. As families of inquiry that have singly and collectively struggled to rebut Michel Foucault's unflattering depiction of them as "dubious disciplines," the social sciences are today in the uncomfortable position of negotiating a series of increasingly intense and confusing disputes about the ontological foundations, epistemological status, and practical relevance of their inquiries. These conflicts, which often take the form of battling dichotomies or binary oppositions, are animated by seemingly irreconcilable views of the proper goals, methodological approaches, and self-image of social and political inquiry. The general character of these controversies—that is, the key assumptions and objectives that animate them and the cleavages they reflect and sustain—reveal what is at stake in this struggle to define the relationship of science to social and political life.

Social Science Wars I

On May 18, 1996, Alan Sokal, a theoretical physicist at New York University, and the editors of *Social Text,* a journal of cultural studies, became at once public celebrities and potential casualties in the latest round of the science wars. Although the very fact of this newfound celebrity was astonishing in its own right, its cause was even more remarkable. By his own account disturbed by "an apparent decline in the standards of rigor in certain precincts of the academic humanities" and "the spread of subjectivist thinking"[1] more generally, Sokal set out to test this conjecture by devising a rather unusual "experiment." Writing an article about the cultural and political implications of recent developments in quantum physics that simultaneously mimicked poststructuralist and postmodernist literary conventions and was generously peppered with erroneous claims and tongue-in-cheek remarks identifiable as such to any undergraduate math or physics major, Sokal submitted his parody for publication in *Social Text.* As Sokal himself describes his now notorious experiment: "Would a leading North American journal of cultural studies —whose editorial collective includes such luminaries as Frederic Jameson and Andrew Ross—publish an article liberally salted with nonsense if it (a) sounded good and (b) flattered the editors' ideological preconceptions? The answer, unfortunately, is yes."[2]

In a special issue of *Social Text* titled none other than "Science Wars," the editors—apparently oblivious to Sokal's errors and jokes and perhaps all too eager to legitimate their own views with the imprimatur of a "hard" scientist—obliged Sokal by unwittingly publishing as serious scholarship his sham, jargon-infested article.[3] After Sokal revealed his hoax in an essay published three weeks later in the journal *Lingua Franca*, the editors of *Social Text* quickly found themselves in the wholly unexpected position of being targeted by their own presumed ally, recipients as it were of not-so-friendly fire.

At first glance, "Sokal's Hoax," as it has become known, would seem an odd candidate for media saturation. Certainly Sokal's prank spotlighted dramatically the virtues of peer review and the obligation of editors of academic journals, whether peer reviewed or not, to consult scholars who know something about the subject matter under review before making editorial decisions about it. Moreover, as a Swiftian satire of one form of insular and inflated academic discourse, Sokal's intervention can be credited with exposing (if admittedly not for the first time) a real issue, namely, that of the relationship between academic and public discourse. In itself, however, this would hardly seem to account for the flaming rhetoric and fierce debate, in both the public and academic press, provoked by Sokal's Hoax. Indeed, when one looks for its larger meaning and significance, consensus seems to recede like an object nearing its vanishing point. Did Sokal's parody, as one journalist alleged, call "into question the intellectual standards of the whole field [of cultural studies]?"[4] Or did it, as the literary theorist (and then executive editor of Duke University Press, which publishes *Social Text*) Stanley Fish maintained, involve an act of intellectual fraud, one that was likely to further deplete the precarious fund of trust on which all scientific and intellectual inquiry depends?[5] Did it, as another journalist claimed, "prove that postmodern American academia is a banana republic?"[6] Or did it, as the historian and philosopher of science Evelyn Fox Keller worried, threaten to demonize the misunderstood field of science studies, thereby further obscuring the legitimate reasons why scholars in that field have drawn on "postmodernist theory" in the first place?[7] Did it, as the physicist Steven Weinberg asserted, serve an important "public purpose, to attract attention ... to a decline of standards of rigor in the academic community?"[8] Or did it, as the sociologist of science Bruno Latour charged, represent "the last acrobatics of Cold War science," with its attendant search for a "new menace" that could halt the precipitous declines in funding for theoretical physics in a post–Cold War world?[9] Did it go "to the heart of debate over left-wing scholarship?"[10] Or, as the historian Ellen Schrecker surmised, did Sokal's effort to rescue the integrity of the "real physical world" naively ignore the "real political" world into which it was launched, in effect fueling conservative attacks on both the "entire academy" and the "public sector," and thereby undermining the progressive ideals the hoax was intended to advance?[11] Or, finally, was the hoax nothing more than media hype—journalists delighting in the spectacle of highbrow academics savaging one another over the supposedly ridiculous question of whether the real world exists?

Whatever the larger public reaction to the Sokal affair, Sokal himself was quite unequivocal in articulating his own understanding of the broader meaning and implications of his act. Conceding at the outset that "the mere fact that the parody was published proves little in itself; at most it reveals something about the intellectual standards of *one* trendy journal,"[12] Sokal held that his purpose was nonetheless both epistemological and "explicitly *political*":[13] to expose certain fashionable forms of irrationalism and epistemic relativism as incoherent and vacuous, and to combat the spread of these pathological ideas to various sectors of the "American academic Left."[14] In Sokal's view, these purposes were intimately connected. The abandonment of Enlightenment commitments to reason, logic, argument, and evidence, as well as the corresponding embrace of "fashionable postmodernist/poststructuralist/social-constructivist discourse," are, Sokal alleges, not only epistemologically misconceived but also "inimical to the values and future of the Left."[15] In addition to highlighting the presumed political implications of epistemic relativism, however, Sokal located within the academy precisely those precincts where the dangers of infection were most acute. Asserting that "the natural sciences have little to fear, at least in the short run, from postmodern silliness," Sokal urged that "it is, above all, history and the social sciences . . . that suffer when verbal game-playing displaces the rigorous analysis of social realities."[16]

Insisting on the linkage between epistemology and politics, Sokal also identified the historical and social sciences as the fields of inquiry most vulnerable to the corrosive effects of epistemic relativism. By his own account, Sokal hoped to open a "dialogue" about the relationship between science and social inquiry, between epistemology and human emancipation. For many scholars in the social sciences, this invitation may have seemed rather dated. Controversies about these issues have, after all, been raging for several decades. And while debates about the relationship between postmodern theory, social inquiry, and social criticism are more recent, they too have been discussed extensively in the literatures of philosophy and social theory over the past few decades. More important, however sincere Sokal's motivations may have been, his ambition to rescue social science from fashionable forms of irrationalism tended to subvert rather than establish the conditions on which any meaningful dialogue might be built. Indeed, while extolling the virtues of objectivity, Sokal all too often misrepresented the views of those he ridiculed.[17] While insisting on the importance of empirical evidence, he frequently failed to provide it.[18] While deploring as "fashionable nonsense" postmodern and poststructural abuses of scientific concepts and theories, Sokal ignored the possibility that some of that nonsense might be due to his own interpretive blindnesses rather than his opponents confusions and lapses.[19] In short, Sokal's desire to initiate a dialogue was compromised by his own epistemic, interpretive, and rhetorical practices, practices that, whatever their intent, often evinced many of the errors his parody was designed to expose and condemn. In so doing, Sokal, like the authors of *Higher Superstition* and other less temperate polemics against postmodernist, social constructivist, and feminist students of science, dissolved complex problems of scientific inquiry into apocalyptic oppositions between imperiled scientists and rapidly advancing brigades of anti-science ideologists.[20]

This missed opportunity was unfortunate. However amusing spectators may find these long and inflammatory volleys of charges and counter-charges, the exchanges themselves are inherently unproductive. Moreover, questions about the meaning of science; about the relationship between the natural and social sciences; about the standards appropriate for the evaluation of social and scientific research; and about the alleged connections between science, social criticism, and social change may, like the return of the repressed, be ignored, disregarded, or silenced but are unlikely to disappear.

Social Science Wars II

Recently, a related debate from within the academy has again migrated to the pages of major newspapers and magazines such as the *New York Times*, the *Guardian*, and the *New Republic*.[21] This new debate, however, shifts Sokal's opposition between Enlightenment reason and postmodern relativism. This time the catalyst was not an assault on epistemic relativism but instead an Internet-fueled protest within the field of political science against the alleged "domination and control" of the discipline and its institutions—its journals, associations, and fellowship committees—by an entrenched "coterie" of methodologically like-minded scholars. Spurred by an anonymous e-mail message sent initially to seventeen sympathizers but quickly forwarded to hundreds of colleagues, Mr. Perestroika, as the author (or authors) of the initial memo referred to himself, decried the methodological colonization of the discipline and its most widely circulated publication outlet—the *American Political Science Review*—by "statisticians," "game theorists," and others whose work focused narrowly on technical methods rather than on salient political issues. Charging that this domination made the champions of methodological diversity an increasingly endangered species, Mr. Perestroika further asserted that the methodological purification of the field, along with the absence of internal democracy within the principal professional association of political scientists, the American Political Science Association, had a number of baleful consequences: it narrowed the scope and diminished the quality of work on political issues, it alienated many of the most creative minds in the field, and it operated to police and discipline younger scholars whose employment and tenure prospects depended upon publication in high-profile journals that were increasingly methodologically monistic.[22]

Like Sokal's manifestos, the Perestroika manifesto asserts that the academic study of society and politics is deeply imperiled. Also like Sokal, the Perestroika movement places questions of rigor, science, and methodology at the center of this crisis. However, in a remarkable transposition, the very terms of analysis are implicitly reconfigured, placed in an alternative constellation of questions, and set on a new and more unstable orbit. For Perestroika's supporters, "rigor" is not primarily a matter of whether academic scholarship should be accountable to high intellectual standards. They agree that of course it should be. The central issues, rather, involve how those standards of rigor are conceived, by whom and through what processes they are defined and authorized, and what (or whose) ends they serve.[23] More generally, many supporters of Perestroika wonder whether a single conception of rigor, defined once and for all and in abstraction from any engagement with concrete social or political problems, makes the study of social and political life more or less "rigorous"—whether, in short, it contributes to increased rigor or to intellectual rigor mortis. Given the extraordinary range and complexity of problems influencing the social and political world, might not a certain degree of methodological pluralism, thoughtful division of labor, and multidimensional inquiry be appropriate?[24]

Just as the Perestroika protesters demand that hegemonic notions of rigor be rethought, they also insist that dominant understandings of science and methodology be recast. Indeed, if Sokal feared that the virus of postmodern relativism represented the principal threat to the intellectual vitality and integrity of the social sciences, the Perestroika revolt implies that the most virulent contagions are not epistemic relativism but methodological monism and epistemological absolutism. Asserting that a misplaced formalism and mathematicization is partly, if not largely, responsible for the notorious failure of Anglophone political scientists to either predict or anticipate the breathtaking disintegration of the Soviet Empire, the Perestroika manifesto advocates a recognition of "diverse knowledges and methodologies"[25]: "political history, institutional history, political sociology, interpretive methodology, constructivists [sic], area studies, critical history, and last but not the least—postmodernism."[26] In short, Perestroika's supporters hold that it is precisely the a priori conflation of science and methodology with formal and quantitative methods that lies at the heart of the current crisis in the study of politics.

Finally, the Perestroika manifesto sketches—without explicitly articulating—a view of the relationship between epistemology and politics that at once accepts Sokal's proposition that the two are intimately related and rejects his conception of that relationship and the causal claim that informs it. Rather than maintaining that epistemological reform is the principal vehicle of political emancipation, Mr. Perestroika posits that political emancipation, in the form of genuinely open, inclusive, and democratic institutional arrangements, is the principal vehicle of epistemological reform. In other words, if Sokal argues that relativist epistemologies need to be supplanted and that doing so will produce a paradigm change in the study and practice of politics, Mr. Perestroika suggests instead that inequities of power and anti-democratic political structures within the discipline of political science need to be supplanted and that this will produce a paradigm change in epistemology. Not incidentally, these changes may also yield theories that better address the asymmetries of power in the societies that social and political scientists purport to explain and understand.

Debating the Foundations of Political Science

Although the Perestroika manifesto has provoked much discussion among members of various alienated constituencies within political science, it is thus far unclear to what extent it will succeed in initiating a broader conversation within the discipline as a whole about many of the questions it raised regarding the nature of political inquiry. Indeed, for some time there has been a growing sense of anxiety about the appropriate methods of social and political inquiry, the relationship between the social sciences and the natural sciences, and the meaning and implications of fealty to the scientific enterprise. In presidential addresses, commission reports, conference themes, and roundtables, worries have been voiced about whether political and social science is too unified or too fragmented, too much like the natural sciences or too unlike the natural sciences, too pre-occupied with the development of general and formal theories or too indifferent to such ambitions. Unfortunately, these concerns are often, like the Perestroika memo itself, expressed in very general or anecdotal terms, and are rarely joined to detailed analysis.[27] As a result, there are surprisingly few recent efforts within political science to explore systematically the key presuppositions animating these debates, to develop philosophically and empirically informed conceptions of the appropriate forms of social and political inquiry, and to map the social role that social science can and should presently play. In part, this failure may be a consequence of recent developments in the academy and the world. Taken jointly, these developments have converged to deprive students of social inquiry of even the few reliable landmarks and stable assumptions that constituted a common starting point from which debates about social inquiry could proceed.

Within the academy, the demise of positivist orthodoxies and the concomitant rise of various "postempiricist" histories, sociologies, and philosophies of science have unsettled the one shared understanding around which many of the above disputes pivoted, namely, the understanding of natural scientific practice. During most of the twentieth century, whether one defended a positivist or hermeneutical or critical conception of social inquiry, whether one endorsed naturalism or anti-naturalism, or whether one advanced a value-neutral conception of social explanation grounded in general laws and theories or a value-laden, ideographic view of social understanding based on practices of interpretation, all agreed that the standard positivist account of scientific explanation accurately described (or at a minimum rationally reconstructed) the epistemic practices of the "hard" sciences. Over the past few decades, however, this consensus has disintegrated. Often working in different disciplines and to very different ends, disparate postempiricist studies of science[28] not only have chiseled away at the assumptions and distinctions that formed the cornerstone of positivism but have gone even further, attacking all idealized, mechanical, rule-governed, or strictly deductive pictures of scientific activity—what Thomas Kuhn famously calls the "textbook" image of science, or what others call the "received" view of science—pictures conceived in abstraction from a detailed examination of the history and practice of ongoing scientific inquiry.[29] Against these images, recent students of science like Peter Galison, Nancy Cartwright, Ian Hacking, Arthur Fine, Donna Haraway, John Dupré, Norton Wise, and Andrew Pickering foreground the complexities, exigencies, and intrinsic messiness of the scientific enterprise, emphasizing how intricately interwoven and laboriously produced is the fabric of even the most advanced sciences.

Alternatively, within the world, the dramatic and unpredicted collapse of the communist regimes of Eastern and Central Europe, the ascendence of new forms and dynamics of globalization, the entrance onto the political stage of new political agents, the growing prominence of cross-cultural and intersocietal relations and conflicts, and the development of increasingly complex forms of power relationships (with the velvet glove of computer terminals, data banks, and Foucauldian self-monitoring taking its place beside the Orwellian image of a boot on a human face) have all conspired to escalate confusion about the proper methods of political analysis. This, in turn, has produced new fault lines around which epistemological and methodological conflicts in the social sciences are organized. Indeed, these new social science wars not only cut orthogonally across the boundaries and alliances that defined previous conflicts, they are also astonishingly pervasive, affecting not only political science but every domain of social inquiry.

Moreover, among scholars' investigations of political science's methodological and theoretical foundations, almost all fall into one of two

categories. First, there are studies that focus exclusively on a single methodological approach such as rational choice theory, critical theory, or
postmodernism, and, second, there are disciplinary histories that chronicle the development of disciplinary anxieties and crises.[30] Although both
approaches have proved valuable for understanding particular dimensions
of contemporary anxieties, each is limited by its own self-imposed par-
ameters. On the one hand, studies of a single methodology may yield a
better understanding of the value and limitations of that methodology,
but by definition such studies are ill-equipped to provide more comprehensive and comparative assessments of disparate methodological approaches and the relationships between them. Disciplinary histories, on
the other hand, may cast considerable light on the historical, intellectual,
and political dynamics that have shaped present crises, and thus may
provide a necessary compass for moving beyond them. Such histories,
however, rarely attempt to chart a course out of them.

Sciences of Uncertainty

By contrast, this project encompasses a third category of investigation,
one that focuses neither on a single method nor on a disciplinary history
per se. The point of this book is instead to examine these debates through
a rigorous and philosophically grounded examination of the conflicted
and contested ontological and epistemological foundations of social scientific inquiry. I maintain that this will not only provide a context in
which current debates about methodology can be better understood; it
will also yield specific proposals for transcending them. The Perestroika
movement offers a new opportunity to examine questions regarding the
nature of science in social scientific inquiry. My project here is to forge
a middle ground in which the distinctiveness of human self-fashioning
and self-interpretation is not forsaken in favor of a narrowly conceived
understanding of scientific analysis. That is, rather than shutting down
discourse, as has been the perhaps unintended but nevertheless very real
consequence of Sokal's approach, I hope to open a genuine "dialogue"
about the relationship between science and social inquiry, between knowledge and the betterment of the human condition.

The questions I pose in this book should be familiar to most students
of social and political inquiry. Indeed, they are among the most venerable
and disputed questions in all of social science. First, I explore the doctrine

of naturalism, that is, the "unity-of-science" thesis, and, more specifically, the claim that theoretical and empirical advances in the study of social and political life will be forthcoming only if students of social and political inquiry imitate the methods, or more exactly the *method,* characteristic of the advanced physical sciences.[31] In some respects, the impulse animating this view dates back to Thomas Hobbes's notorious ambition to enlist the resources of mathematics and the new sciences in the quest for a wholesale reconstruction of social and political thought, one that would finally yield certain knowledge about the basis of social and political order. More recently, however, questions about the methodological unification of science have centered on disputes about one or another model of scientific explanation—whether that model is conceived broadly, as something like a commitment to the covering law model of explanation, or more narrowly, as loyalty to a particular method or methodology (for example, rational choice theory). In either case, controversies about the unity-of-science thesis have typically branched into disputes between those who defend some version of *methodological monism,* that is, the view that there is one proper method for studying both physical nature and social phenomena, and those who champion *methodological autonomy,* namely, the doctrine that the methods appropriate to the study of social life are distinct from those characteristic of the natural sciences, and/or *methodological pluralism,* which denies methodological monism.

Second, I examine questions about the proper forms of social and political inquiry. Historically, debates about the "logic" of social scientific inquiry emerge with the rise of the German historical school in the nineteenth century and its revolt against Hegel's speculative philosophy. Arguing that "historical understanding had to begin with a recognition of its own historicity,"[32] writers such as J. G. Droysen, Leopold von Ranke, and Wilhelm Dilthey drew on practices of textual interpretation to refute the unificationist program of Auguste Comte and to assert the methodological autonomy of historical and social inquiry. For most of the twentieth century, debates about the logic of social inquiry have been structured around the distinction between explanation *(erklären)* and understanding *(verstehen),* and attendant iterations of this distinction by the advocates of the deductive-nomological model of scientific explanation, such as Carl Hempel, and representatives of various hermeneutical and neo-Wittgensteinian positions, such as Hans-Georg Gadamer and Peter Winch.

Third, I investigate the relationship between political science and political practice. Like the previous two questions, this matter also has a long and disputed legacy. As historians of the discipline have shown, political science has been consumed with recurring identity crises almost since its initial appearance on American soil during the latter part of the nineteenth century. While generally agreed that the mission of the discipline was to facilitate intervention in political affairs—in this sense, political science was never conceived as a purely theoretical science—disputes have persisted about the proper mode of intervention and the forms of knowledge and understanding required for it. Should political scientists jettison the imperatives of ethical neutrality and model their discipline along Jeffersonian lines, conceiving of the vocation of the political scientist in a democracy as a normative one charged with the responsibility of educating citizens in the ethos of democracy? Or, perhaps less sanguine about the intellectual and moral capacities of democratic citizens, should they adopt a more Wilsonian model, one that regards political science as an instrument in the service of the administrative state and political scientists as educators and handmaids—or *Staatslehre,* to borrow the more evocative German term—of a scientifically trained and committed administrative elite?[33] Should political science constitute its identity through imitation, looking to other disciplines—such as history, economics, biology, or physics—for its collective imaginary? Or should it proceed in a more independent and inner-directed fashion, forging its own distinctive identity out of struggle with its particular subject matter and the problems it poses?

Fourth, I analyze questions about the relationship between power and method. This too is an issue with a long history, dating at least to Hobbes and Descartes, both of whom pictured method as a form of power and thus initiated the modern preoccupation with method. My concern, however, is primarily with a set of contemporary questions about the ways in which particular methodological commitments enable or constrain one's capacity to identify and act upon opaque power relations that sustain forms of domination. While these concerns are usually articulated in the context of debates about the multiple "faces of power," my aim is to "test" these modes of inquiry by exploring the dimensions of power they reveal or conceal. Since power is often considered the conceptual core of any account of politics, it is also a particularly convenient standard for assessing the value and limitations of disparate modes of social and political inquiry.

Proceeding in what might loosely be called a dialogical fashion, this book proposes answers to these questions by drawing on and rethinking the relationship between four postempiricist views of social and political science—pragmatism, hermeneutics, critical realism, and poststructuralism. While all four of these philosophies are joined in resistance to the absolutist and foundationalist pretensions of logical empiricism, and more specifically to the legacies of scientism and classical empiricism in social inquiry, they are also typically pictured as adversarial models of social science. Indeed, in standard textbook accounts and in the narratives presented by many of their preeminent representatives, these perspectives are plotted as paired dichotomies and oppositions. This device is so common even among those purporting to eschew it that it may sometimes appear as if a particularly sinister form of the cunning of reason is at work, one that inconspicuously reconstitutes oppositions at the very moment in which a writer announces emancipation from them. Thus Richard Rorty, deploying the resources of American pragmatism to circumvent and redescribe standard oppositions between "Galilean" and "hermeneutical" social science, ultimately does so only by first constructing an equally misconceived opposition of his own, this time between pragmatism, on the one hand, and hermeneutics and realism, on the other (see chapters 1 and 2). Similarly, Roy Bhaskar declares at the outset of his influential book *The Possibility of Naturalism*, his intention to overcome the "polarized" disputes between two traditions, a naturalist tradition founded on positivist principles and an anti-naturalist tradition grounded in commitments of hermeneutical or interpretative social science. Yet Bhaskar's own effort to transcend this opposition is parasitic on the construction of another opposition, now between critical realism, on the one hand, and hermeneutics, pragmatism, and poststructuralism, on the other (see chapter 4).

Working from the supposition that these oppositions often reveal less about the world than about the analyst's desire to impose order on it, this book reconceives standard understandings of social and political inquiry in two ways. First, rather than following conventional accounts of the relationships between pragmatism, hermeneutics, critical realism, and poststructuralism, I challenge them. Pursuing a more ecumenical line of argument, I sketch an account of social and political inquiry that foregrounds the links rather than oppositions between pragmatist, hermeneutical, realist, and poststructuralist views. My account is *pragmatist* in its rejection of the foundationalist idea that inquiry can be grounded in a bedrock of language- or interpretation-free access to physical or social reality; in its insistence on viewing inquiry as an open, fallible, communal, and evolutionary process; in its foregrounding of social practice as the object of inquiry and the standard by which inquiries are judged; and in its latitudinarian conception of science as an extension, refinement, and "intensification of the usual methods"[34] of reflection. It is *hermeneutical* in its defense of an ontological and methodological distinction between the natural and social sciences, in its demand that internal understanding constitute the necessary starting point of any adequate social and political inquiry, and in its accent on the indispensability of interpretation in the study of human and social affairs. It is *critical realist* in its aim of integrating the often segregated discourses of hermeneutical understanding and causal explanation and in its effort to redeem a normative and critical conception of social and political science. Finally, it is *poststructuralist* in its recognition of and attentiveness to the inescapable impurities of reason; in its reflexive insistence that, as social practices, the epistemic practices of social science (and the forms of knowledge they yield) must themselves be understood in their specific social, political, and cultural contexts; and in its focus on embodied subjectivity rather than atomistic, disengaged Cartesian conceptions of the subject.[35]

Second, this book reconfigures standard understandings of social and political inquiry by attending more directly to its peculiar nature and the practical challenges it presents. Through the articulation of an alternative account of ontology and method in political science, I sketch a view of political inquiry as a "science of uncertainty."[36] In so doing, I aim to liberate the term "science" from conventional associations with concepts like certainty, unity, and strict determinism. Rather than banishing agency, contingency, ambiguity, and judgment from the study of political life, I take them as its premise. Ultimately, I picture science as a disunified, multivocal, *and* rigorous activity. Moreover, a science of politics conceived in this manner is fundamentally political in a double sense of the word. First, it is political in its aim of informing reflective judgment by elucidating the possibilities and constraints that constitute the horizons of, and give purpose to, political deliberation and action. Second, it is political in its recognition of the inescapably power-laden dimensions of all efforts to define the ontology of the political, that is, what politics is or can be. Glimpses of this recast conception of political inquiry can be found throughout the book but are crystalized in chapter 5, which explores Pierre Bourdieu's political sociology, or sociology of power. Here I bring together a number of different strands of argument, contending that although Bourdieu's "fieldwork in philosophy"[37] has received virtually no attention within political science, its distinctive way of crisscrossing, reconfiguring, and even dissolving many of the boundaries and dualisms constitutive of postwar political theory and science in the United States makes it a particularly valuable source of clues for overcoming tensions both within political theory and between political theory and the discipline of political science. Most important, Bourdieu's articulation of the links between symbolic, institutional, and mental structures provides students of politics with an account of power that contrasts simultaneously with those articulated in the "three faces of power" debate and with those of Foucauldian poststructuralism.

While the final chapter provides one exemplar of a kind of social and political inquiry that integrates rather than segregates the normative and the empirical, theory and research, philosophy and science, constructivism and realism, the earlier chapters, working through detailed investigations of writers such as Rorty, Bhaskar, Bourdieu, Charles Taylor, and Hannah Arendt, develop the arguments about politics and science that constitute the platform from which the final chapter proceeds. Of the five chapters, chapters 1–3 investigate aspects of Rorty's work, although not as an end-in-itself, but rather as a vehicle for exploring a specific set of questions about anti-foundationalist, pragmatist, and postmodernist views of scientific inquiry. It is important to note that Rorty is not only one of the most influential champions of these approaches to social inquiry, he is also one of the only contemporary representatives to articulate detailed accounts of natural science (chapter 1), social science (chapter 2), politics (chapter 3), and the relationship between them (chapter 3). Moreover, as a writer who expresses his views with rare clarity, candor, and wit, Rorty is an almost ideal medium for exploring the value and limits of such approaches.

Chapter 1 examines Rorty's "postmetaphysical" views of science and society. Focusing on his accounts of language, incommensurability, and theory change in natural science, it navigates a position that defends Rorty's premise, namely, that there is no language- or interpretation-free access to physical nature or the social world, yet denies his conclusion, that is, that natural scientific terms and theories can never represent, in better or worse terms, physical nature. Accordingly, I argue that Rorty's position is based on the illicit assumption that realism and representationalism presuppose foundationalism. Drawing on recent literature in the history of science, I defend a nonfoundationalist realism that accents the *disunity* of the scientific enterprise. Indeed, I contend that far from tarnishing the integrity of science, disunity is central to its strength and stability. Among other things, this account undercuts standard versions of the unity-of-science thesis, implying as it does that any authentic imitation of the natural sciences by the social sciences would entail not the unification but the disunification of social science.

Chapter 2 assesses Rorty's view of social science, exploring his endorsement of pragmatist "therapies" as alternatives to stale philosophical debates about social scientific method. Challenging both his specific proposals and his broader reconstruction of debates between the advocates of hermeneutics and the proponents of the covering law model of social science, I contend that Rorty misinterprets the tenets and arguments of hermeneutical writers such as Charles Taylor and Hubert Dreyfus. Indeed, I hold that Rorty himself unwittingly manifests metaphysical commitments anathema to his own postmetaphysical ethos. Inverting Rorty's claims, I conclude that the arguments adduced by writers like Taylor and Dreyfus not only are sound but also are the progeny of precisely the sort of pragmatic and historiographic reflection that Rorty endorses but fails to employ. The problem, therefore, is not, as Rorty holds, that hermeneutical social science is an anachronistic relic of the metaphysical tradition and thus opposed to pragmatism, but rather that Rorty's pragmatism is deeply unpragmatist.

Chapter 3 brings together the prior discussions of Rorty by linking his political theory to his epistemological and methodological positions. Focusing on his efforts to "redescribe" the familiar rationalist and natural rights vocabularies of liberalism in nonmetaphysical terms, I reveal the political consequences of his epistemological position. In short, I argue that Rorty's misconceived philosophy of science yields a political ideal— his "liberal utopia"—that not only fails to engage urgent questions of power, domination, and exclusion, but cannot do so. Methodologically and conceptually unable to engage in social structural analysis, Rorty's alternative not only neglects but precludes radical criticism.

Chapter 4 explores a second response to the most recent crisis in social science, namely, Roy Bhaskar's "critical realism." This view, which brings questions of ontology to the very center of debates about the nature and aims of science, has gained wide purchase among philosophers of natural science. Recently, however, many prominent political theorists have also championed it. What attracts them to realism, and Bhaskar's views specifically, is its claim to offer an alternative to the foundationalist and conventionalist/postmodernist epistemologies that have dominated recent debates about social inquiry. Moreover, Bhaskar's thought is distinguished by an effort to fuse a realist account of scientific explanation with a larger critical and emancipatory impulse. Thus, rather than viewing scientific explanation as a value-neutral enterprise, Bhaskar conceives of social and political inquiry as explanatory and liberating, scientific and normative. Although sympathetic with important elements of this approach, I contend that Bhaskar misconstrues key implications of his project as well as its relation to other theoretical positions, like hermeneutics. In particular, I hold that Bhaskar is insufficiently attentive to the diversity of positions within the hermeneutical tradition and consequently fails to notice both important points of agreement and the real bases of disagreement between many hermeneutical thinkers and his own conception of critical realism. In sum, I argue that far from being a sharp opponent of critical realism, hermeneutical social science complements and buttresses many of its central commitments.

Chapter 5 sketches a final approach to political inquiry, one that is empirically rigorous, yet deeply attuned to the complex interplay between power, knowledge, and interpretation. To this end, I draw on the work of sociologist Pierre Bourdieu. Like critical realists, Bourdieu brings causal and interpretive investigations together, exploring agents' own self-understandings and the mechanisms through which social order is reproduced or transformed. Like the representatives of American pragmatism and hermeneutics, Bourdieu explores the limitations of formal thought and exhibits a concern with fashioning modes of analysis that remain true to the idiosyncracies and messy uncertainties of political life. Unlike many pragmatists and hermeneuticists, however, Bourdieu displays an acute attentiveness to power and power relations. Through the development of his theory of the "social field" and especially his notion of *habitus* (a system of "durable dispositions," into which human beings are socialized, which makes possible and regulates practical activity, while also sustaining and reinforcing the social field that governs that activity), Bourdieu analyzes the enduring structures that make social life possible, as well as the contingent practices that sustain and transform those structures. Most important, his detailed case studies highlight the manner in which power and "symbolic violence" operate, both objectively and subjectively. By exposing the inadvertent ways that relations of domination are perpetuated and legitimated in both everyday life and social and political institutions, Bourdieu explores and brings together the micro-politics of everyday life and the macro-politics of institutional silencing and exclusion. Moreover, by elucidating the operation of "gentle" and inconspicuous relationships of power, Bourdieu politicizes ostensibly "nonpolitical" domains and relationships, thus displaying the inherently political nature of political theory and science. Like sociology, political science at its best is a science that disturbs, disorders, and troubles ("une science qui dérange"[38]).

I conclude by returning to the central issues raised by the Perestroika controversy. Here I explain in detail the ways in which my arguments both elucidate and transform ongoing controversies about methodological monism and methodological pluralism, the status of "hegemonic" methodologies, and the question of naturalism. Analyzing enduring and recent questions of democratic theory and practice, I show the value and limitations of statistical and rational choice research, as well as the vital importance of "critical pluralism" in political inquiry. At the same time, these concluding reflections further clarify the double meaning of "disorder" alluded to in the title of this book. On the one hand, the disorder of political inquiry refers to the often expressed view that political inquiry today is in a state of acute decomposition, decay, and disrepair, and therefore requires systematic reordering. On the other hand, it refers to a central thesis of this book, namely, that disorder in political inquiry is not necessarily something to be feared, repressed, repelled, or expunged. That is, when conceived neither as a chaos of the multiple, nor as a weary recognition of a discipline forever divided into isolated or warring sects, but instead as an active commitment to practices of critical pluralism and modes of constrained disunity, disordered political inquiry may be a positive and even indispensable source of dynamism and renewal.

These final chapters, along with the earlier ones, thus provide a clearer perspective on Sokal's and Mr. Perestroika's two stories of decline and redemption. I suggest that the current "crisis" of political and social science is in part self-fabricated. To the extent that students of political activity misconceive the nature of their subject matter and the relationships between different modes of inquiry, they set for themselves goals they cannot achieve and sustain crises they cannot overcome. The unsurprising result is a profound sense of disciplinary unease and disarray, if not chaos. If, however, one understands better why political science has never been and is not likely to become a "normal" science in Kuhn's strict sense of the term, then it may be possible to begin undertaking substantive inquiries into pressing questions of political life that are grounded in an understanding of the distinctive (and distinctively unstable) ontology of that life.

— 1 —

Science Turned Upside Down

As I noted in the introduction, earlier debates about the methodological unification of science pivoted around the question of whether the human sciences could be transformed into objective sciences. With both the advocates and opponents of a unified science agreeing that the astonishing successes of the physical sciences issued from their possession of theory- and context-independent criteria for choosing between alternative hypotheses and theories, the central issue was whether such criteria could be productively applied in the human sciences. The champions of naturalism contended that they could, maintaining that through a radical transformation of language—that is, a shift from an inherently imprecise, value-laden ordinary language into a precise, intersubjective, and value-free scientific language—the human sciences could finally become objective sciences. Their adversaries, also viewing language as the lynchpin of the debate, inverted these very arguments. Holding that in the human sciences language and human reality are mutually imbricated, anti-naturalists concluded that efforts to explain human activity in a value-free language necessarily distorted the reality it purported to explain.

In addition to their shared image of natural science and preoccupation with questions of language, the proponents of naturalism and their rivals converged on a third issue, namely, the appropriateness of conceiving both the aims and success of the natural sciences specifically in terms of representationalist models of knowledge. That is, both parties agreed not only that natural science progressed (at some level this could hardly be denied), but also that it did so through scientists' ability to close systematically the epistemic gap between their "inner," mental representations of nature and an "external," mind-independent, natural world that those representations sought to "mirror." By carefully assembling a body of neutral, "pretheoretical" observations that would serve to arbitrate between alternative representations of nature, natural scientists, it was argued, slowly but inexorably corrected distorted representations, dispensed with erroneous theories, and thereby insured an unbroken accumulation of reliable knowledge about physical nature. This capacity to "test" and "confirm" independently alternative representations of physical reality, and by extension systematically to overcome errors of representation, was, they believed, the cornerstone of modern natural science.

In this chapter I will discuss a line of thought that shares earlier writers' preoccupation with questions of language, yet rejects both their image of natural science and their commitment to a representationalist construal of knowledge. This line of thought has perhaps been most fully developed in Richard Rorty's writings over the past few decades. It is, however, also found in some of Mary Hesse's essays and in the work of those associated with the "strong programme" in the sociology of knowledge. What unites these otherwise disparate thinkers is a firm conviction that representationalist models of science are unnecessary, self-deceptive, and perhaps pernicious as well. Such models, they argue, rest on a mistaken view of the natural sciences, one that holds that such sciences are somehow less "interpretive" and "subjective" than the human sciences. Against this view, the representatives of "universal hermeneutics" argue that problems of translation, or of the "theory-ladenness" of observational descriptions and statements, are as nettlesome and ubiquitous in the physical sciences as they are in the human sciences. The anti-naturalist attack on the unity of science thesis thus collapses not because the natural sciences possess some external, intersubjective criteria of verification, criteria that can and should be applied to the study of human activity as well, but rather because no such criteria exist even in the physical sciences. As Charles Taylor, in a passage conveying both the drama and irony of this transformation, notes, "This is an extraordinary reversal. Old-guard Diltheyans, their shoulders hunched from years-long resistance against the encroaching pressure of positivist natural science, suddenly pitch forward on their faces as all opposition ceases to the reign of universal hermeneutics."[1]

In what follows I assess this new version of the idea that there are "no interesting differences"[2] between the *Natur-* and the *Geisteswissenschaften*. Using Richard Rorty's work—which I label "linguistic pragmatism"—as one exemplary expression of universal hermeneutics, I develop a position that simultaneously accepts and rejects the key views Rorty advances. On the one hand, I defend Rorty's anti-foundationalist proposition that the success of the natural sciences cannot be attributed either to their possession of language or theory-independent facts of the matter or to the existence of "a permanent neutral matrix for all inquiry."[3] On the other hand, I reject his further inference that there are no interesting differences between the natural and the human sciences. There *are* important differences, but they are not explained by the fact that one is interpretive whereas the other is not. Additionally, I shall argue that the very model of hermeneutics presupposed by thinkers like Rorty is inadequate even as a model for the human sciences. Thus, the "no difference" thesis collapses for two reasons: first, because it fails to acknowledge important distinctions between the natural and the human sciences, and, second, because the model of hermeneutics on which the thesis relies is inadequate even for the human sciences.

To clarify the myriad issues Rorty raises, the following chapter will be confined (1) to an overview of his pragmatist stance, and (2) to an analysis of his account of natural scientific inquiry. More specifically, I will examine his provocative endorsement of a nonrealist, anti-representationalist construal of the natural sciences, suggesting that although the concerns informing this posture are well-motivated, the position remains captive to the foundationalist framework it seeks to subvert. Having completed my discussion of Rorty's views on the natural sciences, I will proceed to examine his accounts of the human sciences and politics.

Before proceeding, it might be useful to say a few words about the unconventional practice of starting an investigation of political inquiry with an examination of natural scientific inquiry. From one perspective, this approach may appear symptomatic of a longstanding tendency to displace and depoliticize questions of political inquiry by analogizing it to other forms of inquiry, whether natural scientific, economic, or philosophic. On this view, efforts to gain clarity about the nature of political inquiry by examining other forms of inquiry can only be self-defeating, as they obscure the distinctiveness of political life by drawing on models used to explain very different types of phenomena. Although I take this line of argument quite seriously, I believe that if we hope to understand better what is misplaced about efforts to unify political inquiry by modeling it on other forms of inquiry—such as natural scientific inquiry—

we must first gain purchase on how and why those arguments are made and what, if anything, is defective about them. This is one of the central tasks of the present chapter. Here I will contend that both traditional (positivist) versions of the naturalist thesis and more recent (postpositivist) versions are fueled by important misconceptions: positivist versions of naturalism err in assuming that scientific inquiry must be unified inquiry, whereas postpositivist variants of naturalism mistakenly presume that the absence of foundationalist unity subverts realism. Against the positivist view, I will argue that the strength and stability of natural science lies precisely in its disunity, and that efforts to unify political inquiry by modeling it on an image of unified natural science are therefore fundamentally misconceived. Against postpositivist views like Rorty's, I will maintain that the disintegration of foundationalist epistemology does not entail the demise of realist construals of natural science or of realist ontologies generally. To the contrary, the belief that foundationalist and realist fortunes are ineluctably linked is itself a vestige of the very tradition that writers like Rorty strive to overcome, namely, the tradition of positivism.

Philosophy, Foundationalism, and Linguistic Pragmatism

Although there are a number of possible avenues into Rorty's unique version of pragmatic, or universal-hermeneutic, naturalism, perhaps the most secure, if not the most direct, route is one that moves first through some of his broader views on questions regarding the nature of modern philosophy and philosophical discourse—for example, questions about the sort of activity that philosophy is; its aims, purposes, and methods; its standards of evaluation; and its proper place in Western culture. To some observers these questions may initially appear remote from or plainly unrelated to current disputes about the nature of causation, the function of theories, the role of experiment, the possibility of reference, or the problem of incommensurability. According to Rorty, however, the very fact that we take *these* problems as the central ones, that we conceive, discuss, and evaluate them in the ways that we do, is precisely what is at issue. Indeed, Rorty maintains repeatedly that it is only against the background of a certain understanding of philosophy that particular philosophical issues acquire their present status and configuration. For this reason, the process of challenging and overcoming dominant views in philosophy often entails not only an articulation of alternatives to existing positions, but also an account of how those issues got formulated in the first place, of how they came to appear so obvious, elemental, and "given." In the absence of such an account, efforts to devise alternatives must either remain sequestered within the precincts of "normal" philosophical discourse, or seem to one's opponents altogether implausible, irrational, or unintelligible.

There is, moreover, a second reason for starting our discussion with an outline of Rorty's views on modern philosophy. This stems from the striking congruence between Rorty's account of the pathologies besetting post-Cartesian philosophy and his diagnosis of the disorders characteristic of current disputes regarding naturalism. In both cases Rorty begins by identifying similar sources of confusion and concludes by offering analogous therapies for these confusions. More specifically, Rorty uses the tools of "linguistic pragmatism" to redescribe issues that he contends have been infelicitously "framed" by the tradition of seventeenth-century epistemology. By showing that there is no "cash value" in allying ourselves with this tradition's model of knowledge, mind, rationality, and truth, he hopes to convince us that these particular construals are not necessarily the only coherent ones, and that the legitimacy of our political, cultural, and scientific practices and institutions is not contingent on finding solutions to these "timeless," "perennial" problems.

Turning now to the narrative itself, Rorty states at the outset of his influential book *Philosophy and the Mirror of Nature* that his principal objective is to "survey . . . some recent developments in philosophy, especially analytic philosophy, from the point of view of the anti-Cartesian, anti-Kantian revolution"[4] initiated by "the three most important philosophers of our century—Wittgenstein, Heidegger, and Dewey."[5] Amplifying this point, he remarks that at bottom what links his "survey" of current developments to "the later work" of this philosophical trinity is not simply a shared discontent with one or another doctrine, thesis, or argument advanced by Descartes or Kant, but rather a profound uneasiness with an entire "self-image" or "conception of philosophy." Although in Rorty's estimation fragments of this self-image can be found as far back as Plato and the dawn of Western philosophy itself, it was most decisively shaped during the Enlightenment, when the founders of modern philosophy—Descartes, Locke, and later Kant—successively brought it into its present, clearly discernible form. Together, they succeeded eventually in fashioning a general picture of what philosophy as a discipline should be, one that is flattering, high-minded, and ambitious, yet also anachronistic, burdensome, and self-deceptive. As sketched by Rorty, this picture contains the following features:

> Philosophy as a discipline thus sees itself as the attempt to underwrite or debunk claims to knowledge made by science, morality, art, or religion. It purports to do this on the basis of its special understanding of the nature of knowledge and of mind. Philosophy can be foundational in respect to the rest of culture because culture is the assemblage of claims to knowledge, and philosophy adjudicates such claims. It can do so because it understands the foundations of knowledge, and it finds these foundations in a study of man-as-knower, of the "mental processes" or "activity of representation" which make knowledge possible. To know is to represent accurately what is outside the mind; so to understand the possibility and nature of knowledge is to understand the way in which the mind is able to construct such representations. Philosophy's central concern is to be a general theory of representation, a theory which will divide culture up into the areas which represent reality well, those which represent it less well, and those which do not represent it at all (despite their pretense of doing so).[6]

On this construal, post-Kantian philosophy becomes a *Fach*, a professional endeavor endowed with a distinctive, and distinctively weighty, task: that of providing secure "foundations of knowledge," that is, of articulating language- and context-independent rules, principles, methodological directives, or meta-vocabularies that could, by virtue of their "global" or transcendental character, serve as "permanent, neutral" arbiters of *all* epistemic claims—"in every field, past, present, and future."[7] Seen in this light, philosophy appears not as one discipline or science among many, but as a privileged discipline, one that "grounds" or undercuts knowledge-claims made in all other areas of culture. In Mark Okrent's words, philosophy becomes henceforth "a science of science, or of knowledge . . . Philosophy [becomes] epistemology."[8]

For Rorty, however, this Enlightenment transformation of philosophy into epistemology and epistemology into the search for a general theory of representation entails something more pervasive than the adoption of a framework for posing philosophical problems. It also involves commitments about the language, style, techniques, and methods used to come to grips with these problems. Rorty connects it, for example, with the dominance of "the treatise" as the central vehicle of philosophical expression and with a bias toward theory and against narrative.[9] Perhaps most importantly, he maintains that it is tightly interlaced both with the hegemony of analytic approaches in contemporary Anglo-American philosophy and with "the linguistic turn" in philosophical thought. Indeed, analytic philosophy's emphasis upon the formal aspects of language, along with its broader aim of "clarifying" or "solving" philosophical problems through the close analysis of concepts or different forms of linguistic statements, appears imperative only if one presupposes that the problems of representation and reference are *the* central problems of philosophy. Likewise, the recent turn toward the philosophy of language as a stand-in for Kantian epistemology seems unavoidable only if one begins by assuming that philosophy is primarily concerned with the relation between mental content and mind-independent objects and processes, and if one further sees language as the medium through which this relationship is articulated.[10]

What Rorty finds especially pernicious about this foundationalist vision of philosophy is not that it is "wrong"—though he frequently makes gestures of this sort. In his mind, such attacks are parasitic upon foundationalism, for they implicitly presume the existence of an Archimedean point from which one can evaluate the claims of foundationalism itself. This, however, only perpetuates the very framework that he recommends we abandon. Therefore, Rorty instead follows Wittgenstein, Heidegger, and Dewey in inveighing against the very idea of a theory of knowledge, maintaining not that such a project is wrong, that what we need is a new and improved theory of knowledge, but that it is deceptive, is self-defeating, and no longer serves any useful human purposes. From this standpoint, foundationalist philosophy should be resisted not because it fails to articulate what knowledge "really is," but because—quite unlike its function during the Enlightenment, where it was an indispensable weapon in the struggle for democracy, religious toleration, and scientific understanding—it now blocks, rather than facilitates, the process of inquiry, and thus fails to aid us in our particular human endeavors.

Consistent with this position, Rorty's "defense" of pragmatism and anti-representationalism emerges not from a new *theory* of language (although, as I will discuss shortly, he does offer an alternative *account* of language), but from a historical narrative tracing the development of modern philosophy. In this narrative Rorty maintains that although foundationalism and traditional philosophy were once at the vanguard of various "progressive" movements—that is, allied with science against religion, with reason against superstition, and with political liberalism against illiberalism—they have now been banished from our broader cultural conversations. According to Rorty, this is because Enlightenment philosophers linked the status of their nascent *Fach* with the status of natural science itself; however, with the decline of faith in science's standing as "the paradigmatic human activity,"[11] philosophers, or at least professional philosophers, lost their privileged authority to serve as both "the moral teachers of the youth"[12] and "the principal vehicles of moral change and progress."[13] In short, the decline of science as the singular locus of truth and meaning initiated a shift of responsibility for moral and cultural transformation, one that moves away from philosophers and toward poets, novelists, filmmakers, literary critics, historians, and ethnographers—those, in short, who expand our imaginative powers through the creation of literary, visual, historical, and other narratives. These new cultural heroes advance liberalism and "human solidarity" not by writing treatises, developing theories of representation, or analyzing the grammar of natural language, but by constructing narratives that make us more sensitive "to the particular details of the pain and humiliation of other, unfamiliar sorts of people. Such increased sensitivity makes it more difficult to marginalize people different from ourselves by thinking, 'They do not feel it as *we* would,' or 'There must always be suffering, so why not let *them* suffer?' "[14]

For Rorty, then, pragmatism—which he defines variously as antirepresentationalism,[15] anti-essentialism,[16] and "the doctrine that there are no constraints on inquiry save conversational ones"[17]—is endorsed principally as a way of bringing philosophy back into what he, following Michael Oakeshott, calls "the conversation of mankind."[18] By shifting the standard of knowledge from representation to social practice, Rorty's pragmatism seeks to circumvent the conundrums associated with Cartesian epistemology and to empower philosophy by restoring its voice in moral, social, and cultural discourse. In this sense, pragmatism is for Rorty much more than a new form of anti-Platonism or anti-Cartesianism—it is also a political philosophy and a strategy for transforming philosophy into an instrument of moral and political change.[19]

As indicated above, however, Rorty's endorsement of pragmatism, regardless of its attractiveness on purely moral or political grounds, cannot ignore entirely traditional questions about the nature of language, truth, and reality. This is the case in part because *any* attempt to explicate what is involved in knowing or understanding something, or to articulate how things "hang together," presupposes at least an account of those concepts (however misguided they may be) that so deeply color our current epistemic and hermeneutic views. Second, such an account is unavoidable because many philosophers argue forcefully that the very attempt to locate some ground between or outside of foundationalism and unrestrained relativism is hopeless, that any retreat from the former necessarily leaves one adrift in some form of idealism, epistemological skepticism, or nihilism. In following this line of argument, these writers reject pragmatism in favor of what Richard Bernstein has termed "a grand and seductive Either/Or. *Either* there is some support for our being, a fixed foundation for our knowledge, *or* we cannot escape the forces of darkness that envelop us with madness, with intellectual chaos."[20] Faced with this "choice," they insist that pragmatism is at bottom simply nihilism in disguise, and that foundationalism of some sort offers the only genuine hope of justifying cultural practices, political institutions, or epistemic claims.[21]

In response, Rorty has sought to develop the notion that "truth [and language] is made, not found" in a way that bypasses the familiar criticisms—by realists, positivists, and others—of German idealism. The initial phase in this process involves an attack upon representationalist construals of reality, as well as a redescription of the relations between language, truth, and reality. Rorty begins by suggesting that we distinguish "between the claim that the world is out there and the claim that truth is out there."[22] "Truth," he maintains, "is a property of sentences"[23] and since sentences cannot exist independently of vocabularies and vocabularies cannot exist independently of human beings, truth cannot be a human discovery: it must be a human creation. "The world," on the other hand, "is not our creation."[24] It "is out there," it includes causes and effects that operate independently of human mental states, but the world "as such" is not a candidate for truth or falsehood. Only descriptions of the world are candidates. Accordingly, since these descriptions are always necessarily descriptions-in-some-vocabulary, and since, as Wittgenstein tells us, the notions of "choice" and "criteria" are applicable only to comparisons between sentences, but not between vocabularies-as-wholes, then the idea of locating some neutral linguistic bedrock from which we adjudicate between the claims of competing vocabularies is equally out of place.

Now Rorty holds that if this Davidsonian/Wittgensteinian account of the relation (or lack thereof) between language, truth, and world is sound, then one is further obliged to abandon not only the idea that language is a vehicle of representation, but also the more deeply entrenched belief that language is a "medium" and that it has some "fixed" task to perform. All of these convictions, he suggests, are products of our enchantment with the notion of an "intrinsic nature," one that language can and should represent and/or express. But this idea, namely, that there is something external to our vocabularies that serves as a noninvidious standard for judging all possible vocabularies, is just what the foregoing account renders incoherent. Rather, Rorty contends, we should avoid the idea that language has any intrinsic purpose or function and should regard it instead as "sheer contingency," as purely "a product of time and chance."[25]

When this pragmatist redescription of the relationship between language, truth, and reality is grafted onto the current debate regarding naturalism, it yields a striking alternative to the standard positions advanced by positivists, hermeneuticists, and realists alike. First of all, Rorty rejects the assumption shared by non-Humean positivists such as Karl Popper and Imre Lakatos, hermeneuticists like Charles Taylor, and realists including Roy Bhaskar and Richard Boyd that the language of natural science mirrors or represents objects, processes, and natural kinds operating independently of human beings and their vocabularies. Vocabularies, Rorty insists, do not latch onto the natural world, nor does "nature" have a special language through which it speaks. Rather, vocabularies are privileged or jettisoned for pragmatic reasons: they make our understanding of some aspect of the world less mysterious; they enable us to make important technological advances; they facilitate more accurate predictions of behavior. As long as some vocabulary assists our inquiries in this way, we rightly privilege it. However, the fact that we privilege it is no indication that it limns reality itself, or even that it must be privileged in all our inquiries. In this respect, the sciences of nature are no different from the human sciences. For both, what matters is the road of inquiry, not the adequacy of representation.

Second, Rorty acknowledges that there are presently crucial differences between the natural and human sciences, but as a pragmatist he denies that these differences have anything to do with the distinct subject matter of the two sciences, with the question of value neutrality, or with the idea that one is interpretive while the other is not. Rather, the differences between the sciences are simply contingent differences between two types of discourses. In the natural sciences, the overriding aims of prediction and control have produced a "normal discourse," one "which is conducted within an agreed-upon set of conventions about what counts as a relevant contribution, what counts as answering a question, what counts as having a good argument for that answer or a good criticism of it."[26] Here, as in all areas of inquiry where such discourses reign, there is a feeling "that we have the right vocabulary at hand."[27] The human sciences, on the other hand, are now characterized by nonnormal or abnormal discourse—discourses in which there are no "agreed-upon practices of inquiry (or, more generally, of discourse),"[28] or where "someone joins in the discourse who is ignorant of these conventions or who sets them aside."[29] They are hermeneutic sciences because hermeneutics is for Rorty "discourse about as yet incommensurable discourses"; it is "the attempt to make sense of what is going on at a stage where we are still too unsure about it to describe it, and therefore to begin an epistemological account of it."[30] This situation, however, is again viewed as a peculiar feature of current practice, rather than a discovery "about 'the nature of human knowledge.' "[31]

Thus, Rorty contends that the line between the human and natural sciences "is not the line between the human and the nonhuman but between that portion of the field of inquiry where we feel rather uncertain that we have the right vocabulary at hand and that portion where we feel rather certain that we do. This does, at the moment, roughly coincide with the distinction between the fields of the *Geistes-* and the *Naturwissenschaften*. But this coincidence may be mere coincidence. In a sufficiently long perspective, man may turn out to be less δεινός [powerful] than Sophocles thought him, and the elementary forces of nature more so than modern physicalists dream."[32] One important consequence of this position is that it separates Rorty not just from empiricists (like W. V. Quine) and realists (like Roy Bhaskar), both of whom link the success of natural science with the quest for value- and context-free theories and explanations, but also from hermeneutic anti-naturalists such as Hubert Dreyfus and Charles Taylor. Responding first to thinkers of the Quine and Bhaskar stripe, Rorty maintains that the successes of natural science have nothing to with its possession of a special method, with its value neutrality, or with its ontological standing. Rather, "Scientific break-throughs are not so much a matter of deciding which of various alternative hypotheses are true, but of finding the right jargon in which to frame hypotheses."[33] Seen in this light, thinkers like Galileo did not—as Galileo himself sometimes declared—succeed in discovering either some special "scientific method" or the language of nature itself. They "just lucked out."[34]

On the other hand, Rorty takes issue with Dreyfus's and Taylor's claim that because the human sciences study self-interpreting beings rather than objects, efforts to generate stable and highly accurate predictive theories of human behavior are all but certain to fail. For Dreyfus, this is because one condition of stable and accurate prediction is the existence of a complete, decontextualized account of the domain under study, that is, an account in which context-free terms, elements, and properties are abstracted from their everyday meaningful contexts, and then systematically interrelated through the formulation of formal rules or laws (which thereby serve as the basis for successful prediction). In physics, for instance, one "predicts and explains everyday changes of place in terms of meaningless, context-independent properties such as mass and position which can be abstracted from the everyday world."[35] In the human sciences, however, practical contexts partly determine what counts as the event one seeks to predict, and therefore any reliable predictive account of human conduct requires that one first bring those contexts under a theoretical net of decontextualized features and rules. But practical contexts are themselves intelligible only against what Dreyfus calls "a background of shared practices,"[36] that is, a flexible, noncognitive, nonrepresentational "totality of cultural practices" that simultaneously lays out a field of possibilities before us and configures what shows up as intelligible to us.[37] Consequently, a precondition of any stable predictive science of human and social conduct is a decontextualized theory of those background practices that partly constitute practical contexts.

Bringing this into sharper focus, we might explore one of Dreyfus's examples. In his discussion of social scientific efforts to examine the concept of talkativeness, Dreyfus cites the Stanford psychologist who, after counting the number of words uttered in the course of a day by both "talkative" and "normal" persons, and finding no significant quantitative differences between them, announced that "the concept of talkativeness is unfounded."[38] Contesting this claim, Dreyfus replies that the psychologist had not discovered anything, but instead misconstrued the concept of talkativeness, and hence the methods of data collection appropriate for investigating it. Indeed, the general agreement regarding who is talkative, Dreyfus avers, "is no illusion"; rather, talkativeness is defined not by the number of words one utters, but by "the meaning of what is said and the situation in which it is said."[39] Talkative persons either speak incessantly of trivialities, or do it at inappropriate times, for instance, during lectures, concerts, and funerals, or when those they are speaking to are rushed or otherwise absorbed with pressing matters. Identifying instances of talkativeness thus demands both a capacity to grasp the situational context in which persons speak and an ability to "dwell in a shared background of practices"[40] (which is precisely why cross-cultural conversations so often leave all parties with a vague feeling that they have missed subtle social codes and crossed boundaries they are not aware of).

For Dreyfus, drawing on and refining Martin Heidegger's influential formulations in *Being and Time,* there are at least two reasons for thinking that a theory of background practices is, if not impossible in principle, clearly unattainable in practice. First, background practices consist not of beliefs or rules (either explicit or implicit), or indeed of any propositional knowledge in the traditional sense, but rather of "habits and customs" embodied in social and bodily *skills*—that is, in a generalized, yet pliant know-how or savoir faire, acquired through social training and imitation, that enables one to recognize precisely the situation one is in and to respond appropriately to it. Most importantly, these skills are so thoroughly context-specific that they can never be articulated fully; thus they resist any theoretic, formulaic, or propositional expression.[41] One might, of course, offer maxims or rules of thumb to a beginner (for example, "Don't split infinitives!"), yet these maxims can (and must) often be broken ("What if my meaning is clear *only* if I split the infinitive?"), and so their application presumes the very skill they seek to explain.[42] In short, any attempt to embody skills in a set of rules and facts is bound to be futile, for one must either grant that the proper application of these rules presupposes a skill (which means presupposing what is to be explained) or fall into an infinite regress.

Second, Dreyfus maintains that one cannot have a decontextualized theory of background practices because the background is holistic. Here Dreyfus holds that any effort to bring our everyday involvements with things like tables under a theoretical umbrella of facts and rules would demand the use of function predicates stipulating in advance all of those myriad situations in which humans interact with tables. Moreover, because our various interactions with tables cannot be isolated theoretically from our involvements with related "equipment" such as chairs, food, pencils, lamps, books, and ping-pong balls, these involvements too would require articulation via function predicates.[43] Yet human involvements with tables are so diverse, and their interrelations with related equipment so complex and polymorphous, that any effort to cover them by adding facts in the form of function predicates would never be adequate to enable someone from a radically different culture to cope with tables as we do. Still less would it enable them to understand the disparate roles they play in novels, films, paintings, and other fictional and aesthetic mediums. Thus any attempt to spell out all of these purposes, interrelations, and involvements in a series of formal propositions would require that each of these propositions include *ceterus paribus* conditions, that these conditions also have conditions, and so on.[44] This task, as Edmund Husserl despairingly conceded during his later years, is literally "infinite."

For Dreyfus, then, the effort to develop a theory of background practices is both futile and "hopelessly misguided,"[45] and this in turn points to the crucial difference between the human and natural sciences. In the human sciences, social background practices define what counts as an instance of some object or event, and thus any theory of human behavior must include a theory of background practices. But since this background can never be fully articulated theoretically and is not fixed, all attempts to formulate predictions based on some theory must remain both incomplete and unstable. In the natural sciences, however, what counts as a given type of object or event, for example, a "force," is determined by its behavior "under ideal conditions such as weightlessness or in a vacuum,"[46] not by skills or practices for picking out examples of scientific theories in the everyday world (even though these skills or practices may be necessary for decontextualizing phenomena or applying theories). Natural scientists can therefore be wrong in their judgments about what counts as an instantiation of some theoretical entity in the everyday world, but in the human sciences there can be no such external check— that is, no check other than the prevailing social practices themselves— on what counts as an instance of some object or event in the everyday world. This, Dreyfus maintains, is the basic disjunction between the two sciences, and it explains why the human sciences are inherently unstable in a way that the natural sciences are not.[47]

In a slightly different way, Charles Taylor has also sought to explain why the human sciences can never attain the explanatory and predictive power characteristic of the mature natural sciences. As developed in several essays over the past few decades,[48] Taylor argues that the principal difference between the natural and human sciences is that the objects studied in the latter but not the former are self-interpreting beings, that is, beings whose being is partly constituted by their individual and social self-interpretations. According to Taylor, this implies that investigations of human phenomena are not just hermeneutic but doubly hermeneutic in the sense that they must take into account not only the interpretations of those engaged in the investigation—this, he maintains, is equally true of the natural sciences—but also the self-interpretations of those being investigated. Moreover, because these self-interpretations causally affect human behavior yet also change, attempts to formulate predictive accounts of human activity using terms abstracted from self-interpretations must necessarily fail, simply because they cannot accommodate the changing structure of causal relations that accompany changes in self-interpretations. In the natural sciences, however, the case is quite different. Here one does not presume that the objects under investigation are causally governed by their self-interpretations, if indeed it makes any sense to speak of atoms or molecules having self-interpretations in the first place. Thus the demand that all scientific accounts eliminate reference to what Taylor calls "subject-related properties," namely, properties, like felt heat or color, that things have "only insofar as they are objects of experience of human subjects,"[49] is at once essential for the development of the natural sciences and deeply misdirected in the human sciences, where self-interpretations are causally efficacious and partly constitutive of the objects under investigation.[50]

In contrast to Dreyfus and Taylor, Rorty rejects the proposition that there are sound philosophical reasons for doubting the possibility of a stable, highly predictive science of human beings. According to Rorty, this is because all attempts to draw an essential distinction between the predictive natural sciences and the unstable human sciences rest on metaphysical or ontological commitments anathema to the pragmatist stance. He thus accuses Dreyfus and Taylor of reverting to metaphysical notions such as "correspondence to reality," or ontological distinctions between people and things, when in fact the only relevant "break" between the two sciences is "a *moral* break,"[51] that is, a break regarding the wisdom of devoting our energies to the prediction and control of human beings, on the one hand, and of atoms and quarks, on the other. Although Rorty shares Dreyfus's and Taylor's uneasiness with scientism in the human sciences, he attacks it exclusively on the moral and pragmatic grounds "that there are more important things to find out about people than how to predict and control them."[52] Insisting that the only interesting barriers to the development of a complete, predictive science of human behavior are moral and pragmatic ones, Rorty avers that, although the physicalist's dream of one day uncovering the "initial conditions" or "the antecedent states of microstructures" governing human behavior "will be too difficult to carry out except as an occasional pedagogical exercise,"[53] there is no reason to question the possibility of such a science. Indeed, he states candidly that "physicalism is probably right in saying that we will one day be able, 'in principle,' to predict every movement of a person's body (including those of his larynx and his writing hand) by reference to microstructures within his body."[54] His only caveats are of two sorts: first, about the pragmatic value of this agenda, that is, about whether, even if such a program were completed, it could aid us in our moral and political deliberations, in evaluating someone's character, and the like;[55] and, second, about its claim to offer not just one vocabulary of human behavior and human beings, but *the* vocabulary of human behavior, or *the* truth about human beings. At no point, however, does Rorty indicate either that there are good reasons for doubting whether physicalism can become a highly predictive science of human behavior, or that such a program, if realized, would force us to reevaluate our entire vocabulary of human agency and action.[56]

Setting aside momentarily Rorty's views on physicalism and prediction in the human sciences, this survey should indicate clearly both the scope and originality of Rorty's thought. By interlocking an interpretation of Deweyan pragmatism and a Wittgensteinian/Davidsonian account of language, Rorty has constructed a powerful narrative about the relation between philosophy, politics, and the sciences, one that intersects, but never converges fully, with any of the prevailing lines of thought on these issues. Moreover, he has done so in a way that is undeniably arresting and attractive. His suggestion, for example, that if only we cast off the burdensome weight of philosophical foundationalism, we can liberate philosophy from its present status as a highly technical professional discipline, must surely command the attention of anyone dismayed with philosophy's withdrawal from broader public discourse and social criticism. Similarly, his contention that this liberation further enables us to avoid seemingly hopeless disputes about objectivity, truth, and method, while also permitting us to preserve both the "thin" vocabulary of the natural sciences and the "thick" vocabulary of the human sciences, is, if nothing else, impressive in its artful circumvention of issues that have left other thinkers in various states of grim resignation. Indeed, it is precisely this delicate and provocative mixture of qualities that has led some commentators to praise *Philosophy and the Mirror of Nature* as the most "devastating critique of professional philosophy"[57] since Dewey and William James, and as "perhaps . . . the most fundamental and challenging contribution to metaphilosophy since Kant created philosophy roughly as we know it."[58]

Without denying the elegance, import, or dramatic power of Rorty's narrative, I will argue below that, once we remove its patina and explore more detailed questions about its implications for the natural and human sciences, as well as for philosophy generally, we find a stance that ultimately raises as many issues as it resolves. Significantly, I will maintain that Rorty proves unconvincing not because philosophy should rightly preserve the furniture of Cartesian- or Kantian-centered epistemology but because his own preoccupation with jettisoning this furniture has produced a species of pragmatism that is both quite thin and disfigured, and still beholden to philosophical foundationalism. In the following, therefore, I will argue that pragmatism, construed broadly, warrants not only the sorts of distinctions suggested by Dreyfus and Taylor, but also a vastly different conception of philosophy and the human sciences. On this last point, I will contend (in chapter 2 and especially chapter 3) that, although Rorty defends pragmatism in large part as a strategy for politicizing philosophy, his own variant obscures rather than exposes critical issues of power and privilege. The ironic result of these efforts is a version of politicized philosophy that fails to illuminate many of the most urgent questions of social and political life.

Rorty's View of Natural Science

As discussed above, one of the most original and controversial features of Rortian naturalism is its unequivocal rejection of representationalist, realist, and anti-realist construals of natural science. Dismissing these standard options, Rorty constructs an anti-representationalist account of language as the primary vehicle for moving "beyond realism and anti-realism."[59] He does this, as we have seen, by distinguishing between "the world," which is "out there," "is not our creation," and consists of "non-linguistic items," and the idea of truth, which "is not out there" because it "is a property of linguistic entities, of sentences."[60] Endorsing the neo-Wittgensteinian position that alternative language games or vocabularies resist any noninvidious comparison because the notions of criteria and choice are not trans-linguistic, but internal to specific language games and vocabularies, Rorty concludes that the very idea of "deciding" between different vocabularies is out of place. We (or the world) no more decide between scientific vocabularies like Aristotle's and Newton's than we (or the world) decide between poetic vocabularies like Blake's and Dryden's. In both cases there are causes, but not reasons, for adopting one or the other vocabulary.[61]

At other times, however, Rorty circumvents—rather than undercuts— the dispute between realists and anti-realists by invoking the pragmatist claim that the controversy about appearance and reality, or about the relation between linguistic and nonlinguistic items, is fruitless and superfluous. On this construal, such debates are the inevitable offspring of an Enlightenment picture of philosophy, language, and the world, one that yields irreconcilable and dispensable dualisms. The way to avoid them is simply to resist the temptation of finding any Archimedean point whatsoever, any point that would allow one to distinguish between statements that represent and fail to represent "reality," or between linguistic items that represent and fail to represent "nonlinguistic items." Thus, in contrast not only with realists, but also with anti-realists such as Bas van Fraassen (who challenges the scientific realist's claim that terms in mature scientific theories represent or correspond to nonlinguistic "facts of the matter," yet accepts realism with respect to ordinary observable entities),[62] Rorty defends what he terms a "radically anti-representationalist view-point."[63] This viewpoint cuts through the various tissues of debate about realism and representationalism by maintaining that "*no* linguistic items represent *any* nonlinguistic items."[64] Rorty, of course, is not asserting that nonlinguistic items do not exist,[65] but that the entire project of determining which class of linguistic statements do or do not represent non-human reality is philosophically "useless." Such projects are "useful when confined to relatively narrow contexts (apparent magnitude rather than real magnitude, non-dairy creamer rather than real cream), but useless when blown up to the traditional philosophical scale."[66] Rorty articulates his position as follows: "It is useless to ask whether one vocabulary rather than another is closer to reality. For different vocabularies serve different purposes, and there is no such thing as a purpose that is closer to reality than another purpose. In particular, there is no purpose that is simply 'finding out how things are' as opposed to finding out how to predict their motion, explain their behavior, and so on."[67]

Considered as a whole, this position constitutes the core of Rorty's linguistic pragmatism, and its crucial feature is a nonrealist, anti-representationalist construal of natural science. The position averts charges of idealism by holding that there are indeed things and causal relations independent of human thoughts and mental states. Yet it also resists the metaphysical realist claim that the vocabulary of modern science mirrors, represents, or corresponds to the vocabulary of Nature itself, that it offers *the* true description of nature and the natural world.[68] Importantly, however, the routes that Rorty takes to arrive at this stance are quite distinct, even if the terminus is identical. In the following pages, I shall examine them separately in order to locate more precisely where each of them errs.

To begin with Rorty's discussion of "alternative language-games," the first issue is whether he is persuasive in holding that there are no non-invidious, meta-linguistic grounds for privileging (ontologically or epistemologically) any one language-game or vocabulary over another. Rorty reaches this conclusion partly by appealing to the aforementioned neo-Wittgensteinian remarks about criteria and truth, partly by appealing to arguments from holism, and partly by trading on Kuhnian notions of paradigms and incommensurability. In all these cases he maintains that the ontological or epistemological privileging of one language-game (or scientific paradigm) over another is futile because it presupposes precisely what cannot be generated: context-free, meta-linguistic criteria for determining truth or correspondence.[69] Absent such criteria, there is no basis for noninvidiously privileging one language-game over another, and hence no grounds for invoking distinctions other than purely pragmatic ones.

Although the general point of this discussion—that comparison and choice between language-games presuppose shared patterns of activity or forms of life, and where no shared patterns or forms of life exist, there is no room for noninvidious comparison or choice—is in my view correct, what is most noteworthy for our purposes is the way in which Rorty takes a highly uncommon situation and uses it as a lever for rejecting *tout court* the possibility of adjudicating conflicts between alternative language-games. He does this primarily by sketching a picture of language-games—as well as vocabularies, paradigms, and discourses—as discreet, self-contained global systems or worldviews that, like Hobbesian atoms in the void, move through space, sometimes passing one another, sometimes colliding with and bouncing off one another, but never penetrating, overlapping, or otherwise engaging one another. Here the incommensurability or incomparability in question is of a global nature, for there is no identifiable body of linguistic practices, common to each language-game, from which one may begin to make each intelligible to the other. Put in the idiom of linguistic philosophy, two such language-games defy translation. They are not simply in conflict, but are fully unintelligible to each other, because they share no basic terms, statements, semantic or syntactic rules, or linguistic practices.

Now this view of global incommensurability is plausible in some cases, especially those where one seeks to compare, evaluate, or translate profoundly alien languages, cultures, practices, or forms of life. For example, in *The Mountain People,* Colin Turnbull describes the behavior of a tribe called the Ik, who, driven out of their traditional hunting grounds and hence living on the brink of starvation, engage in practices that appear so gratuitously and grotesquely cruel—"Men would watch a child with eager anticipation as it crawled toward the fire, then burst into gay and happy laughter as it plunged a skinny hand into the coals"—that one has difficulty deciding whether they have radically conflicting moral practices or none at all.[70] Among historians of natural science, Ian Hacking argues that Paracelsus's "whole system of categories" and "style of reasoning" are so deeply connected with "forgotten styles of thought" that although we can read his words perfectly well, we cannot make him intelligible, nor can we "assert or deny what is being said." In this sense, "Paracelsus' discourse is incommensurable with ours, because there is no way to match what he wanted to say against anything we want to say."[71]

In both of these cases there is some legitimacy in speaking of global incommensurability. Our practices, forms of life, and patterns of thought are so "dissociated" from those of Paracelsus and the Ik that only an act of profound hubris would permit us to assume that we could locate some common or objective criteria for choosing between our vocabulary and theirs.[72] With Paracelsus, as we have seen, the entire "network of possibilities" and "ordering of thought" are so alien from our own that large numbers of statements are not even among "our candidates for truth or falsehood."[73] Here, I maintain, there is a meaningful sense to, and meaningful methodological role for, the notion of global incommensurability. It means that our practices, styles of reasoning, and form of life are, as Hacking puts it, so dissociated from another that we cannot compare them in any strict way. Moreover, it serves as a humbling reminder that in such cases there is no common measure for making epistemic or ontological judgments, and that a stance of epistemic, ontological, and intellectual humility—though not necessarily agnosticism—is appropriate.

Importantly, though, the claim that meaningful sense can be given to the notion of global incommensurability does not itself license a general account of natural science as both nonrealist and anti-representationalist. For the latter, Rortian view turns on the idea that *all* dramatic transformations of vocabularies in the natural sciences are like gestalt shifts: one can move from one vocabulary to another, but can never arbitrate between them, or demonstrate conclusively that one represents reality more accurately than another. The former view, however, implies only that such conclusions may be warranted in specific cases, and if they are to be warranted, this must be shown, not assumed. To do otherwise is to make the mistake of superimposing an image of scientific change on the history of natural science, instead of examining the history of natural science as a prelude to developing an image of scientific change.

To explore questions about the appropriateness of importing a philosophical picture of scientific change into the history of science, we might first ask whether the history of scientific change does in fact provide support for Rorty's nonrealist, anti-representationalist, discontinuous construal of natural science. I contend that if Rorty's construal is understood as a general account of natural science, it does not. It is simply not the case that all changes—or even all dramatic changes—of scientific vocabularies, paradigms, or theories involve ruptures so deep that they defy any ontological or epistemological comparison. To borrow Rorty's favorite example, the shift from Ptolemaic to Copernican astronomical theory, it is true that during Copernicus's time there were no precisely stated, clearly ordered, and universally accepted criteria available for dictating a choice between geocentric and heliocentric theories. As Thomas

Kuhn and others have noted, Copernicus's theory was not, at least during his lifetime, more predictively accurate than Ptolemy's, nor was it more consistent with prevailing scientific doctrines in related fields (in fact, it was less so). It was not even simpler in any unambiguous way, for although it offered a less complicated mathematical apparatus for the explanation of certain qualitative features of planetary movement, it did not reduce substantially the labor that most professional astronomers were engaged in at the time, that is, "the computational labor required to predict the position of a planet at a particular time."[74] In addition, even the objects referred to in the two systems, for example, the sun, moon, earth, Mars, and so on, operated differently in each, so that in one system the earth and Mars were part of the same set of objects, whereas in the other they were not. For these reasons, any "choice" between the Ptolemaic and Copernican systems could not be based on the methodical application of some explicitly stated, universally shared criteria or "algorithm." It would instead be a matter of determining which of these, and also other, disparate considerations were most weighty, and here there was clearly room for disagreement.

What does this example reveal about Rorty's picture of alternative language-games and incommensurability, and about the related issues of comparability and representationalism? At first blush it may appear to support the Rortian image, for, as I have indicated, there was "no neutral algorithm of theory-choice,"[75] no systematic set of criteria, shared by all sixteenth-century natural philosophers, capable of producing a decisive resolution of the controversy. Early converts to the Copernican system like Galileo and Kepler were thus convinced to accept it not because some vocabulary-independent criteria dictated their choice, but because they privileged certain sorts of considerations—for example, simplicity (in the previously mentioned sense of requiring less mathematical apparatus to explain the qualitative features of planets), aesthetic qualities (harmony, purity of circular motion), and congruence with important cultural movements (in Kepler's case, German Romanticism's sympathy to notions of energy conservation)—over others—such as compatibility with the principles of the best established physical theory of the day (Aristotelian physics) or conformity with prevailing religious doctrines. In this respect, Rorty's claims about the futility of locating vocabulary-independent criteria would seem quite powerful, for there appears to be no neutral, independent criteria to which either party might have appealed. Consequently, there appears to be no space for invoking terms like "comparability" or "representability."

But this stance is warranted only if one makes the mistake of conflating the absence of a shared algorithm with the absence (or impossibility) of discourse and arbitration generally. As we have seen, the early debates between Copernicians and Ptolemians were indeed messy and complex. Different parties frequently interpreted the same criteria in different ways, or accorded different relative weights to the same or other criteria, and thus reached divergent conclusions regardless of whether they shared the same list of basic criteria. However, none of this implies either that there is a difference in kind between this debate and more localized debates between those who share the same vocabulary, or that the two vocabularies were so hermetically closed from one another that communication and arbitration were simply impossible. In fact, the evidence contravenes both suggestions. First, the very way in which early converts such as Galileo and Kepler set out to support an infant theory like Copernicanism reveals an acute awareness of the sorts of objections offered by their opponents. For instance, Galileo's effort to develop a new physics that was both prima facie plausible and consistent with the Copernican system indicates a remarkably clear grasp of the typical objections advanced by his Ptolemaic opponents, as well as of the sorts of work requisite for answering those objections. He knew that Copernican astronomy was at odds with the principles of Aristotelian mechanics and that the ultimate fate of Copernicanism rested largely on the ability to construct an alternative physics that was at least independently credible (in the sense that it could explain several well-known phenomena that were neither initially, nor easily, explicable by those working within the Aristotelian and Ptolemaic cosmological traditions), if by no means unambiguously superior (which, at the time, it clearly was not). That his attempts in this regard were rather crude, and that even this contribution did not resolve the debate once and for all, show only that radical and especially infant theories are rarely empirically or theoretically rich enough to produce immediate acceptance based on unambiguously confirming data (and this holds a fortiori in those cases where the aim is to supplant an already well-developed theory). None of this, however, demonstrates that such theories are in general incommensurable and therefore beyond comparison.

Likewise, Kepler's radical revision of Copernicus's system, which made

possible much more precise predictions of celestial movement, was un-
mistakably an attempt to address one of the most salient concerns *shared*
by Copernicans and their Ptolemaic opponents. As Kuhn has remarked,
Copernicus and his allies understood very clearly that predictions of planetary position "were what astronomers valued; in their absence, Copernicus would scarcely have been heard."[76] Notably, neither Copernicus nor
Kepler questioned whether prediction was "the basis on which judgments
would have to be reached if heliocentrism were to survive."[77] To the contrary, both acknowledged this and sought to support heliocentrism
through the formulation of predictions based on it. One of Kepler's signal
contributions to the debate was his refashioning of the Copernican system
in such a way that it yielded predictions that were unambiguously more
accurate than those of its competitors;[78] in this respect Kepler, like Galileo,
clearly sought to fill gaps in the Copernican system "specified by shared
values alone."[79] Of course, even these efforts were not enough to settle
the debate definitively—for prediction, like consistency, was not the only
relevant criterion or value, even if it was the predominant one for professional astronomers of the day—but they do vitiate Rorty's claims
about the impossibility of comparing alternative language-games and
vocabularies-as-wholes. With Galileo and Kepler, what one observes is
not a total lack of communication, shared procedures, and consensus,
but only an absence of some formal, neutral algorithm for choice.[80] The
absence of an algorithm, however, is itself inadequate to support the
Rortian picture of alternative language-games as entirely closed global
worldviews, for this absence is characteristic not only of conflicts between
language-games, but also of disagreements within a language-game.
Making it the standard of comparison would therefore entail a subversion
of the very idea of genuine disagreement. For these reasons, Rorty's dec-
larations about the transformation and incomparability of vocabularies
in natural science cannot be defended as a general account of natural
science, nor can they be applied to one of his own paradigmatic cases of
such a transformation.

More generally, these examples reveal a pair of conspicuous lacunae in
Rorty's account of natural science, lacunae that, taken together, undermine his radically discontinuous, nonprogressive, nonrealist view of scientific development and change. The first of these is his failure to recognize that, even in those cases where communication between the
proponents of different vocabularies, language-games, or theories is

clearly "incomplete"—that is, where their terms, meanings, and/or general conceptual structures vary to the extent that any direct subsumption, translation, or point-by-point comparison is logically impossible—there remain "concrete technical results"[81] that are recognized and achievable by those working within each community. These results constitute a shared domain of phenomena, effects, manipulations, or practical achievements that serve to preserve continuity and stability even in the midst of disorder and at times radical change. Moreover, they provide, as Kuhn points out, a common comparative ground from which proponents of competing theories can apply, with "little or no translation,"[82] shared value criteria such as accuracy, fruitfulness, and scope.[83]

Second, Rorty's picture of alternative language-games as mutually impenetrable world-systems does violence to the ways in which practicing scientists manage regularly to collaborate, communicate, and coordinate actions and beliefs even in situations where the formal conditions of incommensurability hold. Peter Galison, for instance, has recently challenged the traditional vision of modern physics as a single, tightly knit, highly unified community of scientists by showing that, during the last century, the field of physics has been divided into distinct subcultures—in particular, those consisting of the practitioners of, respectively, theory, experiment, and instrumentation—which commonly display all of the hallmarks of Kuhnian and Feyerabendian incommensurability. Furthermore, he argues that this fundamental disunity, far from undercutting the integrity and success of modern science, in fact "brings strength and stability."[84]

As described by Galison, the practitioners of theory and experiment in modern physics are not just divided, but doubly divided. First, they are divided socially and culturally. That is, they consist of sociologically distinct communities (as defined by Kuhn) and subcultures, each with "different meetings, different preprint exchange, different journals," "separate conferences," "workshops," "summer schools," "national and international laboratories," and distinct arenas of community activity (such as laboratories, centers, and institutes).[85] Second, they are divided epistemologically, ontologically, and nomologically, exhibiting all of the features typically used to define incommensurable systems of belief and theories: they have distinct and often incompatible systems for classifying entities and their interactions; different standards for determining the existence of entities; different evaluations of what entities exist; and different understandings of "the *laws* that govern the objects they study."[86] Yet, in sharp contrast to the standard Rortian, Kuhnian, and Feyerabendian pictures, these otherwise disparate subcultures, each representing "distinct communities and incommensurable beliefs,"[87] still manage to engage in productive, coordinated interaction that cannot be described accurately as living in "different worlds," or mere talking "past one another."[88] To the contrary, "the enormously productive use each makes of the other's results seems to speak against such an unbridgeable gap."[89]

This productive communication is achieved, Galison argues, through the formation of "trading zones," that is, local contexts of exchange and interchange, based on and sustained by consensus and robust constraints, which serve "as a social, material, and intellectual mortar binding together the disunified traditions of experimenting, theorizing, and instrument building."[90] As with unlike cultures that locally coordinate rules of exchange while disagreeing dramatically about "the broader (global) significance of the items exchanged,"[91] trading zones represent a locally shared symbolic and spatial site in which actions and beliefs can be coordinated, even in those cases where there exists an "ontological, epistemological, and nomological mismatch between the commitments of experimentalists and theorists."[92] In them, "The two groups can collaborate. They can come to a consensus about the procedure of exchange, about the mechanisms to determine when the goods are 'equal' to one another. They can even both understand that the continuation of exchange is a prerequisite to the survival of the larger culture of which they are part."[93] Most importantly, these groups of "traders" can achieve and sustain collaboration and consensus *despite* large differences "about the implications of the information exchanged or its epistemic status."[94]

Among the case histories that Galison examines is one that has often served as a locus of disputes about incommensurability and revolutionary change in natural science: the case of the shift from prerelativistic Newtonian to relativistic Einsteinian conceptions of mass. According to Kuhn and Feyerabend, and presumably Rorty as well,[95] the vocabularies of H. A. Lorentz, Max Abraham, Henri Poincaré, and Albert Einstein were so different from one another that any noninvidious experimental comparison of their respective theories should have been impossible.[96] Nevertheless, an experimental subculture preoccupied with just this task soon developed, and, with Alexander Kaufmann and Alexander Bucherer providing the crucial impetus, it succeeded eventually in providing results that were "clearly understood by all four of the relevant theorists (Poincaré, Lorentz, Abraham, and Einstein) to be an arbiter among theories."[97] Indeed, after examining Kaufman's results, Lorentz unequivocally admitted defeat, conceding melancholically that "my hypothesis . . . is in contradiction with Kaufman's results, and I must abandon it. I am, therefore, at the end of my Latin."[98] Similarly, Poincaré acknowledged despondently "that at 'this moment the entire theory may well be threatened' by Kaufman's data."[99] Even Einstein, who "was more confident of his theory . . . did not challenge the relevance *in principle* of the results. Quite the contrary: Einstein went to considerable pains to produce predictions for the transverse mass of the electron so that Kaufmann and Bucherer could use their experimental methods to study the theory; he constructed a detailed analysis of Kaufmann's data; and he even designed his own modification of the electron deflection experiments that he hoped someone would execute."[100]

What this and Galison's other case studies suggest is an image of scientific change that moves both between and beyond the classical positivist picture, where "protocol statements" serve as the "rock-bottom" unifiers of all science, thus making possible a smooth, methodical, and cumulative march of scientific development and change; and anti-positivist accounts like Rorty's, Feyerabend's, and Kuhn's, where the absence of any such observational edifice, neutral algorithm, or transcontextual method is adduced as evidence for a noncumulative, nonrealist construal of natural science. In contrast, the foregoing description highlights the manner in which local zones of shared meanings, activities, and beliefs link sociologically, linguistically, and theoretically disparate subcultures of science, with each containing its own distinct and sometimes formally incommensurable goals, vocabularies, and understandings. These local zones, although unconnected by any single transhistorical, transdisciplinary thread—they are not linked by a protocol language or universal translation language, nor can the traders involved state in advance what would constitute a decisive set of experiments or evidence—nonetheless operate as nexuses of communication, collaboration, coordination, and consensus.[101] In so doing, they provide a space for continuity and progression in particular natural scientific disciplines, while simultaneously preserving the discord and disunity that are essential conditions of such an advance.[102]

More specifically, these local trading zones constitute the crucial missing links in an account of science that at once makes sense of the anti-positivist insight that natural scientific development cannot be described accurately as a fully unified, mechanically cumulative process sustained by a single bedrock of universal, "indubitable" knowledge, while avoiding the common anti-positivist implication that "the expressed experience" of communication among scientists possessing different vocabularies and theories is merely a delusion. Instead, the above account reclaims the experience of communication among scientists, without resurrecting a monolithic or methodic account of scientific development.[103] As Galison elegantly summarizes it, "in the trading zone, where two webs meet, there are knots, local and dense sets of quasi-rigid connections that can be identified with partially autonomous clusters of actions and beliefs."[104]

Second, this view makes room for a description of natural science that, unlike Rortian pragmatism, remains faithful to understandings of science embedded in everyday natural scientific practice. It redeems, for example, the background understanding that there is a domain of objects that exists independently of scientists and their practices, that this domain is one of the things that scientists of nature study, that natural scientific theories seek to explain the properties of natural kinds and their causal powers, and that natural science is progressing toward truer and truer accounts of physical entities and their causal powers. All of these things, with the possible exception of the first, are denied by Rorty, Feyerabend, Kuhn, and some "strong" social constructivist accounts of natural science.[105] As we have seen, they are denied frequently on the grounds that realism presupposes the existence of some global language or decision rules, the absence of which undercuts any such ontological pretensions. However, to the extent that anti-positivist aversions to realism rest upon formulations of this type, they are clearly vitiated by the foregoing account of trading zones, where communication, coordination, and consensus occur without the existence of any global common denominator.

Finally, the concept of the trading zone contributes to a picture of scientific development, change, and interchange that is notably richer and more complete than Rorty's—in the sense that it makes room for the idea that scientific change is necessarily a product of countless historical contingencies, while it rejects the proposition that all large-scale change is like a gestalt-shift, and thus either defies explanation or should only be explained pragmatically. Indeed, one of the most striking features of

Rorty's narrative is the absence of any detailed examination of the processes of development, transformation, and interchange that occur when scientific—or any other—communities encounter subcultures employing new or foreign vocabularies, language-games, or theories. Instead, he offers truncated sketches of dramatic and genetically complex shifts, always with the aim of reinforcing his sweeping claims. Although this may appear rather odd for someone who is both a self-labeled historicist and a staunch proponent of historicist understandings of social and philosophical issues, it is not merely a curious and dissonant feature of Rorty's narrative. On the contrary, it emerges directly from his account of alternative language-games. That is, if one begins with the Rortian account of language-games and vocabularies-as-wholes, then detailed historical examination of scientific change loses its status as the primary source material for thinking and theorizing about scientific transformation. Rather, history becomes merely a repository of potential illustrations used to reconfirm what the discussion of language-games has already established: that large-scale scientific (and cultural) change "just happens"—that it results from no act of will, operates according to no translinguistic criteria, has no explanation, and defies characterization as a movement toward a better or worse description of the world. As Rorty, offering his own interpretive summary of Kuhn, describes it, "We did not decide, on the basis of some telescopic observations, or on the basis of anything else, that the earth was not the center of the universe, that macroscopic behavior could be explained on the basis of microstructural motion, and that prediction and control should be the principal aim of scientific theorizing. Rather, after a hundred years of inconclusive muddle, the Europeans found themselves speaking in a way which took these interlocked theses for granted. Cultural change of this magnitude does not result from applying criteria (or from 'arbitrary decision') . . . We should not look within ourselves for criteria of decision in such matters any more than we should look to the world."[106]

Although my earlier discussion of the conflicts between the proponents of geocentric and heliocentric astronomy supports Rorty's contention that these transformations were not the result of a single, universally recognized *experimentum crucis,* of the methodical application of context-free criteria or decision rules, or of some individual or corporate act of will, it is clearly out of tune with his parallel claim that, after a century of "inconclusive muddle," Europeans just happened to be talking in a different vocabulary. As we have seen, such a gloss ignores the myriad ways in which a number of nascent theories were gradually developed, integrated, and refined to produce a well-articulated body of theories, achievements, predictions, and results. Some of these theories, achievements, predictions, and results did, of course, have pragmatic appeal, but over time they became so interwoven and variously buttressed—Kepler's quantitatively superior Rudolphine tables, the development and refinement of instruments for celestial observation, the development and refinement of a system of mechanics compatible with the assumptions of heliocentric astronomy, the aesthetic simplicity of the Copernican system, and the eventual discovery of the phases of Venus, mountains on the moon, spots on the sun, and previously unknown stars—that they correspondingly imposed severe restrictions upon what might be the case. In effect, these theoretical refinements and practical achievements constituted a web of interpenetrating commitments that placed such rigid constraints upon what one could believe or what theories one might hold that support for both heliocentrism and the ontological status of the objects it posited became almost impossible to avoid.

More generally, it is simply a non sequitur to move—as Rorty does—from the legitimate and important observation that innumerable historical contingencies needed to converge for various interlocking theses to be taken seriously at all to the conclusion that after a century of muddle these new theses just happened to triumph. The former assumes only that these transformations were the result of a complex interweaving of historical contingencies, contingencies that defy encapsulation within a single narrative line and therefore require thick, multilayered historical description. By contrast, the latter suggests either that there are no explanations (in a later passage, Rorty refers to "constellations of causal forces" as "random factors"),[107] or that the only explanations are pragmatic ones (some vocabularies are more "useful," because they allow us to better "predict" or "cope" with particular phenomena or issues) combined with references to "luck," "chance," or good fortune.

Perhaps most importantly, the former stance, unlike Rorty's, resists generalized assumptions about the proper interpretation of scientific change. It offers no general account of how or why changes occur, or of the ontological status of those changes. Moreover, it neither presupposes nor licenses a priori realist construals of particular transformations, theories, or entities, but instead urges that ontological issues be examined on a case-by-case basis. By contrast, Rorty's account is dictated by his nonrealist, anti-representationalist picture of alternative language-games and vocabularies-as-wholes. By beginning with the Rortian image of language-games and vocabularies-as-wholes, one where alternative languages and vocabularies are so closed from one another that all interchange necessarily terminates in non- or miscommunication, the gestalt-shift or "no explanation" model of change becomes not simply one option among many, but the only conceivable option. This, however, is precisely what happens in Rorty's narrative. First, his account of language eliminates a priori all descriptions of large-scale change that invoke categories such as comparability, communication, contestation, collaboration, dialogue, and consensus. Second, he fills this vacuum with "no explanation" or pragmatic accounts of change. Finally, he reinterprets all large-scale scientific or cultural change along the lines imposed by his linguistic pragmatism. The result is that Rorty's nonrealist construal of natural science, which is defended largely as the lone nonmetaphysical alternative to the metaphysics of realism and anti-realism, operates in practice as yet another variant of metaphysics, that is, as something that imprints an interpretation of scientific change on the history of science, rather than as something that emerges from it.

Having completed our examination of Rorty's language-game defense of anti-representationalism, and nonrealism, we are now better positioned to evaluate his second, more pragmatist-inspired endorsement of these same positions. As I indicated above, the pragmatist position aims to circumvent both realism and anti-realism by rejecting ontological and epistemological issues as philosophically "useless" remnants of Enlightenment epistemology. According to Rorty, such debates have import only if one starts from the Enlightenment assumption that the justification of our scientific, social, and cultural practices requires the identification of some "unambiguous" epistemic standard prior to and independent of them, and that the absence of such a standard entails a freefall into bottomless relativism. However, once we recognize the futility of locating ahistorical standards of this sort, disputes between realists and anti-realists correspondingly lose their significance. By replacing quarrels about the relation between vocabularies and reality with deliberations about the relation between vocabularies and particular human purposes, we can, Rorty maintains, obviate the problems associated with representational conceptions of knowledge while also avoiding the charge of unrestrained relativism. For example, we can still legitimately privilege the vocabulary of modern positional astronomy over that of astrology, but not on the general grounds that the latter is more "out of touch with reality" than the former. Rather, the pragmatist rejects astrology because its vocabulary is less useful for the specific purpose of predicting planetary motion and simultaneously dismisses questions of representation as "irrelevant" or "misleading" ways of posing this issue.[108] In this manner both the Charybdis of representationalist epistemology and the Scylla of relativism are deftly evaded.

Seen in this light, the pragmatist defense of anti-representationalism and nonrealism is essentially a recommendation to shift the focus of inquiry from abstract ontological and epistemological considerations about the possibility of realist and representationalist vocabularies to pragmatic reflections about the usefulness of such vocabularies for specific inquiries. In short, Rorty's pragmatism eschews both realism and anti-realism not because it offers a better answer to the common questions that realists and anti-realists ask, but because the questions that they ask are "fruitless," "useless," and "boring": they paralyze rather than advance conversations about pressing problems of human choice and action. Ontological and epistemic questions of this sort should therefore be "dissolved" and "forgotten," rather than resolved and removed.[109] Likewise, the burden of proof is again shifted back onto the shoulders of realists and anti-realists, who now must show that questions of ontology or epistemology have some "cash value" in the course of particular inquiries.

In appraising this pragmatist "recommendation of benign neglect," note first that, although Rorty appears to endorse local and conversation-specific standards for determining the utility of ontological discourse, his varied discussions of these issues suggest a more general standard, one that relies heavily upon his already discussed treatment of language-games and vocabularies. Indeed, if one asks in what particular circumstances it might be useful to discuss, rather than "neglect," issues of realism and representation, Rorty responds by reiterating his linguistic distinction between disputes *within* language-games and vocabularies-as-wholes and those *between* language-games and vocabularies-as-wholes. He contends that such discussions are useful only in "relatively narrow contexts" where the dispute is about some particular statement within a vocabulary.[110] On the other hand, these same deliberations are fruitless in those inquiries where the issue is one of deciding between vocabularies-as-wholes. Here the most effective response is not to engage in epistemic or ontological discourse, but to rise above it. By "forgetting" such controversies—either by creating new vocabularies that bypass them altogether, or by examining existing vocabularies on specifically pragmatic, rather than epistemic or ontological, grounds—we circumvent conversational roadblocks and move ourselves further down the road of inquiry.

Like his linguistic defense of nonrealism and anti-representationalism, Rorty's pragmatist view entails that it is *never* useful to appeal to ontological or epistemological considerations as a means of arbitrating disputes between the proponents of alternative theories, language-games, social practices–as–wholes, or vocabularies-as-wholes. On this account, such questions produce only conversational gridlock and should be supplanted by other, specifically pragmatic, questions: Is our aim to predict and control phenomena? Or is it to develop rules for moral deliberation, or habits for political action? By shifting the focus of inquiry from the jurisdiction of ontology or epistemology to the jurisdiction of politics, morality, or particular practical purposes, one jettisons irreconcilable issues and attends instead to solvable, specifically human ones.

For two reasons, I find myself in disagreement with this view. First, to the extent that Rorty's pragmatic distinction between contexts of inquiry where ontological questions are useful and those where they are not relies on his prior arguments about incommensurable language-games and vocabularies-as-wholes, it is clearly misplaced. As I have shown, these arguments rest on the erroneous assumption that communication, collaboration, and consensus are possible only if one possesses in advance of all possible inquiry some "neutral vocabulary which begged no questions against any philosophical position—an ahistorical matrix of all actual and possible philosophical inquiry."[111] But in physics, at least, members of subcultures that are differentiated along social, ontological, and epistemological lines manage regularly to communicate, collaborate, and reach consensus in the absence of any such global common denominator. In these cases, it would be counterproductive to follow Rorty's injunction that we "change the subject" whenever we fail to locate a context-independent, global meta-vocabulary. Far from advancing inquiry in physics, doing so would yield the distinctly anti-pragmatic result of impeding it.

Second, Rorty's recommendation that we replace ontological considerations in our selection of vocabularies with moral, political, or other considerations has the similar anti-pragmatic effect of closing off avenues of inquiry that might otherwise inform specific disputes in both the natural and human sciences. Although there are clearly cases where a stance of ontological agnosticism—as opposed to ontological neglect—may be warranted, there are also instances where ontological considerations inform inquiries by providing reasons for making judgments about a vocabulary or theory that could not be sustained on the basis of moral, political, or instrumental considerations alone.[112] The clearest examples of this type are found in the social sciences, especially in those cases where the proponents of alternative vocabularies differ not on questions about the basic goals of their inquiries ("Is the aim of our inquiry into celestial phenomena to equip us with accounts that articulate the properties and predict the movements of those phenomena, or is it to provide us with a spiritually comforting or morally instructive image of the cosmos?"), but on questions about the explanatory status or scope of a vocabulary or theory. The field of political science, for instance, has a long history of attempts to develop theories of political behavior based explicitly on models imported from the physical or biological sciences. Writers of this persuasion have commonly conceived of their project as one of emulating "the techniques of the students of physical nature,"[113] and have formulated their goal, however distant, as that of reaching "the state of maturity associated with theory in physics."[114] Although many of the proponents of these techniques and methods have recently been more modest in expressing their ambitions, the aspiration to pattern theories of political conduct on models prevalent in the physical or life sciences remains deeply entrenched in the practice of mainstream political science. It is, for example, reflected institutionally in current distinctions between "empirical" and "normative" theories of politics, in disciplinary understandings of terms like "political methodology," in journals, in conference panels, and in professional associations.[115]

In responding to these naturalistic claims, we might adopt the Rortian strategy of questioning the *aims* of such approaches, maintaining that explanation and prediction are not the only—and perhaps not even the central—goals of political inquiry. We might insist, for example, that other, equally legitimate aims are decidedly normative in character and therefore could never constitute part of a field of inquiry that confined itself exclusively to the goals of explanation and prediction. On the other hand, we might maintain that some naturalistic theories of political behavior, even if successful, defy articulation in a language suitable either to policymakers or others interested principally in issues of social change or practical action. We could then reject such theories on precisely these grounds.[116]

When framed in the above Rortian manner, this strategy yields a strong case for methodological pluralism in political science, but it fails to address questions about the likely success of naturalist programs understood in their own terms. Rather, it assumes—in spite of repeated failures—that there are no insurmountable barriers to the development of precise, highly predictive, and general theories of political behavior, and thus that the only grounds for rejecting them are specifically pragmatic or moral ones. This response, however, elides the fact that there are many instances in which objections to theories of political behavior are motivated less by concerns about their usefulness or the moral value of one's goals than by doubts about the likelihood of achieving those goals. Surely, for instance, a parsimonious, highly predictive, transcontextual theory of war, revolution, socioeconomic mobility, political participation, or democratic development would be immensely valuable, regardless of what that theory revealed or how it was practically or ideologically employed. Here, and in other cases, the issues are not primarily pragmatic, moral, or teleological ones, but ones of successful science.

But once one moves from the question of desirability to that of possibility, discussions of ontological questions become unavoidable. Any discussion about whether a transcontextual, highly predictive science of political affairs is possible must include an account of why such attempts have failed repeatedly to produce the results promised by their proponents. Yet one of the most prominent accounts of this failure is the ontological one: the account—articulated in various ways by writers as diverse as Vico, Dilthey, J. S. Mill, and Heidegger, as well as Dreyfus, Habermas, and Taylor—that decontextualization, prediction, and theoretical explanation are notably less successful in the human sciences because the objects studied in those sciences—human and social activity—differ in crucial respects from the objects examined in the natural sciences. Of course, ontological accounts are not the only possible accounts of conspicuous failures in the human sciences—others, including Rorty himself, hold that these failures are a consequence of the relative youth of the human sciences, of the complexity of human activity, or of other factors—but there is nothing prima facie implausible about such explanations, either. To eliminate them from consideration on the grounds that they are "useless," or that they block inquiries by reverting to atavistic metaphysical notions of "essences," is to limit prior to inquiry the possible outcome of inquiry. And this is clearly inconsistent with the pragmatist commitment to advance inquiry through open discourse.

In the following chapter, I will examine in detail competing explanations of the failures of naturalistic theories in social and political science. There I will defend the thesis that the best explanation of these failures is indeed an ontological one. For the moment, however, it is sufficient to demonstrate that Rorty offers no compelling justification for purging ontological considerations from specific methodological inquiries, and that, in the absence of any such justification, the recommendation remains empty.

Conclusion

Earlier in this chapter, I suggested that the central problem with Rorty's linguistic pragmatism was not its rejection of foundationalist epistemology, but its unacknowledged adoption of foundationalist assumptions in a putatively pragmatist account of science. In the previous section, I showed how this was manifested most clearly in his account of alternative language-games, yet was also present in his pragmatist rejection of ontological considerations as unnecessary barriers to the advancement of inquiry. Both of these stances reinforce traditional epistemology and undercut pragmatism by structuring inquiry about natural scientific practice prior to an examination of that practice. The result, as I have indicated, is a nonrealist resurrection of foundationalist canons under the guise of postfoundationalism.

Nevertheless, none of my arguments constitutes a repudiation of pragmatism construed in a more general sense. The basic pragmatist commitment to an inquiry-based rather than philosophically based conception of natural science, along with its emphasis upon the messy, contingent, interpretive, and nonmechanical features of that activity, are essential to an understanding of natural science that moves beyond dogmas about the "logic of science" or formalist accounts of "rational procedure." Similarly, Rorty's and other anti-positivists' concerns about the deification of natural science, about the tendency to see natural scientific knowledge as the model for knowledge in all domains of life, are equally well motivated.

However, as I have maintained throughout this chapter and as I will demonstrate in more detail in the following one, the way to come to grips with these legitimate concerns is not to deny the capacity of natural science to reveal facts about the physical world or to provide us with increasingly true descriptions of physical entities and their causal powers, but to understand the practices through which this is accomplished, as well as the limitations of those practices. This means, in the first place, questioning the putative link between foundationalism (construed as the demand for a "permanent neutral matrix" for all inquiry) and realism. The presumption that natural scientific activity has ontological significance only if it possesses a fully unified, permanent neutral matrix or "heuristic vocabulary" is an artifact of positivism that Rorty and other anti-positivists have been much too eager to accept. Thus, when it eventually became clear that natural science was not a fully unified, mechanical endeavor, anti-positivists like Rorty took this to imply that natural science could only have instrumental but never ontological power. However, I have urged that a better approach to these issues is one that dispenses with all equations that place foundationalist unity on one side and realism on the other. Once this is done, it becomes possible to begin exploring how natural science can be a disunified, untidy, fully human enterprise, yet simultaneously one that is capable of producing more and more accurate descriptions of physical nature.

Similarly, the legitimate discomfort about the natural sciences' epistemic hegemony—the tendency, as Rorty puts it, to "take science as the paradigmatic human activity"—is best relieved not by denying that these sciences' spectacular achievements ever reveal anything about the physical world, but by showing both the preconditions for and limits of these achievements.[117] The Rortian stance, which recognizes these achievements yet refuses to grant them ontological significance, has the virtue of limiting the authority of natural science, but only through a Draconian amputation of ontology from all of natural science. Such an approach is not only suspect in its own terms, but also invites familiar "anti-science" countercharges from its opponents. By contrast, my position, which will be articulated more fully during the next chapter, achieves the same objectives, while avoiding these Draconian measures and the accusations they prompt. In this respect, it remains closer to the spirit of pragmatism than Rorty's own stance.

— 2 —

In Defense of Disunity

As I noted in the previous chapter, Rorty's version of naturalism has variously intrigued, puzzled, and irritated students of social inquiry. Rejecting all ontological and methodological distinctions between the natural and social sciences, Rorty maintains that science is unified in the sense that the basic activities of scientific inquiry, as well as the appropriate prescriptions for overcoming conversational stasis, are identical regardless of whether the objects under examination are electrons or ethnic violence. Indeed, for all inquiries Rorty endorses pragmatist therapies— and especially the pragmatist injunction that the establishment of "rational" methods and standards of evaluation be an open, mutable, communal activity emerging in the course of, rather than prior to, concrete inquiries—as the most effective treatment for those metaphysical maladies impeding progress on specific issues. By dissolving a priori foundationalist questions into concrete practical questions, pragmatists circumvent irresolvable disputes and abet the advancement of particular inquiries. By declaring general methodological and ontological queries "useless," they open the way for a more flexible and experimental approach to current problems. By jettisoning representationalist frameworks, they shift social practice to the center of conversation and inquiry. In a rebuke of the classic hermeneutic distinction between the explanatory, objective, nomothetic natural sciences and the interpretive, textual, ideographic human sciences, Rorty asserts that "from a full-fledged pragmatist point of view, there is no interesting difference between tables and texts, between protons and poems. To a pragmatist these are all just permanent possibilities for use, and thus for redescription, reinterpretation, manipulation . . . The strong textualist simply asks himself the same

57

question about a text which the engineer or physicist asks himself about a puzzling physical object: how shall I describe this in order to get it to do what I want? Occasionally a great physicist or a great critic comes along and gives us a new vocabulary which enables us to do a lot of new and marvelous things."[1] In this view, the natural scientist and the social scientist, as well as the philosopher, the literary critic, and the poet, all engage in roughly the same activity—the pragmatic and instrumental activity of locating or inventing vocabularies that enable us to see, predict, manipulate, understand, and express things that were previously invisible, unpredictable, recalcitrant, opaque, or ineffable.

However, although Rorty finds no interesting differences—that is, no essential ontological, methodological, or epistemological differences—between the natural and the human sciences (or between these sciences and the arts and humanities), he eschews also the standard naturalist assumption that the absence of such disparities entails unavoidably a methodological unity of all the sciences. To the contrary, he contends that there are good pragmatist reasons for thinking that the aims of these two sciences should not necessarily coincide and that their respective configurations should perhaps remain quite distinct. Breaking with all previous variants of naturalism, he maintains that one upshot of the pragmatist stance is "the suggestion that perhaps 'the human sciences' *should* look quite different from the natural sciences . . . and that prediction and control may not be what we want from our sociologists and literary critics."[2] Indeed, to the extent that the term "science" has now become largely an honorific reserved for those areas of inquiry dominated by normal discourse and preoccupied principally with prediction and control, he claims that perhaps it is wrong to "assume that 'a science' is necessarily something we want sociology to be."[3]

In articulating how it is possible, on the one hand, to insist that the basic activity of inquiry in the natural and social sciences is identical, yet, on the other hand, to recommend that in many cases their methods and standards of evaluation should nonetheless remain distinct, Rorty sketches a pragmatist account of the *Geisteswissenschaften,* one that accents redescription, recontextualization, and pluralism while being decidedly anti-essentialist and anti-representationalist. This account, he emphasizes, is not founded on the idea that there is any essence or secret to science in general or the social sciences in particular. Instead, it is tailored expressly to meet the needs of specific sorts of social scientific inquiries. As such, it should be appraised not by reference to any general epistemic or methodological criteria, but by its effectiveness in advancing the diverse inquiries characteristic of the social sciences.

This conception of social science emerges directly from Rorty's pragmatist redescription of the *erklären/verstehen* controversy as well as his attendant criticisms of hermeneutical social science. In what follows, I begin by reexamining this controversy, and then advance a different account of the relationship between pragmatism and hermeneutics, one that radically reconceives the meaning and implications of pragmatism. Specifically, I argue that although some of Rorty's criticisms may apply to particular hermeneutical writers, the core commitments of hermeneutical social science remain immune from his attacks. Indeed, at their best, hermeneutic claims about the meaningfulness of human activity and the inappropriateness of the covering law model are fully pragmatic arguments. That is, they are empirical arguments that assess the value of methodological practices by examining the actual histories of inquiries. This empirically and historically informed version of hermeneutics is, however, at odds with Rorty's linguistic pragmatism in that it rejects the idea that current differences between the natural and social sciences are merely the artifacts of historical and sociological contingencies. Rather, it suggests that a thoroughgoing pragmatism yields the judgment that differences between the social and natural sciences are ontologically based. Importantly, this argument also demonstrates that Rorty's own stance is buttressed by unacknowledged anti-pragmatic and metaphysical commitments. A consistently articulated pragmatism entails, in other words, a rejection of some of Rorty's own putatively pragmatist claims.

Pragmatic Naturalism and the Social Sciences

Since the nineteenth century, the naturalist controversy has been conceived typically as a quarrel about the distinction between *erklären* (explanation) and *verstehen* (understanding) or, as Rorty characterizes it, between the proponents of a "Galilean" or "covering law" model of the social sciences and those who recommend a "softer," "more cozy" hermeneutic model.[4] In this debate, the champions of a Galilean model— writers such as Carl Hempel in philosophy, Milton Friedman in economics, Claude Lévi-Strauss in anthropology, and William Riker in political science—advance the ideal of a "value-neutral" and methodologically unified science, one grounded in the conviction that genuinely scientific accounts are those that explain some set of events (or statements, processes, states, or phenomena) by covering or subsuming them under a net of general, context-free rules or laws. According to this standard view of scientific explanation, explaining an event consists of formulating and systematically interrelating universal rules or laws that, in combination with statements of initial and boundary conditions, can then be used to deduce predictions or retrodictions of events. These predictions or retrodictions then serve as the testing ground or "objective checks"[5] of the proffered explanation, confirming or infirming it. In this way science purportedly avoids contamination by "pseudo-explanation": "metaphors," "vague analogies and intuitive 'plausibility,' " "pictorial and emotional appeals," and "metaphysical" theories.[6] Thus the hallmark of all science and scientific progress is explanation, and this requires both (1) the articulation of general laws and (2) the successful prediction or retrodiction of empirical events.

By contrast, their hermeneutic opponents—figures such as Hubert Dreyfus and Hans-Georg Gadamer in philosophy, Clifford Geertz in anthropology, and Charles Taylor in political science—typically offer two objections to the covering law model, both of which issue from the idea that human beings' self-interpretations of their activities makes the study of human behavior different in kind from that of physical entities. Most commonly, they argue that the covering law model is inappropriate for social science because the objects of social scientific inquiry are self-interpreting (individual and collective) agents and their meaningful actions, practices, norms, intentions, and institutions, rather than "meaningless" events, processes, states, and behavior. What distinguishes social from physical reality is the fact that the former is partly constituted by the intertwined linguistic resources, social practices, and self-interpretations of the "objects" under investigation. Physical objects, by contrast, have no self-interpreting capacity, or if they do, that capacity fails to affect causally their behavior and hence plays no role in scientific explanations of it. For this reason, however, the Galilean drive to purge self-interpretations and meanings in the interest of formulating value-free and decontextualized explanations of human reality is self-defeating. Far from yielding more scientific and objective descriptions of human reality, it distorts that reality.

Second, hermeneuticists contend that because the specific configuration of language, social practice, and self-interpretation is partly constitutive of social reality yet also changes over time and differs from culture to culture, a necessary condition of predictive precision and stability—that is, "conceptual unity," the condition that "all states of the system, past and future, can be described in the same range of concepts, as values, say, of the same variables"—cannot be met in the social sciences.[7] This means not only, as Charles Taylor argues, that some events (for example, the "culture of youth" in the United States during the 1960s and early 1970s or "the Puritan rebellion of the sixteenth and seventeenth centuries")[8] are "radically unpredictable,"[9] but also, as Hubert Dreyfus adds, that the social scientist can *never* state in advance what aspects of linguistic patterns, social practice, and human self-interpretation must remain constant for the continuation of predictive success. Indeed, Dreyfus holds that this condition of inherent instability makes the social sciences "not only incomplete and unstable in comparison with ideal theoretical disciplines such as physics; they are also incomplete and unstable even when compared to disciplines with changing background conditions such as ecology."[10]

If, as these writers argue, the covering law model of explanation is necessarily incomplete or distortive of social reality, then what the social sciences require is a quite different, "interpretive" approach, one that "illuminates" social reality by manifesting the individual or collective meanings, purposes, intentions, or self-interpretations embedded in social activity and practice. In this model, the aim is not to subsume actions or events under a net of universal, decontextualized rules and laws, but to disclose the specific contexts of meaning within which actions, events, and institutions are located, to unfold the processes through which these contexts are transformed and reproduced, or converge and diverge. This approach, hermeneuticists argue, differs in principle from the covering law model. Its object is meaningful human activity rather than meaningless physical events, its goal is understanding rather than explanation, its route is interpretation rather than decontextualization, and its model is the circular process of textual analysis rather than the architectonic process of natural scientific theory construction.

In pragmatically redescribing this controversy, Rorty starts by denying what is assumed as axiomatic by the proponents of both positions: that the quarrel is primarily a quarrel about "methods." Genuine disputes about methods, Rorty submits, presuppose a consensus about the goals to be achieved, and disagreement solely about the means of achieving them. But the quarrels between the proponents of the covering law and interpretive models of social science are clearly not quarrels of this sort. As Rorty asserts, "The two sides . . . are not disagreeing about how to get more accurate predictions of what will happen if certain policies are adopted. Neither side is very good at making such predictions, and if anybody ever did find a way of making them both sides would be equally eager to incorporate this strategy in their view."[11] Similarly, Rorty denies that the controversy pivots on disagreements about "the competing goals of 'explanation' and 'understanding.' "[12] Although he agrees that "this contrast is real enough," he adds quickly that "it is not an issue to be resolved, only a difference to be lived with."[13] Reiterating the pragmatist point that there is no logical, intrinsic, or otherwise obvious contrast between vocabularies that describe human beings "in nonevaluative, 'inhuman' terms" and those that describe humans in "teleological" or evaluative terms, Rorty urges that the insistence on such rigid oppositions is as misplaced as "the notion that microscopic and macroscopic descriptions of organisms are opposed ways of doing biology."[14] In both cases, the relevant question is not whether there is an essential distinction between different vocabularies but whether one or another vocabulary is "more useful for a certain purpose."[15]

According to Rorty, what sustains this curious and awkward pas de deux is a miscast conviction on the part of both sides that there is some intrinsic connection between two distinct requirements for the social sciences: (1) the requirement that "it should contain descriptions of situations which facilitate their prediction and control";[16] and (2) the requirement that "it should contain descriptions which help one decide what to do."[17] Instead of recognizing that it would be "nice" but is not necessary "to have a single vocabulary which is useful for every possible purpose,"[18] both sides assume mistakenly that neither of these requirements can be fulfilled "unless the other is also."[19] Hence, the followers of hermeneutics presume that, because Galilean vocabularies are not usually useful vocabularies for moral reflection, they fail to get at what people are " 'really' doing," whereas the advocates of value freedom conclude that, once social science finds the right vocabulary for prediction and control, it will then be our "duty" to begin making policy decisions on the basis of an " 'objective' and 'scientifically based' " ethics.[20]

Rorty holds that in both cases what gets overlooked is the idea that there may be nothing particularly unsettling about having one vocabulary for prediction and another for deliberation. Indeed, the notion that social scientists *must* unite these distinct requirements carries force only if one assumes precisely what needs to be shown: "that only a certain vocabulary is *suited* to human beings or human societies, that only *that* vocabulary permits us to 'understand' them."[21] Locked in their common commitment to the idea of a privileged vocabulary, both sides search for a single core "which is definitory of the human," as well as a single vocabulary fashioned expressly for the task of revealing our human essence. For Rorty, however, this shared belief in a single privileged vocabulary is no basis for a productive philosophical debate about either the human condition or the social sciences, but instead "is the seventeenth-century myth of Nature's Own Vocabulary all over again."[22] The idea that the social sciences must somehow assimilate in a single vocabulary objectives ranging from predictive accuracy to policy proposals to the promotion of just and honorable human relations is, he holds, compelling only as long as one remains within the dubious intellectual ambit of Enlightenment epistemology. But once we follow Dewey, Heidegger, Wittgenstein, and Freud in recognizing that humanity is not "a natural kind with an intrinsic nature"[23] but simply "a web of relations to be rewoven,"[24] and that vocabularies are not mediums of representation but rather "instruments for coping with things,"[25] then the idea that there are "two 'methods' " or two goals becomes incoherent. Rather, we circumvent the problem altogether by acknowledging that there is neither an intrinsic connection nor an intrinsic absence of connection "between being able to predict and control people of a certain sort and being able to sympathize and associate with them, to view them as fellow citizens."[26]

Importantly, Rorty remains sympathetic to the hermeneutical movement in the social sciences, but only to the extent that it is conceived solely as a protest against the "fetishism" of behaviorist social scientists and their preoccupation with "being 'scientific.' "[27] Understood in this way, the movement is a well-motivated effort to remind us that "narratives as well as laws, redescriptions as well as predictions, serve a useful purpose in helping us deal with the problems of society."[28] However, when hermeneuticists begin drawing principled distinctions between human beings and physical entities, and subsequently use these as a toehold for driving a methodological wedge between the social and natural sciences, their "protest goes too far."[29] In Rorty's view, such extrapolations rest on a pair of specious assumptions about the possibility of epistemically privileging a particular vocabulary. He claims, first, that the hermeneutical insistence on an ontological and methodological distinction between the social and natural sciences presumes a nonexistent contrast between objects that are constituted by "webs of meaning"—such as human beings—and objects that are not, like purely physical entities. Rorty rejects this contrast, contending that semantic webs are no less necessary for the constitution of fossils, for example, than they are of human beings. In both instances the objects are constituted only by placing them in relation to other similar and different objects: "To say that human beings wouldn't be human, would be merely animal, unless they talked a lot is true enough . . . But one could equally well say that fossils wouldn't be fossils, would be merely rocks, if we couldn't grasp their relations to lots of other fossils. Fossils are constituted *as* fossils by a web of relationships to other fossils and to the speech of the paleontologists who describe such relationships. If you can't grasp some of these relationships, the fossil will remain, to you, a mere rock. *Anything* is, for purposes of being inquired into, "constituted" by a web of meanings."[30]

Moreover, Rorty avers that the same hermeneutic essentialism that fuels this spurious contrast between the natural and social sciences also generates a second misconception, "the mistaken assumption that somebody's *own* vocabulary is always the best vocabulary for understanding what he is doing, that his own explanation of what's going on is the one we want."[31] Rorty maintains that this affirmation of "privileged access" to one's own behavior or culture—a stance that he attributes specifically to Charles Taylor, but that has been linked to others as well—is yet another byproduct of the confused seventeenth-century notion that the aim of science was to discover nature's own language.[32] This notion, he suggests, engendered in turn the idea that the explanandum was epistemically privileged, that it was epistemologically illegitimate for scientists to impose an alternative vocabulary or explanation on it. Not surprisingly, Rorty rejects this claim of epistemic privilege. He notes that there are indeed cases where we "rightly wave aside" the agent's own vocabulary or explanatory account of his or her behavior, for instance, when we encounter or explain the behavior of psychotics or extremely "stupid" people.[33] In these cases, we make no effort to describe their behavior in their own language, and proceed instead to "attribute intentions and actions to them in terms they do not accept and may not even understand."[34]

Significantly, Rorty agrees that as a "general hermeneutical rule" it is good to take into account agents' self-interpretations of their activities, but he insists that this rule is rooted in pragmatic and moral, not epistemological, considerations.[35] Thus, when social scientists, trial lawyers, and others ask people to explain their behavior, they should do so either because a good explanation might save them the time and trouble of searching for their own account, or because Western moral codes dictate it, but *not* because agents have privileged access to their own motives or because texts are different in kind from fossils. As Rorty explains,

> Taylor's claim that we need to look for *internal* explanations of people or cultures or texts takes civility as a methodological strategy. But civility is not a method, it is simply a virtue. The reason we invite the moronic psychopath to address the court before being sentenced is not that we hope for better explanations than expert psychiatric testimony has offered. We do so because he is, after all, one of us. By asking for his own account in his own words, we hope to decrease our chances of acting badly. What we hope from social sciences is that they will act as interpreters for those with whom we have difficulty talking ... Thus, for example, the contrast which Hirschman draws between good and bad political science ... seems to me a contrast between fellow feeling and moralizing condescension—between treating men as moral equals and as moral inferiors.[36]

In short, methodological choices issue from neither ontological nor scientific considerations, but from pragmatic and moral ones. When making such choices, social scientists should avoid asking questions like "Is this vocabulary more or less objective, or more or less scientific than another?" and instead ask, "Is this vocabulary more or less useful, or more or less sensitive than another?"[37]

In a moment I will explore these claims in more detail, but for now it is perhaps useful to sketch briefly what Rorty sees as the "cash value" of his pragmatist redescriptions. If, as he suggests, both Galilean and hermeneutical approaches are offspring of the same essentialist parents, then what should social science look like ideally, and how should social scientists conduct their inquiries? As I have indicated, Rorty proposes a pragmatic and moral turn in the social sciences. Social scientists, he urges, should abandon their preoccupation with abstract questions about "objectivity," "scientific method," "epistemic privilege," and "ontological differences" and instead focus their attention on pragmatic issues, that is, on deliberations about concrete alternatives to particular problems. This shift to a thoroughly anti-essentialist and pragmatic social science would not, he believes, eventuate in the banishment of either Galilean or hermeneutical approaches from the *Geisteswissenschaften,* but it would advance inquiry by discarding pointless disputes about "criteriology" and forcing each side to justify methodological choices by demonstrating the promise of their approach for solving particular practical problems.[38] Ultimately, Rorty believes that this movement away from social scientific foundationalism and essentialism would have the salutary effect of blurring traditional disciplinary boundaries, and would probably—though not necessarily—yield a situation whereby Galilean approaches would be applied in instances where the aim is prediction and control, while narrative-based approaches would prevail in cases where one's concerns are morally motivated.[39]

Without a doubt, there is much in this vision that social scientists would likely, or do, find attractive. Rorty's emphasis on blurring traditional boundaries, his distaste for endless quarrels about scientific method, his privileging of practical application over abstract method, his proposed division of labor between predictive and normative inquiries, his emphasis on peaceful coexistence, and even his ultimately very modest proposals for reform are often echoed by a wide range of social theorists and scientists.[40] However, although I agree that Rorty expresses a number of laudable sentiments, it is nonetheless worth asking whether he dissolves deep and longstanding conflicts among social scientists a bit too effortlessly. Is it, for example, really the case that essentialism and foundationalism are the only, or even the most serious, impediments to progress in contemporary social scientific inquiries, or that fuzziness and universal antiessentialism are adequate for removing these impediments? Likewise, is it the case that difficult ontological or methodological issues can be avoided or dissolved merely by turning one's attention to concrete practical problems, or does the turn to particular problems sometimes force these issues back upon us, whether or not we choose to recognize it?

To explore these questions, I shall first reconsider Rorty's account of the *erklären / verstehen* dispute. Specifically, I will examine whether Rorty's attack on hermeneutical social science is either convincing or consistent with his putatively pragmatic commitments. I thus ask: Is it the case, as he suggests, that all hermeneutic invocations of ontological and methodological differences between the sciences are merely cozier versions of traditional metaphysics and epistemology? Is the effort to defend internal understanding at bottom simply a category mistake, a confusion of methods and morals? Are hermeneutical writers like Dreyfus and Taylor in fact committed to the idea that there is one right vocabulary for understanding human and social life? In answering these questions, I will offer an interpretation of hermeneutics that is consistent with the cardinal concerns of pragmatism yet notably different from Rorty's. This, I contend, raises a further, and more troubling, question regarding the pragmatism of Rorty's pragmatism.

Hermeneutics Revisited

As indicated previously, Rorty offers three responses to hermeneutic claims for the autonomy of the social sciences, all of which issue from the supposition that hermeneutic pleas for methodological autonomy fail because they are based invariably on illicit essentialist and foundationalist convictions. First, Rorty alleges that Charles Taylor and others sanction a form of epistemic privilege, one that entails that valid accounts of actions and practices must be internal in the sense that they must employ the vocabulary of the agent or culture in question and must ultimately grant epistemic priority to agents' or participants' own account of their activities. Second, he contends that hermeneutic arguments for autonomy presuppose a false contrast between objects that are partly constituted by webs of meaning and objects that are not. Finally, Rorty holds that hermeneutic social scientists share with the proponents of value-freedom the mistaken assumption that two distinct requirements for the vocabulary of the social sciences—the requirement (1) that it should contain descriptions that facilitate prediction and control, and (2) that it should contain descriptions that inform our moral deliberations—must necessarily be connected, that finding the "right" vocabulary for satisfying one of these requirements implies that we have also found the right vocabulary for satisfying the other.

Let us begin with the first charge. Rorty maintains that Taylor commits two crucial and interrelated errors: first, Taylor fails to recognize that an agent's or culture's own descriptions are not always correct, that sometimes their explanation "is so primitive, or so nutty, that we brush it aside";[41] and, second, he assumes mistakenly that when one considers an agent's own account, one does so not for moral but for ontological or epistemological reasons. The first allegation is undoubtedly serious. If Taylor's position grants epistemic priority to agents' or participants' own understanding of the meaning of their actions, then the pervasive moral and legal practice of holding people responsible for actions that they deny would have no basis. Likewise, the common conviction that social scientists are capable of producing accounts of actions or practices that are clearer, more enhanced, or more illuminating than participants' own would be equally groundless.

This, however, is not a view that Taylor holds. Taylor never maintains that "somebody's *own* vocabulary is always the best vocabulary for understanding what he is doing."[42] Rather, Taylor argues that grasping actions and practices internally is the necessary starting point of all interpretation and understanding: "The very nature of human action requires that we understand it, *at least initially,* in its own terms; that means that we understand the descriptions it bears for the agents. It is only because we have failed to do that that we can fall into the fatal error of assimilating foreign practices into our own familiar ones."[43] Taylor's point is clearly not that agents' own accounts of their activities are incorrigible but that an understanding of the specific meaningful context within which an action or practice occurs is a precondition for formulating any accurate account or appropriate evaluative standards. Without such an understanding one runs the risk of imputing meanings, intentions, practices, and standards of judgment on an agent or culture without first ascertaining whether those meanings and intentions could exist or whether the standards of assessment are indeed appropriate.

To bring this issue into clearer focus, Taylor, in his essay "Interpretation and the Sciences of Man,"[44] has noted that the practice of "negotiation" is central to a wide range of social activities, from corporate buyouts to determining salaries, ending wars, resolving trade disputes, and getting a divorce. This practice, however, as well as the attendant practices of breaking off or concluding negotiations, never occurs in socially or linguistically isolated space but appears only against a background of shared meanings, concepts, rules, distinctions, norms, and understandings. It requires, for instance, shared understandings regarding bargaining (the making of offers and counteroffers, concessions, and tradeoffs) and the distinct autonomy of the various parties involved (the respective parties must conceive of themselves as conflicting on some issue or issues, and their representatives must be capable of acting independently of each other), norms and distinctions between willed and coerced agreements (agreements reached while one party holds a large, loaded gun at the temple of the other party are not typically considered negotiated agreements) and between bargaining in good and bad faith (it is bad faith to stonewall all efforts to reach a settlement or to accept conditions one has no intention of fulfilling), and rules (rules for conducting and breaking off negotiations). According to Taylor, this family of understandings, distinctions, norms, and rules is constitutive of the practice of negotiation in the sense that it occupies collectively a specific region of "semantic 'space,' " a region without which the very practice itself cannot exist.[45] Thus, in traditional Japanese villages where social life is founded upon "a powerful form of consensus, which puts a high premium on unanimous decision,"[46] one finds no corresponding conception of bargaining between autonomous parties or of pressing for maximally favorable terms of agreement. Hence, there exists no practice of negotiation. The villagers do, of course, discuss issues and adjust their differences, but their vocabulary carves up semantic space in such a way that our notion of bargaining and practice of negotiation cannot possibly have the same resonance for them that it has for us. And this implies, in turn, that the difference between contemporary Western societies and that of the villagers is a difference not just "of vocabulary, but also one of social reality."[47]

Significantly, Taylor's account does not entail, as Rorty alleges, that one's "own explanation of what's going on is the one we want"[48] but, rather, that language and social practice delimit the possible range of meanings that can be ascribed in a particular situation. On Taylor's view, certain shared or "intersubjective" semantic configurations, norms, social practices, and meanings not only constitute specific practices like negotiation, but also circumscribe the field of intelligible possibilities for individual belief and action. Thus, in traditional Japanese villages where the field of semantic space, social practice, and shared meanings leaves no place for those norms and meanings "constitutive of negotiation themselves,"[49] the practice of negotiation literally cannot exist. In such instances, the question of whether an agent is engaging in a practice is not exclusively or even primarily one of what the agent says she or he is doing but also one of what that agent could possibly be doing. As Taylor argues, "Actors may have all sorts of beliefs and attitudes which may rightly be thought of as their individual beliefs and attitudes, even if others share them . . . They bring these with them into the negotiations, and strive to satisfy them. But what they do not bring into their negotiations is the set of ideas and norms constitutive of negotiation themselves. These must be the common property of the society before there can be any question of anyone entering into negotiation or not. Hence, they are not subjective meanings, the property of one or some individuals, but rather intersubjective meanings, which are constitutive of the social matrix in which individuals find themselves and act."[50]

Concomitantly, Taylor emphasizes that because contexts of shared meanings, norms, social practices, and institutions constitute an intersubjective social reality that is ontologically prior to individual beliefs and actions, they also determine the meaning of someone's conduct independently of that person's own vocabulary, descriptions, or subjective mental states. In other words, it is not only the case that, in the absence of shared linguistic and social practices, certain actions are inconceivable. Taylor also maintains that certain movements or utterances in the appropriate context have definite meanings regardless of whether that person recognizes it or not. Taylor, for instance, notes that the very way in which we comport ourselves in public space reveals a sense of our dignity and power that we may neither recognize nor acknowledge. As he explains, "Our style of movement expresses how we see ourselves as enjoying respect or lacking it, as commanding it or failing to do so. Some people flit through public space as though avoiding it, others rush through as though hoping to sidestep the issue of how they appear in it by the very serious purpose with which they transit through it; others again saunter through with assurance, savoring their moments within it; still others swagger, confident of how their presence marks it: think of the carefully leisurely way the policeman gets out of his car, having stopped you for speeding, and the slow, swaying walk over as he comes to demand your licence."[51] Notice that in these hypothetical cases the agents themselves might be entirely unaware of the specific meanings attached to their behavior or even deny that it has any meaning whatsoever. The policeman, for instance, might protest that his manner of walking to your car has no meaning, that he was seeking neither to command your respect nor to intimidate you, display his macho attitude, or manifest his institutional power. Indeed, it might even be the case that he, or the person whom he has stopped, lacks any explicit understanding of the distinction between private and public contexts or of notions such as deference and dignity. Nevertheless, if the policeman's conduct marks these distinctions—if, for instance, we observe that he does not normally walk in the same "carefully leisurely" manner when working in his yard, when walking his dog, or when called into his sergeant's office—then Taylor's claims about the meaning of his comportment are not vitiated. What remains primary in this and other instances is not the agent's own descriptions, or his or her mental states, but the broader intersubjective context within which that action occurs.[52]

It should now be apparent that the principal upshot of Taylor's argument is not that agents' own descriptions of their conduct are epistemically privileged but that any accurate understanding of human activity must *begin* by grasping action internally. Indeed, Taylor denies unambiguously that human and social explanations must be framed in the participants' vocabulary.[53] Nonetheless, he insists that any adequate social scientific theory or interpretation must account for the participants' own self-understanding, and this necessarily requires a prior understanding of their self-understanding, as well as some connection between their vocabulary and the more sophisticated or rigorous social scientific one. Any concept, theory, or interpretation that is unrelated entirely to the agents' or cultures' own self-understandings and practices is perforce inadequate simply because these self-understandings and practices are partly constitutive of social reality.[54]

Significantly, this epistemological claim rests not only on ontological considerations about human beings—for example, that they are beings whose being is partly constituted by their individual and social self-interpretations—but also on historiographic considerations about the fortunes of theories and methods that omit reference to the meaningful social context that situates human action. For instance, Taylor points to the case of behavioral political science, where efforts to formulate a verification procedure consistent with the dictates of the covering law model yielded accounts of political activity that both failed to predict and misdescribed important political movements. According to Taylor, behavioralists, unlike physicalists or cognitive psychologists, sought not to exile meanings altogether but rather to house them entirely in the "subjective realm" where they could be treated as "colorless" facts describing an agent's beliefs, attitudes, or opinions toward some objective state of affairs, for example, a legislative proposal or an institution. Here, Taylor argues, behavioralists eliminate not meaning in toto, but "inter-subjective meanings," that is, meanings that are irreducible to a convergence or consensus of individual subjective beliefs or psychological states because they "are constitutive of the social matrix in which individuals find themselves and act."[55] Precisely because intersubjective meanings shape, rather than operate within, the horizon of "intelligible possibilities" for subjective beliefs—as Joseph Rouse explains, they "make *either* consensus or dissensus possible"—the failure to include them in accounts of social activity leads inexorably to incomplete and misdescribed accounts of that activity.[56] Indeed, Taylor holds that the failure to recognize the constitutive role of intersubjective meanings made it impossible for behavioral political scientists to predict or understand phenomena such as the emergence and practices of the counterculture during the 1960s. Divested of any conceptual resources for including intersubjective or common meanings in their political inquiries, they were destined to interpret countercultural challenges as strategic bargaining maneuvers within a matrix of cultural and political relations based on production and negotiation, rather than as a challenge to the configuration of the matrix itself. Taylor contends that such misunderstandings not only made these challenges appear more trifling than they were, but also masked crucial questions of power and ideology.[57]

This account also illuminates what is mistaken about Rorty's attendant claim that when one takes into consideration a person's own explanations or self-understandings of his or her conduct, one does so for moral— that is, out of moral respect for the agent (whether an actor or author) as "a human being like ourselves"—rather than epistemic or ontological reasons.[58] In fact, Taylor's argument is precisely the opposite: the issue of internal understanding is an epistemological one in the sense that it is about what constitutes a potentially successful scientific practice. Taylor's stance is that theories, vocabularies, or explanations of social activity that abstract from the meaning structures that house that activity obscure the very reality to be disclosed and thus fail to yield either insight into or stable predictions of it. Such theories and explanations are, moreover, doubly dangerous. They both misdescribe the phenomena under investigation and do so in the name of a scientific practice that extols the avoidance of such distortions as one of its signal virtues.

By contrast, Rorty's insistence on moral rather than epistemic privilege is inadequate precisely because it replaces what for Taylor is a necessary starting point for any accurate social scientific understanding with a fully subjective standard, namely, the social scientist's personal moral commitments. Rorty maintains, in other words, that the social scientist's obligation to grasp a text, action, or cultural practice internally is altogether unrelated to issues regarding the epistemic integrity of her interpretations or explanations. Rather, it is dependent exclusively on the individual social scientist's moral respect for the dignity of the author, actors, or culture under examination. As Rorty states, "The difference between his [i.e., the agent's] description and ours may mean, for example, that he should not be tried under our laws. It does not mean that he cannot be explained by our science."[59] This, however, assumes precisely what needs to be demonstrated, namely, that there is, or will eventually be, a reliable,[60] explanatory, and highly predictive social scientific vocabulary that is unconnected to the specific meaning structures of everyday human activity, or, in the case of textual interpretation, that one can formulate an accurate or useful interpretation of a text such as Machiavelli's *The Prince* without first understanding anything about Renaissance Italy or the differences between the ancient Roman concept of *virtù* and modern notions of virtue.[61] The truth is that social scientific efforts to bypass agents' or cultures' own understandings of their activities or to transform them into a language consistent with the dictates of the covering law model have failed repeatedly to produce anything like a "Copernican Revolution"[62] in social science or the "general theory of motion in physics or of life in biology."[63] As we have seen, Rorty himself grants that "the last fifty years of research in the social sciences have not notably increased our predictive abilities."[64]

Formulating this point rather differently, we might say that the problem with Rorty's position is his assumption that the issue for social scientists is one of choosing between two quite different but equally feasible vocabularies of social analysis, one that is, broadly speaking, thick, context sensitive, and hermeneutic and another that is thin, context independent, and Galilean. Because these two vocabularies are equally adequate in their own terms, the issue for social scientists is, he suggests, a subjective and moral one, not unlike the subjective and moral considerations involved in choosing and delimiting one's subject matter. Hence, the decision to choose one vocabulary over another is simply a decision about whether to treat one's subject matter as fellow human beings or as objects, not a question about how best to grasp and describe human and social conduct.

I contend that the problem with this stance lies not in its logic but its premise, namely, that both vocabularies are equally adequate in their own terms, one being useful for moral reflection and understanding human beings as agents, the other being useful for prediction and control. As I have emphasized, and as even the most avid proponents of a Galilean vocabulary acknowledge, there is presently no general and highly predictive theory of politics or social activity, be it behavioralism, cognitivism, operationalism, systems theory, or some variant of rational actor theory.[65] Nor, as the foregoing suggests, should this be surprising. As J. S. Mill observed more than a century ago (and as writers such as Taylor have underscored), "man" is a "complex and manifold being, whose properties are not independent of circumstance, and immovable from age to age . . . but are infinitely various, indefinitely modifiable by art or accident."[66] For this reason, the elegant simplicities of "pure" and abstract Galilean theories only intermittently conform with the muddy and mutable realities of social and political action.[67]

Importantly, this claim that internal understanding should be viewed as a precondition of social scientific practice rather than as a subjective moral option is not simply an ontological thesis but is fundamentally a historical one as well. As I have held, the epistemic privileging of internal understanding does not, as Rorty often assumes, presuppose a return to traditional foundationalist epistemology or a priori ontology.[68] As historians of philosophy, including Rorty,[69] have often noted, the principal ambition of foundationalist epistemology is to defeat radical skepticism by developing anterior to inquiry a set of context-independent rules, principles, methodological directives, or meta-vocabularies that underwrite the epistemic integrity of all inquiries in all fields. It should be evident, however, that the epistemic privileging of the sort I defend has nothing in common with foundationalist epistemology. My approach neither entails that such privileging is a precondition of all inquiry[70] nor demands a priori rules and principles of the type required to silence the radical skeptic. Rather, it starts from comparative and historiographic evidence regarding the fortunes of particular inquiries.[71] It is therefore neither foundationalist nor essentialist in Rorty's sense but is better described as an a posteriori and context-sensitive epistemology, one designed to assess the reliability and promise of theories and methodological strategies through an examination of the histories of scientific inquiries.

Let us now turn to Rorty's second objection: the charge that hermeneutic arguments for the autonomy of the social sciences fail because they presuppose an unwarranted contrast between objects that are partly constituted by webs of meaning and objects that are not. According to Rorty, hermeneuticists, in their urge to draw sharp, in principle distinctions between the social and natural sciences, overlook the fact that in order for *anything* to be identified as something, it must first be embedded in a larger vocabulary or web of meanings. Not only human activities such as wars, revolutions, and negotiations, but also physical entities such as fossils and protons appear as what they are only against a shared background of language and social practice—what Thomas Kuhn calls the "disciplinary matrix" of a science. Distinguishing one fossil from another, and distinguishing both from pieces of reinforced steel or concrete, thus presupposes at least a tacit understanding of various interrelated concepts, categories, and semantic distinctions, as well as various skills, for instance, the ability to operate complex scientific instruments. In this sense, Rorty contends, there is no interesting difference between the paleontologist's activity of distinguishing fossils from rocks and the social scientist's efforts to distinguish revolutions from rebellions. Each inquiry presupposes a background web of meanings and practices that partly constitute the objects under investigation, just as each aims to bring some object or objects of study into a coherent relation with other objects.

Now it should be clear that I agree with Rorty's claim that there is no language-independent, pretheoretical access to either nature or social life, and in this sense both physical entities and human actions are partly " 'constituted' by a web of meanings."[72] Without a grasp of the relevant vocabulary of modern physics, as well as significant amounts of scientific training, the physicist's bubble-chamber photograph appears, as Kuhn has aptly remarked, not as "a record of familiar subnuclear events," but simply as "confused and broken lines."[73] Nonetheless, there is something deeply wrong with Rorty's concomitant suggestion that because the natural and social sciences share these particular features, there are "no interesting differences" between the activities of physicists and social scientists, or that, because both activities are interpretive, they are so in identical ways. Most significantly, Rorty's claim that the objects of study in both the natural and social sciences are partly constituted by webs of meaning fails to address what writers such as Taylor and Dreyfus identify as the crucial distinguishing feature of the two sciences, namely, the *doubly* hermeneutic character of the social sciences.[74] Like Rorty, Taylor and Dreyfus agree that a shared background of meanings and practices is a precondition not only of natural scientific, but of any scientific practice. The notion of a science without a vocabulary or disciplinary matrix is, they maintain, incoherent; hence "the very idea of . . . an interpretation-free understanding of what ultimately is [or of anything] does not make sense."[75] Moreover, Taylor and Dreyfus both hold that because this shared background includes theoretical and technical presuppositions and practical skills that can never be made fully explicit, interpretation and judgment are unavoidable features of all natural scientific practice. As Peter Galison correctly notes, and as Dreyfus and Taylor would surely agree, natural scientific "procedures are *neither rule-governed nor arbitrary*."[76] Rather, they operate within a necessarily flexible but not entirely elastic hermeneutic circle of interpretation.

Taylor and Dreyfus further contend, however, that in the social sciences interpretation is required not only because a shared background of meanings is a precondition of all inquiry, because data are theory laden, and because scientific skills and practices can never be made fully explicit—all of which hold in the natural sciences as well—but also because the objects are themselves self-interpreting agents. This means, as Dreyfus states, that in social science, "studying human beings as self-interpreting beings requires interpretation within *the full hermeneutic circle* of shared significance, whereas to have a science of any object including human beings as objects requires only the circularity of working within a theoretical projection."[77] On this construal, social science is distinguished by virtue of its doubly hermeneutic character: it requires both (1) a grasp of the background webs of meanings and practices that are the precondition of all science and all intelligibility, and (2) an understanding of the background self-interpretations of the objects (persons, groups, cultures, classes, and the like) being studied. Moreover, this second feature places constraints on the first, namely, that social scientific vocabularies must retain some connection to the self-interpretations of the objects being studied.

This second element of interpretation—that is, interpretation of the self-interpretations of the objects under study—is precisely what Rorty's "no interesting differences" account of science omits. It is, however, the basis of hermeneutic arguments for the methodological distinctiveness of the social sciences. The claim is that, although there may be some metaphorical or nonmetaphorical sense in which physical nature "speaks" through effects, reactions, resistance, and the like, there is no historical evidence indicating that these physical effects, reactions, or resistances are causally affected by physical entities' "self-interpretations" or that physical entities even have self-interpretations. To the contrary, natural scientific debates about the existence or nonexistence of physical entities, the status of competing theories, and the reliability of particular experiments, procedures, equipment, calculations, and data are all premised on the belief that natural phenomena behave in stable (and often stubbornly stable) ways.[78] Significantly, these stable ways of behaving are deemed so in part because, as Sandra Harding remarks, "Physical nature does not organize itself culturally."[79] For instance, when experimenters at one physics laboratory fail to replicate the results of those at another, the assumption is not that the behavior of the physical entities examined in those laboratories is causally governed by the entities' disparate self-interpretations or cultural practices, or that the entities speak different languages, but that the equipment in those laboratories, or the experimental and interpretive practices of the scientists working in those divergent settings, differ.

In the social sciences the situation is strikingly different. Here, too, one finds stability in the sense that vocabularies, meanings, and patterns of behavior frequently persist over extended periods of time, yet one also finds that these same vocabularies, meanings, and patterns of behavior are, as Richard Ashcraft has stated, "neither fixed nor permanent."[80] Rather, they exhibit a manifest "open-endedness," one that is apparent not only in the transformations over time of people, cultures, and institutions, but also in the varieties of behavior exhibited from person to person, culture to culture, and time to time. These variations, of course, are no less an object of any adequate social science than are the well-documented phenomena of social and linguistic stability and reproduction. But as hermeneuticists such as Taylor and Dreyfus have observed, numerous attempts to bring the evident varieties of social activity under a single "conceptual net" have had fortunes quite different from analogous efforts in the natural sciences.

We have already explored one effort to abstract from the meaning structures of everyday social existence, namely, Taylor's discussion of behavioral political science and its failure to predict or understand the significance of countercultural challenges during the 1960s. This, however, is only one instance of problems and failures attending all social scientific efforts to circumvent the contextual and self-interpretive aspects of human and social life. During the past several decades, not only behavioralism but also Lévi-Strauss's structuralism, David Easton's systems theory, and Gabriel Almond's functionalism have all attracted considerable interest among social scientists, only to fall gradually out of favor as initial expectations failed to be met. More recently, in the fields of artificial intelligence and cognitive science, researchers attempting to explain or simulate human behavior by linking a set of decontextualized rules with facts (in the case of artificial intelligence) or mental representations (in the case of cognitive science) have encountered profound difficulties in explaining or simulating even very basic forms of intelligent human behavior—for example, in programming computers capable of properly inferring the meaning of statements such as "The spaceship photographed Seattle, flying to Mars."[81] Likewise, recent assessments of rational actor theories in political science have found that, in spite of practitioners' increasingly impressive mathematical and formal skills, these theories frequently avoid potentially falsifying evidence only by examining a highly selective group of cases, by arbitrarily restricting the domain of application, or by formulating "slippery" or "vaguely operationalized" predictions.[82] On the other hand, in those instances where rational actor theories have generated reasonably precise predictions or retrodictions, the results have failed to establish a convincing case in support of the approach.[83]

This clear discontinuity between the natural and social sciences is something that cannot be dismissed, and any adequate treatment of the relation between these sciences must account for it. We have already seen that Rorty is well aware of this discontinuity and offers an explanation of it. To recall, he makes two distinct but interrelated defenses of the idea that these discontinuities are only contingent, not essential, differences between the natural and social sciences. First, Rorty contends that there is no reason in principle why human and social behavior must be any less amenable to decontextualized explanations and predictions than natural phenomena, and hence, that there is no basis for supposing that past and current differences between the sciences are products of anything more than sundry historical and sociological contingencies as well as luck. Thus, although there may be pragmatic reasons for questioning the usefulness of a normal, highly predictive science of social life, the only nonpragmatic impediments to the development of such a science are time and resources. Second, Rorty maintains that hermeneutical arguments about essential or in principle differences between natural and human phenomena all rest on unwarranted metaphysical theses about the essence of humans beings, for example, that " 'humans differ in their essence from nonhumans by being self-describing and thereby capable of altering their essence,' "[84] or on differences between two distinct kinds of being, being "in-itself" and being "for-us."[85] Rejecting these options, Rorty inveighs that "as a good pragmatist, I want to replace the notion of 'discovery of essence' with that of 'appropriateness of a vocabulary for a purpose.' "[86]

Let us start with the first claim. Rorty is surely correct to point out that presently there is no universally accepted philosophical proof (in the Cartesian sense that doubt would be self-contradictory) of an essential ontological or methodological distinction between the natural and social sciences. Moreover, not only Rorty but also many others are convinced that there simply is no in principle distinction to be made. However, given Rorty's profound distrust of all foundationalist enterprises, it is unclear why he would regard the absence of philosophical proof against the unity-of-science thesis as a compelling reason to presume either that a stable, general, and highly predictive social science will eventually be forthcoming or that social scientific inquiry would be best advanced by operating on such an assumption. Such commitments, if they are to be sustained in the absence of any unimpeachable proofs or absolute certainties, must themselves be advanced on the very pragmatist grounds that I have identified, that is, on the grounds of a comparative historiography of natural and social scientific inquiries.[87] In other words, Rorty must show that, although the social sciences may be maturing more slowly than sciences like physics or chemistry, the basic developmental patterns remain quite similar—for example, that social science demonstrates a slow, uncertain, and nonmechanical but nevertheless distinct movement toward increasing predictive success, or that through a combination of labor, discipline, and ingenuity social scientists exhibit over time a similar capacity to increasingly "stabilize" the phenomena under investigation.[88] Such an account, if provided, would furnish Galilean social scientists with strong pragmatic reasons for remaining confident about the ultimate success of their project.

But Rorty never provides such an account. Instead he relies on the unavailability of any in principle arguments against the naturalist thesis as sufficient evidence for accepting it. But this is neither logically nor pragmatically defensible. Logically, the absence of an in principle proof against the possibility of an idea is clearly not a compelling reason to hold that idea. Following this logic, one might as easily hold that chemists should exchange their modern laboratory equipment for pentagrams, since no one has ever proven in principle that alchemy must necessarily fail.[89] Pragmatically, Rorty's appeal to the absence of in principle arguments is unpersuasive because it invokes a standard of belief that inevitably engenders precisely the sort of philosophical deadlock that his pragmatism aims specifically to avoid. After all, Rorty's anti-naturalist opponents could deploy the same reasoning to insist that the absence of any indefeasible proof that a covering law model must succeed is reason enough to assume that it must fail.

Turning to Rorty's second claim—that all efforts to draw an essential distinction between the objects of the natural and social sciences rest on outmoded metaphysical doctrines about the essence of human beings or on equally outmoded metaphysical distinctions between the in-itself and the for-us—it should be apparent that here, too, his charges miss the mark. Although the position I have outlined rests on a claim about ontological differences between physical nature and human beings, it is manifestly not a metaphysical thesis in the sense that most pragmatists presume when they describe metaphysics pejoratively as a "sterile" or "vain" activity. What pragmatists such as C. S. Peirce, William James, and Dewey (and even Rorty) typically dislike about "the Western metaphysical tradition" are, for example, its preoccupation with a priori cosmology and speculation (especially as expressed in nineteenth-century German idealism); its tendency to privilege the fixed, finished, and immutable over the temporal, empirical, and changeable (as found in Greek philosophy and American Platonism); its emphasis on locating ultimate origins or causes; and its search for what Hilary Putnam has called a "God's-Eye point of view." In these and other instances, pragmatists attack metaphysical modes of thought for committing one of two (or both) interrelated errors—first, the error of blocking the road of inquiry by articulating standards of reason, knowledge, or reality prior to or independent of specific ongoing inquiries, and second, the error of devaluing both the empirical world and engaged human activity.[90]

But my account of the differences between the *Geistes-* and *Naturwissenschaften* commits none of these sins. As I have argued, it is through and through an a posteriori and empirical defense of ontological differences, one that is fully consistent with the pragmatist ethic of viewing inquiry as an ongoing and evolving social practice. Indeed, far from being a product of disembodied exercises in first philosophy, the ontological and methodological distinctions adumbrated above emerge from examinations of the fortunes of different types of natural and social scientific inquiries. By contrast, Rorty's refusal to entertain ontologically based arguments of any sort, along with his unwillingness to consider the possibility that vague allusions to luck and historical contingencies may not provide the best framework for understanding why social scientific predictions and explanations conforming to the covering law model of science have thus far been entirely unforthcoming, indicate metaphysical commitments of the type that earlier pragmatists did find anathema. Both of these refusals, whether intended or not, have the effect of limiting, antecedent to inquiry, the direction and outcome of inquiry. And this is inconsistent with pragmatism's emphasis on the central role of open discourse in the advancement of inquiry.

It is time to examine the last of Rorty's three responses. Here Rorty's claim is that hermeneutic social scientists, like their Galilean opponents, mistakenly assume that two distinct requirements for the vocabulary of the social sciences—first, that it should contain descriptions that facilitate prediction and control, and second, that it should contain descriptions that inform our moral deliberations—are intrinsically connected, that the best vocabulary for coping with one requirement must also be the best vocabulary for coping with the other. According to Rorty, this hermeneutic and Galilean fealty to the idea of a single synoptic vocabulary for "understanding" human beings is ultimately an expression of a social scientific version of "the seventeenth-century myth of Nature's Own vocabulary."[91] Like the earlier adherents of that notion, hermeneutic and value-free social scientists both mistakenly presume that vocabularies are something more than mere pragmatic "instruments for coping," that their purpose is to represent the intrinsic nature of things. As Rorty sees it, this mutual metaphysical commitment sustains a debate that could otherwise be terminated by simply admitting that there is nothing wrong with having one vocabulary for prediction and another for moral and political deliberation. As Rorty puts it, "I am not saying that we are doomed to predict in one vocabulary and deliberate in another, but only that it is no disaster if we do so."[92]

On this point Rorty also misconstrues what is at issue in the hermeneutic attack on Galilean social science. Indeed, it should be clear that the hermeneutic position I have articulated is manifestly not, as Rorty avers, a social scientific corollary of the idea of "Nature's Own Vocabulary."[93] Rather, I hold that the very idea of either physical nature or human beings having a vocabulary that is intrinsically their own is possible only if one first subscribes to some version of Plato's theory of the Forms, one in which representations and essences are held to exist independently of human beings and their practices.[94] However, one central premise of the preceding account is that all human understanding of reality is possible only through language and interpretation. Hence, even if essences, representations, and vocabularies exist independently of human language, interpretation, and practice, they are not cognitively accessible to human beings.

Similarly, the pragmatically informed conception of hermeneutics that I have sketched does not assume that there is necessarily one right vocabulary for all human and social inquiries. Neither, however, does it entail that all vocabularies rest on equally secure or insecure epistemic ground. Instead, it posits only that careful historical reflection on the fortunes of inquiries is the most reliable guide for making methodological choices in those instances where social scientists have neither a clear logical compulsion to privilege one methodological strategy over another nor the luxury of waiting until the pragmatic ideal of unrestrained inquiry pursued indefinitely finally yields a consensus. Seen in this way, pragmatism and hermeneutics are not really specific vocabularies at all; they are attempts to establish ways of intelligently proceeding based on where inquiries are at any given time, on both short- and long-term goals, on the viability of various assumptions, and on systematic reflection regarding what has and has not been fruitful and illuminating in the past. As Taylor aptly remarks:

> How else to determine what is real or objective, or part of the furniture of things, than by seeing what properties or entities or features our best account of things has to invoke? Our favored ontology for the micro-constitution of the physical universe now includes quarks and several kinds of force, and other things I understand only dimly. This is very different from how our ancestors conceived things. But we have our present array of recognized entities because they are the ones invoked in what we now see as the most believable account of physical reality.
>
> There is no reason to proceed differently in the domain of human

affairs. If we cannot deliberate effectively, or understand and explain people's action illuminatingly, without such terms as "courage" or "generosity," then these are real features of the world.[95]

Conclusion

By now it should be clear that, far from being an expression of the metaphysical tradition and hence an enemy of pragmatism, hermeneutic social science can and should be viewed as consistent with it. Likewise, hermeneutic commitments to an ontological and methodological distinction between the natural and social sciences, and to the idea that "a people's self-understanding must be among the things which any adequate theory can explain,"[96] are not only compatible with pragmatism but are also the offspring of it. With this in mind, we might profitably restate the conflict between Rorty and hermeneutical social science: the problem is not that hermeneutical social science is unpragmatic, but that Rorty's pragmatism is not pragmatic enough.

— 3 —

The Politics of Redescription

In the essay "Method, Social Science, and Social Hope," Rorty contends that perhaps the most important challenge facing social scientists today is that of reinvigorating the long dormant Deweyan ideal of social science. This ideal, which flourished in America for a period prior to the advent of behavioralism, accents above all "the moral importance of the social sciences—their role in widening and deepening our sense of community and of the possibilities open to that community."[1] Rather than following the path of figures such as Michel Foucault (who, Rorty claims, also adopts the "pragmatist line," but unlike Dewey emphasizes the darker aspects of the social sciences, the ways in which they "have served as instruments of 'the disciplinary society' "),[2] Rorty urges pragmatists to devote their energies to the positive task of enlarging human solidarity, that is, of expanding the scope and depth of our liberal democratic community by showing us how others who do not share our particular cultural practices or form of life, who look strange, or who act differently are ultimately also " 'one of us.' "[3] This transformation of both our sensibilities and our sense of community is accomplished, Rorty says, not by locating something universal that binds us all together but by describing what unfamiliar people are like and redescribing what we ourselves are like.[4] By interpreting people, cultures, institutions, and practices in ways that make us more sensitive to the details of human pain, suffering, and humiliation; by promoting an appreciation of the cardinal liberal values of tolerance, diversity, and freedom; and by fostering an awareness of the contingency of all communities, pragmatists contribute to both a "strengthening of liberal institutions"[5] and "a renewed sense of community."[6]

Now if the principal aim of this Deweyan/Rortyian vision of social science is the widening and deepening of a flexible, pluralistic, open, and tolerant "bourgeois liberalism,"[7] then the means to this end lie in the somewhat vague interpretive practice that Rorty labels "redescription." As conceived by Rorty, redescription is an intellectual practice employed specifically for the purpose of radically transforming or replacing a calcified but well-entrenched vocabulary. Such a practice is necessary because, following from his neo-Wittgensteinian account of alternative vocabularies and language-games, in those cases where one's aim is to uproot a well-established and "time-honored" vocabulary, standard forms of argument prove invariably to be "inconclusive or question-begging."[8] This, he says, is because the proponents of the time-honored vocabulary always demand that any arguments against it be phrased in their vocabulary. And this implies that their opponents must show that certain features of the entrenched vocabulary are internally incoherent or inconsistent, or that they " 'deconstruct themselves.' "[9] But these demands, Rorty holds, can never be met, for the current vocabulary defines what is coherent, consistent, and meaningful speech in the first place.[10] Thus, the attempt to uproot an entrenched vocabulary through *argument* is always at best inconclusive, simply because there are no noninvidious common criteria of evaluation or comparison. For this reason, Rorty maintains that "interesting philosophy is rarely an examination of the pros and cons of a thesis. Usually it is . . . a contest between an entrenched vocabulary which has become a nuisance and a half-formed new vocabulary which vaguely promises great things."[11]

In these instances, what is required is not careful argument but an ability to show how things might look when rearranged and placed in a different light. As Rorty explains, this "method" of philosophy

is the same as the "method" of utopian politics or revolutionary science (as opposed to parliamentary politics or normal science). The method is to redescribe lots and lots of things in new ways, until you have created a pattern of linguistic behavior which will tempt the rising generation to adopt it, thereby causing them to look for appropriate new forms of nonlinguistic behavior, for example, the adoption of new scientific equipment or new social institutions. This sort of philosophy does not work piece by piece, analyzing concept after concept, or testing thesis after thesis. Rather, it works holistically and pragmatically. It says things like "try thinking of it this way" . . . It does not try to pretend to have a better candidate for doing the same things which we did when we spoke in the old way. Rather, it suggests that we might want to stop doing those things and do something else. But it does not argue for this suggestion on the basis of antecedent criteria common to the old and new language games. For just insofar as the new language really is new, there will be no such criteria.[12]

In short, redescription is not an attempt to enunciate " 'the right description' "[13] but an attempt to avoid or dissolve intractable problems, conflicts, or anomalies by reweaving the fabric of our current ways of speaking into a new vocabulary, one "that cuts across the vocabulary we have so far used in our . . . deliberations."[14] The aim of the redescriber is not to offer arguments against the currently familiar vocabulary, but to "make the vocabulary I favor look attractive by showing how it may be used to describe a variety of topics."[15] If successful, the redescriber will contribute to intellectual progress by creating new metaphors and modes of speech that over time succeed in becoming literalized.[16]

Because the practice of redescription is resolutely not an attempt to engage in, but to avoid, "normal" philosophical and conceptual argumentation, efforts to evaluate it on these grounds are in Rorty's view fundamentally misconceived. They are misconceived for the obvious reason that they presuppose precisely the normal vocabulary and practices of justification that the redescriber seeks to circumvent and replace. As one sympathetic critic has noted, to ask Rorty "for a conceptually adequate account of redescription would be to demand a philosophically responsible account of irresponsibility."[17] Although I would maintain that there are indeed cases in which it *is* possible to argue for or against the introduction of a new vocabulary,[18] here I am primarily interested in examining Rorty's redescriptive practice in its own pragmatic terms. That is, I want to see to what extent his redescriptive efforts facilitate the preservation and extension of freedom and pluralism, help us to determine which social and political traditions and practices should endure and be extended and which may need reconstruction or abandonment, and provide us with a promising exit from particular conflicts and dilemmas. In this chapter, therefore, I will explore what is perhaps Rorty's most ambitious effort at redescription, his attempt to redescribe liberalism by sketching a picture of what he calls a "liberal utopia." By examining some of the problems implicit in this particular exemplar of redescription, I hope to identify some of the limitations of Rorty's redescriptive practice. However, before examining these questions, it is first necessary to describe in more detail Rorty's understanding of current impasses in social and political thought, as well as his vision of a postmetaphysical liberal utopia.

Redescription Applied

Rorty's postmetaphysical redescription of liberalism is, among other things, an attempt to offer a way out of what he sees as a prototypical case of philosophical deadlock in contemporary social and political theory, namely, the stalemate regarding the relation between the private and public domains of life, or, as Rorty redescribes it, the conflict between, on the one hand, the desire for private autonomy and self-creation, and, on the other hand, the desire for solidarity and social justice. Rorty contends that these conflicting impulses constitute the principal tension between two distinct and ultimately irreconcilable types of thinkers, each with its own philosophical vision, as well as its own understanding of selfhood, community, and freedom: *ironists* such as Nietzsche, Proust, Heidegger, and Nabokov, and *liberals* such as "Marx, Mill, Dewey, Habermas, and Rawls."[19]

Rorty begins by noting that, in at least one respect, the two types of thinkers are quite similar: both are "historicist" in the sense that they reject any and all attempts at theoretically, theologically, or metaphysically grounding our "most central beliefs and desires."[20] Like Rorty, both types repudiate the idea "that there is any such thing as 'human nature' or the 'deepest level of the self,' " as well as the notion that there is "an order beyond time and change which determines the point of human existence and establishes a hierarchy of responsibilities."[21] To the contrary, they all "insist that socialization, and thus historical circumstance, go all the way down—that there is nothing 'beneath' socialization or prior to history which is definitory of the human."[22] In this respect, these authors have helped release us from the grip of "theology and metaphysics," and have prepared the way for a future, "postmetaphysical culture," one organized around "an endless, proliferating realization of Freedom, rather than a convergence toward an already existing Truth."[23]

However, apart from their common animus to the idea of metaphysical grounding, these two types of historicist writers are motivated by dramatically different desires. For ironists like Nietzsche, Heidegger, and Foucault, "the desire for self-creation, for private autonomy, dominates."[24] These writers are interested primarily in the quest for "private perfection," in the self-creation of a distinctive, autonomous life, one that is not, as Harold Bloom says, either "a copy or a replica."[25] As such, they are exemplars of "what private perfection . . . can be like"; but at the same time they distrust processes of socialization, which they tend to view as "antithetical to something deep within us"—such as the will to power, libidinal impulses, or Being.[26] By contrast, liberal authors like Mill, Dewey, Habermas, Rawls, and Isaiah Berlin are animated primarily by "the desire for a more just and free human community."[27] They see their work not as a personal quest for autonomy, but as "a shared, social effort—the effort to make our institutions and practices more just and less cruel."[28] Indeed, Rorty calls these figures liberals precisely because (borrowing Judith Shklar's definition of "liberal") they "think that cruelty is the worst thing we do."[29] However, this overriding regard for social justice and the cessation of cruelty places them deeply at odds with their ironist counterparts, whose pursuit of private perfection seems frequently imbued with a decidedly anti-liberal proclivity for " 'irrationalism' and 'aestheticism.' "[30] For this reason, liberals like Rawls (in his earlier writings) and Habermas continue to search for a postmetaphysical anchor for their politics, hoping in this way to harness the threat of unbridled ironism.

In discussing this often acrimonious conflict between "writers on autonomy" and "writers on justice," Rorty holds that the standard philosophical solutions all seek to reconcile these antagonistic stances by uniting them under a single, more synthetic theoretical or philosophical view, one that "would let us hold self-creation and justice, private perfection and human solidarity, in a single vision."[31] Hence, we find debates between neo-Kantian rationalists like Habermas, neo-Nietzschean anarchists like Foucault, communitarians like Michael Sandel, and philosophically oriented liberals like Rawls and Ronald Dworkin—all seeking to reconcile opposing claims by bringing them under a more synoptic philosophical view. Rorty maintains, however, that these manifold proposals are plausible only if one first assumes that the ironist and liberal visions are not fundamentally "incommensurable" but are merely opposed. But, he insists, they *are* incommensurable: "The vocabulary of self-creation is necessarily private, unshared, unsuited to argument. The vocabulary of justice is necessarily public and shared, a medium for argumentative exchange."[32] Because of this ineradicable incommensurability, there "is no way to bring self-creation together with justice at the level of theory."[33]

Rather than endeavoring to unify these forever incommensurable stances in a single philosophical vision or to terminate the conflict by granting priority to the demands of one side over those of the other, Rorty instead recommends that we look at the relation between these two types of writers "as being like the relation between two kinds of tools— as little in need of synthesis as paintbrushes and crowbars."[34] One kind of writer, the ironist, teaches us that there are indeed legitimate virtues other than social virtues, that some people do succeed "in re-creating themselves."[35] These writers serve us by bringing to light our own "half-articulate need" for self-transformation and by encouraging us to become "one whom we as yet lack the words to describe."[36] Conversely, liberal writers prompt us to recognize the gap between the commitments embodied in "the public, shared vocabulary we use in daily life"[37] and the actual character of our current institutions and practices. By pointing out the ways in which these institutions and practices fall short of our implicit commitments, these writers help give focus to our "sense of obligation to other human beings."[38]

As a way of preserving what is most valuable in both types of thinkers, Rorty advocates not a theoretical solution but, rather, a satisfactory practical "compromise." In this compromise, each party is recognized as being "right," but only within a particular domain.[39] The challenge, Rorty believes, is to reconcile ourselves to the fact that our "final vocabulary" (that is, those fully contingent and foundationless but nevertheless irreducible and authoritative words that constitute the linguistic ground for all of our claims about knowledge, morality, and the good life)[40] contains "two independent parts," one crucial for the private project of self-creation, the other indispensable for the public project of human solidarity.[41] Our imperative, he emphasizes, is not to unify but to *accommodate practically* these two "equally valid, yet forever incommensurable" parts.[42]

For Rorty, the most suitable modus vivendi is one that grants the ironist's demand for autonomy and self-creation yet insists that the pursuit of this goal be strictly a private affair. Ironists, Rorty writes, are figures who are defined in part by their acute awareness of the arbitrariness and contingency of their own final vocabulary. Unlike nihilists, ironists have commitments, but unlike metaphysicians, their commitments are wedded to "a sense of the contingency of their own commitment."[43] Indeed, precisely because ironists are "never quite able to take themselves seriously,"[44] they continually entertain and experiment with other vocabularies, hoping through this ongoing process to fashion an increasingly self-made self, one that is not simply a reflection or effect of one's predecessors, historical circumstances, or local culture. However, although this unending process of questioning, redescribing, and reweaving one's inherited vocabularies, of exploring and creating new ones, is central to the ironist's quest for an ever more autonomous, self-created final vocabulary, Rorty denies emphatically that this activity plays any positive role in public life. "Irony," he states, "seems inherently a private matter," something that "is of little public use."[45] More importantly, Rorty warns that when nonliberal ironists such as Nietzsche, Heidegger, and Foucault seek to bring their redescriptive practices into the public domain, they typically abandon their ironic appreciation of the contingency of their own vocabulary and instead become convinced that they have hit upon some deep truth about the way in which public institutions repress inherently the desire for autonomy. Failing to recognize that autonomy "is not the sort of thing that *could* ever be embodied in social institutions,"[46] ironist public philosophers are led to dismiss too easily both liberalism and its attendant institutions. When this happens, public ironists become "at best useless and at worst dangerous."[47]

To circumvent these potential hazards of public ironism, Rorty offers an elegantly clear and simple prescription: we should "*privatize* the Nietzschean-Sartrean-Foucauldian attempt at authenticity and purity" and enforce this by insisting upon "a firm distinction between the public and the private."[48] On this view, the ironist's desire for autonomy and self-creation, as well as the utopian vision of a culture characterized by an endless proliferation of alternative descriptions (what Rorty calls a "poeticized culture"), are all to be welcomed as legitimate and even exemplary private ideals. As long as they "do it on their own time—causing no harm to others and using no resources needed by those less advantaged," ironists are free to be "as privatistic, 'irrational' and aestheticist as they please."[49] Such freedom from coercion is not only tolerable but also is, Rorty claims, "the aim of a just and free society."[50] In the public realm, however, things are altogether different. This is the realm of what Wilfred Sellars calls "we-intentions," of shared practices and self-interpretations that define us not as individuals, but as part of a larger moral community.[51] Here our paramount concern is with public issues of social justice, and in such public matters discourse must begin necessarily from within a common vocabulary, one that permits both argument and rational consensus. This, of course, does not imply that public vocabularies must remain forever immune from criticism and transformation, but it does entail a "mild ethnocentrism," one based on the idea that public discourse must start from "the way *we* live now," and that "people [and communities] can rationally change their beliefs and desires only by holding most of those beliefs and desires constant."[52]

For "us" citizens of "the secular modern West," this shared and public vocabulary is unavoidably that of liberal democracy, with its characteristic accent on averting cruelty and "the humiliation of human beings."[53] Rorty openly accepts the idea that these core commitments can never be buttressed by appeals to transcendental or ontological arguments, but he maintains that such philosophical reinforcements are not needed in the first place. All that is required to sustain a commitment to liberal democracy is a comparative historical narrative about the way in which its customs and institutions have, on the whole, made these societies less cruel and more free (in the aforementioned sense of tolerating a greater range of self-expression, and providing more leeway for people to pursue whatever private projects they may wish) than nonliberal societies.[54] Such an account could not, he acknowledges, rationally convince just anyone of liberalism's superiority, for unless one already shares our moral sensitivity to acts of cruelty and humiliation, as well as our appreciation of the pleasures devolving from freedom, diversity, and toleration (that is, unless one already accepts some of the "words" in liberalism's "final vocabulary"), such comparative accounts have no persuasive force. This absence of ultimate ground, however, is in Rorty's view no cause for despair, both because the demand for a "noncircular" justification of our social practices is itself incoherent and, more notably, because our own ungrounded ground is all we need for *our* social deliberations.[55]

Although at first reading this resolutely nominalist, historicist, and "postmodernist" conception of liberalism might appear to be hopelessly at odds with the standard canon of liberal thought, Rorty contends that in fact it remains in tune with the basic commitments both of J. S. Mill's liberalism and of Jeffersonian democracy.[56] For example, he tells us that, although the *practical tasks* of reducing cruelty and of balancing public and private commitments require perpetual deliberation and social experimentation, "my hunch is that Western social and political thought may have had the last *conceptual* revolution that it needs. J. S. Mill's suggestion that governments devote themselves to optimizing the balance between leaving people's private lives alone and preventing suffering seems to me pretty much the last word."[57] On the question of how best to close the divide between liberal ideals and the often depressing (and cruel) realities of life in contemporary liberal states, Rorty rejects the idea that what we need is a "radical critique" of liberal thought and instead insists that "contemporary liberal society already contains the institutions for its own improvement."[58] Indeed, the "only way to avoid perpetuating cruelty within social institutions" is simply to continue extending those institutions emblematic of liberalism, that is, to continue "maximizing the quality of education, freedom of the press, educational opportunity, opportunities to exert political influence, and the like."[59]

Seen in this light, Rorty's fully developed ideal polity—his "liberal utopia"—is a clear repudiation both of Habermas's attempt to eradicate all ironism and ground social democratic practices in a universalist "communicative reason"[60] and of Foucault's putative hope for a "total revolution" that would embody our autonomy in our institutions.[61] Rather, what emerges is a dualistic, compartmentalized vision not only of the self but also of the relation between the public and the private spheres. On the private side of this divide is the ironist's preoccupation with autonomy and passion for continual redescription—both esteemed as exemplary impulses in the quest to achieve private perfection. Here we find the realm of negative freedom and the absence of other-regarding obligations, and, hence, the realm of fantasy, play, incommensurate metaphors, and self-creation. On the public side of the divide is the liberal's commitment to the minimization of pain, cruelty, and humiliation through the expansion and refinement of "the institutions of bourgeois liberal society."[62] This is the realm not of idiosyncrasy and aesthetic invention but of "solidarity" and we-intentions. Here the highest virtues are those of the public citizen, the person engaged in common public discourse about ways to minimize cruelty, achieve social justice, and extend human solidarity. As a polity composed of citizens who have dispensed with attempts to synthesize philosophically the public and private spheres, Rorty's utopia stands as a picture of a transformed culture freed of such Enlightenment neuroses, one that seeks only to devise various practical and political measures to balance these "equally valid" yet dualistic commitments.[63] Likewise, the ideal resident of this polity, the "liberal ironist" (an unlikely combination of the private ironism of Proust and Derrida and the public liberalism of figures such as Dewey and George Orwell), is one who renounces the Enlightenment-induced longing for a unified and centered self and in- stead strives merely to negotiate the competing demands of "a private ethic of self-creation and a public ethic of mutual accomodation."[64]

For Rorty, this redescription of Enlightenment liberalism terminates in a new and more compelling vision both of liberal politics and of the relation between the public and private spheres. By abandoning the out- dated vocabularies of theology, metaphysics, and foundationalist philos- ophy, Rorty believes that we provide the conditions for a revitalized public and private life, one that consists of an "intricately textured collage of private narcissism and public pragmatism."[65] Moreover, he insists that the absence of such vocabularies does not leave us without the tools necessary for defending liberal commitments to freedom, tolerance, plu- ralism, and the like (as some critics maintain it does) but rather reinvig- orates those commitments precisely by underscoring in detail both their practical advantages *and* their historical contingency. Such a story may lack the sense of epic drama found in the "grand" treatises of Enlight- enment philosophy, but it is no less capable of engendering a commit- ment to human solidarity.

This vision of a liberal society, founded entirely upon "our loyalty to other human beings clinging together against the dark, not our hope of getting things right,"[66] is unquestionably one of the more ambitious ef- forts to rejuvenate liberalism's most attractive ideals—namely, its moral commitment to toleration, pluralism, and the avoidance of cruelty and its preoccupation with developing a mix of rights, liberties, and institu- tions that protect individuals and minorities against the all-too-familiar dangers of absolutism, totalitarianism, and other forms of unrestrained statism. By detaching these aspirations from the rigid and abstract phil- osophical structures in which they have frequently been encased, Rorty proposes a vision of liberalism that departs both from classical social contract and natural rights versions and from those offered by contem- porary foundationalist liberals like Ronald Dworkin, Robert Nozick, and the early John Rawls.[67] However, apart from the evident originality of Rorty's liberal utopia, one must still pose the basic pragmatist questions: What is the cash value of this redescription? Does it offer us a *useful*

alternative to foundationalist liberalism, one based on a clear understanding of "the patterns of the past and the needs of the present?"[68] Or,
by contrast, does the very way in which he seeks to escape from the
pathologies of conventional foundationalist philosophy leave him without
the resources required for expanding and ultimately realizing liberalism's
most admired ideals?

Contingency, Self-Creation, and Change

Perhaps these issues can be defined more sharply if we begin by examining what is clearly *the* connecting thread running throughout Rorty's
narrative. This is the rather elusive but frequently invoked notion of contingency.[69] In its broadest sense, Rorty construes contingency as the idea
that things and events "might have been otherwise."[70] Understood in this
way, the term "contingency" typically stands at one end of a set of oppositions whose other term is variously "necessity," "essence," "intrinsic,"
or "unconditioned." These latter terms, as I have indicated, are themselves
tightly intertwined with notions of a common "human nature," a telos,
a divine order, or some other principle of legitimacy that is privileged
precisely because its status is independent of our particular historical location and social practices. At a minimum, then, Rorty's accent on contingency is tied closely to his denial of the idea that there is anything
"'beneath' socialization or prior to history that is definatory of the
human."[71]

Unfortunately, this account is not in itself highly informative, for it is
at best an extremely general and purely negative construal. When Rorty
speaks of contingency in a more specific manner, however, he typically
uses the term in one of two ways. The first use links it to notions of
novelty, innovation, originality, and creativity. In these instances
(common in his chapter "The Contingency of Selfhood" in *Contingency,
Irony, and Solidarity*) contingency is meant to pinpoint some domain or
space that is devoid of any immanent nature or logic and therefore also
open to innovation, transformation, and redescription. Here contingency
refers to the abundant possibilities inherent in the recognition of historicity: because our inherited practices and forms of life are not ontologically fixed but are culturally and historically constituted, they can (although never all at once) be questioned, transformed, and redescribed.
Understood in this way, Rorty's invocation of contingency moves between

a restatement of the undeniable fact that human beings and human history are something more than the combined effects of culture and nature and a voluntarist notion that the only impediments to human change and transformation are those set by the human will itself.

At other times, Rorty uses the term "contingency" in a quite different manner, identifying it not with the powers and possibilities of human innovation but with notions of chance, luck, accident, randomness, or fortuitousness. This connection is made explicit in a number of different passages: "Poetic, artistic, philosophical, scientific, or political progress results from the accidental coincidence of a private obsession with a public need";[72] Galileo "just lucked out";[73] "the idea of human solidarity is simply the fortunate happenstance creation of modern times";[74] the scattered references to "random factors" and constellations;[75] and the invocation of Philip Larkin's metaphor of the "blind impress."[76] It is, however, also implicit in Rorty's radically decentered conception of human subjectivity, as well as in the recurrence of haunting and despondent passages on the theme of human powerlessness. Whether explicit or implicit, however, the meaning of contingency in all of these passages is essentially the same: it implies uncontrollable and unpredictable forces or events that shape our lives decisively.

What is significant about these construals of contingency is the way in which they accent Rorty's equivocations regarding the potentialities and limits of individual and collective action. As we can see from his dual use of the term, Rorty vacillates between an "anything goes" vision of human agency—in which our capacities for personal or social transformation are limited only by the powers of our individual or collective imaginations— and a vision in which human efforts to shape one's self and one's world are every bit as uncontrollable as in the most deterministic and totalizing philosophical systems. Here Rorty finds himself locked in the same dichotomy between voluntarism and determinism that he associates with metaphysical and foundationalist enterprises.[77]

In fact, neither of these construals is typical of everyday life. Our capacity for self-creation or imagination is *not* unlimited; it is instead partly constituted, and therefore also partly constrained, by past and present cultural and linguistic practices. These practices not only privilege certain imaginative and creative efforts over others but also partly constitute the categories of "novelty" and "originality," thus distinguishing them both from "the old" and from eccentricity, insanity, silliness, and the quixotic.

Indeed, as many have pointed out, the absence of any "great" women artists or philosophers in the standard canon of Western culture reveals more about the ways in which categories like originality and genius have been constructed than about the artistic or intellectual talents of women.[78] Conversely, it may be true that there are countless unanticipated and uncontrollable events that in one way or another shape the course of our lives, but precisely *what* effect they have on us and *how* we respond to them is neither fully predetermined nor entirely a matter of "chance." Rather, these things are delimited both by material forces and by the horizons of our individual and social self-understandings—horizons that simultaneously make meaning possible and limit the possible domain of meaning.

Rorty, of course, is not entirely unaware of these problems. He acknowledges at times that our creative capacities are not unlimited and that even purely chance events can be understood and confronted in different ways. He tells us, for example, that there are "no fully Nietzschean lives ... no lives which are not largely parasitical on an unredescribed past and dependent on the charity of as yet unborn generations."[79] Unfortunately, Rorty fails to appreciate fully the social and political implications of this insight. If novelty and imagination are themselves partly constituted by language and social practice, and if (as I have indicated) language and social practice place flexible and contestable but nevertheless real restrictions upon what is and is not intelligible, who has the right to speak, whose speech and what forms of speech are taken seriously, and what counts as a problem and what counts as a solution to some problem, then questions about the pursuit of and capacity for self-creation and change are not just personal and private questions, nor are they just questions about whether we should "drop" worn-out vocabularies and metaphors in favor of newer, more useful ones. Indeed, precisely because what counts as a "worn-out" or "useful" vocabulary is itself partly constituted by the social and linguistic practices of our communities, questions about self-creation, change, and the usefulness of vocabularies all presuppose a specific social, political, and ideological context that cannot be erased even if it goes unnoticed.

This discussion of contingency and the public/private dichotomy suggests a profound tension in Rorty's redescriptive efforts. Although his accent on contingency, along with his rigid separation of the public and the private, are both intended to open up spaces for increased pluralism, novelty, play, self-creation, and human solidarity, they tend instead to pass over or mask just those forces that not only limit the range of possible projects but also structure the level, quality, and possibility of participation in cultural and political conversations. If we ask what features within Rorty's narrative encourage these problematic construals, we find at least two, one deriving from Rorty's understanding of politics and the political and one (which is more "methodological") concerning the relation between theory (and narratives) and practice.

Starting with the second, one of the most puzzling features of Rorty's redescriptive practice is the conspicuous gap between his formal pronouncements regarding the heuristic value of particular genres and the content of his own writings. Formally, Rorty tells us that certain sorts of books are particularly "relevant to our relations with others, to helping us to notice the effects of our actions on other people."[80] These are, first, books that "help us to see the effects of social practices and institutions on others" and, second, "those which help us see the effects of our private idiosyncrasies on others."[81] Beyond these very general categories Rorty places few restrictions—apart from the stipulation that theories and treatises are *not* well-suited for these tasks—upon the types of books that might illuminate these issues. Apparently, anything from "the reports . . . of government commissions" to novels like *Sister Carrie* and *Black Boy* are possible candidates for moral and political edification.[82] In keeping with his anti-theoretical, anti-universalist posture, however, he emphasizes the importance of narratives that focus on particular exemplars or offer what Clifford Geertz calls "thick description." He observes, for example, that "ethnography," "concrete examples," "detailed historical narratives," and "detailed description of what unfamiliar people are like and . . . redescription of what we ourselves are like" are all particularly effective ways of enlarging our moral sympathies and political understanding.[83]

What is significant here is not just the observation itself (which is, after all, common among those who question the practical benefits of transcendental theorizing) but the extraordinary disjunction between these recommendations and Rorty's own narrative practice. That is, within the corpus of Rorty's writings, there is almost *no* "detailed description" of "the effects of our social practices and institutions on others," nor any "detailed historical narratives" mapping the genesis and effects of those practices. In fact, it is striking that although Rorty acknowledges the existence of deep and disturbing social problems—he laments, for example, "the unending hopelessness and misery of the lives of the young blacks in American cities"—he never describes in any detail the broader context or "social field" in which those problems are embedded, nor does he locate particular social practices that contribute to and sustain these problems.[84]

This failure to offer any detailed description of the social field or particular social practices leads inevitably to a number of difficulties. It sustains, for example, Rorty's problematic construal of contingency. As we have seen, when he asserts that "man is always free to choose new descriptions (for, among other things, himself),"[85] or when he speaks of poets and other original thinkers inventing radically novel and incommensurate metaphors that eventually become literalized, he veers toward an extreme form of voluntarism—one in which, as Roy Bhaskar puts it, we are "always free to choose *any* description."[86] This stance appears credible *if* we examine only the most palpable and formal types of social constraints. But once we observe in narrative detail the role that linguistic and social practices play in constraining, disposing, and directing (even if not determining and compelling) our descriptions and redescriptions, Rorty's voluntaristic understanding of contingency and choice appears both facile and complacent.

To take one example, the sociologist Pierre Bourdieu, in a study of modes of classification in French academic institutions, examined the individual files of a professor of philosophy at a *prèmiere supérieure* in Paris.[87] Through the inspection of grades and comments on the written and oral work of students of different social origins, Bourdieu found "a simple and clearly visible relation" between a *hierarchy of epithets* (evaluative comments ranging from "simplistic," "silly," and "insipid" to "lively," "cultivated," and "masterly") and a *hierarchy of social origins,* a ranking based on "the importance of the cultural capital" inherited from their parents (determined by factors such as the residence and profession of the pupils' parents).[88] Students from the middle classes (there were no students from the lower classes, nor any male students, since the files were taken from an all-girls' school) and the provinces "were the prime target of negative judgments—and of the most negative among them, such as simplistic, servile or vulgar . . . Even the virtues which are attributed to them are negative too: academic, painstaking, careful, conscientious."[89] By contrast, students from the class with the most cultural capital "almost entirely avoid the most negative judgments, even in their euphemistic forms, as they do the petty-bourgeois virtues, and they most often find themselves granted the most sophisticated qualities."[90] Moreover, he found that in those instances where students from different social origins received the same grades, the remarks were "all the more severe and more brutally expressed, less euphemistic, as the social origins of the pupils decrease."[91]

As Bourdieu notes, both technical aptitudes, such as the capacity to construct an argument or to grasp the specialized vocabulary of particular authors, and personal and physical qualities constitute part of the disparate criteria of professorial judgement. Especially in students' oral work, these latter " 'external' criteria" become prominent, and here too there is a tight connection between students' social origins (as expressed in one's accent, body language, and style of speaking) and the professor's remarks on their work and talents: "The 'external' criteria, most often implicit and even rejected by the institution, have even greater importance in the remarks on oral work, since the criteria already mentioned are compounded with all those concerning speech, and, more specifically, *accent, elocution and diction,* which are the surest, because the most indelible, marks of social and geographical origins, *the style of the spoken language,* which can differ radically from written style, and finally and above all the *bodily 'hexis',* manners and behavior, which are often designated, very directly, in the remarks."[92] Bourdieu's point is clearly not that philosophy professors or professors from other disciplines self-consciously conspire to reproduce in the academic field the social hierarchies characteristic of the society in which they live. If this were the case, the process could hardly be sustained in the way that it is.[93] Rather, he claims that it is the very way in which the academic field itself is structured that "makes it unthinkable" for both professors and their pupils to recognize "the social significance of the judgments."[94] Hence, the manifestly brutal epithets used to describe pupils' work (epithets that, Bourdieu rightly observes, "would not be permissible in ordinary usage") and the "complacency and freedom of symbolic aggression" are possible only because they operate in disguise.[95] As Bourdieu remarks:

It is because they think that they are operating a purely academic or even a specifically "philosophical" classification ... that the system is able to perform a genuine *distortion of the meaning* of their practices, persuading them to do what they would not do deliberately for "all the

money in the world." It is also because they believe that they are making
a strictly academic judgement that the social judgement which is masked
by the euphemistic implications of academic (or, more specifically, philosophical) language can produce its characteristic effect . . . The transmutation of social truth into academic truth (from "you are a petty
bourgeois" to "you work hard but lack brilliance" [*vous étes travailleur
mais pas brillant*]) is not a simple game of writing which has no consequence but an operation of social alchemy which confers on words
their symbolic efficiency, their power to have a lasting effect on practice.[96]

This example shows that although Rorty would like to separate clearly
private projects of self-creation from public projects of social justice, in
the realm of everyday life these projects inevitably spill over and causally
intermix. For the middle-class student from the provinces whose project
of self-creation includes the desire to teach philosophy, these concerns
are neither abstract nor trivial nor easily eradicable. Indeed, they are the
sort of thing of which deep personal conflicts are made, for in this case
it may involve either disavowing or eradicating aspects of her identity or
history, or—having come to believe that she genuinely is "lacking philosophical talent"—deciding that her preferred project is not one for
which she is suited.[97] In either instance, however, the private project of
self-creation cannot be neatly distilled from the social practices, mechanisms, hierarchies, and power relationships that operate, sometimes inconspicuously and sometimes quite nakedly, in the public domain. To
the contrary, private projects are always and unavoidably structured by
public forces.

Rorty would no doubt agree that in practice the line between the private pursuit of self-creation and the public pursuit of social justice is
often fuzzy and that one of the principal aims of social science is to reduce
this fuzziness by identifying previously unrecognized forms of cruelty in
public institutions that constrain the private pursuit of self-creation. Nevertheless, he would—and does—insist that it is important to think of
these two spheres as distinct and "forever incommensurable" universes
and to make this distinction the basis of our political deliberations. This
response, however, fails to address the crucial question of why the public
and private spheres *should* be viewed as linguistically and conceptually
exclusive and incommensurable categories, if, as Rorty himself recognizes,

history and human experience clearly indicate that they are not. In other words, if, as writers such as Carole Pateman argue, the evidence of history and everyday life shows that these two spheres have never been simply divided, but have always been intimately and "inextricably interrelated" as well,[98] then the proper starting point for deliberating about these spheres would seem to be precisely this evidence, rather than the arbitrary and abstract separation that Rorty defends. Indeed, it appears that in his effort to correct those writers who seek to unify the public and private spheres via an abstract theoretical synthesis, Rorty simply inverts the problem by positing an equally misleading and abstract separation—one that, far from being a redescription of the public and private spheres, merely follows the time-honored liberal practice of insisting solely on a division of these spheres, while ignoring their historical and conceptual interrelations. The result is a description that is not in any substantive way a redescription and a proposed solution/compromise that remains detached from the political realities that it seeks to inform.

This point, of course, does *not* imply that the public/private distinction has no meaningful social or political purpose but rather that philosophical solutions or pragmatic redescriptions that clearly contravene the lessons of history and everyday experience should be received with skepticism. This is especially the case when those solutions or redescriptions are ones that reenshrine patterns of thinking that have historically legitimated and sustained patriarchal or oppressively hierarchical forms of social relations. As many feminists have observed, however, the classical liberal dichotomy between the public and the private spheres, founded on the idea that these two spheres are ontologically separate and unrelated "but equally important and valuable,"[99] has served historically as a mainstay of patriarchical relations in both the public and private spheres.[100] Moreover, to the extent that this philosophical separation eventually became internalized in individual and social bodies, it has, as Pateman points out, functioned ideologically to mystify and delegitimize those aspects of experience that denied the separation.[101] For these reasons, many feminists have advocated a conception or ideal of the social order that is markedly different from the classical liberal and Rortyian versions. This conception "looks toward a differentiated social order within which the various dimensions are distinct but not separate or opposed, and which rests on a social conception of individuality, which includes both women and men as biologically differentiated but not unequal creatures. Nevertheless, women and men, and the private and the public, are not necessarily in harmony. Given the social implications of women's reproductive capacities, it is surely utopian to suppose that tension between the personal and the political, between love and justice, between individuality and community will disappear with patriarchical-liberalism."[102]

The preceding analysis demonstrates the way in which Rorty's reluctance to examine the complicated interweavings of past and present social practices leaves him without any analytic resources for either assessing the costs of those practices or indicating how we might preserve, extend, criticize, or challenge them. All of these endeavors presuppose that we first have some understanding of how social and linguistic practices interact; of the various privileges, distinctions, and distortions that they enshrine; and of the role they play in constituting our individual and collective self-interpretations. This requirement, of course, does not entail a return to grand theory or, a fortiori, to totalizing conceptions of society. It does, however, imply an empiricism of sorts, namely, a willingness to examine closely how these practices developed, what their effects are, and how their benefits and burdens are parsed among different individuals and groups in society. In this regard, the recurring theme of powerlessness, along with the corresponding admission that we "have no clear idea of what to work for,"[103] should not be conceived as being out of tune with the more celebratory temper of Rorty's narrative. Rather, both motifs are natural consequences of the type of narrative that Rorty constructs, one that—ironically—implicitly shares the theorist's and traditional philosopher's animus toward all forms of empiricism and detailed historical and sociological description.[104]

Redescription and Politics

Let us turn now to Rorty's postmetaphysical vision of liberalism. Rorty's redescription of classical liberal thought proceeds, as we have seen, through a nonrationalist, nonuniversalist redescription of the hopes and aims of a liberal society. The key maneuver in this redescription is his recommendation that philosophers and political theorists drop their efforts to fuse theoretically the impulses for self-creation and justice. They should instead be content to recognize the import and legitimacy of both impulses, while carefully circumscribing the domain in which each is allowed to flourish. By insisting on a firm distinction between the public and private spheres, Rorty contends that irreconcilable philosophical disputes can be transformed into concrete practical questions about how best to balance the incommensurable demands for self-creation and human solidarity. Striking adequate compromises between these two demands is, Rorty inveighs, the most important practical issue in liberal societies, but the skills required to negotiate such compromises are quite different from those of the theorist or traditional philosopher.

In examining this redescription, we might begin by posing the sort of instrumental, pragmatist questions that Rorty himself encourages us to ask: What is the practical benefit of this redescription? Does it illuminate or help us to resolve concrete social or political questions? Does it, in the spirit of Dewey, help us to determine or usefully consider which social practices we must preserve, cultivate, or extend and which we must refashion or jettison—especially once we have dispensed with the hope of solving these questions through the application of neutral, context-independent criteria or theories? Here, Rorty's pragmatic liberalism is at its weakest. Even if one finds convincing his claims about the impossibility of philosophically or theoretically synthesizing "Nietzsche with Marx or Heidegger with Habermas,"[105] it is difficult to see how Rorty's description of a liberal utopia could operate as an effective starting point or heuristic device for coming to grips with current social and political dilemmas. For instance, Rorty's insistence on a firm distinction between the public and private spheres may usefully remind us of the obvious dangers of eradicating the distinction altogether, but it does nothing to answer the truly difficult question of how that distinction is to be negotiated in practice. In current political debates about abortion rights, prayer in the school, family leave, governmental regulation of the economy, welfare payments to the poor, domestic violence, and the like, the issue under dispute isn't whether or not some distinction should be drawn between those aspects of life that are immune from governmental regulation and those that are not (this is instead the common starting point of the debate) but where, how, and on what basis that distinction is to be drawn.

Indeed, if we examine current ideological conflicts in the United States, what is striking is the way in which conservatives and liberals seek to defend diametrically opposed agendas through appeals to Rorty-like distinctions between the public and private spheres.[106] Broadly speaking, conservatives view markets and economic affairs generally as the realm of freedom, autonomy, innovation, and self-creation. They accept economic inequality as an unfortunate but inevitable effect of free markets, arguing that whatever cruelties the market may inflict on individuals, such cruelties are still less severe than those that would result from governmental efforts to regulate economic affairs and redistribute wealth. On the other hand, they argue that cultural, moral, educational, and lifestyle issues are issues of public concern, for without a consensus on basic moral and cultural questions, civility, decency, and public life generally cannot be sustained. Conversely, liberals contend that these same cultural, moral, educational, and lifestyle issues belong in the private sphere, the sphere of negative freedom, autonomy, irony, and self-creation. They maintain that questions of moral belief, lifestyle choice, and the like are quintessentially private questions; as such, they should remain free from state regulation and coercion. By contrast, the demands of justice and the obligation to minimize cruelty require more control over economic affairs and the distribution of wealth than an unregulated market provides. Moreover, they argue that civility, decency, and civic-mindedness are best preserved, not through the institution of moral and cultural orthodoxy, but by ensuring humane living conditions and attenuating extreme economic inequalities.

This brief sketch of current political conflict illustrates the severe practical limits of Rorty's redescription of classical liberalism. Not only does his proposed separation of the public and private spheres fail to provide a clear alternative to or exit from current ideological combat, but it also fails to even be a redescription in the strict sense of the word. As we have seen, both conservatives and liberals already appeal to distinctions identical to Rorty's own, yet they make these appeals in defense of diametrically opposed social and political policies. Hence, Rorty's distinctions between autonomy and justice, self-creation and human solidarity, and private narcissism and public pragmatism are better understood as restatements of positions that both conservatives and liberals endorse, the difference being that they interpret these distinctions in very different ways.

Rorty, of course, would surely reply that only someone still under the spell of metaphysics and theology could demand something more than the narrative that he provides, for only such a person believes that there are things like a special method or general a priori principles that determine what counts as rational or moral action in particular circumstances. As a pragmatist, however, he cannot—and need not—appeal to any neutral, context-independent principles or criteria for determining the outcome of specific conflicts. At most, he can recommend a possible locus of public deliberation, while supplementing this recommendation with a narrative describing its potential benefits and the potential dangers of competing alternatives. In politics, as in other areas of inquiry, the loyal pragmatist construes "rational" or "just" policies as those that emerge as a result of "undistorted communication" or of "free and open encounters of present linguistic practices and other practices with suggestions for new practices."[107] The actual resolution of particular conflicts can thus occur only through "free and open" public deliberations, not through the development of ahistorical theories of morality, politics, or justice.

This response might be credible if Rorty either convincingly demonstrated that "undistorted communication" or "free and open encounters" were indeed accurate descriptions of current political discourse in the United States or offered detailed analyses of current impediments to such encounters, along with proposals for removing them. But Rorty rejects both of these options. He concedes openly that, for all of American liberalism's virtues, there is still a clear and undeniable gulf between the ideal of free and open encounters and current political realities. Yet he also fails to examine those social practices and institutions that inhibit the development of a more free, open, inclusive, and democratic public discourse. Instead, he offers vague suggestions that avoid entirely the difficult practical issues. For example, he says that "discoveries about who is being made to suffer can be left to the workings of a free press, free universities, and enlightened public opinion" and that "the only way to avoid perpetuating cruelty within social institutions is by maximizing the quality of education, freedom of the press, educational opportunity, opportunities to exert political influence, and the like."[108] Such statements may, as far as they go, be true, but they elide all the troublesome questions about the particular measures required to realize these abstract aims. Can one, for instance, seriously hope to maximize the quality of education and educational opportunities without improving teacher-to-student ratios, without paying teachers salaries comparable to those in other respected professions, without increasing the number of days a year that children are sent to school, and without providing the necessary equipment for instruction?[109] And if not, how does one propose to finance these reforms in an age of fiscal uncertainty and increasing voter distrust of government generally? In short, Rorty's utopian dream of "building new and magnificently equipped schools in the inner cities"[110] may be an honorable one, but this dream only raises further and considerably more contentious questions about the types of political, economic, cultural, and institutional transformations that might be required to make this utopia a reality and about the forms of collective action that are likely to be the most effective instruments of such changes.

These, of course, are only a few of the many issues that arise as soon as one moves from the level of abstract sentiments to the terrain of social and political action, yet Rorty's narrative repeatedly stops short of any serious or systematic exploration of them. In place of a detailed inter-pretation of the social context and genesis of problems like the "crisis in education," Rorty offers sweeping and unsupported generalizations about "an increasingly greedy and heartless American middle-class" that lets "the quality of education a child receives become proportional to the assessed value of its parents' real estate" or that "is unwilling to pay the taxes necessary to give poor blacks a decent education and a chance in life."[111] Such claims are themselves deeply contentious, yet even if one grants that middle-class greed and racism are part of the problem, this too would seem to require further analysis and interpretation: Is the American middle class as fully unitary as Rorty assumes, or is it a complex collection of different social groups and communities (whites, African Americans, Asian Americans, urban and rural, northern and southern, men and women, white collar and blue collar, Christian, Jew, and Muslim) with disparate and frequently conflicting interests, sensibilities, and social sympathies? Was it just a matter of "chance" or "accident" that this class, or segments of this class, became increasingly greedy, selfish, and racist during the past twenty-five years? Was this a matter of "choice"? And if not, what are the social, political, economic, institutional, and historical sources of this shift in social sensibilities? Unfortunately, Rorty never pursues these questions. Instead, he quickly closes off the conversation by declaring that "it seems to me a fact [that] we need no fancier theoretical notions than 'greed,' 'selfishness,' and 'racial prejudice' to explain these phenomena . . . When I am told that to appreciate the significance of these facts I need a deeper understanding of, for example, the discourses of power of late capitalism, I am incredulous."[112]

Here again, Rorty's legitimate suggestion (that there is a point at which further analysis of pressing social problems can become an evasion of or substitute for, rather than a supplement to, political action) obscures the larger question of whether his remarkably vague proposals, along with his global claims about the causes of current social dilemmas, are accurate, compelling, or pragmatically useful (in Rorty's own sense of identifying a " 'pressure point for initiating change' ").[113] As I have argued, Rorty's recommendations not only fail to help identify pressure points for change; they represent a flight from that very task. In this respect, his original Deweyan ambition of transforming philosophy into an instrument of moral and political change—of bringing it back into "the conversation of mankind"—is abrogated by his own reluctance and inability to explore precisely those questions that are morally and politically urgent. Oddly, Rorty's preoccupation with avoiding a return to foundationalism, metaphysics, and Truth have left him so resistant to all forms of systematic analysis that his alternative to foundationalism is in many ways every bit as aloof from the complexities of ongoing social and political issues as the foundationalist philosophy that he sought to replace.

Conclusion

To return to the questions I posed at the outset, I hope to have shown that "redescription," as well as the broader Deweyan aim of reinvigorating social science and philosophy, must involve something more than just overcoming foundationalism or theoretical hegemony. It also means creating a space for the development of detailed portraits of our institutions and practices, of how they develop, of the effects they produce, and of the issues to which they give form. In addition, this means recognizing that the absence of an Archimedean point implies that issues of power are always potentially at stake in constituting, sustaining, or transforming our social practices. Rorty's own work is a testament to the fact that one can all too easily fuse sophisticated views about epistemology and philosophical foundationalism with political positions that are, however well intentioned, at best misconceived and at times self-stultifying. If we hope to avoid these problems, perhaps we should combine postmetaphysical insights on the status of knowledge not simply with "thin" global stories about the past, but also with detailed histories of practices and power.

— 4 —

Reclaiming the Language of Emancipation

Roy Bhaskar's Critical Realism

In the preceding chapters we examined the possibilities and limitations of Rorty's linguistic pragmatism. Though purporting to map a way out of the fierce conflicts presently dominating academic discourse about philosophy, politics, and social inquiry, Rorty's pragmatism ultimately fails to achieve its ambitions. It fails to do so, moreover, precisely because it absorbs large traces of the very modes of thought it aims to supplant. Consequently, Rorty's laudable effort to recast and reinvigorate both philosophy and political inquiry fails on its own terms.

This chapter will investigate controversies gathered around a second response to the "social science wars," one identified with a family of writers who variously characterize their position as "scientific realism," "critical realism," "transcendental realism," "qualified naturalism," or "critical naturalism." These writers—figures such as Roy Bhaskar, Richard Boyd, Rom Harré, and John Searle in philosophy; Jeffrey Isaac, Ian Shapiro, and Alexander Wendt in political science; Tony Lawson in economics; and Margaret Archer, Derek Layder, William Outhwaite, Andrew Sayer, and Erik Olin Wright in sociology—share Rorty's profound discomfort with standard empiricist and hermeneutical understandings of science,[1] as well as his naturalistic conviction that human and social affairs can "be studied in the same way as nature."[2] By contrast, however, the proponents of "realism"—that is, those who hold minimally "the theory that the objects of scientific inquiry exist and act, for the most part, independently of scientists and their activities"—directly challenge Rorty's counsel that ontological controversies about the "objects" of natural and social scientific inquiry should be "bypassed" or "forgotten."[3] Instead, realists argue that this casual indifference to ontology is both unthera- peutic and exceedingly pernicious. Such prescriptions, realists hold, not only prevent students of science and social inquiry from fully tran- scending classical empiricism's most questionable and dogmatic assump- tions, but also shield from critical scrutiny the implicit ontological commitments that ineluctably constitute and direct all inquiries. Conse- quently, the proponents of realism insist that any effort to study social and political life systematically must, explicitly or implicitly, proceed from a sound—and specifically realist—ontology. Deprived of such a basis, social scientific inquiry is destined to precipitate a variety of conceptual and empirical confusions, confusions that, if taken up and implemented in social policy or internalized in political and social practice, may well yield not just futility but also injustice and disaster.

In addition to the realist's effort to bring questions of ontology to the very heart of debates about the nature of political and social inquiry, there is a second respect in which realism departs markedly from the perspectives outlined by pragmatists like Rorty, by the advocates of the covering law model, and by some proponents of an interpretive or her- meneutical social science, for example, Peter Winch's early reflections on the nature of social science.[4] Rather than viewing the covering law model of explanation and hermeneutical modes of understanding either as sep- arate "tools" to be deployed for distinctive but rarely overlapping pur- poses or, more strongly, as opposed and irreconcilable perspectives, re- alists simultaneously reconceive and incorporate key dimensions of both approaches to develop a more synthetic model of social and political inquiry. Specifically, realists strive to articulate a conception of scientific inquiry that grants equal dignity both to the emphasis on causal expla- nation that is the lynchpin of the covering law model and the interpre- tation of meanings that is the hallmark of hermeneutical approaches. In short, by reconstruing causality along non-Humean lines and joining it to an account of intentionality, realists purport to integrate dialectically the often sequestered discourses of technical control and moral relations, of causality and intentionality, and of explanation and understanding. Implicitly rejecting the imperatives of what in another context Michael Walzer refers to as "the art of separation,"[5] realists maintain that what is required is an approach that moves simultaneously between these two discourses, bringing into interplay and proximity what are often conceived as unbridgeable dualisms.

Finally, realism is distinguished by its effort to redeem a promise stretching back to the birth of political theory itself, namely, the promise of enlisting social inquiry in the specifically critical project of overcoming false beliefs, misunderstandings, self-defeating practices, oppressive social arrangements, asymmetrical relations of power, and crippling ideological distortions, all of which intensify human misery and social injustice while diminishing human dignity and freedom. This emancipatory ambition, realists argue, has in recent years become deeply endangered. Indeed, realists contend that in very different ways the ostensibly incompatible movements of positivism, hermeneutics, and postmodernism have all contributed to this condition.

In responding to these challenges, realists navigate an argumentative course that tacks simultaneously between accommodation and critique. On the one hand, realists acknowledge the existence of insuperable epistemic limits to human and social knowledge, limits that foreclose the possibility of a foundational, highly predictive science of human affairs. Maintaining that at least one necessary condition of any such science, namely, experimental closure, does not obtain in the social sciences, realists such as Roy Bhaskar reject as inapplicable the aspiration to develop a stable and highly predictive science of social and political inquiry.[6] On this view, prediction can never operate as an appropriate criterion of the adequacy of social scientific explanations, nor can any logic of social scientific inquiry be identical to that of the natural sciences. Moreover, because social inquiry is created by finite, mutable human agents and social practices that it also takes as its subject matter, its theories, explanations, interpretations, and practices must be viewed as fallible, revisable, and nonabsolutist.

On the other hand, realists insist that none of these provisos and limitations is inconsistent with the conviction that there are better and worse interpretations of social phenomena, that the social world has a definite (if mutable) structure, and that, among other things, science aims to, and sometimes does, produce true statements about the world. Indeed, although realists do not develop the point, the grammar of terms like "fallibility" and "revisability" presupposes the existence of states of affairs, ideals, and standards of evaluation by which we gauge failure and success, adequacy and inadequacy, illumination and obfuscation, and clarity and confusion. We may (and must), of course, consider even the prevailing benchmarks as themselves fallible idealizations, and thus we may revise them in light of countervailing evidence. But this in no way undercuts the basic point that these terms presuppose a normative perspective. And this means not only that normative commitments are inescapable and that any "totalized" critique of truth or reason must therefore founder under the weight of familiar self-referential paradoxes, but also that such critiques ironically jettison the very language of fallibility that in general, or in other specific contexts, they wish to invoke.[7]

Seen in this light, social scientific realism is both a cautionary project of retrieval and a radical enterprise. Although repudiating philosophical foundationalism, it remains animated by a desire to reclaim from contemporary forms of skepticism the possibility of obtaining principled and rational judgments regarding human interests, freedom, social and political norms, and social and economic justice. Arguing that this desire can only be redeemed by first rethinking the very basis of social and political inquiry, realists join an ontological and conceptual critique of prevailing forms of social inquiry with a defense of a normative conception of social and political science. In this respect, realism is above all a call for a transformed mode of social scientific inquiry, one that conceives the terminus of social investigation as neither the production of general and predictive laws of human behavior, nor the clarification of the meaning of actions for the agents performing them, but rather the identification of the "darker" elements of social practices. As Ian Shapiro, in a passage that at once recalls and implicitly challenges writers such as Foucault and Derrida, puts it: "What centrally concerns the principled critic is those opaque dimensions of social practice that are causally implicated in the atrophy of practices into systems of domination. Critical arguments that expose these particular darker dimensions of actions and practices offer the hope of enhanced knowledge that can illuminate major sources of such atrophy. They therefore hold out to the people to whom they are addressed the continuing possibility of authentic action in their dealings with others."[8]

Although one or another form of "realism" now constitutes the predominant ontological view within the philosophy of natural science and has recently gained considerable purchase among social scientists and theorists, the precise nature of this view, of what it entails and what it does not, remains controversial.[9] In part, this is due to the fact that the term "realism" has both a complex etymological and philosophical pedigree and a wide variety of meanings. Moreover, it is often linked to a dizzying mélange of modifiers—"internal," "external," "scientific," "metaphysical," "constructive," "critical," "hermeneutic," "relational," "theoretical," "moral," "modal," "transcendental," "commonsense," "pragmatic," "experimental," "empirical," "dialectical," "naive," "realism with a capital 'R,' " and "realism with a small 'r,' " to name some of the most common variants—some of which refer to quite prominent differences, and others of which seem largely compatible or redundant.[10] So multiform are the current understandings of realism that one advocate, Jarrett Leplin, has remarked that "like the Equal Rights Movement, scientific realism is a majority position whose advocates are so divided as to appear a minority."[11]

To circumvent the difficulties attending any effort to survey comprehensively all variants of realism, this chapter will be restricted primarily to the investigation of one species of it, scientific or critical realism,[12] and one writer's exemplary articulation of its commitments, Roy Bhaskar's. Since the 1975 publication of *A Realist Theory of Science,* Bhaskar has been widely recognized as one of the most tireless and resourceful champions of scientific realism, and without question he has been one of the principal catalysts behind realism's growing appeal among students of political and social life. Indeed, Bhaskar's account of realist social theory, developed initially in *The Possibility of Naturalism* and augmented in a number of subsequent books, has recently (and not inaccurately) been described as "something of a canonical statement of 'critical social realism.' "[13] Similarly, fellow realists such as Andrew Collier have praised Bhaskar's achievements lavishly, calling his work "the most exciting development in Anglophone philosophy in this half-century."[14] Quite apart from its broad influence and generally favorable critical reception, however, Bhaskar's writings comprise what is arguably the most philosophically detailed depiction of the theoretical commitments and entailments of what he calls critical realism. His work is therefore an especially appropriate point of departure for analyzing the relationship between critical realism and issues explored in previous chapters.

In order to assess both the possibilities and the limitations of Bhaskar's critical realism, I will proceed in a rather unconventional manner. Rather than adopting the model of much of the secondary literature on critical realism, which often oscillates wildly between unmitigated praise and polemical condemnation, what follows shall combine elements of sympathetic explication, positive reconstruction, and direct critique. By interpreting Bhaskar's positions charitably yet critically, I hope to identify its most compelling features while also exploring its central tensions, elisions, and misconceptions. I do so in part to advance a qualified endorsement of critical realism, and in part to resituate debates about the relationship between critical realism and other approaches to social inquiry, such as hermeneutics and pragmatism. By recasting the terms of the debate I hope to open theoretical space for a more ecumenical line of argument, one that resists the tendency to regard hermeneutics, pragmatism, and critical realism as necessarily opposed or incommensurable research programs. I shall maintain that the distance between these positions is much shorter than Bhaskar and others think. Moreover, even in those instances where they differ significantly, clarifying precisely where and why they differ reveals something important about the relationships between these positions and the ways in which controversies between them should be understood and mediated.

As should be clear from the preceding remarks, this analysis of critical realism is intended not only as an exploration of one particularly influential and misunderstood strand of contemporary social and political inquiry, but also as an important link between the foregoing chapters and the subsequent final chapter. In short, the present discussion provides an opportunity both to refine a number of arguments developed previously, and to anticipate my investigation of Pierre Bourdieu's theories of practice and power.

In what follows, I begin by briefly considering Bhaskar's accounts of the philosophical enterprise and the philosophy of science, that is, of how they are related to yet distinct from ongoing scientific activity and of how they can variously inform and transform the work of practicing scientists. Here I emphasize that, for Bhaskar, the philosophy of science is something less than what Rorty calls a "superscience," but something more than a catalog of what practicing scientists do. More importantly, Bhaskar connects the philosophy of science with "the project of human self-emancipation,"[15] contending that this latter ambition constitutes one of the principal motivations behind realism.

Although I endorse much of this realist vision, in the third part of the chapter I take up and question one particular feature of Bhaskar's account, namely, his view of the relationship between critical realism and hermeneutics. Here I maintain that Bhaskar's defense of critical realism as an alternative to positivism and hermeneutics is predicated upon a positioning of the latter two modes of thought as dichotomous pairs (nomothetic/ideographic, explanation/understanding, causal analysis/interpretive analysis, and so forth), pairs that are also inconspicuously joined by a shared commitment to an anti-realist ontology. Contesting this argumentative strategy, I shall contend that Bhaskar's manner of framing the problem prejudices the outcome of his analysis. More specifically, I will show that Bhaskar's account of the dialectical oppositions between these two modes of thought rests on a prior but unnoticed consolidation of diverse and even competing views *within* positivism and hermeneutics. By conflating, for instance, the views of particular post-Wittgensteinian philosophers such as Peter Winch or continental philosophers like Hans-Georg Gadamer with those of hermeneutical theory generally, Bhaskar both sets up a number of binary oppositions that can then be dialectically transcended by his own account of critical realism and precludes from consideration those currents of hermeneutical thought that are neither irrealist nor anti-realist. Thus, by recovering some of the philosophical remainders of Bhaskar's account, I hope to secure a vantage point that enables me to identify concordances that Bhaskar's analysis obscures. Moreover, by using this vantage point to gain a rather different perspective on Bhaskar's conception of critical realism, I hope to identify some of the unnoticed ways in which the legacy of positivism continues to haunt aspects of his own critical framework, configuring and disfiguring various elements of it.

In challenging Bhaskar's understanding of the relationship between hermeneutics and critical realism, I reconsider four central theses about hermeneutical theory that constitute the cornerstone of Baskar's analysis: first, the view that hermeneutical writers accept a positivist account of natural science and an empiricist ontology; second, the assertion that the proponents of hermeneutics adopt an empiricist view of causality; third, the claim that hermeneutics lacks critical resources and implicitly defends the status quo in the sense that it can at best "illuminate" subjective meanings and "disclose" deep or implicit understandings of social norms, institutions, and practices, but cannot provide evaluative standards by which to criticize those meanings and understandings or the forms of life in which they are embedded; and, fourth, the proposition that hermeneutics, by virtue of its commitment to anti-naturalism, also evinces an anti-scientific animus. Drawing on the work of Charles Taylor and Hubert Dreyfus, I defend a conception of hermeneutics that not only is invulnerable to these charges but that, properly understood, enables one to project a critical spotlight back on some of the deficiencies of Bhaskar's own account.

Through these repositionings and redescriptions, I shall develop a conception of realism that sustains the view that overcoming positivism entails something more and different than a "benign neglect" of ontology (as with Rorty's pragmatism) or the embrace of one form or another of empiricist ontology (as with behavioral social science or philosophers such as W. V. Quine and Bas van Frassen). At the same time, however, this conception clears the way for a more flexible and pragmatic approach to social and political inquiry, one that attends more closely to the domain of the political, the vagaries and uncertainties of political life, and the demands and limits of political inquiry.

Critical Realism as a Philosophy for the Sciences

Within the social sciences, the recent rise of interest in critical realism can be traced both to its perceived intellectual attractions and to its potential contribution to the practical tasks of understanding and ameliorating pressing social and political problems. As I have already briefly indicated, critical realism's intellectual appeal lies in its promise of offering a viable alternative to a trinity of influential positions within the social sciences: empiricism, hermeneutics, and postmodernism. In Bhaskar's view, each of these positions provides important clues about the nature and aims of social scientific inquiry, yet each remains afflicted by serious pathologies. Curing these maladies therefore requires something more than minor recalibrations of their premises. It demands a fundamental rethinking of the research programs themselves.

As sharp critics of earlier forms of philosophical foundationalism, however, critical realists must first face up to the questions that their own proposals raise. Namely, if foundationalism is indeed a misconceived enterprise, then what role, if any, can philosophy play in the arbitration of disciplinary disputes about theory and methodology? If, in other words, philosophy no longer sees itself as that discipline that legitimates or debunks claims of knowledge made in all other fields of study, then why is a *philosophical* reconsideration of these problems necessary at all, and by what authority can philosophy, or any particular philosophy of science, legislate epistemological solutions to them? Does not the abandonment of foundationalism, of the quest for an Archimedean lever, entail, as Rorty has famously suggested, an acknowledgment that standards of evaluation—or, as pragmatists like Rorty put it, warranted assertibility—do not and cannot rest on anything more than what is acceptable to, or the present consensus of, a particular local community (of inquirers, professors, and the like)?

In his effort to carve out a role for philosophical reflection without simply reverting to the notion of philosophy as a foundational discipline, Bhaskar begins by recasting the terms of the issue. Bhaskar asserts that, although the demise of philosophical foundationalism, understood as "the quest for incorrigibility or an unhypothetical starting point,"[16] leaves philosophy with a diminished and less pretentious role, it does not signal an end to philosophy *tout court.* Citing Kant, who similarly attacked Descartes's foundationalist metaphysics while defending a distinctive role for philosophy, Bhaskar avers that "I am taking it to be the function of philosophy to analyse concepts that are 'already given' but 'as confused.' "[17] That is, philosophy in this more modest sense starts not from a set of indubitable beliefs upon which one builds a system of certain knowledge, but rather from particular practices and experiences that are "universally recognized, if inadequately analysed."[18] Bhaskar assumes that there are "universally recognized" experiences and practices such as science, politics, and the like, and that our understanding of them is often implicit, opaque, confused, or contradictory. Although philosophy cannot provide global, ahistorical, and epistemically indefeasible standards of evaluation and analysis, it can gain some critical purchase on these practices and experiences, purchase that is not merely local in the Rortian sense.[19] Most notably, it can develop transcendental arguments that demonstrate what human subjects or the world must be like in order for certain practices or features of experience to be possible at all. It can, moreover, clarify and make explicit the background understandings implicit in some practice or concept, identify tensions and inconsistencies internal to it, reveal distortions of it, and issue challenges to it.[20] What is central to this conception of philosophy, which interestingly redefines the philosophical enterprise in such a way as to make it less a professional discipline or disciplinary matrix than a method and mode of reflection on specific practices and problems,[21] is that all of these activities begin not from a theory of knowledge developed anterior to any investigation of specific practices, but from within established, taken-for-granted practices and experiences.[22]

In articulating this conception, Bhaskar draws repeatedly on images of philosophy as a "midwife" and, especially, an "under-labourer."[23] Like Locke's "under-labourer," who tries to clear "the ground a little," removing, as Locke caustically puts it, "some of the rubbish that lies in the way to knowledge,"[24] Bhaskar views the primary purpose of the philosophy of science as one of underlaboring on behalf of the sciences. By clearing "the ideological ground" of obstacles that inhibit the advancement of "the sciences, and especially the human sciences," philosophical underlaborers help to fulfill a necessary condition of the improvement of science.[25] And by better interpreting and representing the phenomena they study, these underlaborers also advance rational change in human and social life. Fusing his claims for critical realism with his emancipatory vision of the human sciences, Bhaskar argues that interpreting the world correctly is a necessary condition of rational change, and that critical realism supplies an equally necessary metatheoretical basis for correct or accurate interpretation. As such, critical realism, by identifying "the structures at work that generate . . . events or discourses,"[26] is "a necessary but insufficient agency for human emancipation."[27]

Whereas Bhaskar's conception of philosophical underlaboring draws on Locke, his defense of realism proceeds not from Locke's empiricism but from the style of transcendental argument first developed in the Transcendental Analytic of Kant's *Critique of Pure Reason*. This argument, which in its most general form starts from an indubitable feature of our experience and then regressively asks what must be the case in order for that feature of experience to be possible, is deployed most famously in Kant's attack on classical empiricism. Intentionally adopting the empiricists' own starting point, namely, experience, Kant poses the question: what must be necessary in order for experiences, ordered in time, to be possible at all? To this question Kant replied that our succession of representations must be synthesized, that is, they must be absorbed, connected, and unified in a single consciousness, a unity that Kant refers to as the "unity of apperception."[28] But to characterize an experience as mine, to distinguish myself and my experiences from an array of other things, presupposes a prior distinction within experience between objective and subjective orders. Without such a distinction, Kant holds, it would be impossible ever to have an experience *of* something, and if one cannot have this, that is, an experience without an object, then one cannot have an experience at all without presupposing a prior distinction between subjective experience and an objective order of things. It is, Kant maintains, therefore a necessary condition of having any experience at all that one regards at least some of those experiences as perceptions of an order of objects that are independent of oneself. Thus, starting from the thoroughly uncontroversial assumption that there is a succession of experiences, Kant purports to dissolve a pair of questions that had haunted the classical empiricists: first, the question of the existence of the external world—of how, beginning with "bundles" of experiences or sense impressions, it is possible to mount a compelling defense of the common-sense belief in the existence of an external world; and, second, the question of personal identity—of how, if experiences are nothing more than "bundles" of perceptions, as Hume claimed, those bundles are tied together.[29]

In his argument for realism, Bhaskar appropriates Kant's mode of transcendental argument while rejecting his idealism. That is, rather than arguing regressively from *experience* in order to establish conclusions about both its unity and the categories of the mind that project a structure onto the world, Bhaskar inverts the starting point, asking the following: what must the *world* be like in order for science and, more specifically, experimental activity to be possible? This inversion is revealing, since it both signals Bhaskar's own substitution of transcendental realism for Kant's transcendental idealism and because it accents a feature of scientific activity that the positivist tradition at once exalted and ignored. For although positivists notoriously made experiments the unambiguous arbiters of alternative theories and hypotheses, and thus placed them at the epicenter of their epistemology, they paid almost no attention to the activity and practice of experiments. Indeed, as the historian of science Peter Galison has correctly noted, "It is ironic that the very philosophers who called themselves logical empiricists had virtually no interest in the *conduct* of experiments."[30]

Although Bhaskar also does not examine in any detail the conduct of experiments,[31] he does provide a philosophical analysis of experimental activity, something that, he claims, "no-one or virtually no-one"[32] has done. This analysis begins, not surprisingly, with a Kantian question: how are experiments possible? That is, if scientific experiment sometimes enables us to intervene spectacularly in the world, if it sometimes provides us with quite precise knowledge of natural entities' properties and causal powers, and if it sometimes permits us to isolate particular effects and mechanisms, then what must experimenters presuppose for their commonly recognized practices and achievements to be possible or even intelligible? What assumptions and distinctions can they not help but invoke if their practices are to make sense? Bhaskar holds that at least two presuppositions are unavoidable. First, experimentation presupposes the existence of what Bhaskar refers to as *"intransitive objects of knowledge."*[33] These objects, or this "dimension" of reality of which they are a part, comprise the realm of real entities, structures, and mechanisms possessed of causal powers and tendencies that can and do operate independently of both human beings and those conditions—social and experimental practice—that permit human beings to gain access to them.[34] For instance, "the specific gravity of mercury, the process of electrolysis, the mechanism of light propagation" are all objects of knowledge "which are not produced by men at all."[35]

Bhaskar argues that experimental practice "presupposes the ontological independence of the objects of experience from the objects of which they are the experiences."[36] Without a prior distinction between our perception of an object and the object of our perception, or, as Bhaskar puts it, between experiences and events, the concept of perception would, he argues, have no clear meaning or application, nor would it be clear why experimental science attached any significance to it. When, for instance, Galileo and Kepler look at the morning sun and see a horizon dropping, whereas Simplicious and Tycho Brahe do likewise but insist conversely that they observe the sun rising, all nonetheless assume the existence of something they see.[37] Likewise, when two microbiologists look in turn at a prepared slide, one might see "a cluster of foreign matter . . . an artifact, a coagulum resulting from inadequate staining techniques," whereas the other views "the clot as a cell organ, a 'Golgi body.' "[38] However unlike these perceptions may be, both presuppose, in their initial perceptions and in the controversy those perceptions incite, a categorical distinction between experiences and events. Indeed, Bhaskar contends that in the absence of such a distinction, one cannot sustain either an intelligible conception of scientific change or a coherent account of the need for scientific training.

In addition to the presupposition of intransitive objects of scientific investigation, Bhaskar argues that transcendental inquiry yields conclusions regarding "the structured character of the objects investigated under experimental conditions."[39] To grasp this point, one must recall that from the empiricist standpoint the identification of causal laws—which in this tradition are understood as constant conjunctions of events perceived— is the cornerstone of both experimental activity and scientific explanation, forming as they do the basis of predictive statements that in turn confirm or disconfirm scientific theories and explanations. Bhaskar argues, however, that constant conjunctions of events rarely if ever obtain in "open systems" characteristic of the everyday social or natural world. If they did, experimental practices would be pointless. Rather, it is only by artificially controlling and skillfully manipulating experimental conditions–that is, by establishing "closed systems" that isolate the *explanandum* from a variety of extraneous influences—that scientists *produce* constant conjunctions and obtain accurate predictions. Scientists, therefore, are not passive observers or receivers of sense data, but causally active agents in the production of the constant conjunctions they identify.

While this deduction may initially appear rather insignificant, Bhaskar holds that profoundly important consequences proceed from it. First, it implies that the standard Humean account of causation, which identifies causal laws with constant conjunctions of events, must be wrong; as Bhaskar insists, "There must be an ontological distinction between them."[40] Indeed, divested of any ontological distinction between causal laws and their empirical grounds, one would be committed to the logically "absurd" view that "scientists, in their experimental activity, cause and even change the laws of nature!"[41] For this reason, "A real [ontological] distinction between the objects of experimental investigation, such as causal laws, and patterns of events is thus a condition of the intelligibility of experimental activity."[42] It is precisely this distinction that the Humean theory of causation, like the "flat undifferentiated ontology of empirical realism"[43] generally, denies.

Second, Bhaskar maintains that transcendental analysis of experimental activity yields a commitment to what he terms the transfactual activity of laws, that is, their endurance and operation outside the closed systems in which they are identified.[44] If the practice of experimental science is to be intelligible, Bhaskar urges, one must assume that causal laws identified under conditions of experimental closure continue to apply outside of those contexts, namely, in open systems where empirical regularities are not typically forthcoming.[45] If they did not, then causal laws would have no application outside of experimental and laboratory settings and thus would possess no scientific or practical significance. As Andrew Collier rightly notes, experimentation would thereby cease to "tell us what we want to know—i.e., how things work when we are not experimenting on them."[46]

On the basis of the foregoing distinctions and presuppositions, Bhaskar advances a conception of experimental activity and scientific explanation that departs dramatically from orthodox empiricism and idealism alike. Rejecting the empiricist idea that the identification of constant conjunctions of events constitutes the principal object of science, Bhaskar posits instead that the fundamental goal of scientific inquiry is to locate those relatively enduring causal structures, mechanisms, and powers that produce or enable events and experiences. In fact, he maintains that the very assumption that causal laws are transfactual or universal presupposes a prior assumption that causal mechanisms are independent from the events they generate. As Bhaskar states,

> The world consists of things, not events. Most things are complex objects, in virtue of which they possess an ensemble of tendencies, liabilities and powers. It is by reference to the exercise of their tendencies, liabilities and powers that the phenomena of the world are explained . . . On this conception of science it is concerned essentially with what kinds of things they are and with what they tend to do; it is only derivatively concerned with predicting what is actually going to happen. It is only rarely, and normally under conditions which are artificially produced and controlled, that scientists can do the latter. And, when they do, its significance lies precisely in the light that it casts on the enduring natures and ways of acting of independently existing and transfactually active things.[47]

In short, Bhaskar argues that any adequate ontology of science must be a depth ontology. That is, it must conceive of the world as complexly structured and stratified, and must carefully distinguish between different ontological levels or "domains." Specifically, it must differentiate not only between mechanisms and the events they generate, but also between a triad of ontological domains within reality: the domain of the real (the realm of structures, mechanisms, and relations), the domain of the actual (the realm of events and behavior) and the domain of the empirical (the realm of experiences or sense data). Moreover, only on the basis of such distinctions, Bhaskar believes, can one make sense of the idea that causal laws are indeed transfactual but typically *"out of phase"* with phenomena in open systems. If, he argues, one follows the empiricist in ontologically compressing reality into the exclusive domains of the actual and the empirical,[48] then the normic statements those laws express would be "immediately falsified in open systems," thus leaving science "without any epistemic credentials."[49]

In his effort to reconstruct scientific explanation in a way that reconciles both the experimenter's remarkable ability to identify causal laws through intervention, manipulation, and control of phenomena, and the absence of strict empirical regularities in open systems, Bhaskar first redefines the concept and role of causal laws. Rather than construing laws as constant conjunctions of events or as correlations between variables (of the form "if x then y"), critical realism conceives of laws "as designating the activity of generative mechanisms and structures independently of any particular sequence or pattern of events," and of "generative mechanisms" as "nothing other than the ways of acting of things."[50] Laws, in short, refer to underlying mechanisms and "tendencies of things,"[51] which generate phenomena manifest in empirical events. These mechanisms, which may be physical (gravitational forces, neurophysiological processes), social (social norms and structures), psychological (defense mechanisms), or otherwise, possess enduring powers, properties, and dispositions, acting in accordance with both universality and natural necessity.

Although Bhaskar conceives of laws as transfactual and universal, it is important to emphasize that these laws do not, except in closed systems, yield strict counterfactual or subjunctive statements. Instead, the existence of multiple mechanisms operating simultaneously within open systems, along with the impossibility of stating exhaustively all of the possibly relevant factors contributing to the generation of an empirical event, suggest that causal laws issue in what Bhaskar calls "transfactual or normic statements."[52] These statements are empirically grounded—they are factually instantiated in laboratory and experimental settings, or (in social scientific inquiry) through other forms of empirical scrutiny—but express only tendencies and characteristic patterns of behavior, not empirical invariances. As Bhaskar puts it, laws "leave the field of the ordinary phenomena of life at least partially open . . . They situate limits but do not dictate what happens within them."[53] For example, clinical depression, grounded in some combination of neurophysiological, social, and psychological laws, structures, and mechanisms, is characteristically manifested in tendencies toward despondency, inactivity, difficulty in thinking and concentration, and the like. These tendencies can, however, often be mitigated or overcome through the intervention of other causal mechanisms: civil, cultural, and political structures that afford opportunities for other-directed activities; the transformation of structural features of one's life; state and nonstate structures that provide health assistance; various medications; and forms of therapy that identify the source of the condition (in trauma, loss, and so forth). Importantly, causal mechanisms may often but need not be directly observable. Just as Newton famously inferred from observable phenomena the existence of universal laws of motion, gravitational forces, and the impenetrability of bodies, so in general is "transdiction" a legitimate mode of inference.[54]

As with any account of science that places such a heavy explanatory burden on the role of causal laws and mechanisms, questions quickly arise regarding the relationship between different ontological "strata," the laws and mechanisms operative at each level, and the appropriate level(s) of explanation. Indeed, if nature and the social world are stratified, and if explanations of events refer to generative mechanisms operating at multiple levels, then what kinds of research programs are appropriate for explaining the phenomena in question? Does critical realism ultimately endorse some version of reductionism, whereby the "better" explanation is always the one at the most basic level? If not, does it countenance some form dualism or exceptionalism, such that laws at one level of reality cannot be formulated or do not hold at another, more basic level? Or, finally, does critical realism posit a variant of nonreductive interaction between different mechanisms operating at different levels? If so, what is the nature of these interactions?

To avoid choosing between the antinomies of reductionism and exceptionalism, Bhaskar defends a version of the third alternative, one that proceeds through an elaboration of the doctrine, first developed in biology, of "emergence." In a characteristic formulation, Bhaskar defines emergence as "a relationship between two terms such that one term diachronically or perhaps synchronically arises out of the other, but is capable of reacting back on the first and is in any event causally and taxonomically irreducible to it."[55] Less abstractly, emergence is a doctrine about the necessary dependence but ultimate irreducibility of more complex forms of organization on (or to) less complex forms of organization, or of higher-level terms and properties on (or to) lower-level terms and properties. In this sense, emergence is the idea that complex forms of life and organization emerge from and are limited by more basic forms, but are not always predictable from or reducible to them. It is almost universally conceded, for example, that because human beings are among other things part of the physical and biological furniture of the world, human life is based upon, restricted by, and emergent from physical and biological laws. Unlike the thesis of reductionism, however, the doctrine of emergence eschews the idea that the dependence of human life on physical and biological imperatives means that all aspects of that life can be reduced to and are explicable by the laws of biology and physics, as, for instance, the Boyle-Charles law was reduced to the kinetic theory of gases. Rather, it suggests that the laws governing operations and entities at one level are not reducible to laws operative at a more basic level, even though the former may depend upon and be constrained by the latter. In this sense, higher-order laws remain partially autonomous from, and irreducible to, lower-level ones.

These relationships can perhaps be better understood by considering briefly one of Michael Polanyi's examples.[56] Discussing "the art of making bricks," Polanyi observes, "It relies on its raw materials placed on a level below it. But above the brickmaker there operates the architect, relying on the brickmaker's work, and the architect in his turn has to serve the town planner. To these four levels there correspond four successive levels of rules. The laws of physics and chemistry govern the raw material of the bricks; technology prescribes the art of brickmaking; architecture teaches the builders; and the rules of town planning control the town planners."[57] Notice that, within this hierarchy, each level contains its own rules or laws (the laws of physics and chemistry stipulate that certain substances, such as water, do not possess the properties requisite for making bricks), which in turn constrain higher-level activities (the architect may utilize glass bricks for decorative and design purposes, but not as basic structural elements of large buildings). At the same time, lower-level laws and rules remain in various ways "under the control" of those at the next higher level (not only is it the case that one cannot derive or predict the architect's chosen use of bricks from the laws of physics and chemistry governing their constitution, but it is also true that the architect's design is constrained by the town planner, building codes, and the like). In short, each level is subject to what Polanyi calls "dual control": "First, by the laws that apply to its elements in themselves, and, second, by the laws that control the comprehensive entity formed by them."[58]

Although this account of emergent order remains quite sketchy and at best incomplete, Bhaskar contends that only some variant of it can ultimately yield an intelligible conception of science and a critical social science. Indeed, he argues that the principal alternatives to the theory of emergent powers—reductionism and idealism—either preclude meaningful conceptions of agency and rationality or violate fundamental assumptions of modern science. On the one hand, reductionism entails either that physical laws completely determine all human activity and thus that the transformation of the world through human agency is impossible, or that human agents possess causal powers independent of physical and biological laws, in which case they also possess the power to violate the seemingly inviolable laws of nature. On the other hand, idealism, by failing to acknowledge the existence of objects outside of thought, makes thought and emancipation "unconditioned and irrationality . . . inexplicable."[59] As Bhaskar declares, "Emancipation depends upon the untruth of reductionist materialism and spiritual idealism alike . . . Emancipation depends upon explanation depends upon emergence. Given the phenomenon of emergence, an emancipatory politics or therapy depends upon a realist science. But, if and only if emergence is real, the development of both are up to *us*."[60]

Finally, Bhaskar posits one further distinction, a distinction between two "dimensions" of knowledge: the intransitive and the transitive.[61] As discussed previously, the intransitive dimension comprises the realm of real entities, structures, and mechanisms possessing causal powers and tendencies that are capable of operating, and frequently do operate, independently of both human beings and the conditions—namely, social and experimental practices—which enable human beings to gain access to them. In this dimension we again find the realm of "*ontological depth*."[62] By contrast, the transitive dimension refers to that body of antecedently produced, corrigible, and changing knowledge that is constantly being "used to generate the new knowledge."[63] Instances of such knowledge are "the antecedently established facts and theories, paradigms and models, methods and techniques of inquiry available to a particular scientific school or worker."[64] Because this dimension is the realm of historically, socially, and culturally produced experimental activity and scientific theories, its "objects" are, as the label "transitive" suggests, both mutable and incapable of existing independently of human beings.

Bhaskar argues that an intelligible account of experimental activity, along with an image of scientific development that attends equally to the twin features of growth and change, is possible only on the basis of a prior commitment to the notion of ontological depth and a related distinction between the transitive and intransitive dimensions of knowledge. The empirical realism of positivist and idealist philosophies of science—which is also adopted by the dominant empiricist and behavioralist approaches in social and political science,[65] and which Bhaskar claims is uncritically accepted even by their hermeneutic and interpretivist opponents—lacks any such commitment to the concept of ontological depth and thus cannot sustain a convincing, or even intelligible, account of science.

Taken together, these arguments constitute a significant departure from standard positivist, idealist, pragmatist, and postmodern conceptions of science. By articulating a defense of ontological stratification and emergent powers, distinguishing between open and closed systems, and reconceiving causal laws as expressions of "tendencies of things," Bhaskar emphatically rejects both the covering law model of explanation and the corollary proposition that explanation and prediction are symmetrical. Rather, Bhaskar's account shifts from the margin to the center a conception of scientific explanation that emphasizes the construction of models of real structures and causal mechanisms that, if they "were to exist and act in the postulated way would account for the phenomenon in question."[66] Moreover, by redirecting the scientific eye away from the discovery of general laws and the cataloging of empirical conjunctions and toward the identification of structures and mechanisms that constrain and cause actions and events, Bhaskar foregrounds the complexity, indeterminancy, and uncertainty that are such prominent features of phenomena operating in open systems. Additionally, by pairing epistemic relativism with ontological realism, Bhaskar acknowledges the significance of constructivist and historical accounts of science that accent both the complex work involved in the scientific enterprise and its changing nature, yet also holds that these ineradicable features can only be made intelligible against the backdrop of a realist ontology. Finally, by insisting on the importance of adducing empirical support for our explanations and theories, Bhaskar incorporates empiricist correctives to the reifications and metaphysical assumptions of some social theories—for instance, orthodox Marxism, historicism, and Parsonian structural functionalism—while abandoning empiricism's own conspicuous dogmas—its flattened ontology, its strict distinction between observational and theoretical terms and statements, its embrace of a similarly strict distinction between facts and values, and its commitment to a reductivist program that excludes in principle the thesis of emergent powers while privileging mechanism and methodological individualism.[67] Urging the necessity of empirical scrutiny, critical realism demands, for instance, that if one wishes to explain sexual inequalities such as the underrepresentation of women in legislative bodies by their lack of particular cognitive or intellectual capacities, one must produce empirical evidence, grounded in present biological and psychological knowledge, corroborating this postulated explanatory mechanism. Appeals to mechanisms that in principle resist empirical scrutiny are perforce not explanations at all.

However one may assess Bhaskar's general picture of science, it remains at this point a rather indistinct and liminal depiction of *social scientific* inquiry. What, specifically, does this position countenance when it is transposed onto questions of social and political inquiry? What are its concrete implications? Is a realist science of society and political affairs possible at all? If so, how might it help us to better comprehend and address pressing social and political problems, to better clarify and shape the ends and means appropriate to political life? To these issues we will now turn.

Critical Naturalism and the Stakes of Social Inquiry

As we have observed, the principal appeal of Bhaskar's critical realism resides in its deployment of transcendental arguments that seek to undercut foundationalism, skepticism, and idealism alike while reconciling the opposed insights of empiricism and rationalism. By demonstrating that one must presuppose the existence of a structured and stratified world independent of our perceptions in order to make sense out of phenomena that even skeptics and idealists do not question, Bhaskar, in a phrase that strongly echoes Karl Marx's dictum that "all science would be superfluous if the outward appearance and the essence of things di-

rectly coincided,"[68] purports to show that the "essence" of science "lies
in the *movement . . .* from manifest phenomena to knowledge of the structures that generate them."[69] If, however, this is indeed the case, the question becomes: To what extent is a similar movement possible in the study
of social life? Do human and social "objects" possess properties and
powers required for them to be suitable objects of *scientific* investigation?
Are manifest social and political forms and practices similarly generated
by underlying structures and mechanisms? Are they "real"? And if so, are
they cognitively accessible to us?

In answering these queries, Bhaskar steers a careful course between
unqualified naturalism and hermeneutical anti-naturalism. In short, he
argues that, although human and social "objects" are irreducible to natural objects, the study of the former can be scientific "*in exactly the same
sense,*" even if "*not in exactly the same way*" as the latter.[70] On the one
hand, human and social objects can be objects of scientific study in the
same sense as natural objects because human and social reality, like natural reality, is ontologically emergent and stratified in the manner outlined above—that is, it is stratified into the distinct levels of the real, the
actual, and the empirical. As such, the goal of social science, like that of
natural science, is to identify those underlying structures and causal
mechanisms that conjuncturally interact to generate social phenomena.
What these structures and mechanisms may be, what properties and
powers they may possess, the ontological level at which they operate, and
the status of the substantive social theories in which they are embedded
are on this view issues to be resolved through ongoing empirical investigation rather than philosophical fiat. Nonetheless, Bhaskar holds, contra
hermeneutical anti-naturalists, that critical realism fully funds the proposition that there is a basic symmetry between the study of human and
social life and the study of the natural world, namely, that both can be
studied scientifically.

On the other hand, contra positivism, Bhaskar urges that any convincing defense of naturalism must be a "qualified" defense, that is, one
that recognizes various ontological, epistemological, and relational limits
on it. Most importantly, this entails an *ontological limit* deriving from
"the activity-, concept-, and space-time-dependence of social structures."[71] If, Bhaskar argues, one wishes to defend persuasively the view
that social structures are adequate analogues for the mechanisms that
generate natural events, then that defense must begin by acknowledging

frankly three critical distinctions between them. First, unlike natural mechanisms and structures, social structures have no existence independently of the very human activities they govern; second, they do not exist independently of agents' conceptions and self-understandings of their activities; and third, they are only relatively enduring.[72] Although certainly contestable in some of these specific formulations, the broader proposition that Bhaskar intends (or should intend) to underwrite is simply that human and social reality is partly constituted by the interrelationship between language, self-interpretation, and social practice, and therefore contains ineradicable hermeneutical and historical dimensions.[73] Moreover, this indissoluble link between language, social practice, and human reality implies, first, that even though the objects of natural scientific inquiry are presumed to exist and operate independently of human activity and our descriptions of them, this assumption is unwarranted in social science, simply because human and social reality does not exist in a relationship of exteriority to language and social practice.[74] Thus, on the one hand, it makes perfect sense for natural scientists to theorize about physical mechanisms that are presumed to possess properties and causal powers independent of human agents and their descriptions of them, yet, on the other hand, the concept of a revolution or a power elite or a betrayal of trust necessarily presupposes the existence of corollary linguistic resources and distinctions, as well as wider contexts of social practice in which those distinctions are situated. Second, because language is partly constitutive of human and social reality and conceptual change is a basic feature of all language, human and social mechanisms possess a mutability and fragility that natural mechanisms do not. So, although concepts such as noblesse oblige may have once functioned as mechanisms for explaining and understanding relationships and interconnections between lord, vassal, and serf, the gradual decline of premodern notions of a supernatural hierarchy of persons, along with the advent of concepts of free labor, natural equality, and alienable land, as well as the attendant rise of modern capitalism, contributed to the radical transformation of this causal mechanism in the industrialized West. In sum, the ubiquitous presence of these and other historically shifting complexes of causal mechanisms suggests not only that social mechanisms possess greater "space-time specificity" than natural ones, but also that the urge to ground social inquiry in universal laws is misguided in a way that similar efforts in the natural sciences are not.

Apart from these ontological limits, Bhaskar locates a second, *episte-mological limit:* the intrinsic openness of social systems. That is, in contrast to natural systems where experimental closure enables researchers to identify empirical regularities, social phenomena manifest themselves only in open systems where such regularities fail to obtain. This absence of genuine experimentation, and hence "of crucial or decisive test situations in principle,"[75] implies, Bhaskar argues, that the criteria for theory assessment in social inquiry cannot be predictive, but instead must be exclusively explanatory.

Finally, Bhaskar identifies a third, *relational limit* on naturalism. The social sciences, he maintains, are distinctive from the natural sciences in that the former but not the latter have an internal and potentially circular relationship to their subject matter.[76] Unlike natural objects, the existence and behavior of which are independent of our theories of them and the processes through which we come to know them, no such independence obtains in the arena of social inquiry. This entails, somewhat trivially, that some objects of social scientific inquiry—for instance, social scientific institutions and practices, the sociology of social science, and so forth—cannot exist independently of social science. More significantly, it implies "a causal interdependency between social science and its subject matter."[77] That is, on the one hand, social science itself is often causally "affected or conditioned by"[78] the society and social relations on which it depends and of which it is a part; and, on the other hand, social scientific theories possess the power to transform the very practices and relationships they are intended to illuminate and explain. Sometimes, of course, this latter, circular relationship between theory and practice yields quite salutary insights, as when social scientific inquiry exposes hidden or unnoticed biases, false beliefs, and relations of domination, thereby initiating future possibilities of reform. There is, however, also a more disturbing possibility, namely, that social scientists, through the circulation throughout society of their descriptions and theories of society, can manufacture the kinds of objects and self-understandings necessary to validate their theories. This situation, in which descriptions and theories, through education, may manufacture the material required for their validation and thus become self-fulfilling prophecies, is also entirely unique to social science. Moreover, this causal connection between social scientific theory and practice and its objects of inquiry suggests that a commitment to reflexivity in social scientific inquiry is not optional but mandatory for preserving the integrity of it. Without it, social scientific inquiry is all too easily enlisted in the service of various ideological agendas.

Finally, Bhaskar identifies a fourth crucial difference between the natural and social sciences: the latter but not the former are "intrinsically critical" and normative (or, in Bhaskar's terminology, "value-impregnating") sciences. At first glance this remark may seem odd, for there is a quite unambiguous sense in which the sciences of nature are every bit as critical and normative as the sciences of social and political life. Like social scientists, natural scientists commonly criticize rival theories and explanations of natural phenomena, and do so with the intention of affecting (through support or opposition) public policies or prevailing norms, beliefs, and practices within and outside their scientific communities. In this sense, they too are engaged in critical and normative projects. Although Bhaskar would certainly agree, he maintains that the social sciences are distinctive because they include not one but *two* types of critical investigations: first, investigations of social objects, that is, social institutions, practices, norms, and facts; and second, scrutiny of beliefs about them, for instance, beliefs about the organization, rules, and roles governing institutions; about the meaning and point of social practices; about the basis of authority of social norms; and the like.[79] Unlike the physical sciences, where the subject matter in question not only has no beliefs but also remains profoundly indifferent to our beliefs about it, this relationship does not hold for students of social and political life. Here the latter (like all scientists) investigate and criticize their own beliefs about the objects they study, yet *also* investigate and criticize the beliefs of the objects they study. Furthermore, as indicated previously, changing interpretations of and beliefs about social objects may well yield a transformation of the objects themselves. When, for instance, social critics or scientists redescribe an institution such as the family, viewing it not as a "haven in a heartless world" but instead as a site of child abuse, domestic violence, ideological reproduction, and the control and exploitation of women, this redescription potentially transforms social understandings and individual and social self-interpretations of the institution, as well as the constellation of causal relationships of which it is a part. Moreover, to the degree that such redescriptions conflict with other self-interpretations and truth claims, they are implicitly critical of them. And to the degree that institutions such as the family are fundamentally normative in character (which almost all, if not all, institutions are), these criticisms also represent, *ceteris paribus,* a call to action, one directed both at a transformation of the institution and at the erroneous beliefs that buttress it. Indeed, given what Bhaskar claims is the inherently value-impregnated character of social objects, the human sciences cannot be anything other than normative and critical.[80]

On the basis of this logic Bhaskar purports simultaneously to have refuted Hume's law—namely, that one cannot logically derive value conclusions (an "ought") from factual premises (an "is")—and to have demonstrated the possibility of an "explanatory critique" in social science—an idea that would appear oxymoronic from the standpoint of more orthodox positions in the philosophy of social inquiry.[81] Fusing causal knowledge of the conditions of action and belief (the explanatory element of explanatory critique) with a conception of critical rationality (the critical element), Bhaskar writes, "If we possess (i) adequate grounds for supposing that a belief P (about some object O) is *false* and (ii) adequate grounds for supposing that S *explains* P, then we may, and must, pass immediately to (iii) a negative evaluation of S (CP) and (iv) a positive evaluation of action rationally directed at the removal of S (CP)."[82]

Although this model of explanatory critique is at points so exceedingly abstract and formal that it is difficult to evaluate, in its general outline it suggests a possible "middle way" between foundationalism and conventionalism, causal theory and interpretive theory, scientism and pure conviction.[83] Drawing on both Kantian and Hegelian-Marxian currents of thought, Bhaskar articulates a form of critical realism that is, in Jeffrey Isaac's words, "*doubly* 'critical.' It is epistemologically critical in the Kantian sense, in its understanding of the presuppositions of valid knowledge. And it is also critical in the Hegelian-Marxian sense, in its aspiration to unmask unnecessary forms of social determination, to underwrite normative social criticism, and to inspire practical social change informed by a scientific understanding of historical limits and possibilities."[84] More generally, by challenging the equation of positivism and science, an equation that Bhaskar contends was too congenially accepted by the proponents of hermeneutics and Frankfurt School critical theory alike, Bhaskar opens the possibility of a reconciliation of science and normative political inquiry, one that pivots around an empirically grounded depth analysis of political thought and action. By investigating underlying causal mechanisms that enable and constrain the surface play of observable social activity, critical realism abandons positivism and empiricism without renouncing the quest for causal theory. By refusing to take the social and political world as given, critical realism joins with earlier strands of critical theory in recognizing that current understandings of ourselves and the world may be distorted and naturalized in ways that blind us to alternative possibilities, yet also breaks with those forms of philosophical reflection—particularly among some followers of the Frankfurt School—that are hostile to the very idea of empirical social science.[85] Finally, by developing an account of explanatory critique, critical realism purports to transcend the limitations of purely proceduralist approaches to normative political inquiry—approaches associated most closely with the influential work of John Rawls and Jürgen Habermas—through the development of a form of ethical naturalism that reclaims the Aristotelian and Marxian languages of "real" or "human" or "objective" interests.[86]

In short, Bhaskar's critical realism represents something more than a distinctive position within the philosophy of science; it is also constitutes an important and unique position within contemporary critical social theory and critical social science. In recent decades the identity of critical theory as an intellectual discourse and political practice has altered dramatically. Once associated primarily with modernist currents of thought stretching from Marx to the Frankfurt School, contemporary forms of critical theory frequently break, often sharply, with many of the modernist and Marxist assumptions that animated the tradition through the first half of the twentieth century. On the one hand, poststructuralists like Michel Foucault have developed forms of critical thought that jettisoned the modernist belief in the power of science and reason to fuel "grand" projects of human emancipation. On the other hand, new social movements and the rise of identity politics have produced forms of critical practice that rejected Marxist orthodoxies that identified the proletariat as the key agent of social transformation and political emancipation. Indeed, many of the partisans of these new social movements, which draw eclectically on feminist thought, liberation theology, postcolonial theory, critical race theory, queer theory, and many other forms of thought and practice, were severe critics of those aspects of Marxist thought that granted epistemic privilege to the proletariat and political priority to class politics.[87]

In many ways, Bhaskar's critical realism constitutes an effort to bridge and transcend these increasingly conspicuous rifts in critical theory. That is, Bhaskar aims to develop a form of critical theory that at once defends the scientific enterprise and attacks both positivism and scientism. It abandons epistemological foundationalism while remaining loyal to a conception of emancipatory critique. It acknowledges the central importance of conventionalist and constructivist critiques of science and society while resisting radical skepticism. It jettisons the exclusive focus on the proletariat in favor of more diverse and inclusive forms of radical democratic politics. In all of these respects, Bhaskar aims simultaneously to reconceive and reweave disparate strands of critical theory.

Having now sketched in broad brush the contours of Bhaskar's critical realism, it is time to pose the normative, theoretical, and pragmatic questions that his model of social inquiry invites. What, if any, are the specific limitations of Bhaskar's realism? If there are limitations, how morally, politically, and epistemologically significant are they? What modifications do they demand? Do they suggest an abandonment of the project itself? In answering these questions, we will observe that, although Bhaskar's critical realism requires significant recasting, it would nonetheless be unwise to abandon it entirely. Indeed, I will contend that, suitably reconceived, critical realism allows us to rethink important questions of social inquiry.

Ontology, Causation, and Social Criticism

As we have observed, Bhaskar's critical realism positions itself as an alternative to the Manichean struggles of positivist and hermeneutical epistemologies of social science. Indeed, in a strikingly provocative gesture, Bhaskar maintains that underlying the surface glow of binary oppositions are a number of undetected commonalities, commonalities that indicate that in fact the proponents of hermeneutics are so deeply infected by the positivist virus that their proposed inoculants to it actually contain toxic quantities of it.[88] Unmindful of the ways in which their own discourse is constituted by the modes of thought it is designed to displace and transform, advocates of hermeneutics unwittingly assimilate what they intend to repudiate. More specifically, Bhaskar contends that hermeneutical thought assimilates four constitutive features of positivism, all of which distort its understanding of science and social inquiry. First, Bhaskar asserts that the champions of hermeneutics accept "an essentially positivist account of natural science, or at least (and more generally) of an empiricist ontology."[89] Second, he holds that, having adopted an empiricist ontology bereft of ontological depth, hermeneutical writers also necessarily embrace an empiricist and essentially Humean view of causality.[90] In fact, Bhaskar claims, it is precisely by adopting this view of causation that the advocates of hermeneutics are led into two related errors, first of restricting the scope of causal explanation exclusively to the domain of natural science and thus denying the possibility that human and social affairs are causally explicable, and second of viewing causal explanation and interpretive understanding as incompatible enterprises.[91] Third, Bhaskar claims that having "in effect [ceded] natural science to positivism,"[92] hermeneutical accounts of social inquiry are driven to challenge not just positivism but also the commitment to science itself.[93] Finally, Bhaskar alleges that hermeneutics shares with positivism a nonnormative, nonemancipatory conception of social and political inquiry, one that precludes rational criticism of agents' beliefs about their interests and intentions, the meanings of their actions, and the like.[94]

It is largely on the basis of these charges that Bhaskar advances critical realism as an original and attractive exit from the impasses of contemporary social inquiry. Situating critical realism as a sublation of dialectical oppositions between positivist naturalism and hermeneutic anti-naturalism, Bhaskar purports to incorporate and transcend these antithetical views. But does he succeed? More precisely, does he provide an accurate and convincing account of the relationship between positivism, hermeneutics, and critical realism? If not, what is the political and epistemological significance of his mischaracterization? What losses might it entail, and what possibilities might it foreclose?

Although I agree that critical realism stands at some remove from positivism, its relationship to hermeneutics (and other traditions, such as pragmatism) is generally much more complex and less antagonistic than Bhaskar suggests. This can perhaps best be illustrated by reviewing in some detail the charges adumbrated above. Let us begin with the first, namely, the claim that proponents of hermeneutics adopt an essentially positivist account of natural science. This contention is critical to Bhaskar's argument precisely because it underpins many of his corollary allegations, such as the claim that the advocates of hermeneutics adopt an empiricist conception of causality. If it is vindicated, then many of the subsequent charges would ostensibly follow. Turning from the views of Peter Winch to contemporary hermeneutical philosophers such as Taylor and Dreyfus, it is manifestly clear that Bhaskar's allegations apply at most to a particular subset of writers associated with hermeneutics and not to the "tradition" in toto. In fact, Taylor, in an analysis of Richard Rorty's nonrealist pragmatism, declares unequivocally his commitment to a realist account of natural science. Moreover, he maintains that current forms of nonrealism—for example, Rorty's pragmatism and some forms of postmodernism—represent the latest expression of a mode of thought that remains parasitic on, even while purporting to be a radical alternative to, the miscast epistemology of Vienna School positivism. In a passage that leaves little room for interpretive ambiguity, Taylor writes, "I reject Rorty's non-realism. Rather I believe that non-realism is itself one of the recurrently generated *aporiai* of the tradition we both condemn. To get free of it is to come to an uncompromising realism."[95] Later in the same essay, Taylor emphatically reaffirms his commitment to a realist construal of natural science: "Similar things could be said of the claim that there are electrons or quarks, or that there is no such thing as phlogiston or caloric. To balk at this is to slide back into the bad old non-realism of the Vienna positivists, with their untenable distinction between 'observables' and 'theoretical terms.' What is meant to be so wrong with correspondence talk here?"[96] In short, Taylor, arguably the leading representative of hermeneutics in the world today, clearly contravenes Bhaskar's twin assertions about the hemeneutic tradition. Far from accepting "an essentially positivist account of natural science" and an "empiricist ontology," he definitively repudiates them.

Similarly, Dreyfus, in an analysis of Heidegger's view of natural science that also reflects his own, rejects internal realism and anti-realism (in both its instrumentalist and idealist incarnations) alike, defending instead a position he terms "hermeneutic realism." This stance strives to vindicate as coherent "natural science's background realism" and the idea that "dasein can detach itself from its concerns and so can reveal entities that exist independently of us."[97] Concomitantly, however, it jettisons the metaphysical realist view that natural science can ever provide "a theory of *ultimate* reality."[98] By contrast, Dreyfus's hermeneutic realism is simultaneously a "plural" or "multiple" realism, one that remains receptive to the idea that different theories may answer different kinds of questions and therefore reveal different aspects of nature or reality.[99] Thus, although modern science may provide the "one right answer as far as physical causality is concerned,"[100] this does not preclude the possibility that other theories may better reveal or illuminate other aspects of nature or the real. As Dreyfus puts it, "Natural science can be getting it righter and righter about how things *work* even if there is no one right answer to how things *are*."[101] Although Bhaskar does not articulate a view on this latter issue, it should be evident from the foregoing that hermeneutic realism in no way entails a positivist account of natural science, nor does it presuppose or otherwise embrace an empiricist ontology. Indeed, Dreyfus maintains that, although one can never stand outside current scientific practice and establish through metaphysical argument that science must be about the discovery of natural kinds and their causal powers, neither can one undercut realism by insisting on an ontology that purges all nonobservables from the domain of scientific knowledge.[102] To the contrary, hermeneutic realism provides an account of how scientists can develop and test theories, grounded in empirical data and subject to empirical debate, about entities, their properties, and their causal powers, even if those entities—quarks, quasars, electrons, and the like—cannot be directly experienced, nor their properties and powers directly observed. In short, Dreyfus's realism differs from both earlier variants of anti-realism (like those of Kuhn, Nelson Goodman, and Hilary Putnam) and currently fashionable forms of "deflationary realism" (as developed by philosophers such as Donald Davidson). It is instead a "robust realism," one that supports "the claim that *we can have access* to things as they are in themselves independent of our practices."[103]

If Taylor and Dreyfus abjure positivist accounts of natural science and are committed to a thoroughgoing, "uncompromising" realism, then Bhaskar's second charge, that is, that the hermeneutical tradition embraces a Humean account of causation, is also without warrant. As I argued briefly in chapter 2, the hermeneutic defense of an ontological distinction between the natural and social sciences is itself *based* on a causal claim, namely, the claim that agents' self-interpretations and self-understandings cause actions, whereas physical entities have no self-interpretations, or if they do, there is no evidence that those self-interpretations are causally efficacious.[104] Similarly, the hermeneutical claim that actors' self-interpretations cause actions is precisely the basis of the equally important thesis that any explanatory social theory must take self-interpretations, common meanings, and beliefs into account as evidence.

Accordingly, what distinguishes Taylor's and Dreyfus's position, as well as the hermeneutic stance being developed here, is neither, as some allege, its outright rejection of causal explanation nor, as Bhaskar maintains, its embrace of an empiricist conception of causality. Rather, these views are animated by their challenge to empiricist conceptions of causality and, more broadly, to sweeping and monolithic notions of causation that demand that *all* causal relations necessarily be expressible in correlational or nomological form.[105] In fact, contrary to the claims of Bhaskar and other critics of hermeneutics, Taylor directly challenges *both* empiricist views of causality and the views of post-Wittgensteinian philosophers such as G. E. M. Anscombe, Anthony Kinney, and A. I. Meldon who, in their zeal to attack Cartesian and empiricist conceptions of thought and action, effectively sever all links between causal explanation and the explanation of action by denying that "motives, desires, intentions, [and] acts of the will"[106] constitute causes of the actions one explains by them.[107] Declaring this view "quite mistaken,"[108] Taylor contends that "in the broad sense of being concerned with how actions come about, explanations by desire or intention are thus undeniably causal."[109]

To better appreciate what this account involves, it may be helpful to return to Bhaskar's favorite source of critique, Hume. In his accounts of causation in *A Treatise of Human Nature,* Hume identifies three empirical relations—contiguity, priority (or succession) in time, and constant conjunction—as essential to the concept of causation.[110] To take one of Hume's most famous examples, when one billiard ball strikes another, and the ball that was previously at rest subsequently moves, it is the copresence of these three relations that vindicates the ascription of a causal relation between the two objects. That is, the moving ball's collision with the ball at rest is the cause of the latter's motion and is so precisely because of the presence of these three relations between antecedent and consequent. From Hume's perspective, which grounds all secure knowledge in observation and experience, this and other causal relations do not involve relations of necessity simply because observation yields nothing more than a "constant conjunction" or "regular correlation" between events. Consequently, only if one steps outside the framework of empiricism can one posit the existence of hidden powers or forces that join in relationships of necessity antecedent and consequent events.

Although this "regularity" theory of causation has been the target of considerable criticism since the demise of logical positivism, it has also proven to be a remarkably resilient position within the philosophy of science and the social sciences.[111] As a general account of causation, however, it remains deeply inadequate. This is the case not only because it notoriously conflates ascriptions of causality with constant conjunctions and thus in principle cannot provide grounds for distinguishing causal from noncausal conjunctions, but also, as Barry Stroud notes, because in doing so it either divorces the concept of causality from the idea of having a good reason to believe (that observed A will be followed by observed B) or a priori defines reasonable belief in terms of observed constant conjunctions.[112] In either case, Hume's account forecloses the possibility of having good reasons for belief or nonbelief independent of observed regularities.

More generally, this view fails to consider the possibility that an account of an action may be causal (in the most common, basic sense of showing what "produced" or "brought about" some change or event) without being grounded in observed constant conjunctions. To better grasp this point, it may be useful to suspend momentarily analyses of complex or controversial cases of causal attribution, as well as a priori investigations of causation. Instead, let us turn briefly to an examination of what might be called the mundane phenomenological genesis of the root notion of causal attribution. That is to say, if we reflect on the kinds of experiences from which our root notion of causation and causal attribution is derived, it is evident that such attributions are built on basic, ordinary bodily experiences such as pushing, pulling, holding, rubbing, squeezing, lifting, and blowing. By squeezing an egg, for instance, we cause it to break. By rubbing two pieces of wood together, we cause the dry grass to catch on fire. By placing a stone in our hand and making certain complex motions of the arm and fingers, we cause it to travel through the air in a parabolic arc.[113] From these epistemically "primitive" and fundamental experiences, we gradually become acquainted with both the world and our own powers and capacities (or lack thereof) to intervene and manipulate, to produce or prevent events, and thereby to change ourselves and our environment. Likewise, it is on the basis of this everyday experience and knowledge that we develop our core, first-order conception of causation as that which produces or brings about something. As Richard Miller suggests, these experiences provide the concept of causation with "its point and its unity."[114] More broadly,

> in all elementary varieties of causation . . . typical cases are of interest as a means of control. By learning about pushes and other elementary mechanical causes, we learn how to change trajectories. By learning about motivations, we acquire the basic means of changing conduct,

namely, persuasion. By learning how to give sensations and feelings, we learn how to change the course of others' inner lives. Our interest in changing some process by affecting another gives point to our having a concept of causation, just as our interest in nutrition gives point to having a concept of food—even though plenty of food is not nutritious.[115]

Importantly, even when we ascend from these mundane, prescientific instances of causal primitives to engage in inquiries that raise more complex, second-order issues of causal attribution, the former are never entirely displaced or superceded, but remain in the background as important orientations, benchmarks, or paradigm cases on which we draw. In fact, it is only on the basis of a prior familiarity with them that we can engage in, and extend the meaning of causality to, these more sophisticated causal inquiries. Thus, the primitive, first-order understanding of causality is neither inferior to nor complementary with second-order notions. Rather, the former makes possible the latter.[116]

Significantly, however, this epistemically primitive understanding of causation, as well as the explanations it countenances, is not easily reconciled with the Humean precept that causal statements link antecedents and consequents via constant conjunctions or lawlike correlations. When, for instance, I posit my being tripped as the cause of my newly chipped tooth, I may provide an ostensibly convincing causal account of this event yet be unable to cast it in correlational or covering law form. Does this, as the Humean account would imply, mean that the claim is not really causal at all, that it fundamentally misconstrues the defining features of the concept and the rules governing its use? If one accepts without examination Hume's definition, the obvious answer to this question is "yes." Singular statements, Hume and his allies argue, must be instantiated in lawlike regularities in order to be causal. On the other hand, if causation is conceived in its core sense as showing what has brought about an event, then the answer is "certainly not." In the latter instance, singular causal attributions can also be vindicated by identifying relevant counterfactual conditionals, that is, conditionals stating that if the putative cause—some event or state—had not obtained, the effect would not have occurred. So, when I maintain that if I had not been tripped I would not be visiting my dentist today, I make a singular causal statement that is both contingent in the Humean sense—for instance, I might have fallen—and falsifiable in the Popperian sense. It is not, however, apparent that this causal claim is deduced or is deducible from a causal law or lawlike regularity. Rather, in instances of this sort, causal attributions are typically supported by counterfactual or subjunctive conditionals, which are themselves situated in a larger context of determinate circumstances, conditions, structures, and meanings. Through this process, one builds evidential support for claims of causal relations without necessarily being able to frame those claims in nomological or correlational terms.[117]

Although the idea that causal attributions must be nomologically deducible is currently the predominant view within the social sciences, many explanations in contemporary social science, including a number of quite widely acclaimed studies, utilize counterfactual rather than nomological conceptions of causation. For instance, in an effort to explain the comparative absence of class-based political parties and movements in the United States (a phenomenon often referred to as "American exceptionalism") and, more broadly, the fragmentation of conflict and bargaining in American politics, Joshua Cohen and Joel Rogers pinpoint six "deeply rooted" factors or features. According to Cohen and Rogers, these factors—constitutional design, geography and natural resources, uneven economic development, racism, ethnic and religious divisions, and state repression—have perdured and reinforced one another throughout U.S. history, contributing decisively to the production and reproduction of a narrow, nonideological, interest-group politics rather than one anchored around broad, class-based coalitions and cleavages.[118] And this, they further maintain, constitutes a significant barrier to democratic participation and action, one that simultaneously threatens the legitimacy of the political system and contaminates the policy-making process.

Although the factors that Cohen and Rogers identify, as well as the inferential claims they advance about their consequences, are certainly both causal and counterfactual in the sense sketched above, the authors do not articulate (nor do they indicate a desire to articulate) their explanation in the form of general laws connecting the six cited factors with the absence of class politics in the United States. Nor, as one might argue, is it clear that Cohen and Rogers's explanation is best understood as an "explanation sketch,"[119] to borrow Hempel's term. This view presumes that the ultimate integrity of an explanation qua explanation rests on the possibility of linking under an umbrella of general laws and initial conditions the *explanandum* and its *explanans*. But it is not at all evident why Cohen and Rogers's hypothesis, in order to be an explanation (in the ordinary sense of overcoming an "obstacle" or making "what was unintelligible intelligible"),[120] must be understood as a vague indication of laws and initial conditions waiting to be fleshed out in a form consistent with the covering law model (or in any nomological form). To the contrary, it is a perfectly intelligible explanation, regardless of its adequacy. Moreover, the explanation's power or weakness, adequacy or inadequacy, persuasiveness or unpersuasiveness rest not on its congruence with the logical form of the covering law model or any other nomological model of explanation, but on its capacity to marshal evidentiary support in defense of the postulated crucial factors. That is, if Cohen and Rogers's explanation is inadequate, it is so because it misconceives or overestimates the role of particular institutional structures (such as federalism), because it overlooks the failure of labor leaders to make aggressive efforts to organize and recruit women, because it omits any consideration and comparative assessment of rival hypotheses such as the Hartz thesis, and so forth.[121] As Philip Gaspar states, "If Cohen and Rogers' explanation is deficient, it is because it ignores salient factors (e.g., the political weaknesses of the U.S. working-class movement during crucial periods), not because it fails to provide a covering law."[122]

Similarly, in *Power and Powerlessness*, John Gaventa's celebrated analysis of quiescence and rebellion in central Appalachian mining communities, the author explores a family of practical and theoretical questions that lie at the heart of any critical theory, namely, questions regarding the sustained existence of political quiescence and inaction under conditions of profound political and economic inequality.[123] As Gaventa asks, "Why, in a social relationship involving the domination of a non-élite by an élite, does challenge to that domination not occur? What is there in certain situations of social deprivation that prevents issues from arising, grievances from being voiced, or interests from being recognized? Why, in an oppressed community where one might intuitively expect upheaval, does one instead find, or appear to find, quiescence? Under what conditions and against what obstacles does rebellion begin to emerge?"[124] In answering these questions about political inaction—questions that cannot even be recognized as problems from within the methodological borders of positivism and behavioralism—Gaventa holds that the miners' quiescence (and rebellion) is a result of power relations, and particularly power relations belonging to what Steven Lukes terms the second and third dimensions of power.[125] To establish this causal claim, Gaventa draws explicitly and frequently on a variety of counterfactual analyses. Through historical and comparative investigation, for instance, Gaventa demonstrates that in similar situations during the 1890s, early 1900s, 1920s, and 1930s, when the power of the élite declined, miners in various parts of the region did in fact rebel.[126] Significantly, however, Gaventa never casts his causal claims in nomological form. Rather, his recurrent emphasis on locating "*relevant* counterfactuals"[127] strongly suggests that his causal attributions are not meant to be understood in these terms. In these and other cases, what matters are relevant similarities and differences embedded in specific contexts of explanation, not lawlike generalizations of the form "if A then B."[128]

Gaventa's study has rightly been cited as an important work of empirical social science that implicitly evinces realist commitments.[129] In its quest to locate underlying structures and causal mechanisms, in its commitment to transdiction, and in its general skepticism toward empiricist or "event-centered" ontologies, Gaventa's work displays a striking affinity with the views of critical realists such as Bhaskar. It is also, of course, an evocative ethnography and historical narrative, one that displays great hermeneutical sensitivity. In this respect, Gaventa's study is perhaps best understood as an exemplar of a sophisticated methodological pluralism that, by joining hermeneutical and realist commitments, achieves in the domain of empirical research the kind of *Aufhebung* that Bhaskar purports to realize at the level of social theory. Nonetheless, by eschewing a nomological conception of causation, Gaventa's study represents an important departure from Bhaskar's critical realism. It might therefore appear that his study is not after all a true exemplar of critical realism, or at least of Bhaskar's version of it.

Here, however, I would suggest that instead of searching for new exemplars one would do well to revise one's conception of critical realism. Indeed, given Bhaskar's and other realists' professed repudiation of epistemological foundationalism, rejection of prediction as a criterion of social scientific explanation, and corollary defense of what Ian Shapiro and Alexander Wendt term "more flexible, question-driven standards of causal inference,"[130] the central question, I would maintain, is not whether the absence of a nomological conception of causation compromises Gaventa's account but whether critical realists should insist on conceiving of a structurally layered, multipurpose concept like causation in ways that exclude

in principle the sorts of counterfactual claims Gaventa advances.[131] Given
the notorious difficulties of sustaining the view that causal relations are
supervenient on underlying causal laws, this insistence seems curious.[132]

Like the proponents of Humean regularity theory and the covering law
model, realists might reply that the appeal to a counterfactual analysis of
causation, however well intended, is ultimately empty, since counterfactuals must themselves be sustained nomologically (in the Humean sense)
and thus must ultimately be reducible to a regularity theory of causality.
Indeed, it is often argued that, for statements of causal relations between
states of affairs to be genuinely explanatory, they must be supported by
generalizations or causal laws. Although arguments of this sort are not
uncommon, they rest on a specious inference from the fact that a causal
claim can be challenged to the conclusion that any claim *must* depend
on another more basic one that is epistemologically unchallengeable. But
the idea that all claims must be reducible to an epistemologically basic
claim that defies challenge is patently foundationalist, a position that hermeneuticists, realists, and pragmatists alike reject. Moreover, if the foregoing account of the relationship between causal primitives and second-
order causal attributions is sound, then the nomological analysis of
causation inverts the actual relationship between causality and laws. Instead of causal attributions being supervenient on universal laws, it is
laws that are parasitic on causation.

In short, the foregoing analysis outlines an alternative construal of causation, one that need not be explicated exclusively in correlational or
nomological form. Deploying counterfactual conditionals, it is possible to
pick out cases of singular causation without being prepared to articulate
them as lawful correlations. This, I should stress, does not preclude the
possibility or appropriateness of ever going beyond primitive causal attributions to build a nomological science. Like efforts to provide a definition of causation that is valid in all contexts, the idea that it is *never*
possible or salutary to build a nomological science violates the pragmatist
injunction that such issues be resolved on the basis of evidentiary considerations emerging out of an examination of the history, development,
and objectives of specific ongoing inquiries. What the account adumbrated above does contravene, however, are a priori claims that causal
ascriptions must be lawlike or nomological. Ironically, the Humean account, which putatively grounds its analysis of causation in observation
and experience, rests on just this sort of a priori assertion about what

governs claims of causal attributions. As such, it renders otiose the very causal primitives from which the concept of causation is derived.

We are now in a position to state more precisely the relationship between critical realist and hermeneutical understandings of causality. Pace Bhaskar, it is not the former's rejection and the latter's adoption of the Humean theory of causation that fundamentally distinguish critical realism and hermeneutics. The truth is that neither Taylor nor Dreyfus endorses the Humean account.[133] Rather, these views are distinguished by the former's embrace and the latter's rejection of the notion, derived at least in part from Hume, that causal attributions must be grounded in lawlike statements or correlations. That is, although Bhaskar draws on the distinction between open and closed systems to contest the positivist view that adequate explanations in social science must be predictive, he leaves untouched another cornerstone of positivism, namely, the idea that causal attributions must instantiate a nomological or correlational relation between similar kinds of events. In fact, Bhaskar's account implicitly assumes that, if social theories could be scrutinized under conditions of experimental closure, then both constant conjunctions and the causal laws that sustain them would, in principle and presumably in practice, be forthcoming. It is unclear, however, how this claim might be justified. It cannot be based on any direct empirical evidence, since Bhaskar's claim that experimental closure in social inquiry is impossible entails that no such empirical evidence exists. If, on the other hand, it is justified analogically, that is, on the basis of an analogy between the natural and social sciences, then it presupposes what needs to be shown, namely, that these sciences are similar in all relevant respects. In neither case does Bhaskar adduce a convincing justification for his key assumption.

Let us now turn to Bhaskar's third allegation, namely, the charge that hermeneutics shares with positivism what, in a deliberately paradoxical phrase, I will term the "norm of antinormativity," that is, the view that social scientific explanation (or understanding) is essentially acritical, nonnormative, and nontransformative in the sense that it neither aims to locate nor is capable of providing grounds for appraising the phenomena that it studies. Drawing again on Peter Winch as a representative figure, Bhaskar argues that Winch's Wittgensteinian approach to philosophy, which views problems of philosophy as "problems about the conditions, limits, and forms of *language*,"[134] reduces questions of ontology to questions of language and thereby eradicates any distinction between language and reality. This "linguistic fallacy"[135] transforms both philosophy and social science into an entirely linguistic affair, one in which the elements of language derive their meaning not by virtue of their relationship to some object but rather from their use in what Wittgenstein famously termed a "form of life." On this view, the exclusive aim of philosophical and social inquiry is to elucidate the meanings of concepts informing human activities and forms of life by identifying the conceptual connections between various internally related linguistic elements. As Brian Fay puts it, "Philosophy [and social science] is an essentially hermeneutical endeavor, one in which the role of the philosopher is to unearth the meaning of the complex ways fundamental concepts function in particular forms of life. This is a kind of conceptual anthropology. The philosopher seeks to uncover the various uses of certain abstract, essential terms as a way of rendering explicit the deep meaning of what we do; as a way of enlightening us as to how others different from ourselves conceive the world and live in it; and as a way of enlarging our understanding of the possibilities of living a human life."[136]

However, having collapsed entirely the distinction between concepts and world by conceiving of society as not simply concept dependent but also "entirely conceptual in character,"[137] Bhaskar maintains that Winch is driven to a form of conceptual idealism, one in which ideas and conceptualizations are held to exhaust social reality and in which agents' own conceptualizations are deemed incorrigible.[138] From within this perspective, it is impossible to ask questions about the adequacy of our concepts for grasping and understanding the social world. Social science, like philosophy, can at best describe the meaning of concepts and deflate the pretensions of those who purport to hold the key to reality as such. It cannot provide evaluative standards for assessing the concepts it describes or for arbitrating between competing concepts or forms of life. Hence, Winch's view of philosophy (and social science) as "*uncommitted enquiry*":[139] "To take an uncommitted view of such competing conceptions is peculiarly the task of philosophy; it is not its business to award prizes to science, religion, or anything else. It is not its business to advocate any *Weltanschauung*."[140] Or, as Wittgenstein, whose thought Winch purports to explicate, wrote, "Philosophy may in no way interfere with the actual use of language; it can in the end only describe it . . . It leaves everything as it is."[141]

Whereas other commentators have tried to counter these readings with more generous interpretations, my strategy here is rather different. Dodging the vexed question of whether Bhaskar's readings of Winch and Wittgenstein are the most credible ones, I would like instead to explore the status of Bhaskar's more general claim that views like those attributed to Winch "are quite characteristic of the hermeneutical tradition generally."[142] In other words, I shall ask: Is it the case that the hermeneutical thinkers *characteristically* "transpose" positivist views in a manner that renders criticism impossible? Do they routinely commit the "linguistic fallacy"? Do they implicitly or explicitly "leave everything as it is"? If, as I will argue, the answer to these questions is a resounding "no," then his claims about the hermeneutical tradition are simply erroneous. This, it goes without saying, would be the case regardless of one's views about the adequacy of Bhaskar's readings of Winch and Wittgenstein.

Before proceeding, it might be useful to add a brief word about the notion of uncommitted enquiry adumbrated above. Although at one level this view of philosophical and social inquiry clearly does abandon one of the principal objectives of critical theory as it has often been conceived, namely, as a foundational enterprise charged with the task of providing objective or context-independent standards for evaluating the social and political phenomena it investigates, at another level it does not simply leave philosophy impotent and social life untouched, as a superficial reading of Wittgenstein's phrase of philosophy leaving "everything as it is" might appear to suggest. Even on Winch's own deflationary understanding of philosophy and social science as descriptive inquiries that aim exclusively to illuminate the meanings of concepts nested in specific forms of life, these endeavors do not necessarily leave unaltered the self-understandings and practices they investigate and the agents to whom they are addressed. Both in their effort to debunk grandiose inquiries that claim to reveal "the essence of intelligibility as such"[143] and in their interpretations of the meanings of opaque, puzzling, or strange self-interpretations and practices, hermeneutical inquiries can transform self-understandings, yielding a modified and less impoverished perspective on the object of analysis and on ourselves. By, for instance, suspending the impulse to apply indiscriminately "our" vocabulary and standards to the analysis of alien and ostensibly atavistic practices and beliefs such as Azande witchcraft or Islamic fundamentalism, hermeneutical investigations may not only render intelligible what would otherwise appear irrational, but may also transform our understanding of those cultures and practices and, by extension, ourselves and our relationship to them.[144] Likewise, clarifying the ways in which conceptualizations of collective identities like nationhood and nationality figure in particular forms of life may not yield specific normative prescriptions for resolving disputes about identity and recognition in multicultural societies and global politics, but it may, by modifying the disputants' understanding of the nature and genealogy of their conflicts and identities, reconfigure the basis of dialogue and conciliation. In these ways, even Winch's "uncommitted" hermeneutics does not necessarily leave unaltered the self-understandings and practices it explicates.[145]

More strongly, however, the twin propositions that hermeneutical inquiries assume the incorrigibility of lay accounts and that "the chronic failure of the hermeneutical tradition lies in its inability to sustain the conditions necessary for a *non-idealist critique of ideas*"[146] rest on pinched notions of "traditions" (or, in Bhaskar's favored construction, "the tradition") as univocal and self-contained rather than as multivocal, heterogenous, internally conflicted, and promiscuously interacting organisms. In so doing, Bhaskar both betrays his own professed allegiance to (a suitably reconceived) hermeneutics and commits an error that strikingly mirrors one committed by Winch in his analysis of forms of life. Just as Winch's early work erred in conceiving of forms of social life as singular, unified, and autonomous, thereby neglecting both their internal tensions and their overlapping character, so Bhaskar errs by conceiving of traditions in this manner. This mistake, in turn, drives Bhaskar to exile from his narrative those strands of hermeneutical thought that disrupt the tight positioning of hermeneutics and positivism as binary oppositions in need of dialectical transcendence. Failing to acknowledge that there is not one but are many hermeneutical outlooks, Bhaskar subsumes the many into the one and thereby excludes from analysis those strands of thought within hermeneutics that reject the conceptual idealism he criticizes.[147]

This performative contradiction between Bhaskar's philosophical defense of hermeneutics as an essential feature of all social scientific inquiry and his violation of hermeneutic principles in his own interpretive practice suggests that, in spite of Bhaskar's aggressively transformative conception of his critical realist philosophy (asserting not immodestly that it aspires to nothing less than "an anti-Parmenidian revolution, reversing 2,500 years of philosophical thought"),[148] he remains in many ways under the influence of an all-too-familiar mode of philosophical interpretation, one that frames philosophical controversies as transhistorical, transcontextual disputes between opposing "schools" and "traditions." This approach, however, makes it exceedingly difficult to chart connections between problems of philosophy and problems of everyday human life, and hence undercuts efforts to achieve the kind of transformation Bhaskar envisages.

As for the hermeneutical tradition's alleged conceptual idealism, it should be clear from my discussion in chapter 2 that influential hermeneutical thinkers such as Charles Taylor, Hubert Dreyfus, Hans-Georg Gadamer, Alasdair MacIntyre, and Fred Dallmayr, to name only a few, unequivocally repudiate both the incorrigibility thesis and the view that meanings are not only partly constitutive of social reality but are also exhaustive of it. As I explained, far from embracing the incorrigibility thesis, writers such as Taylor argue that understanding an agent's or people's actions and practices in their own terms is a necessary precondition of any adequate understanding or criticism of those actions or practices.[149] Moreover, they defend this regulative injunction simultaneously on historical, political, and epistemological grounds, arguing, first, that all accounts must rely on the agents' or cultures' own understandings and aspirations to identify their *explanandum*,[150] and, second, that the injunction operates as an indispensable constraint on the familiar tendency of social scientists and laypersons to project ethnocentrically their own language(s) of self-understanding onto the agents, events, and social practices they study. This latter constraint is of particular urgency in encounters marked by significant asymmetries of power, where the dominant party can confidently presume that it already possesses the correct terms for describing the other precisely because it does not have to contend with the kinds of resistance and refutation that are possible when power relations are equal. Possessing the privileges of power, not the least of which is the ability to live a fiction without having to recognize it as such, dominant parties can complacently reaffirm their own identity without engaging in the identity risk that attends all efforts to achieve real understanding. Thus, only by insisting on such a constraint can one hope to minimize, for example, the symbolic and actual violence resulting from the now widely recognized imputations and distortions characteristic of theories of development that dominated American political science during much of the 1950s and 1960s. These theories, which posited that all political systems performed certain basic functions (although they performed them in different ways and within different political structures), projected as universal features of political systems functions, such as "interest-aggregation and-articulation," particular to societies punctuated by a notable degree of individuation. By conceiving their own parochial model of political systems as a universal and culture-transcendent one, these theories of political development not only failed to illuminate but also actively distorted the political practices of those societies where such forms of individuation did not exist.[151]

Importantly, this defense of internal understanding as a precondition of any adequate social scientific inquiry does not preclude but enables interpretation and criticism of lay accounts for the aforementioned reason that any genuine disagreement or criticism presupposes understanding. In fact, hermeneutical thinkers such as Taylor ally internal understanding and evaluation, holding that if one purpose of social and political inquiry is attainment of a clarity and coherence that facilitates more effective coping and intervention in the world, and if, further, the best measure of the adequacy of a social theory is its capacity to enable one to cope or intervene more effectively, then this goal can be achieved only if one first grasps the languages, norms, institutions, and practices through which agents understand and act in the world. Precisely because "man" is "a self-interpreting animal"[152] whose social reality is partly constituted by the interdependent relationship between structures of meaning and interpretations of them, adequate understanding of an action, practice, ritual, or the like presupposes a prior understanding of that agent's or culture's understanding. Such understanding, however, need not stop at this point. From the proposition that grasping an action, practice, or text internally is a precondition of any adequate understanding of it, it simply does not follow that one must either capitulate meekly to it or abstain from criticizing it.

In short, Bhaskar is surely correct in arguing that, if one eviscerates the distinction between concepts and world and holds that "society is entirely conceptual in character,"[153] it becomes senseless to ask how well those concepts describe the world and equally senseless to maintain that an agent's self-understanding of his or her actions is partial, occluded, or distorted. Unfortunately, his corollary allegation, namely, that this position is characteristic of hermeneutical thought generally, on which he premises his broader charge that the tradition of *verstehende* social inquiry precludes genuine criticism, rests on no similarly convincing evidence. To the contrary, it is clear that some leading proponents of hermeneutics unequivocally reject conceptual idealism and its anti-critical, anti-normative entailments. Taylor, for instance, has taken up this issue explicitly in a number of writings, arguing against precisely the views that Bhaskar ascribes to Winch (and that Taylor labels, revealingly, "vulgar Wittgensteinian")[154] and in defense of a position that Taylor designates as "realist" (and that Philip Petit terms "evaluative realism").[155] Inverting the common belief that hermeneutical or Wittgensteinian conceptions of social inquiry demand, first, that explanations of social phenomena must be framed in, or include, the language of the agents themselves, and, second, "that the agents' self-understanding be regarded as incorrigible,"[156] Taylor argues, as I have already briefly suggested, that understanding what actors are doing in their own terms is a precondition for but not a sufficient condition of any adequate understanding or evaluation. As we have seen, it is a precondition because all *human* understanding requires a grasp of and ability to apply correctly the agents' language of self-understanding and "desirability characterizations"—that is, that agents' "aspirations, what he finds admirable and contemptible, in himself and others, what he yearns for, what he loathes, etc."[157] Absent such an understanding, Taylor submits, one cannot even identify the *explanandum*. This does not imply that the agents' own conceptions or self-descriptions must also constitute all or part of the *explanans*. In fact, exactly because "the main proposition of interpretive social science" is "that an adequate account of human action must make the agents more understandable," understanding "generally demands that we go beyond" the agents' own self-descriptions. As Taylor says, "Understanding someone cannot simply mean adopting his point of view, for otherwise a good account could never be the basis of a more clairvoyant practice."[158]

Examining the considerations articulated above, we can now see that Bhaskar is again too anxious to subsume hermeneutical thought under the banner of a particular interpretation of Winch. Moreover, having unsettled Bhaskar's positioning of the hermeneutical tradition as a form of conceptual idealism and hence as an inverted image of positivist excesses, we are now in a position to reassess the relationship between hermeneutics and critical realism. Here I argue that, in fact, the elective affinities joining critical realism with a variety of hermeneutical thinkers is much broader and deeper than Bhaskar and many others presume. To see this, we need only to summarize the preceding arguments and points.

1. On the crucial issue of the relationship between the natural and social sciences, Bhaskar's "qualified anti-positivist naturalism"[159] proceeds through different argumentative channels but arrives at almost exactly the same conclusions as contemporary hermeneutically oriented anti-naturalists such as Taylor, Dreyfus, Habermas, and Gadamer, as well as some earlier hermeneutical writers such as Heidegger. These writers largely share and in some respects augment Bhaskar's account of the ontological, epistemological, and relational limits of naturalism. Taylor, for example, is at one with Bhaskar in acknowledging what the latter terms "the chief epistemological limit on naturalism,"[160] that is, the "open-systems" problem.[161]

2. Like almost every other prominent advocate of hermeneutics, Taylor agrees entirely with what Bhaskar posits as the primary epistemological implication of this "epistemological limit" on the naturalist thesis, namely, that "the social sciences . . . *cannot be predictive.*"[162]

3. Hermeneuticists and Bhaskar agree that the social sciences explore a social reality that is both "preinterpreted" and concept dependent, and that by virtue of this fact, the norms, actions, practices, institutions, and structures that are the central objects of social scientific inquiry do not exist independently of human beings.

4. Like Bhaskar, hermeneuticists such as Taylor and Dreyfus abjure empiricist ontologies and the Humean account of causality, while defending forms of realism.

5. Many if not most hermeneuticists join Bhaskar in repudiating the incorrigibility thesis and its attendant conception of social inquiry as an acritical, nonnormative enterprise.

From the sketch of hermeneutics adumbrated above, we see that critical realism and hermeneutics are not identical currents of thought, but neither are they incommensurable or deeply at odds. On almost all of the central issues regarding the symmetries and asymmetries between the natural and social sciences, the two positions converge. Both, for instance, defend a realist ontology and reject strong social constructivist accounts

the discourses of interpretation and causal analysis, of understanding and explanation, and of explanation and emancipation, Bhaskar maps an alternative to the familiar play of dualisms that have both dominated postwar debates in social and political theory and encouraged reductive forms of either/or logic. In addition, critical realism has the distinct advantage of offering a compelling account and justification of a variety of contemporary research practices that do not fit comfortably on either side of these undifferentiated categories. Indeed, it is precisely this promise that has prompted historical sociologists, advocates of the case study approach, structuration theorists, neo-Marxists, methodological pluralists, and even quantitatively minded scholars to draw on Bhaskar's model of social scientific inquiry. Attracted to Bhaskar's claim that it is possible to jettison both the predictive criterion of social explanation and the worship of observables without thereby abandoning either the project of explanation or the scientific enterprise, a variety of scholars have seen in realism a theory of social scientific inquiry that converges with their own implicit views and that provides an escape from the bogeymen of foundationalism and conventionalism/postmodernism, abstract universalism and unconstrained relativism, scientism and anti-science.[167]

While acknowledging these notable virtues, I have stressed that there is more than one way to hold a bogeyman at bay. Or, rather, I have been suggesting that before devising a strategy for doing so, it is important to first identify who he is. By failing to disaggregate different strands of thought within the traditions he criticizes, Bhaskar's philosophical narrative ultimately obscures fundamental continuities between critical realism and various hermeneutical approaches. In doing so, he at once exacerbates divisions he aims to overcome and undercuts his efforts to transform society and social scientific inquiry. Additionally, Bhaskar's illicit subsumption of the hermeneutical tradition hides from view important differences in, for instance, conceptions of causation.

These limitations, although certainly significant, do not warrant a wholesale repudiation of realism. To the contrary, what is required is an account that attends more adequately to its continuities with other currents of postfoundational thought, such as pragmatism, hermeneutics, and some forms of post-structuralism. In the following chapter, therefore, I will explore yet another effort to develop a realist theory of social inquiry that is nonetheless sensitive to the vagaries and uncertainties of social and political life.

— 5 —

Sciences That Disturb

> What we find out in philosophy is trivial; it does not teach us
> new facts, only science does that. But the proper synthesis of
> these trivialities is enormously difficult, and has immense im-
> portance. Philosophy is in fact the synopsis of trivialities.
> —Ludwig Wittgenstein[1]

Pierre Bourdieu's "Fieldwork in Philosophy"

Over the past four decades, Pierre Bourdieu has developed one of the
most theoretically challenging and empirically rich accounts of human
and social conduct available today. From his ethnographies of the peas-
antry in colonial Algeria to his theory of practice, from his accounts of
symbolic power and symbolic violence to his detailed studies of the structure and operation of specific social fields, Bourdieu's writings have significantly contributed to debates in such disparate areas as anthropology,
law, art history, sociolinguistics, media studies, literature, and, to a lesser
degree, philosophy. It is curious, however, that in spite of the astonishing
breadth, distinctiveness, and influence of Bourdieu's oeuvre, Anglophone
political theorists have yet seriously to engage it. Unlike disciplines such
as sociology, anthropology, and education, where one might justifiably
bemoan the "recurrent misinterpretations"[2] and misappropriations of
Bourdieu's writings, in political theory (and a fortiori political science)
the principal difficulty is one of locating any interpretations or appropriations at all. There are, to be sure, isolated references to his theories
of symbolic power, symbolic violence, and social reproduction, but vigorous discussion of the broader contours of his thought and its bearing
on the study of politics has thus far failed to occur.

This neglect of Bourdieu's contribution to social and political inquiry
is unfortunate. Precisely because Bourdieu's work crisscrosses, reconfigures, and even dissolves many of the boundaries and dualisms consti-

tutive of postwar political theory and science in the United States, an investigation of it may provide valuable clues for overcoming tensions and cleavages both within political theory and between political theory and the larger discipline of political science.[3] Moreover, Bourdieu's articulation—via the concept of habitus—of the links between symbolic structures, institutional structures, and mental structures provides an account of power—a concept that many consider the master term of political inquiry—that contrasts simultaneously with those articulated by the protagonists in the "three faces of power" debate and with poststructuralist conceptions of power such as Michel Foucault's. Finally, by joining his theoretical inquiries with concrete empirical investigations of particular social and political institutions, Bourdieu attends to the more direct practical interests of political theorists and political scientists. Indeed, Bourdieu's efforts to identify the precise ways in which contingent social norms, practices, and structures become "naturalized" is intended to open new spaces of political agency and resistance, to liberate social and political actors by enabling them to shape and act upon those forces that previously shaped and acted upon them, and to facilitate interventions in those chains of causality that restrict the development of more vital democratic institutions and practices.

In what follows, I focus primarily on the issue of how Bourdieu's mode of socioanalysis might advance our understanding of particularly urgent and nettlesome political problems. To do so, I begin by briefly positioning his writings in a threefold context: political, intellectual, and theoretical. By sketching the cluster of problems that initially prompt Bourdieu's rethinking of classical debates in social theory, as well as the conceptual architecture he develops in response to them, I hope to open a clearing for examining Bourdieu's contributions to two areas of political inquiry, specifically, the politics of language and speech and the study of power relations. More generally, I argue that Bourdieu provides unmined resources for investigating vexing problems of democratic theory and practice, and particularly for combating perversions of those political values inextricably linked to democratic forms of life: freedom, equality, and social justice. By joining a phenomenological account of embodied conduct with a depiction of social fields and institutions as both materially and symbolically stratified, Bourdieu articulates a sociology of power that productively explores both the micro-politics of everyday life and the macro-politics of institutional silencing and exclusion. Furthermore, through his analyses of the unperceived ways that symbolic forms become instruments for constituting and sustaining structured inequalities, Bourdieu brings together the often sequestered issues and domains of democracy, culture, civil society, and institutional justice. Finally, by directing the sociological and historical gaze back on the disciplinary habitus itself, Bourdieu fashions a lens not only for seeing what is passed over, for bringing "the undiscussed into discussion,"[4] but also for understanding and overcoming the disabling (as opposed to enabling) constraints and soft censorships that social fields place on those who labor within them.

In sum, I contend that Bourdieu's defiance of longstanding inter- and intradisciplinary boundaries, as well as the specific way that he defies them, are two of the things that make his work instructive. For those who believe that the strict separation of the normative and the empirical, of theory and research, of philosophy and science tends to impoverish rather than purify the study of politics, Bourdieu offers a conceptual vocabulary and set of concrete exemplars that transcend these increasingly sterile and artificial oppositions. In so doing, he provides political theorists and political scientists with a compelling map of a "third way." This way, I argue, lies at the horizon of his theory of practice.

From the Practice of Theory to the Theory of Practice

Although there are numerous routes into Bourdieu's body of work, perhaps the most dependable if not direct leads first through the practical and philosophical concerns out of which it emerged. Indeed, in his preface to *The Logic of Practice* and elsewhere, Bourdieu warns that without a grasp of the specific issues animating his thought—if seen, as he puts it, solely as "theoretical 'theses' "—"the essential point I try to put over in this book . . . would be liable to lose its meaning and its effectiveness."[5] In the case of *The Logic of Practice,* however, the practical and philosophical issues go back to an early and decisive moment in his intellectual formation—namely, his "fieldwork" on Algerian peasant communities between 1956 and 1961. Initially as a conscript in the French army and later as a philosopher engaged in ethnographic research, Bourdieu found himself as a participant observer in the middle of Algeria's agonizing and bloody struggle for independence. "Appalled," in his words, at "the gap between the views of French intellectuals about this war and how it should be brought to a close, and my own experiences,"

Bourdieu set out "to write a book with the intention of highlighting the plight of the Algerian people and, also, that of the French settlers whose situation was no less dramatic, whatever else had to be said about their racism, etc."[6] In particular, he writes, "I was . . . concerned about the associated utopianism since in my view it was not at all helpful, even for an independent Algeria, to feed a mythical conception of Algerian society. Here again I found myself between camps as far as intellectual life was concerned."[7]

Although this effort initially culminated in the 1958 publication of *Sociologie de l'Algérie,* it is, I would argue, significant that Bourdieu has repeatedly revisited and reworked the theoretical ideas informing his early analyses.[8] As Bourdieu notes, the need to reconcile theoretical and practical intentions converged in his ambition to "to work towards a scientific analysis of Algerian society," one that sought "to understand and explain the real foundations and objectives of that struggle."[9] In effect, his Algerian fieldwork became the focus of an emotionally charged series of intellectual and epistemological experiments, forcing him to reflect on how one might bring "together the scientific and the ethical or political vocation," and forge, as he puts it, "a kind of militant craftsmanship, as remote from pure science as from exemplary prophecy."[10] Bourdieu's fieldwork therefore raised, in a dramatic and urgent manner, concrete questions of interpretation, power, and knowledge. At the same time, it issued in broader reflections about the relation between epistemology and politics, between what one holds epistemologically and what one can or cannot say politically.

If, on the one hand, Bourdieu's fieldwork in Algeria formed the practical context of his thought and compelled him to contend with issues that, as he claims, were "in a sense presented by reality itself,"[11] on the other hand, his theoretical reflections on that reality were organized primarily around the dominant disputes and oppositions characteristic of the French intellectual "field" during the 1950s and 1960s, as well as the moral and methodological dilemmas they occasioned. According to Bourdieu, "the most fundamental, and most ruinous"[12] opposition, both in postwar French intellectual life and in the social sciences generally, is the one obtaining between two "perspectives" or modes of theoretical knowledge: subjectivist and objectivist, or as he often characterizes it, social phenomenology and social physics. These oppositions, he contends, represent two radically different and "apparently irreconcilable" views of

knowledge, ontology, method, and practice, with each being "equally indispensable to a science of the social world," yet each remaining inadequate as general frameworks for understanding human and social conduct.[13] Transcending them is therefore not only advantageous, but is also,
he holds, the "most constant and important intention of my work."[14]

Subjectivism, Bourdieu claims, is epitomized by Jean-Paul Sartre's existentialist phenomenology, but also variously embeds rational actor
theory, Alfred Schütz's phenomenological sociology, and some variants of
ethnomethodology (to this list we might add behavioralism and social
contract theory, in both its classical—for example, Hobbesian—and contemporary—for example, early Rawlsian—forms.)[15] Above all, subjectivism is punctuated by one or more of three distinct but often overlapping types of privilege: first, an epistemic privileging of "primary
experience," of its immediate natural character; second, an ontological
privileging of the atomistic, isolated, and willful subject as the author of
meaning and value and hence the ground of human and social reality;
and, third, a methodological privileging of individual acts as the exclusive
unit of individual and social explanations, that is, methodological individualism. For subjectivists, social reality is seen as the product or "ac-
complishment" of the free, conscious decisions of individual actors endowed with a transparent grasp of the "life-world" that they inhabit,
reproduce, and occasionally transform.

By contrast, objectivism designates the ambition to explain and predict
practice by locating "objective regularities (structures, laws, systems of
relationships, etc.) independent of individual consciences and wills."[16]
Premised on the idea that scientific knowledge of social reality entails a
"methodical break" with the primary experience of the social world, objectivism strives to identify and systematize formal, decontextualized
rules, laws, or deep structures governing practice and representations of
practice. Although Bourdieu variously associates this impulse with Dur-
kheimian sociology, Saussurian linguistics, Althusserian Marxism, and
Foucauldian archaeology, objectivism finds perhaps its purest and most
powerful expression in Claude Lévi-Strauss's monumental quest to identify formal codes and universal mental structures generative of all myth
and kinship structures.

For Bourdieu, subjectivism's signal merit is its recognition that much
human experience involves a "taken-for-granted," "self-evident" appre-
hension of the world, and that any account of social reality that bypasses

entirely agents' practical comportment in or self-understanding of that reality must perforce be inadequate—in this sense Bourdieu agrees with the anti-mechanistic and subjectivist proposition that "social agents construct social reality."[17] He argues, however, that subjectivists' singular focus on the primary, lived experience of the social world forecloses the possibility of posing questions about the social preconditions of such immediate, lived experience. This is because subjectivism is a mode of knowledge of primary experience, but primary experience, Bourdieu submits, "by definition, does not reflect itself."[18] Hence, questions about the preconditions of that experience, that is, about the objective conditions necessary for the production of subjective apprehensions of and orientations toward the world, are not only unanswered but cannot even be formulated from within the subjectivist ambit. Moreover, addressing subjectivism's privileging of the conscious, atomistic subject as the author of social reality, Bourdieu echoes other critics of methodological individualism in alleging that such a "philosophy of the subject" is incapable of explaining how a social reality that is putatively the product of free, conscious decisions made by isolated subjects can account for enduring objective configurations and regularities. In short, if the social world is merely the product or aggregate of individual choices, how can one account for the existence and persistence of well-documented objective regularities?

Importantly, Bourdieu contends that subjectivism's failure to explore the "structural constraints that influence interactions"[19] and form the basis of agents' subjective representations is not simply epistemologically and ontologically naïve, but is morally and politically suspect as well. Bourdieu observes, for instance, that Sartre's subjectivist philosophy of action entails an "ethical voluntarism," one in which humans freely choose either to live continuously in "the pure transparency of the subject," or, conversely, to remain an inert thing or passive object fully determined by external, mechanical forces.[20] Although this insistence on free choice and "absolute responsibility" rightly underscores the dual facts that humans are responsible for who and what they are in ways that rocks and other animals are not, and that politics and morality are possible only to the extent that strict determinism is false, it also has the disquieting consequence of dodging—in Bourdieu's view, it cannot even pose—questions about differential constraints on agents' choices, or how agents come to have particular subjective representations. In fact, Bourdieu ar-

gues that, in the absence of any recognition and investigation of the structural constraints on actions, subjectivism merely inverts objectivism's illicit universalization of "the theorist's relation to the object of science"
by itself universalizing "the experience that the subject of theoretical discourse has of himself as a subject."[21] In Sartre's case, this meant universalizing "his own experience as a pure, free-floating subject."[22]

However, whereas Bourdieu stresses the profound limitations of subjectivism, he is equally critical of objectivist modes of thought. According
to Bourdieu, objectivism's paramount virtue lies in its demand that the
social scientist break with two debilitating subjectivist illusions: "the illusion of transparency" (the idea that one can adequately understand and
explain institutions by understanding "the intentions of which they are
the product") and "the illusion of immediate knowledge" (the idea that
one can satisfactorily understand and explain social life by describing
scientifically the familiar prescientific experience of it).[23] Overcoming
these illusions is, he asserts, an indispensable prelude for investigating
questions that subjectivism necessarily excludes, namely, questions about
the specific conditions—structural conditions and objective regularities—
that make possible everyday perception and experience of the world.

Notwithstanding these merits, Bourdieu maintains that objectivism
commits critical errors of its own. Most importantly, it errs in conceiving
of practice as a mechanical, atemporal *"execution"* of independent rules
or logical operations, one in which the observer substitutes an ahistorical,
theoretical model for the reality of practice itself.[24] According to Bourdieu,
this substitution is pernicious not because it bypasses subjective, phenomenological qualities per se,[25] but because it omits properties of practices—
specifically, the tempo of events—which partly define what counts as an
event or object. Thus, any model of practice that excludes its temporal
dimensions is in principle incapable of deriving accurate and stable predictions of that practice, simply because what counts as an object or event
in everyday practice is partly a function of the tempo of the situation. In
his critique of Lévi-Strauss's formal, reversible rules of gift exchange,
Bourdieu draws on his early fieldwork in Kabylia to show precisely how
this process works and what is at stake in the objectivist detemporalization
of practice. If, he notes, a gift is "reciprocated" too quickly—for instance,
if the recipient immediately returns exactly the same object—it is not, as
Lévi-Strauss's formal model implies, a countergift, but a refusal of the gift
altogether and hence an insult.[26] In everyday practice, a countergift "must

be deferred and different,"[27] yet what counts as "deferred" and "different" are determined by the tempo and contextual meanings that objectivist theories like Lévi-Strauss's necessarily omit. In Bourdieu's words: "It is all a matter of style, which means in this case timing and choice of occasions; the same act—giving, giving in return, offering one's services, paying a visit, etc.—can have completely different meanings at different times, coming as it may at the right or wrong moment, opportunely or inopportunely."[28] Bourdieu's point is that by disregarding the temporal elements of practice and contextual meaning generally, Lévi-Strauss's "automatic laws" cannot reliably identify the very practice they purport to explain and predict.

This error, like subjectivism's errors, has not only metatheoretical but also social and political implications. Objectivism, by transforming actors and action into "epiphenomena of structures," "regulated automatons who, like clockwork, follow mechanical laws existing outside their consciousness,"[29] effectively erases uncertainty and hence agency from the landscape of practice. In so doing, it also banishes power from the realm of social and political practice. On the objectivist model, power (in the sense of "power to") resides exclusively in the independent rules and structures that causally determine actors', or rather subjects', behavior. It is therefore entirely external to human practice in the sense that although it may pass through human beings, it is wholly outside the control of human beings. Thus, it is only by breaking with objectivism's " 'monothetic' model" that it becomes possible to reintroduce power and uncertainty into human practice. Once again using Lévi-Strauss's structuralist model of gift exchange as a foil, Bourdieu shows that once temporality and context are reinserted into the analysis of gift exchange, difficult issues of power, politics, judgment, and strategy are simultaneously reinscribed. Time, as it were, transforms a rigid mechanical model into a flexible and unstable field of opportunities and constraints. Here the subtle social and political aspects of gift-giving—that is, the manner in which gift exchanges may create uneasy and unstable bonds of mutual obligation, or become mediums for conferring honor or dishonor on the parties involved—which are inaccessible to strict structural analysis, can be observed and understood.[30] As Bourdieu remarks, "To abolish interval is also to abolish strategy. The period interposed, which must be neither too short (as is seen clearly in the gift exchange), nor too long (especially in the exchange of revenge murders), is quite the opposite of the inert gap of time, the time-lag, which the objectivist model makes of it. Until he has given back, the receiver is 'obliged,' expected to show his gratitude towards his benefactor, or at least to show regard for him, to go easy on him, pull his punches, lest he be accused of ingratitude, and stand condemned by 'what people say.' "[31]

Significantly, Bourdieu claims that one way in which power operates is through a subjective misrecognition of the meanings implicit in an action, practice, or ritual. He argues, for example, that in societies like Kabylia where relations of domination are not perpetuated by "objective mechanisms like the self-regulating market" or the state, they must be constantly created and sustained through the careful cultivation of personal bonds.[32] But this more personal, "elementary" form of domination can be maintained only so long as the participants fail to recognize it for what it really is—an act of domination. Thus, its operation requires that the participants subjectively transmute the relationship from an interested one into a disinterested, "enchanted" relationship. Paradoxically, "to be socially recognized, it must be misrecognized."[33]

This "euphemization" occurs, Bourdieu contends, primarily through the establishment of commitments attached to the ethic of honor, namely, "trust, obligation, personal loyalty, hospitality, gifts, debts, [and] piety,"[34] all of which create bonds that the participants perceive as disinterested and legitimate even though they support relations that are quite literally suffused with power. Bourdieu urges that, although gift exchanges may appear as symmetrical personal relations devoid of power and domination, they may also operate as a form of what he provocatively calls "symbolic violence," a "gentle, invisible violence, unrecognized as such," and therefore "chosen as much as undergone."[35] Through the unperceived transfiguration of the cycle of exchange, giving becomes a way not just of receiving, but of possessing. A person who does not or cannot reciprocate a generous gift with an equally generous countergift thus incurs "a lasting obligation,"[36] one that requires the adoption of a peaceful and obsequious posture toward the giver. Once again, Bourdieu's point is simply that objectivist models that abstract from subjective understandings cannot explain or identify objective relations of domination the condition of which is subjective misrecognition.[37]

In examining the disturbing phenomena of symbolic violence and symbolic domination, Bourdieu returns repeatedly to the notion of "misrecognition" as a nonobjective precondition for their existence. Moving from the culturally distant case of Kabylian gift exchange to more familiar terrain, Bourdieu describes how particular forms of linguistic competence—for instance, the ability to speak "correct" English or to speak with an accent characteristic of the dominant groups or classes—become vehicles of domination and symbolic violence through a collective misrecognition in which dominant and dominated speakers alike "authorize" and confer legitimacy upon an essentially imposed "cultural arbitrary." Thus, in formal settings where "official" modes of speech are socially authorized as the norm, one often finds silent and impalpable, yet also insidious forms of symbolic violence in which dominated speakers (those less skilled in the use of the authorized mode of language) desperately seek to correct, either consciously or unconsciously, the stigmatized aspects of their pronunciation, vocabulary, and syntax. At the limit, these desperate efforts at self-censorship and "euphemization" result in a self-stultifying "disarray which leaves them 'speechless', 'tongue-tied', 'at a loss of words', as if they were suddenly dispossessed of their own language."[38] By misrecognizing the socially imposed dominant mode as a naturally dominant mode, dominated speakers unconsciously participate in the perpetuation of the violence from which they suffer. Objectivism, by abstracting subjective experience from its model of practice, cannot account for the subjective misrecognition that is a necessary condition of symbolic violence.[39]

Now even if one remains broadly sympathetic both to Bourdieu's specific arguments about the limitations of objectivism and subjectivism, and his more general (if less original) charge that the oppositions between these perspectives are not only false but are also the chief impediment to the development of a truly scientific theory of society and practice, one question remains: how does Bourdieu propose to transcend these crippling dichotomies? More specifically, how does he reconcile, on the one hand, the objectivist insight that human practice and representations of practice are partly the products of objective structures and conditions that constrain and bear upon agents, and, on the other hand, the subjectivist recognition that any account that purports to explain how these structures are established, transformed, or sustained must reintroduce agents' subjective experiences, practical aptitudes, and representations? And how does Bourdieu do this in a way that avoids simply reproducing a social scientific corollary of Cartesian dualism, one in which the categories of agent and social world are external to one another? In striving to answer these questions and thereby dissolve the multiple antinomies constitutive of modern and contemporary social theory, Bourdieu formulates a set of interlocking concepts that can be modified and put to use in divergent settings. Of these, three concepts are fundamental to his enterprise: "habitus," "field," and "capital."

For Bourdieu, habitus is unquestionably the most crucial concept. Indeed, it is through his account of habitus, and of the interplay between habitus and field, that he hopes to rescue "the whole real universe of practices"[40] from the abstractions of objectivism and the voluntarism and mentalism of subjectivism. In typically Bourdieuian parlance, habitus are defined as "systems of durable, transposable dispositions, structured structures predisposed to function as structuring structures, that is, as principles which generate and organize practices and representations that can be objectively adapted to their outcomes without presupposing a conscious aiming at ends or an express mastery of the operations necessary in order to attain them. Objectively 'regulated' and 'regular' without being in any way the product of obedience to rules, they can be collectively orchestrated without being the product of the organizing action of any conductor."[41] More concretely, the habitus is a system of "socially constituted dispositions"[42] that lie at the intersection of social structures and practical activity. According to Bourdieu, these dispositions are the embodied product of an individual's history, experience (especially early childhood experience), and social location, becoming over time an ethos, a set of flexible but enduring "mental structures" and "bodily schemas" that organize and orient comportment in private and public space. Being initially defined in terms of the "objective potentialities"— that is, "things to do or not to do, to say or not to say," all of which are shaped in turn by objective structures of social existence such as "hierarchies of age, power, prestige, and culture"—in which it is situated, and being gradually modified in accordance with the ever-changing circumstances of one's life, the habitus generates regular and immediate responses to a wide variety of situations without recourse to strategic calculation, conscious choice, or the methodical application of formal rules.[43] Like the skilled intuition that enables jazz musicians to improvise collectively without a musical score, the habitus, as an embodied practical sense, generates directed and skilled improvisations in everyday situations.

As indicated by this description, the most significant features of the dispositions generated by the habitus are their durability (they endure over time), their transposability (they can be flexibly adapted, through the use of "practical metaphors" and "analogies," to generate responses and practices in fields outside of the one in which they were initially developed), their historicity (they are inextricably intertwined with the forces of history—they are "embodied history, internalized as a second nature and so forgotten as history"), and their nonmechanistic, nonrepresentational, embodied directedness (they become a "feel for the game," a "practical sense," or a "socially constituted nature," one that is inscribed and carried in such minute details as gestures, speech, silence, table manners, posture, dress, and style).[44] Perhaps most importantly, Bourdieu conceives the habitus as reciprocally constituted by social practice (social practice places limits on what is and is not thinkable or intelligible, on what are possible and sensible responses and what are not)[45] and constitutive of social practice (the various hierarchies characteristic of different social fields, the reproduction and transformation of social structures, and so forth). As Bourdieu submits, "There is an ontological complicity between the habitus and the social field."[46]

If the habitus is Bourdieu's conceptual vehicle for describing the genesis and generation of agents' practical sense *(le sens pratique)* and comportment in everyday life, it remains incumbent upon him, first, to explain the generation and coherence of the habitus, and, second, to offer an account of the concordances and discordances between different habitus, and hence of the ways that similar or divergent social contexts inculcate those concordant and discordant dispositions. He must do this, moreover, without lapsing into a determinist variant of objectivism. Although Bourdieu uses a number of terms to articulate the way that specific social contexts and settings reciprocally shape and are shaped by the habitus— "market," "game," and "field" are his preferred locutions—the principal term for our purposes is "field." As Bourdieu, in an extraordinarily abstract passage, provisionally defines it, a field is "a network, or a configuration, of objective relations between positions. These positions are objectively defined, in their existence and in the determinations they impose upon their occupants, agents or institutions, by their present and potential situation *(situs)* in the structure of the distribution of species of power (or capital) whose possession commands access to the specific profits that are at stake in the field, as well as by their objective relation to other positions (domination, subordination, homology, etc.)."[47] In short, a field is a structured space of social positions that is also a structure of power relations. The various "positions" within this space are occupied either by agents or by institutions, and the relations between the positions determine, at any given time, the structure of the field. The objective positions that agents or institutions occupy within a field—for example, dominant or dominated positions—are determined by their possession of the forms of "capital" valorized in that particular field. Perhaps most importantly, fields are the spaces within which the dispositions of the habitus become incorporated, and the practices generated by the habitus serve in turn to reinforce or modify the configuration of the field.

To this rather skeletal description, a number of points must be added. First, the concept of field is above all a relational concept. That is, agents and positions are not treated as autonomous, isolated elements, but are defined in terms of their relations with other agents and positions. Similarly, agents' strategies always operate within a nonmechanical, yet mutually impacting causal context. Here Bourdieu's notion of the social field draws on and resembles closely the field concept in physics: "The field which cannot be reduced to a single aggregate of isolated agents or to the sum of elements merely juxtaposed is, like a magnetic field, made up of a system of power lines. In other words, the constituting agents or system of agents may be described as so many forces which, by their existence, opposition or combination, determine its specific structure at a given moment in time. In return each of these is defined by its particular position within this field from which it derives its positional properties which cannot be assimilated to intrinsic properties."[48] Second, all fields are governed by "specific laws of functioning"[49] that determine both the conditions of entry into the field (economic capital, professional degrees, social connections, and the like) and the specific relations of force within it. These field-specific laws imply, moreover, that fields are to greater or lesser degrees autonomous from one another in the sense that capital accrued in one field cannot necessarily be "converted" into an equivalent volume of capital in another field (economic capital may be the dominant form of capital in one field, whereas forms of symbolic capital may dominate in others) and that entry into one field does not guarantee entry into another. Third, fields are always sites of struggle and competition, and thus are historically dynamic. Like players in a game, agents in the field compete to attain the rewards offered by the field (material or symbolic profit), and to dictate the configuration and rules constitutive of the field. Fourth, relations exist not only within fields but also—as indicated by the second point—between them. That is, different fields are themselves organized hierarchically within larger fields of power and class relations (while also possessing, as discussed, a "relative autonomy" from these fields). Finally, all agents within particular fields share certain fundamental interests—principally an interest in the "worth" of the "profits" that field offers. In Bourdieu's terms, a precondition of the existence of a field is *illusio,* a "commitment to the game" itself.[50] Although the rules of the game may be arbitrary constructions, agents must invest them with an intrinsic significance to play the game at all.

Fields, then, are semiautonomous, contextually and hierarchically defined spaces that serve as arenas for social activity, competition, and conflict. In contrast to rather nebulous and undifferentiated terms like "society" and "community," Bourdieu's employment of the field concept facilitates an analysis of the social world as structurally differentiated and stratified, without reducing it to a set of discrete and self-contained micro-worlds. Using this model, one can, for instance, investigate the scientific field as a distinct domain governed by laws and logics irreducible to those in other fields—for instance, political or artistic fields—yet still explore its relationships to other fields and its position in larger social fields and fields of power. In such cases, questions about the specific configuration of a field, its degree of autonomy, and its precise relation to other fields are necessarily empirical ones. In this way Bourdieu's field concept vitiates the internalist/externalist dichotomy characteristic of many studies of scientific practice, that is, the tendency to treat specific scientific communities either as local cultures isolated from other scientific communities and larger social forces, or as mirror reflections of larger social, political, and cultural views.[51] At the same time, it challenges the mechanistic causality of strict structuralist and functionalist approaches by emphasizing not just the interrelation but also the inseparability of habitus and field.

Bourdieu's third central concept is that of "capital." As he employs it, the concept shares with ordinary usage the idea of a stock of accumulated goods. However, in an effort to obviate the twin defects of "finalist economism" (which assumes that all practices can be explained as functions of conscious optimizing strategies aimed at maximizing economic profit) and economic reductionism (which posits economic relations as the substructure of all social relations), Bourdieu argues that practices "can obey an economic logic without obeying narrowly economic interests."[52] By this he means that *every* field—whether of science, art, philosophy, or religion—operates in accordance with an economy in the sense that the agents within it "invest" resources, produce goods, and compete for profits. But this, he maintains, does not imply that in all fields the investments are economic capital or the profits are economic profits. Even the devout parish priest must have an interest or investment in sacerdotal authority. If he did not, Bourdieu holds, his commitment to his vocation would be inexplicable. This, however, does not mean that his investment is intended to produce economic profits; to the contrary, in the religious field such acts typically provoke censure and condemnation. Rather, he is invested in something different—salvation or communal honor.

Thus, "to eschew the alternative of purely material and narrowly economic interest and of *disinterestedness*,"[53] Bourdieu conceives of capital as differentiated into a quartet of forms: economic capital (that which is "immediately and directly convertible into money"),[54] social capital (social connections with prominent or influential people), cultural capital (cultural knowledge or educational credentials), and symbolic capital (social honor and prestige). According to Bourdieu, both hierarchies among different forms of capital and its overall distribution in a field contribute to the structure of the field. Similarly, an agent's position within a particular social field is determined by the volume and form of capital that agent possesses, which in turn structures her or his horizon of sensible strategies. To take an example, middle-class parents might lack the economic or social capital needed to secure access to lucrative jobs for their children, but those parents may send them to prestigious schools in order to convert that cultural capital into an esteemed, well-paying job. Bourdieu emphasizes, however, that although disparate forms of capital may at times be directly convertible into other forms (and that economic capital is generally the most easily convertible form of capital), they are not *automatically* convertible.

In short, Bourdieu's theory of practice can be seen as an attempt to transform static, one-dimensional views of social space into a larger differentiated, stratified, and multidimensional view. By appealing to homologies existing both between habitus and social fields and between different social fields, Bourdieu claims to account for social stability, order, and reproduction. Conversely, by emphasizing both that the habitus allows for continuous improvisation, and that social structures, as products of history, contain tensions, oppositions, and contradictions, he provides for history, change, resistance, and social transformation. Bourdieu's conception of the habitus thus entails the inseparability of sociology and history, for the very conditions that generate, reproduce, and transform the habitus are themselves inescapably historical in nature.

Ordinary Violences

Having outlined Bourdieu's conceptual tools and theoretical framework, it is time to indicate some of the concerns—particularly in the domain of politics—that they inform. In this respect, three issues merit particular attention. First, Bourdieu's theory of practice facilitates a more rigorous and illuminating exploration of what is sometimes referred to as "the politics of everyday life": those inconspicuous forms of violence, domination, denigration, and exclusion in everyday affairs that go unnoticed precisely because they are so ordinary and "unremarkable."[55] Like other recent writers, Bourdieu is interested in those opaque power relations that contribute to and sustain various forms of domination not only within formal legal and political institutions (though he has much to say about this as well), but also in spheres of life commonly thought to lie outside of the arenas of power and politics.[56] What he offers is not only a sophisticated theory of how structures of domination and subordination emerge, persist, and mutate, but also detailed descriptions of how, for instance, certain authorized forms of language surreptitiously exclude specific groups and classes from participation in certain activities or power within various institutions. By bringing to light those power-infused patterns of behavior that, in a characteristic turn of phrase, go without saying because they come without being said, Bourdieu helps to correct the tendency—found in liberal democratic, civic republican, and rational actor theories alike—to define politics and the political in ways that categorically separate it from and oppose it to everyday life.[57] Indeed, if one joins Ian Shapiro in defining politics broadly "as ranging over all human relationships in which power is or has the potential to become a significant factor,"[58] then Bourdieu's study of what (rewriting Judith Shklar) might be called "ordinary violences" might plausibly be seen as an effort to explore and redefine the ontology of the political.

Second, Bourdieu's theory provides what is arguably the most concrete model for investigating the role that the body plays not only in orienting practical activity but also in carrying and encoding histories and cultural understandings. Following Merleau-Ponty's declaration that "I am my body,"[59] Bourdieu contends that the body "is not something that one has . . . but something that one is."[60] As such, it is not a possession—something that we can own, brandish about, or stand outside of as we wish—but a state of being. Once again, by carefully describing the manner in which embodied styles, gestures, accents, postures, mannerisms, affects, and expressions encode and reproduce a panoply of social hierarchies and divisions (for instance, of class, gender, ethnicity, education, and age), Bourdieu demonstrates that one's "bodily hexis" is not only constitutive of all intelligibility, but also "constitutes a veritable *embodied politics*."[61] Recently, cultural theorists, feminists, and political theorists of varying persuasions have explored the myriad ways in which the materiality of the body becomes both a vehicle for the operations of power in society and "a site of struggle."[62] Bourdieu's central claim—which in its broad contours parallels arguments made by other writers, but is worked out systematically in his accounts of the ontological complicity between the habitus and the social field—is that all theories of politics and society that abstract from embodied agency are incapable of adequately theorizing power relations and hence of locating crucial mechanisms of domination and subordination.[63] At a minimum, such a list would include, on the one hand, contemporary forms of rationalism, for example, rational actor theories, Habermasian communicative rationalism, and Rawlsian contract theory,[64] and, on the other hand, some forms of postmodernism, anti-foundationalism, and discourse theory, such as Baudrillard's semiotics and Foucault's early archaeological studies.

Finally, Bourdieu's case studies describing the operation of symbolic power and symbolic violence—as opposed to his general theory of symbolic capital, which is much more problematic—contribute to an understanding of power relations, particularly to a better grasp of how diverse forms of domination persist even after their legal basis has been proscribed.[65] Indeed, although there is nothing original in announcing that the eradication of legally sanctioned inequalities has failed to eliminate racism, sexism, and other forms of domination and oppression, it is much more difficult to describe precisely how these softer modes of domination operate both institutionally and in everyday face-to-face interactions. As we have seen, Bourdieu offers a detailed account of how forms of social misrecognition quietly sustain and legitimate patterns of domination even among those who have no conscious desire to do so. By locating specific

mechanisms through which social differentiation is transmuted into relations of domination, he explains how various forms of domination may
persist even after their juridical basis has been abolished.

To better illustrate these claims, let us consider briefly one application
of Bourdieu's theory of practice. In this regard, perhaps the most appropriate point of departure is his work on linguistic competence and symbolic violence. This focus on language is especially fitting for our purposes, because the claim that language and politics are deeply linked has
been central to political thought at least since the time of classical Athens.
In Thucydides' *History*, for example, speech and language are portrayed
as mediums for organizing the world and acting in it, and for this reason
the presence or absence of speeches becomes a barometer of Athens's
changing political fortunes.[66] Similarly, Aristotle's celebrated definition of
man as a political animal is fully intelligible only if it is first linked to a
second and equally well-known definition of man as a creature endowed
with *logos*, which means not only reason and thought but also, and most
importantly, language and speech. More recently, speech and language
have been the foci of political writers as dramatically dissimilar as Foucault, Habermas, Catherine MacKinnon, and Quentin Skinner. However,
perhaps the most provocative, and certainly one of the most influential,
recent formulations of the link between politics and language remains the
one articulated in Hannah Arendt's *The Human Condition*. In this work
Arendt holds that the very essence of politics is speech—specifically,
public speech made possible by a shared language. Divested of the capacity to speak and accordingly to listen, to persuade and to be persuaded,
politics would be inconceivable, supplanted instead by "sheer violence,"
which, she adds forebodingly, is necessarily "mute."[67]

In her wide-ranging discussion of speech and action, Arendt makes
three important claims. First, she argues that public speech and action
are ineluctably linked, and hence that one who is rendered speechless is
correspondingly rendered incapable of action. "Speechless action," she
says, "would no longer be action because there would no longer be an
actor, and the actor, the doer of deeds, is possible only if he is at the
same time the speaker of words."[68] Second, she asserts that public speech
and action are uniquely definitory of a human life. To be deprived of
speech and action, of "word and deed,"[69] is to be deprived not simply of
a right or a capacity, but of human identity itself. As she puts it, "A life
without speech and without action is . . . literally dead to the world; it has

ceased to be a human life because it is no longer lived among men."[70] Third, Arendt places strict limits on the functions of political speech and hence the preconditions of politics. Most importantly, she maintains that genuinely public space and public speech exist and flourish only to the extent that the members of these "publics" renounce any ambition to manipulate, deceive, or dominate, and instead strive only to persuade.[71] Hence, she argues that power, as opposed to force, strength, or violence, "is actualized only where word and deed have not parted company, where words are not empty and deeds not brutal, where words are not used to veil intentions but to disclose realities, and deeds not used to violate and destroy but to establish relations and create new realities."[72]

Although these claims have been the subject of considerable controversy, one of the things that makes them simultaneously intriguing and elusive is the highly abstract level at which they are posed. Indeed, Arendt is uninterested, at least in *The Human Condition,* in issues of how manipulation and domination operate concretely in language, how people are rendered speechless even when they are not formally excluded from discourse and deliberation, or how private conditions and institutional structures affect one's capacity for public participation. These, however, are precisely the issues that engage Bourdieu. What Bourdieu does is extend, emend, and complicate Arendt's views by analyzing precisely how power relations operate in concrete linguistic exchanges. Recalling Arendt's own distinction between speech and violence, Bourdieu describes his aim as one of exploring the principal conditions of " 'non-violent' communication,"[73] or what Arendt would term the conditions of possibility of political speech.

Bourdieu's account of linguistic competence begins from an assumption that may appear indisputable, but that he alleges is neglected by most linguists and philosophers of language—that language is not exclusively a medium of communication, but is also a mechanism of distinction, domination, and violence.[74] As such, the ways in which language is used, the social relations of the speakers, the forms of speech, the setting of speech, and the style of speech—all of which are inconsequential to those who picture language exclusively as a medium of communication—become vital to an understanding of the meaning of linguistic exchanges. Using the concepts of habitus, field, and capital as the cornerstone of his account, Bourdieu argues that just as the habitus inculcates a system of durable dispositions that govern our practice, so there is also a linguistic habitus that instills durable dispositions governing our linguistic practices. As the product of a specific habitus, these dispositions are inscribed in the body as part of a "total body schema," one in which "one's whole relation to the social world is expressed."[75] Through various forms of linguistic-bodily discipline, individual agents develop what Bourdieu calls an integrated "articulatory style" that reveals their class position, social position, and at times more specific identities. Although these distinctive and contrasting styles are revealed principally in accents, gestures, intonations, and other bodily techniques for speaking, Bourdieu contends that in France they are also broadly disclosed in two different words for the mouth, each of which has its own cluster of popular usages. Members of the French lower classes, for instance, typically speak with a large and open mouth *(la gueule)*, which is associated with "manly dispositions" that rule out censorship ("prudence and deviousness as well as 'airs and graces' "), and with a valorization of virility that frequently manifests itself in verbal or even physical violence *(casser la gueule, ferme la gueule—* "smash your face in," "shut your trap"). By contrast, members of the bourgeois classes typically speak with a more closed, pinched mouth *(la bouche)*, which is "tense and censored, and therefore feminine."[76]

Importantly, Bourdieu emphasizes that among the dispositions inculcated by the habitus is a sense of the value that one's "linguistic products" will receive in specific markets such as school or the labor market. He maintains that within various social fields differential values are placed on different linguistic products, meaning that, although there may be no formal barriers to speech within a particular field, there are practical barriers to authoritative speech, that is, speech that is recognized as legitimate and worthy of attention. As Bourdieu states, "A speaker's linguistic strategies (tension or relaxation, vigilance or condescension, etc.) are oriented . . . not so much by the chances of being understood or misunderstood (communicative efficiency or the chances of communicating), but rather by the chances of being listened to, believed, obeyed."[77] In other words, hierarchies of linguistic legitimacy and authority (what Bourdieu terms "a high or low acceptability level")[78] informally regulate the operations of linguistic markets, privileging certain linguistic competences as "correct" and "acceptable," while censoring others.

According to Bourdieu, agents lacking the linguistic competence valorized in a particular social or institutional domain are faced essentially with three options.[79] First, and least commonly, they may contest the legitimacy of the dominant language by refusing to recognize it, thus initiating what Bourdieu calls "linguistic conflict."[80] Such instances, he asserts, occur most often during "paradoxical" or "crisis situations," where "the tension and corresponding censorships are lowered."[81] Second, they might try to *euphemize* their expressions by putting them into the forms that are positively sanctioned by the market. These efforts, however, are usually futile, because linguistic competency involves not only grammar and diction, but "all the properties constituting the speaker's *social personality*."[82] Unlike articles of clothing, these "properties"—accent, pronunciation, temperament, and bodily comportment—are inscribed in the body over the course of a lifetime and cannot be exchanged or abandoned at will. Furthermore, even in instances where euphemization is possible, it is often achieved only by negating (or being perceived as negating) aspects of one's own social or personal identity,[83] or by narrowly circumscribing the range and content of what can be expressed.[84] Finally, and most typically, speakers lacking the sanctioned forms of competence in a particular social domain may simply withdraw themselves from those domains, as in the case of the peasant who, "in order to explain why he did not dream of becoming mayor of his village even though he obtained the biggest share of the vote, said (in French) that he 'didn't know how to speak' (meaning French), implying a definition of linguistic competence that is entirely sociological."[85] Less anecdotally, Bourdieu writes that "speakers lacking the legitimate competence are *de facto* excluded from the social domains in which this competence is required, or are condemned to silence. What is rare, then, is not the capacity to speak, which, being part of our biological heritage, is universal and therefore non-distinctive, but rather the competence necessary in order to speak the legitimate language which, depending on social inheritance, re-translates social distinctions into the specifically symbolic logic of differential deviations, or, in short, distinction."[86]

What is so disturbing about these forms of censorship and exclusion is not only the fact that they raise troubling questions about the de facto and de jure basis upon which any shared or authorized language is constituted, and hence about the basis of politics itself, but also the fact that they often operate in ways that escape conscious recognition on the part of those involved. As Bourdieu puts it:

> The distinctiveness of symbolic violence lies precisely in the fact that it
> assumes, of those who submit to it, an attitude which challenges the

usual dichotomy of freedom and constraint. The "choices" of the habitus . . . are accomplished without consciousness or constraint, by virtue of the dispositions which, although they are unquestionably the product of social determinisms, are also constituted outside the spheres of consciousness and constraint. The propensity to reduce the search for causes to the search for responsibilities makes it impossible to see that *intimidation,* a symbolic violence which is not aware of what it is (to the extent that it implies no *act of intimidation*) can only be exerted on a person predisposed (in his habitus) to feel it, whereas others will ignore it. It is already partly true to say that the cause of the timidity lies in the relation between the situation of the intimidating person (who may deny any intimidating intention) and the person intimidated, or rather, between the social conditions of production of each of them. And little by little, one has to take account of the whole social structure.[87]

By highlighting the distinctiveness of this process—namely, the manner in which it operates causally and materially, yet also in the absence of any overt force or conscious intention—Bourdieu draws attention to what I will call a second dimension of violence. Speaking generally, the one-dimensional view designates the standard social scientific conception of violence as involving above all an agent's coercive use of physical force (either directly or through the use of various instruments).[88] This view, which is evident in Max Weber's influential definition of the state as "a relation of men dominating men, a relation supported by means of legitimate (i.e. considered to be legitimate) violence,"[89] defines violence expressly in terms of three basic elements: (1) a relation of domination, (2) a use of tools or physical force directly on the body, and (3) its instrumental, means-end character. Indeed, so common is this conception that even Arendt, who in "On Violence" criticizes almost all previous writers (including Weber) for their failure to distinguish adequately between violence and other terms such as power, authority, strength, and force, includes in her definition two of these elements, differing only on a rather technical rendering of force as "the energy released by physical or social movements."[90]

Bourdieu, by designating as violent relationships involving neither instrumental calculation nor the use of physical force or instruments directly on the body, seeks to call attention to an inconspicuous mode of domination that operates routinely precisely because it is so "gentle."[91]

Such violations are not, Bourdieu emphasizes, *identical* to the brute and horrific physical violence of torture or rape. Symbolic violence clearly lacks the intentional and instrumental quality of brute violence, and works not directly on bodies but through them. Nonetheless, symbolic violence shares with ordinary usage both an accent on relations of domination and subordination and a tight connection to breaches or violations of human dignity. In cases of symbolic violence, however, these relations of domination and breaches of human dignity are decoupled from any conscious intention to dominate or injure, as well as from any threat to use, or overt use of, physical force (as when we speak of "violent denunciations," of having been "done violence," or of having our trust "violated"). By extending the concept of violence to the symbolic domain, Bourdieu spotlights an often unnoticed mechanism for instituting or reproducing relations of domination. And to the extent that such mechanisms go unnoticed, they remain outside the purview of political deliberation or remedial action.

Although much of Bourdieu's work on symbolic violence explores its operation in the spheres of culture and everyday social relationships, he has also devoted considerable attention to explicating the ways that institutions, by implicitly privileging particular types of linguistic competence, bodily comportment, and other markers of social location, position agents in relationships of domination and subordination, including some and excluding others. Through these unrecognized biases, which benignly mask the asymmetries of power they legitimate and sustain, the larger project of forging institutional arrangements that both embody and strengthen democratic forms of life is subverted. In *The State Nobility (La noblesse d'État),* for instance, Bourdieu traces the pathways through which French educational institutions, and particularly élite schools such as the *grandes écoles,* certify and consecrate those who, on the basis of their educational credentials, attain key positions within state and economic institutions. In his analysis of the systems of academic classification deployed in these educational institutions, Bourdieu argues that, far from being neutral arbiters of intellectual excellence and achievement, these taxonomies and modes of classification systematically valorize the dispositions characteristic of the cultured bourgeoisie, who typically possess the greatest amounts of cultural capital. In the workings of this "classification machine," accent, pronunciation, bodily hexis, style, and manners, which are, as Bourdieu notes, among the most powerful instruments of social marking, become key criteria for distinguishing the academically precocious from *academica mediocritas*.[92] In short, these ostensibly neutral schemes of academic classification become potent mediating devices in the transmutation of social and cultural inequalities into academic inequalities and thereby into political inequalities. Through this transmutation, made possible by a misrecognition of social and cultural categories as neutral and meritocratic academic categories, the democratic and "liberating" ambitions of the French educational system are frustrated and the reproduction of political, economic, and educational élites is sustained.

For our purposes, two aspects of this story, one political and one theoretical, are particularly significant. Politically, by implicitly premising institutional power and voice on possession of linguistic and cultural competences that are neither equally distributed nor redistributed through education, democratic ideals of equal opportunity, access, and participation are deeply undermined.[93] Indeed, if mastery of linguistic and bodily practices so deeply anchored to contingent social origins and hence to ascription are shibboleths for inclusion or voice within institutional arenas, then the most elemental aspect of the idea of democracy—that is, the conviction that ordinary people are capable "of self-government, of sharing in the deliberate shaping of their common life"—is thereby threatened.[94]

Yet this account raises a further theoretical, or metatheoretical, problem. Insofar as the symbolic violence and domination produced by educational institutions and transmitted through other institutions result neither from formal legal exclusion nor a conscious intention to dominate, they remain constitutively unrecognizable by, and *politically* unrecognizable to, many currently influential theories of institutions. For instance, conceptualizations of institutional arrangements as "complex composites of rules"[95] (for example, majority voting rules) that structure the "decision situation" of individual actors leave undetected exclusions enacted through bodily comportment and linguistic practices that, unlike formal procedural or boundary rules, are not ordinarily catalogued in constitutions, written regulations, bylaws, or legal codes and are not the product of conscious calculation or choice. In fact, to the extent that the violences and exclusions Bourdieu explores are nondiscursive in the sense that they occur in and through an unformulated, embodied understanding, they remain in principle inaccessible to models that view institutional arrangements as composites of rules.[96] This is because, as Larry Kiser and Elinor Ostrom state, institutional rules are inherently "language-based phenomena."[97]

It is therefore in these ordinary violences that are neither simply consented to nor simply imposed that Bourdieu's analyses become most politically pertinent. If, as Arendt argues, the denial of public speech is the denial of a properly human existence, then questions about the specific mechanisms of exclusion from public discourse, or the basis upon which one is included in that discourse, are political questions of the first order. As I have been arguing, they are also the questions that Bourdieu's accounts of language, power, and symbolic violence instructively address.

Conclusion

In advancing this account of Bourdieu's thought, as well as a defense of its social scientific and especially political significance, I emphasize that I am neither endorsing without qualification his work nor suggesting that his theoretical framework can and should serve as the basis for a "normal science" of society or politics.[98] Although Bourdieu sometimes fosters the impression that he thinks such a normal science might be possible,[99] he much more frequently rebukes proposals of this sort. In his calls for heterodoxy in the social sciences,[100] in his endorsement of "specific rigors" over a "faith in a rigor defined once and for all and for all situations,"[101] and in his ongoing efforts to revisit and refashion his ideas, Bourdieu evinces a view of inquiry that is much closer to the spirit of pragmatism and hermeneutics than to any variant of methodological monism.

Ultimately, Bourdieu's work is perhaps most fairly judged by the degree to which it satisfies the moral, political, and pragmatic standards he himself articulates. The crucial questions are therefore the following: does it enrich the practice of social theory and social science, helping to make these endeavors critically engaged and empirical, without thereby rendering them anti-scientific or scientistic? Does it illuminate crucial issues of power, domination, and resistance? Does it provide students of politics with a vocabulary and set of analytical tools for diagnosing and combating the violences characteristic of everyday social life and social institutions? Does it challenge disabling dogmas and complacent certitudes? Does it help us think more cogently about alternative social and political arrangements, arrangements that are more democratic, more capacious, and less corrupt? I hope that by now, the answers to these questions are clear.

Conclusion: Pluralism, Power, Perestroika, and Political Inquiry

Throughout the previous five chapters I have been advancing an argument that joins key elements of pragmatism, hermeneutics, critical realism, and poststructuralism, articulating in the process a conception of social and political inquiry that is simultaneously scientific *and* critical, rigorous *and* heterodox, structured *and* patchwork. In so doing, I have also sought to challenge both unificationist calls for a normal science of politics and "anything goes" variants of methodological pluralism. Rejecting the terms of debate that such formulations impose, I have instead sketched a picture of political inquiry as disunified and heterogeneous, but not fragmented or unconstrained. Like the productive forms of disunification that I discussed in chapter 1, my defense of disunity affirms both the value of methodological and theoretical heterogeneity *and* the need to establish trading zones, that is, dense, local border territories that serve as sites of intellectual communication, commerce, collaboration, and exchange, binding together without homogenizing disparate traditions and cultures of inquiry. In this effort, however, I am largely alone. The methodological disputes that have animated political science over the past decades have generally oscillated between the untenable polarities of unification and ill-defined pluralism, quantitative and qualitative methods, explanation and understanding, causal analysis and interpretation, mathematical representation and narrative description. Observing these shifts, one might well conclude that students of political inquiry are locked in a peculiarly pernicious form of Nietzsche's eternal recurrence of the same, one in which the *Methodenstreit* is fought (with brief interruptions) again and again and again.

Nowhere is this more apparent than in the Perestroika controversy cited at the outset of this study. In the few years since the Perestroika memo was first circulated, it has arguably become the single most important topic of conversation in the discipline, eliciting numerous symposia, conferences, panels, roundtables, journal articles, and proposals for disciplinary reform. Indeed, the Perestroika movement has now become widely recognized as a movement that aims not just to spark debate about the institutions and practices of academic political science, but also to transform them. It is therefore not entirely surprising that a leading scholar in the field, David Laitin, has recently drawn an analogy between the threat of proletarian revolution that swept through Europe during the nineteenth century and the revolutionary ambitions animating the Perestroika movement today. Simultaneously recalling and rewriting the final sentence of Marx's *Communist Manifesto,* Laitin began his essay on the Perestroikan "challenge" by declaring ominously that "the specter of an insurgency haunts political science."[1]

Whether one reads Laitin's remark as serious statement or ironic gesture, it is clear that the movement has unsettled, if not as yet revolutionized, both the discipline and its flagship association, the American Political Science Association. Particularly at the institutional level, the movement's advocates have spearheaded or added significant momentum to a number of recent developments and reforms: the introduction of a new association-sponsored journal, *Perspectives on Politics* (whose first editor, Jennifer Hochschild, was one of the signatories of the Perestroika-inspired "Open Letter to the APSA Leadership and Members");[2] the selection of scholars closely linked to the Perestroika cause (Theda Skocpol and Suzanne Rudolph) as presidents of the APSA (thereby doubling the total number of women selected as president of the APSA during its century-long existence); the formation of an Organized Section in Qualitative Methods; the creation of an interuniversity Consortium on Qualitative Research Methods; and the first contested election of APSA officers since the Vietnam War period.

At the methodological level, however, matters look quite different. Here even some of Perestroika's allies have bemoaned "the impoverished state of the existing methodological debate,"[3] contending that for all of the heat generated by the Perestroikan challenge, neither its critics nor its champions have to date provided much methodological light. If one were to take a recent symposium of disciplinary luminaries as an accurate barometer of the quality of contemporary debate, one might reasonably conclude that thus far discussions have consisted mostly of banalities and platitudes.[4] In this symposium, for instance, Rogers Smith, a widely respected scholar of American political thought, reaffirmed the truism that *"the core value of all genuinely scientific inquiry is intellectual honesty,"*[5] and Russell Hardin, an eminent proponent of rational choice research, declared with equal vagueness that students of politics should "only do good work and be serious about getting something right."[6] Other remarks included hortatory encomiums (in the name of "border crossing," "interdisciplinary communication," "relevance," and "methodological pluralism"),[7] familiar cautionary tales (about, for instance, the dangers of overspecialization),[8] broad and unsubstantiated analogies (between, for example, the practical value of medical science at the start of the twentieth century and the practical value of economic understanding today),[9] and well-meaning if breathtakingly expansive proposals to develop a more inclusive definition of the "core" of the discipline (such as proposals to organize the discipline around "the study of rules, rule-governed behavior, and the effort to change rules through force or through discussion, debate, and choice").[10] With few of Perestroika's sympathizers providing a convincing intellectual defense of methodological pluralism and few of its critics advancing a spirited and substantive justification of methodological monism and disciplinary unification, it is not difficult to understand why students of political inquiry from Stephen White to John Dryzek to Laitin might lament "the paucity of sustained methodological reflection."[11] It is also understandable why Dryzek and Laitin, who disagree on virtually every other issue raised by the Perestroika controversy, might jointly hold that "the dispute is mostly political rather than intellectual."[12]

In my concluding remarks I hope to rectify this imbalance by attending more directly to the key methodological issues raised by the Perestroika protest. I do so, however, not to privilege methodology over politics or to suggest that a proper conception of methodology will eliminate questions of power from political inquiry, but to articulate a better understanding of the relationships between methodology and power, and between political inquiry and political life. In what follows, I should emphasize that my remarks are not intended to provide either an exhaustive genealogy of the controversy or a quick and easy exit from the current *Methodenstreit.* To the contrary, this study is animated, among other things, by a desire to illustrate the complexity of the problems raised

by the Perestroika movement, and to demonstrate how deeply misconceived are proposals that promise the psychic and epistemological com-
forts of a quick fix. However reassuring it may be to propound simple
solutions to complex problems, I would caution that if epistemological
comfort can be purchased only at the price of understanding, then this,
certainly, is no bargain.

My emphasis on epistemological caution, however, should not be confused with a stance of epistemological neutrality. Throughout this study
I have argued that much hinges on the epistemological and methodological choices that we make. These choices, I contend, are fateful, for in
making them we simultaneously embrace key assumptions about the nature of the objects we study *and* partly constitute (or reconstitute) our
own identities as inquirers. In my concluding remarks, I hope to clarify
further the stakes of contemporary debates about the proper methods of
political inquiry by making explicit the benefits of the form of critical
pluralism that I defend. This position, I will show, diverges in important
respects from those articulated both by the proponents of hegemony and
by many of the advocates of Perestroika. Against the former, I contend
that although quantitative methods and rational choice analysis can illuminate many important problems of social and political life, they
cannot illuminate all of them. Moreover, when practitioners of these
methods fail to incorporate into their research the forms of hermeneutical
and critical reflection that I have described, they invite methodological
abuses that yield in turn social and political misunderstanding. For both
of these reasons, the quest for a single paradigm of political inquiry, one
that will finally yield a "normal" science of politics, is deeply misconceived. Consequently, energy is better devoted to the task of identifying
the limits of dominant modes of research than to the project of shoring
up the conviction that such limits do not exist.

Against the latter, I argue that, although political inquiry at its best
requires plural methods and an abiding interest in problems of politics,
vague endorsements of "pluralism" and "problem-driven" inquiry all too
easily elide or distort central questions of both political inquiry and political life. At one level, of course, the injunction that students of politics
avoid "theory-driven" work that "dictates always opting for the description that calls for the explanation that flows from the preferred model or
theory"[13] is entirely consistent with the anti-reductionist position outlined
in this study. If "problem-driven" research entails nothing other than

opposition to forms of reductionist myopia that leave one unable to entertain seriously alternative descriptions, theories, or models, or, more
generally, resistance to forms of methodological or theoretical fetishism
that aim to vindicate one's favored approach rather than confront
pressing issues of political life, then there is in my view no reason not to
endorse it wholeheartedly. However, when these otherwise salutary interventions are grounded in a sharp opposition between, on the one hand,
"theory-" and "method-driven" work, and, on the other hand, "problem-
driven" work, the defense of a problem-driven conception of political
inquiry may unwittingly fuel distortions and misunderstandings of its
own. Most importantly, they may obscure the fact that problems and
theories are often tightly intertwined, such that many problems are detectable as problems only from the standpoint of an alternative theory.
Just as feminist theorists have often maintained that classical liberal
theory rested on a distinction between the private and the public that
defined out of existence problems of power relations in the domestic
sphere, so have the critics of behavioralism maintained that its criteria of
scientific explanation expelled the category of nonaction from the domain
of scientific inquiry. In both of these cases, critics did not start from a
theory-free examination of "problems" and then ascertain which methods
or theories were most appropriate for understanding or explaining them.
Instead, identifying the problems qua problems required a different theoretical understanding.

I will confine my remarks to three topics that have been central to the
Perestroika controversy: first, the question of methodological pluralism
and methodological monism; second, the issue of "hegemonic" methodologies and their place in the reformulated conception of political inquiry sketched herein; and, third, the issue of naturalism. I shall conclude
with a few general reflections about the present and possible future state
of social and political inquiry.

Perestroika and Methodological Pluralism

Although it is surely hazardous to issue sweeping proclamations about an
institutionally amorphous protest movement that has articulated its concerns primarily through discussions on an e-mail list, it is, I believe, safe
to assert that demands for greater intellectual and methodological diversity have constituted one of the Perestroika movement's pivotal rallying

points. Indeed, attacks on what John Mearsheimer terms "methodological parochialism" and concomitant appeals to methodological pluralism have been central themes both of the original Perestroika manifesto and of virtually all Perestroikan commentary on the present state of the discipline.[14] At the same time, many of Perestroika's most active participants have targeted the goal of greater methodological diversity within the discipline of political science as the movement's single most important "immediate objective," if not the raison d'être of the movement itself.[15] I therefore take it as uncontroversial that demands for methodological pluralism constitute a key part of any Perestroikan program of disciplinary reform.

Although Mr. Perestroika's calls for methodological pluralism have proven thus far to be both rhetorically and strategically effective—so effective that to date virtually no one, including representatives of the reigning "hegemony," has sought to challenge them—one might worry nonetheless that its very potency as a rallying cry has contributed indirectly to the scarcity of sustained methodological analysis.[16] In fact, however appealing the image of a methodologically and intellectually diverse discipline may be, a moment's reflection reveals that methodological pluralism, no less than political pluralism, can never be coherently defended *as such.* Absent any effort to link methodological commitments to political understanding and practice, and to deploy the latter as standards for assessing the value of the former—in short, absent any conception of truth—appeals for greater pluralism and diversity amount to little more than an invitation to abandon all epistemic and political distinctions in favor of a laissez-faire approach to questions of methodology. But in its own way, this view is just as flattening and anti-intellectual as the most oppressive form of monism or hegemony. It is also self-refuting. Suppose, for instance, that we grant the central claim of the laissez-faire pluralist and deny the existence of any basis, however qualified or contingent, on which we might assess competing methodological precepts or practices. It would follow that we would also have no basis for holding that the laissez-faire pluralist's views are in any meaningful sense better than those of his adversaries. But if this is the case—that is, if the laissez-faire pluralist has *no* basis for holding that his views are better than his opponent's—then what's to recommend them? And if there is nothing to recommend these views, then why should we hold them?[17] The point here is not to demonstrate that the thesis of methodological pluralism is indefensible, but to show that it cannot be defended as such. If one wishes to defend it, one must demonstrate how, why, and in what contexts it yields a more adequate understanding of social and political phenomena, how it enables us to cope more effectively with the world around us (or to understand under what conditions or to what degree "coping more effectively with the world around us" may be something that one should not wish to do). Without such an account, the defense of methodological pluralism easily devolves into a form of sloganeering, one that avoids rather than engages difficult questions of analysis and judgment.

Although to date none of the published statements of Perestroika supporters have explicitly endorsed this self-defeating strategy, the tendency to celebrate pluralism without clearly specifying its meanings complicates and perhaps even impedes efforts to achieve substantive disciplinary reform. In the first place, the very emptiness of what Dryzek calls "empty pluralism"[18] makes it an ill-suited catalyst for genuine reform. As a symbol that is entirely innocuous precisely because it is devoid of content, it offers the dubious prospect of a consensus that is itself empty (in either its lack of content or virtually unlimited pliability). In short, rather than pursuing the more strenuous but potentially more productive strategy of advancing substantive accounts of what "pluralism can and ought to mean"[19] and then making those accounts the focal point of vigorous and even agonistic discussions of vexing methodological and political issues,   · invocations of an abstract and empty pluralism encourage a resolution of current controversies that is painless but also superficial. Requiring neither difficult reflection nor any serious effort to persuade, this "solution" erases differences instead of engaging them. As a result, it may well reinforce the status quo that Perestroikans strive to unsettle.

In addition to inviting a shallow consensus that yields peaceful coexistence at the expense of methodological understanding, Perestroikans' reluctance to clarify the meaning and scope of pluralism, like their opponents' reluctance to specify their views, has provided an opportunity for others to do the clarifying for them. Not surprisingly, these opportunities have been seized by some of Perestroika's harshest critics. In one recent case it issued in a series of sharp allegations of intellectual complacency ("mostly we hear a desire for pluralism rather than a defense of best practices")[20] and irresponsibility (pertaining to "the unqualified call for pluralism advocated by many in the perestroika movement").[21] In both, the criticisms assume that Perestroikans largely defend not an empty pluralism but some version of the position that I refer to as "laissez-faire pluralism." Whatever one's view of these allegations, there is little question that just as nature abhors a vacuum, so too does much political and intellectual debate.[22] A disinclination to spell out one's own views entails the risk that, for better or worse, they will be spelled out by someone else.

Hegemonic Political Science and Methodological Monism

If methodological pluralism has emerged as both a source of consensus and one of the principal goals of the Perestroika movement, then it is surely fair to say that the other dimension of this stance, namely, the critique of methodological hegemony or monism, is an equally central theme of the movement. As with pluralism, however, the precise nature of the alleged hegemony can at times seem rather elusive. For some, the single most important feature of the present hegemony is its "methodism" or "method-driven" mode of inquiry, suggesting that it is the general obsession with method rather than commitment to any single method that is most disturbing. At other times, the target of critique is described more specifically "as hard science, technicism, quantification, and an attempt to impose a 'normal science' discipline on political science."[23] Most commonly, it is depicted as an amalgam of rational choice theory and quantitative (particularly "large-N") modes of research. But even this characterization can be puzzling, purporting as it does an alliance among approaches that, as John Dryzek has noted, "are not easily unified or even reconciled at the methodological level."[24]

Although these characterizations all differ in interesting ways, my primary concern here is with the dominant conception of hegemony understood as a compound of rational choice theory and quantitative analysis. On this construal, the central allegation is one of methodological bias that is rooted in a miscast view of scientific rigor. Perestroikans claim that notwithstanding methodological tensions that may trouble efforts to cast the present hegemony as methodologically unified, the champions of rational choice and quantitative methods largely converge in their animus toward "qualitative approaches," a rather eclectic category that variously includes case and small-N studies, interpretive and ethnographic research, historical institutionalism, political history, semiotics, feminist theory, critical theory, poststructural inquiry, and postmodern analysis. These approaches, Perestroikans assert, are deemed deficient because they fail to conform either to rational choice conceptions of science, which view the construction of formal models as essential attributes of good scientific practice, or to large-N quantitative conceptions, which view the testing of variables taken from large samples as an indispensable feature of the scientific method.

In keeping with my broadly contextualist approach to questions of social and political inquiry, the present study ratifies neither sweeping denunciations of rational choice and/or quantitative methods as always nothing more than scientism masquerading as science, nor the self-assured proclamations of those who view these same methods as unifying paradigms of social scientific inquiry, paradigms that will ultimately yield a stable and cumulative science of social and political life.[25] By contrast, I contend that we would do well to cast a wary eye on the starkly dualistic, Manichean rhetoric that joins and sustains both of these positions. Instead of consolidating all rational choice and quantitative scholarship under a single label—conceiving its practitioners, for example, as either methodological Napoleons or Newtons—I propose a more differentiated approach. This approach is less fixated on providing unqualified negative or affirmative answers to questions about the value of rational choice and quantitative approaches than on exploring the particular types of questions and avenues of research that are opened and foreclosed by variants of one or another approach. My central claim is that we are likely to gain better purchase on the stakes of methodological debates if we examine closely the potential gains and losses that attend the use of particular methodological approaches in specific contexts. By seeing more perspicuously how different approaches structure the process of knowledge production and thereby configure what we can or cannot understand or say politically, we are better positioned to grasp, and are better equipped to assess, both the epistemological *and* political implications of methodological choices.

This, in fact, is how I have proceeded in my own effort to defend Bourdieu's work as an exemplar of pluralism in social scientific inquiry. Here I have proceeded both philosophically and empirically, showing the kinds of entities, properties, concepts, and methodological commitments that must be invoked if one is to understand key features of social and political life. My case for an approach that incorporates elements of hermeneutics, pragmatism, critical realism, and poststructuralism is situated, therefore, in a broader analysis of the kinds of methodological and conceptual resources that one must possess if one is to understand adequately enduring and vital features of social and political life (such as power relations). To better grasp how this approach works in practice, we might briefly return to Bourdieu's account of the concept of symbolic violence. As we have seen, Bourdieu construes symbolic violence as a very specific type of violence, namely, one that is enacted symbolically through agents' joint misrecognition of the meanings implicit in their actions. Identifying particular cases of symbolic violence and grasping its peculiar features therefore require among other things, a hermeneutical analysis that operates at two distinct levels: first, an analysis of agents' own subjective understanding of the meanings of their actions, and, second, an analysis of the subjectively misrecognized meanings implicit in those actions. It follows from this observation that methodologies and research traditions that eschew either or both of these levels of analysis—this includes both objectivist models of social inquiry that abstract from subjective meanings and understandings, and subjectivist models that aim exclusively to retrieve subjective understandings—foreclose by methodological fiat the very possibility of pinpointing this particular category of power relations. This, in turn, prompts two additional conclusions: first, that these (objectivist and subjectivist) methodological frameworks and research traditions cannot fulfill by themselves one of the most significant tasks of social inquiry, namely, the task of understanding and making visible key mechanisms of power and domination; and, second, that hermeneutical investigation must be an indispensable part of any such task.

Bourdieu's account of symbolic violence is important, however, not only because it foregrounds the critical role of interpretation in understanding and explaining power relations, but also because it advances strong claims about the role of the body as both a source of intelligibility and a mediating factor in social relations of power. Indeed, Bourdieu holds that many forms of symbolic violence operate directly through the flexible, embodied, noncognitive, and socially constituted dispositions incorporated in the habitus. In sharp contrast to forms of domination sustained through the threat or actuality of brute physical force or violence, Bourdieu maintains that symbolic violence operates gently, subtlety, and inconspicuously through an "ontological complicity" between the habitus and the social field, between subjective and objective structures. Moreover, because this form of domination frequently operates not just through words, but also through understandings enacted in gestures, accents, intonations, and other modes of bodily comportment, illuminating it requires an account that is liberated from the conceptual confines of what Bourdieu terms "intellectualist" epistemologies, that is, epistemologies that view understanding as "residing [exclusively] in thoughts or representations."[26] It requires, in short, an account of *embodied understanding.* Here too, Bourdieu's account challenges directly any hegemonic or unificationist ambitions that may be harbored by the champions of intellectualism. Whether this intellectualism assumes the form of discourse theory, semiotics, or any of a wide range of contemporary forms of rationalism, the failure to incorporate a conception of embodied understanding precludes it from providing a satisfactory account of power relations or of social practice more generally. As such, they cannot—short of simply excluding from the domain of political inquiry all mechanisms of power and authority that operate through agents' embodied relations— provide the exclusive framework or model of political inquiry. At best, they can supply important resources for investigating particular aspects and classes of social phenomena.

In short, my defense of methodological pluralism is a thoroughly pragmatic one, deriving its commitments from both an examination of the history of inquiries and from detailed investigations into the kinds of methodological and conceptual resources that are required to gain purchase on vital tasks of social and political inquiry. Like Dewey's pragmatism, it abandons the foundationalist "quest for certainty,"[27] substituting in its place historical and contextualist standards of assessment. Moreover, just as these standards provide the cornerstone around which I have developed my defense of methodological pluralism and autonomy, so too do they provide the most appropriate basis for contesting that defense, if indeed one wishes to do so. Those who would challenge my position should do so not by developing anterior to social practice abstract accounts of what constitutes knowledge of it, but by contesting the particular interpretations of the history of science on which the argument is premised.

The Contest of Methodological Disunity

My recommendation is that a similar approach should animate contemporary efforts to assess quantitative and rational choice modes of analysis.

That is, rather than asking whether these forms of analysis, by virtue of their putative correspondence to some model of natural scientific inquiry, can and should serve as the cornerstone of a "normal" and methodologically unified science of political life, I propose that we strive to identify the possibilities and limits of each, that we aim to locate the contexts or problem fields in which the application of quantitative and rational choice methods is likely to be most and least fruitful.

With respect to statistical methods, the clear advantage is breadth. Statistical surveys of large populations can provide valuable information about those populations, information that by definition would be unobtainable or unverifiable through the use of case study or small-N research. At a minimum, then, well-conducted statistical research can serve important *descriptive* purposes, enabling students of politics to develop a clearer and more comprehensive profile of large populations at any given moment or (in the case of longitudinal studies) over extended periods of time. This can be particularly valuable when complemented by the use of "thicker," more detailed descriptions of actions and practices.[28] In addition, it can serve crucial *explanatory* purposes. Although it is certainly true that even the most well-established statistical correlations do not independently yield causal explanations, statistical analyses can and often do contribute, either directly or in conjunction with nonstatistical forms of evidence and argument, to the identification of causal mechanisms that underpin those correlations. In so doing, they may sustain precisely the kinds of realist explanations that I defended in chapter 4.

One recent example of the descriptive value of statistical research is Robert Putnam's widely discussed study, *Bowling Alone: The Collapse and Revival of American Community*.[29] In this book, Putnam takes up a theme that has long preoccupied students of democracy in general and American politics in particular: the grand Tocquevillian theme of the relationship between democracy and civil society. In the travels that produced his classic study of American cultural and political life, *Democracy and America*, Tocqueville was profoundly struck by the sharp contrast between the centralized, bureaucratized political institutions characteristic of his native France and the deliberately decentralized governmental institutions of the early American republic. Reflecting on this difference, Tocqueville posited that the latter institutions supported and sustained a number of practices indispensable to the survival of well-functioning democracies: they (1) foster the development of a rich array of locally based social and

civic associations, (2) stimulate the formation of vertical rather than hor-
izontal relations of political power, (3) nourish a spirit of self-help and
local liberty, and (4) encourage public regard for long-term self-interest
(which he termed "self-interest rightly understood"). Perhaps most importantly, Tocqueville held that the dense web of social and civic associations that constitute what scholars now refer to as "civil society" operates
as a critical antidote to the pathogen that is most destructive of healthy
democratic polities: "administrative" or "soft" despotism. This new and
disturbing form of despotism, which Tocqueville describes as milder and
more benevolent yet also more enervating and pervasive then traditional
forms of despotic rule, infects the body politic in a quite distinctive way.
Instead of operating through direct coercion or policies and tactics that
explicitly limit or repress individual liberty, it cultivates in the individual
forms of alienation and self-absorption that divert attention from public
affairs, attenuate bonds of sympathy beyond one's immediate circle of
friends and family, and thereby drain the will of any commitment to
engage in collective action in the name of broad public purposes.[30] In
Tocqueville's view, the tendencies toward self-absorption, withdrawal, apathy, and political fragmentation are most effectively remedied by those
intermediary associations that largely constitute civil society. These associations empower men and women by bringing them outside of themselves, enabling them to join together in common action, to strengthen
norms of reciprocity, and thereby to understand better the meaning and
value of "communal" or political freedom and citizenship.

Although students of politics have often invoked Tocqueville's thesis
about the links between associational life and the health of democratic
societies to celebrate or (more commonly) bemoan the condition of
American politics, the evidence supporting these triumphal and declen-
sionist narratives has often been either anecdotal or selective.[31] Although
it is widely known, for example, that participation in national, state, and
local elections has been declining for the past four decades, and that
union membership has dropped precipitously since the mid-1950s,
Putnam's study brings this familiar data together with exhaustive research
on everything from participation in bowling leagues and reading groups
to philanthropy and volunteering to the observance of stop signs and the
explosive growth of the legal profession. The result is an extraordinarily
rich and encompassing portrait of changes in American civic life over the
past several decades. Not only does Putnam draw on a much wider palette

of evidence than other studies to support his broadly Tocquevillian argument, but his work also has great value independently of whether one finds his thesis about the decline of social capital and civic engagement over the past several decades fully convincing, or his prescriptions for renewal adequate.[32] That Putnam deploys this remarkable array of empirical evidence while also subjecting it to critical scrutiny and openly acknowledging its limitations only adds to his achievement.

In addition to its potential descriptive value, statistical research can and does advance crucial explanatory aims. One particularly compelling example of the explanatory value of statistical analysis involves the national controversy regarding voting irregularities in Palm Beach County (PBC), Florida, during the 2000 presidential election. Beginning on election day, thousands of voters complained of difficulty in understanding the "butterfly ballot,"[33] a difficulty that, they maintained, resulted in the casting of erroneous or invalid votes. Within three days after the election, 5,000 to 7,000 PBC voters had signed affidavits stating that the ballots' confusing butterfly design had caused them either to vote mistakenly for the Reform candidate, Patrick J. Buchanan, rather than the Democratic candidate, Al Gore, or to inadvertently vote twice, thus disqualifying their ballots.[34] Ultimately, eleven groups of PBC voters filed lawsuits seeking redress, asserting that the confusing design of the ballot had caused them to make errors in their presidential votes. Perhaps most significantly, the volume of complaints far exceeded the official margin of victory (537 votes) of the Republican candidate, George W. Bush, over Gore. If voter allegations were true, the confusing ballot design tipped the presidential vote in Florida in favor of Bush, thus providing him with Florida's twenty-five electoral votes and victory in the national election.[35]

Because the Supreme Court of Florida dismissed the lawsuits on statutory grounds (claiming that the ballot did not substantially violate statutory requirements and therefore was not illegal), it did not address what is arguably the most important political question raised by the ballot controversy: the question of whether the ballot design caused Al Gore to lose the presidential election. Certainly there was substantial anecdotal evidence that pointed in this direction, from the sworn affidavit testimony of thousands of voters to the unexpectedly large number of Buchanan votes (3,407 votes, according to the uncertified PBC count) in a strongly Democratic county. When joined with the results of experimental studies indicating that the butterfly ballot format "is more confusing than a single-column ballot" and "may cause systematic errors in voting,"[36] a strong prima facie case can be made in support of the claim that the butterfly ballet tipped the Florida election, and hence the national election, in favor of George W. Bush.

But is it possible to adduce evidence and arguments that yield still firmer conclusions regarding the effects of the butterfly ballot on the election results, evidence that, for instance, does not rest on statements of voters whose claims of error may be incorrect or who may be motivated to lie? If so, how might these conclusions be reached? In this case, two crucial facts about the election—first, that the ballots did not indicate either the political party affiliation or the name of the individual voter, and, second, that most voters failed to keep the stub from their ballot— preclude the possibility of determining through direct ballot inspection the veracity of voters' claims that they had mistakenly voted for the Reform Party candidate, Patrick J. Buchanan, instead of Gore. As Jonathan Wand and his associates correctly remarked, "Inspections may clarify the number of voters who marked their ballot in support of the various candidates, but . . . inspections cannot tell us how many voters marked their ballot for a candidate they did not intend to choose."[37] Although the absence of any direct evaluative method might appear to indicate that claims about the extent and effects of ballot confusion, however plausible prima facie, defy systematic empirical scrutiny, Wand et al. managed to circumvent these obstacles by assembling a powerful body of statistical evidence. This evidence, mostly of the comparative variety, enabled them to assess the trinity of key propositions underpinning allegations that the butterfly ballot decisively altered the outcome of the election: first, the proposition that Pat Buchanan received an "anomalously large" number of votes in PBC; second, the proposition that these anomalies were overwhelmingly the result of systematic voting errors caused by the butterfly ballot; and, third, the proposition that these voting errors were not only systematic but also asymmetric, depriving Gore of votes substantially greater in number than Bush's margin of victory in Florida.

Regarding the first proposition, Wand et al. demonstrated that Buchanan's vote in PBC far surpassed any reasonable expectations. They did so, first, by comparing it with his vote in every other county in the United States in 2000 (none of which evinced anomalies as large as those in PBC); second, by comparing it with the PBC vote for the Reform candidate in the 1996 election (which, in contrast to the 2000 election, was not anomalous); and, finally, by conducting a "natural experiment," one that compared the results of PBC voters who used butterfly ballots (election-day voters) and those who did not (absentee voters). This important "experimental" evidence revealed that "county voters supported Buchanan on election day at a rate (.0085) approximately four times that of absentee voters (.0022)."[38] It also strongly confirmed the second proposition, since it demonstrated that "if election day voters had cast ballots for Buchanan at the rate that absentee voters did, he would have received . . . 854 election-day votes. In fact, he received 3,310 election-day votes. By this method one might gauge the number of accidental votes for Buchanan because of the butterfly ballot as follows: 3,310–854 = 2,456 votes."[39] Finally, Wand et al. used both precinct- and ballot-level data, first, to show that the butterfly ballot caused asymmetrical voting errors that cost Gore more votes than Bush, and, second, to estimate the number of votes that Gore lost as a result of the butterfly effect (which they concluded was "more than 2,000").[40] In short, the authors' statistical analyses yielded "very strong evidence" that "had PBC used a ballot format in the presidential race that did not lead to systematic biased voting errors . . . Al Gore would have won a majority of the officially certified votes in Florida."[41]

If the preceding examples show that well-conceived quantitative and statistical analyses, used either in tandem with or in lieu of other forms of evidence, advance not only descriptive but also explanatory aims of social inquiry, then what, if any, defects might these forms of inquiry most commonly evince? How, why, and when do they slide off their rails? My central claim is that they typically do so when they are driven by misconceived understandings of ontology and scientific explanation, understandings that, either at the stage of research design and data collection or at the later stage of interpreting empirical data, neglect or obfuscate crucial hermeneutical and contextual factors. Errors at both of these stages mar, for example, one of the most influential works of comparative politics, Gabriel Almond and Sydney Verba's *The Civic Culture*.[42] In their investigation of "the political culture of democracy," Almond and Verba used survey research to explore across five national cultures—the United States, Great Britain, Germany, Italy, and Mexico—two venerable questions of democratic theory and practice: questions of "civic virtue and its consequences for the effectiveness and stability of the democratic polity," and of "the kind of community life, social organization, and upbringing of children that fosters civic virtue."[43] Drawing on interviews of 5,000 people, Almond and Verba advanced two major claims. First, they argued that a particular type of political culture "fit" democratic political systems, and that culture, which they term the "civic culture," is precisely the one that thrives in Britain and the United States but is less well-established in Germany, Italy, and Mexico.[44] Second, they held that the civic culture supportive of stable democratic polities is not, as the "classical" theory of democracy would have it, a widely participatory and activist culture. Rather, it is a "mixed political culture," one in which large numbers of citizens "take the more passive role of subject" and those who do participate actively retain "traditional, non-political ties, as well as . . . [a] more passive political role as a subject."[45]

Notwithstanding its reputation as a "modern classic"[46] of comparative political analysis, both the assumptions informing Almond and Verba's study and the conclusions drawn from it have been subjected to sharp criticisms, many of which foreground the dangers, both epistemological and political, of interpretive errors and elisions. On the one hand, Alasdair MacIntyre has attacked the design of Almond and Verba's survey, arguing that the authors' failure to attend to cross-cultural variations in the meaning of key terms like "pride" biases the central "finding" that the political cultures of Britain and the United States are superior to those of Germany, Italy, and Mexico in the sense that they better support a "stable democratic process."[47] According to MacIntyre, Almond and Verba's effort to measure affective orientations—that is, citizens' "feelings about the political system, its roles, personnel, and performance"—like "pride" in one's government[48] by asking respondents to rank order a list of items "in terms of the amount of pride they took in them"[49] yields not objective measures of "the realities of political life,"[50] but crude caricatures of it. The authors' mistake, MacIntyre contends, is an interpretive one. It consists of a failure to recognize the partly constitutive role that institutions, practices, and self-interpretations play in defining the actions, attitudes, and concepts that one studies. Arguing along Wittgensteinian lines, MacIntyre holds that the identification of attitudes (such as pride) cannot be made independently of an identification of the objects toward which those attitudes are directed. We identify, for example, the concept of fear in terms of the objects toward which it is directed—in terms, that is, of concepts like danger and harm—rather than the other way around.[51] Comparing political attitudes across national or cultural boundaries therefore presupposes a prior specification within each culture of the political institutions and practices toward which those attitudes are directed, one, moreover, that reveals that those institutions and practices are largely the same across the units (nations, cultures, and so forth) in question. Barring this prior identification, there simply is no way of knowing whether one is engaging in a valid comparison of attitudes.

This is precisely what Almond and Verba fail to do. Instead of first ascertaining whether the concept of pride has the same meaning across the five national cultures that they study, they implicitly assume that it does. Indeed, it is on the basis of this assumption that the authors of *The Civic Culture* conclude that Italians have less commitment to, and identify less strongly with, their government than do their British and American counterparts. In MacIntyre's view, these conclusions are unwarranted. Strongly contesting the assumptions that generate them, MacIntyre posits that

> in fact the concept of pride ("...si sente piu' orgoglioso...") in Italy is not the same as that pride in England. The notion of taking pride in Italian culture is still inexorably linked, especially in the South but also in the North, to the notion of honor. What one takes pride in is what touches on one's honor. If asked to list the subjects which touched their honor, many Italians would spontaneously place the chastity of their immediate female relatives high on the list—a connection that it would occur to very few Englishmen to make. These notions of pride and honor partially specify and are partly specified by a notion of the family itself importantly, if imperfectly, embodied in the actualities of Italian family life. Hence we cannot hope to compare an Italian's attitude to his government's acts with an Englishman's in respect of the pride each takes; any comparison would have to begin from the different range of virtues and emotions incorporated in the different social institutions. Once again the project of comparing attitudes independently of institutions and practices encounters difficulties.[52]

Although MacIntyre offers no data of his own to support what some might contend is an antiquated notion of Italian male honor, his larger point remains sound, namely, that with respect to attitudes such as pride, the objects toward which those attitudes are directed are not the same across the national cultures of Italy and Britain.[53] In Italy attitudes of pride are intimately connected to an ethic of honor. Ones takes pride, for example, in being an honorable man, a notion that, MacIntyre points out, is itself importantly directed toward and embodied in the practices and background understandings of Italian family life. By contrast, one is deemed contemptible, disgraceful, and dishonorable if, among other things, one is unwilling or unable to defend the honor of one's family. This, MacIntyre contends, is quite different from British conceptions of pride, which are not linked in the same way to an ethic of honor and the affairs of one's family. Consequently, the fact that Italian respondents, when asked to rank order a list of items based on the degree of pride they took in them, ranked the activities of government lower than British or German respondents does not constitute a persuasive evidential basis for the claim that Italians have less affective attachment to, or care less about, government and political life than their counterparts in Britain or Germany. In short, if the concept of pride occupies, as Charles Taylor might say, a different region of semantic space in these distinctive national cultures, then the seemingly "neutral" and "objective" strategy of comparing political attitudes across national or cultural boundaries by aggregating responses to survey questions that ignore these conceptual differences may well occlude more than it clarifies. Moreover, to the extent that these occlusions are treated as brute "facts," they perform double duty as forms of ideological legitimation and delegitimation, both consecrating the political cultures of Britain and the United States as ideal models of stable democratic polities and insulating them from critical scrutiny.[54]

Whereas MacIntyre's analysis draws attention to the critical role that interpretive issues play in the design of Almond and Verba's study and in comparative analysis generally, others have focused more directly on questions regarding the interpretation of empirical data, showing how the theoretical assumptions informing one's interpretations may bias the conclusions one reaches. Carole Pateman, for instance, argues convincingly that the liberal and empiricist assumptions informing Almond and Verba's analysis (and the work of many other empirical democratic theorists) yield highly questionable readings of their empirical data, readings that are in many ways quite inconsistent with their claim to identify the constituents—the social and political attitudes and underlying orientations—of a *democratic* political culture. More specifically, these readings yield a conception of political culture that simultaneously celebrates "the role of political apathy and disinterest"[55] in the Anglo-American political system and forecloses investigation of the ways that class- and sex-based differences (in patterns of political participation and feelings of political competence) might temper or contravene the authors' buoyant claim of a tight fit between the civic culture and liberal democracy. As Pateman summarizes, "Empirical democratic theory, and the argument of *The Civic Culture,* thus mystifies and obscures, rather than clarifies, the significance of its own data, and fails to explain why there is a fit between the balance of the civic culture and the political structure of liberal democracy."[56]

Pateman's analysis pivots around the interpretation of two key relationships: first, the relationship between subjective feelings of political competence and levels of political participation, and, second, the relationship between socioeconomic status (SES) and feelings of political competence. As Pateman observes, Almond and Verba posit a vital link between a democratic political culture and feelings of political competence. After reviewing a variety of data showing relationships between subjective competence and adherence to democratic values, beliefs about the value of participation, levels of actual participation, and the like, Almond and Verba declare that "the self-confident citizen appears to be the democratic citizen."[57] Yet side by side with this resounding affirmation of a link between feelings of subjective competence and democratic citizenship are data demonstrating that levels of subjective confidence, like the levels of political participation to which they are correlated, are not distributed randomly. They are instead distributed in a class- and sex-based fashion. That is, persons from lower SES backgrounds and women constitute a disproportionately large percentage of those citizens evincing low levels of subjective confidence, whereas individuals from higher SES backgrounds and men constitute a disproportionately large percentage of respondents displaying high levels of subjective confidence. In short, the attitudes and orientations that Almond and Verba identify with democratic citizenship, as well as patterns of political participation that they describe, are "divided on the basis of SES and sex."[58]

At a minimum, Pateman contends, these findings severely complicate the authors' assumption that one can speak unequivocally about "*the* political culture or *the* civic culture of Britain and the United States."[59] In fact, the presumption that "there is a model of civic culture at hand," and that this model "is relevant across the whole community," is belied by their own evidence, which "suggests that, if there are not two political cultures, then the civic culture is, at the least, a systematically *divided* political culture . . . The nice balance of the civic culture . . . is, in fact, a balance based on the virtual absence of working-class citizens from political life."[60] The existence of these systematic divisions, moreover, prompts still more pressing questions of interpretation. For if the civic culture is a political culture that is divided along the lines of SES and sex, then a further question immediately arises: "What is democratic about the civic culture?"[61] Pateman's answer is unambiguous: "Very little at all, except that it encompasses universal suffrage. The civic culture is a democratic culture that reverses the central focus of democracy since its origins in ancient times, although it retains the traditional assumption that democracy can exclude half of humankind."[62]

Although the claim that this culture is the one best fitted to "the democratic political system"[63] may appear astonishing, Pateman shows that in fact the conclusion is dictated by the authors' own implicit identification of classical liberal theory with democratic theory. Because "liberal theory . . . has always argued that it is middle- and upper-class males who are best 'fitted' for political participation and decision making," the question of class- or sex-based exclusions (either formally or indirectly) from political participation and decision-making cannot even be posed as problems from within a framework that conflates liberal theory with democratic theory. Unaware of the manner in which their ideological assumptions about democracy fuel their conclusions about the political culture best suited to it, Almond and Verba affirm as factual "findings" about the political culture of democracy what is in truth a particular, and particularly contested, conception of democracy and its relation to political culture. As Pateman states, "What they are doing is offering us a more sophisticated but very familiar answer to the problem of how liberalism can accommodate universal suffrage, without disturbing social inequalities or the predominant political role of the (male) middle-class."[64]

Now even if one concedes that MacIntyre and Patemen spotlight important dangers that arise when quantitative researchers elide fundamental questions of interpretation and meaning, one might nonetheless question the broader significance of this exercise. It might be argued, for example, that even if these errors are real, they are errors characteristic of an earlier, less methodologically advanced generation of research. The best work *today,* our skeptical interlocutor might reply, displays none of these mistakes. The preceding examples, however convincing in their own right, demonstrate little if anything about the limitations of contemporary research.

Although a systematic investigation of the prevalence of these types of errors lies well beyond the purview of this book, it is possible to respond to this objection in a more modest and circumscribed fashion, namely, by examining one exemplar of precisely the kind of rigorous, contemporary quantitative research that our hypothetical interlocutor defends. If I can demonstrate that this exemplar exhibits methodological defects similar to those adumbrated above, then it must be granted that these problems are neither obsolete artifacts of an earlier generation of research, nor are they confined exclusively to undistinguished, uninfluential work. They appear instead in scholarship that is widely, indeed, lavishly praised for its methodological sophistication.

Adam Przeworski et al.'s *Democracy and Development: Political Institutions and Well-Being in the World, 1950–1990* is just such an exemplary study. Composed by a research team headed by a leading scholar of comparative politics, this "widely acclaimed" study has been celebrated as "an excellent book," "a great book," "a truly commendable contribution," and "one of the most important books in comparative politics in the last decade."[65] Moreover, it has been exalted as a work of considerable "methodological sophistication," with one breathless reviewer calling it "a landmark, standard-shattering body of research" whose "data collection efforts and technical expertise ... inspire awe."[66] Przeworski et al.'s study, moreover, engages an issue of considerable interest: the relationship between political regimes (or, more precisely, two political regimes, democracy and dictatorships) and economic development (or, more broadly, "economic well-being"). Working from "historical observations of 141 countries between 1950 ... and 1990,"[67] the authors discover a number of what they term "surprising" patterns. They find, for example, that although transitions to democracy are not the product of a certain level of economic development, democratic regimes are more likely to survive crises as they become more affluent. By contrast, poor countries that make transitions to democracy are more vulnerable to crises, and hence more susceptible to transitions back to "dictatorships." Moreover, they find that although economic growth rates under democratic and dictatorial regimes were virtually the same, democracies have lower birth rates, which in turn produce faster per capita income growth. They thus conclude that political regimes impact demography more than economics. Finally, they find that among poor countries, "regimes make no difference for growth, quantitatively or qualitatively."[68] However, because those democratic regimes that occasionally arise in impoverished states are extraordinarily fragile, the poor "are much more likely to be ruled by dictators," who thereby contribute substantially to their citizens' misery.

Appropriately for a study that aims to explore "systematically the origins and the consequences of political regimes,"[69] the authors begin by taking up questions regarding the definition and classification of various regime types. Acknowledging the minefield of dangers that appear as soon as one tries to define a concept as contested and variously appropriated as "democracy"—the authors note, for example, that " 'democracy' has become an altar on which everyone hangs his or her favorite *ex voto*"— Przeworski et al.[70] settle on a narrow, formalistic, and largely Schumpeterian definition of democracy as "a regime in which those who govern are selected through contested elections."[71] This definition is then operationalized through the articulation of four classificatory rules: (1) "the chief executive must be elected";[72] (2) "the legislature must be elected";[73] (3) "there must be more than one party";[74] and (4) "alteration,"[75] that is, elections must yield observable alterations in office. By contrast, states that violate one or more of these rules fall into the residual category of dictatorships, which, the authors tell us, is "perhaps better denominated as 'not democracy.' "[76]

It should be evident that this Schumpeterian conception of democracy is not without its virtues. As many of those billions who reside in states where electoral competition does not exist would be quick to point out, competition among ideas is an integral part of contemporary conceptions of democratic legitimacy.[77] Schumpeter's view, which aims to institutionalize this competition through the medium of elections, addresses directly this key aspect of democratic legitimacy. Second, there are obvious merits to Schumpeter's strategy of controlling power by transforming it into an object of electoral competition. As Ian Shapiro notes, this approach "disciplines leaders with the threat of losing power in the same way that firms are disciplined by the threat of bankruptcy, and it gives would-be leaders the incentive to be responsive to more voters than are their competitors."[78] Third, as Shapiro also remarks, competitive elections provide incentives for those who lose to remain actively committed to processes of democratic persuasion rather than resorting to the twin temptations of political violence or apathetic resignation. By institutionalizing "the perpetual possibility of upsetting the status quo,"[79] competitive elections can foster valuable forms of political stability. Finally, Schumpeter's definition is methodologically attractive, since it is more easily operationalized than substantive conceptions. As a result, it is well suited both to the binary system of classification that the authors adopt and to transhistorical, large-N studies where the coding of data can become a particularly nettlesome issue.[80]

Although Schumpeter's minimalist, formalistic conception of democracy directs attention to crucial features of democratic institutional structures and practices, it is important to recall that Przeworski et al. invoke this conception in their effort to develop a general and operational definition of democracy, one that identifies necessary and sufficient conditions for classifying regimes as democratic (or not). Seen in this light, Przeworski et al.'s approach becomes more problematic. In the first place, the authors' operational definition of democracy invites the charge that they have without warrant privileged methodological convenience over the hermeneutical obligation to begin with and attend closely to its meanings within and across specific social-historical contexts, and to its etymology.[81] Etymologically, of course, " 'democracy' is derived from *demokratia,* the root meanings of which are *demos* (people) and *kratos* (rule)."[82] As both an idea and ideal, democracy is from its inception linked to this root notion of rule by the people. Indeed, the phrase itself, however difficult to parse and interpret in practice, identifies a key feature by which democracies ancient and modern are distinguished from other political regimes and modes of rule, such as aristocracies, monarchies, tyrannies, oligarchies, and the like.[83] It is a notion, moreover, that begins to take more specific form during the modern age, when democracy becomes increasingly joined to conceptions of popular sovereignty and self-government. In short, whether understood as rule by a specific economic or social class ("common people"), a corporate body possessing a collective will (as in Rousseau's general will), or majority coalitions, democracy has been distinguished both historically and etymologically from forms of élite rule that severely restrict popular participation and consent.[84]

Yet Przeworski et al.'s definition, which insists on multiparty electoral competition but leaves the question of competition among (or in the name of) whom entirely unspecified, erases this distinction. In fact, Przeworski et al. are quite explicit about this erasure, arguing that participation should be studied as a separate variable rather than imported into the formal definition of democracy.[85] It is, however, far from clear why participation is any less basic to the concept of democracy than the characteristics included in the authors' own definition, and, therefore, why the former, in contrast to the latter, constitutes a dubious or illicit effort to decide "definitionally"[86] the meaning of democracy.[87] If anything, one would presume that participation would claim priority over contested elections, since the latter are generally conceived as specific institutional mechanisms through which popular sovereignty is expressed. In any event, the exclusion of participation from Przeworski et al.'s definition of democracy raises fundamental questions about the objectivity of the enterprise and the adequacy of the definition. As Lisa Wedeen has correctly noted:

> Another problem with Przeworski et al.'s notion of electoral contestation is that it does not require widespread political participation. This absence may facilitate coding transhistorically, but it denies the context-specific ways in which we customarily understand democratic relations between rulers and ruled. Would a country in which contestation meant competition among a small, restricted elite be a democracy in any meaningful sense of the term today? Surely the formal (and perhaps *de facto*) disenfranchisement of large numbers of people disqualifies a political regime from being democratic in most of our ordinary language uses of the word. If highly restricted suffrage can nevertheless count as democracy, then the reasons for insisting on a multiparty system seem arbitrary and unhelpful. It is unclear why a one-party system could not be democratic if divergent interests might be represented. Indeed, as Boriana Nokolova points out, it is not even clear why, according to the minimalist view, elections should be held at all if divergent interests can be represented without citizens voting.[88]

More generally, Przeworski et al.'s ambition to articulate a formal and procedural definition of democracy that pivots around the notion of contested elections reclassifies as external and peripheral to democracy features that are historically and grammatically (in the Wittgensteinian sense of the word) central to it. Most importantly, the authors' effort to circumvent substantive questions of representation, responsiveness, and accountability (or to settle a priori disputes about the meaning of such concepts by defining them in terms of contested elections)[89] shifts to the margins issues that have always been at the very center of democratic struggles, namely, issues of power and popular control. If democratic accountability is reducible to the act of reelecting or removing from office executives and legislators, then questions about "citizens influence and . . . direct impact on the choices and actions of those who govern"[90] become by definition external to democracy. If representative democracy is defined entirely in terms of contested elections, then not only are questions of substantive representation—of "how democratic rulers should act once elected, and what their duties and obligations as rulers are, or should be"—rendered incidental to democratic life,[91] but also "the criterion of political success becomes, rather than governance as such, the ability to capture elections."[92] In short, rather than viewing issues of representation, accountability, responsiveness, and control as indispensable to any proper understanding of democracy and contested elections as one, though not the only, mechanism for achieving these ends, Przeworski et al. transform one mechanism of democratic control into the essence of democracy. In so doing, they consign substantive issues of accountability, representation, and the like to the status of variables that bear only indirectly on questions of democracy.[93]

It should be emphasized that these definitional disputes are not, as some might allege, "merely semantic." Rather, they reside at the epicenter of the theoretical framework that organizes Przeworski et al.'s study. If, for example, questions of accountability and control, as well as protections of basic human rights, are deemed integral to any adequate conception of democracy today, then one must conclude that the authors have misclassified as democratic Brazil during the last years of its military dictatorship (1979–1984) and Guatamela during a notoriously repressive period of military rule and "generally fraudulent elections (1966–81)."[94] Moreover, if one included in one's definition of democracy the kinds of considerations that I have just discussed, a strong case could be made for employing a fundamentally different system of classification, namely, a ratio scale as opposed to the authors' nominal classification.

Although Przeworski et al.'s study is in many ways more sophisticated and rigorous than Almond and Verba's, its methodological defects are strikingly similar. Both studies, I have argued, elide important questions of interpretation, language, meaning, and power. In both cases, moreover, these elisions yield consolidations, conflations, and distortions that compromise the authors' ability to illuminate or solve the issues they raise. Indeed, although both studies strive to investigate and answer significant questions of democratic politics, they construe democracy in a manner that either obscures the problems they aim to address (as with Almond and Verba's conflation of classical liberal theory and democratic theory), or that leaves out much of what is central to democratic life (as with Przeworski et al.'s minimalist conception of democracy). Consequently, in both cases it is often unclear what is specifically democratic about their explorations in democratic theory. Indeed, just as Pateman pointedly asks whether there is anything democratic about the purportedly democratic civic culture, so does Wedeen argue "that Przeworski et al. might be better off avoiding the term 'democracy' altogether. The overall objective of this large-*N* study would then be to explain the relationship between contested elections and economic development, without producing a general account of democracy that would seem to foreclose thinking about political participation and accountability within and outside of electoral confines."[95] Finally, in both cases the authors' claims of scientific impartiality are belied by biases that conflate aspects of Anglo-American democracy with democracy *tout court*.[96]

Let us turn now to the other half of hegemonic political science, rational choice theory. Like my analysis of quantitative and statistical forms of reasoning, my broad objective has been to unsettle rather than reinforce the sharp oppositions that have structured recent debates about the role of rational choice analysis in political inquiry. Indeed, given the multiple and often conflicting commitments that characterize contemporary work in the field, sweeping generalizations of any type are difficult to sustain. Here again I would argue that it is more fruitful to examine the lines of research and possibilities for understanding that particular variants of rational choice theory open and foreclose, than to issue universal dicta about its intrinsic value or limitations.

On the one hand, rational choice and game theoretic analysis can and often do advance interpretive and transformative aims that have long been associated with the traditions of hermeneutics, pragmatism, critical realism, and some variants of poststructuralism. Typically, they do so, first, by rendering intelligible actions and predicaments that may appear prima facie to be the product of irrationality or confusion, and, second, by showing that these problems can only be overcome through forms of collective action. In cases, for instance, where agents engage in self-frustrating or "suboptimal" forms of behavior, it is often exceedingly tempting to presume that these agents are irrational "cultural dopes," victims of ideological manipulation, deeply confused about their interests, or simply stupid. By attending closely to the structure of agents' inter-actions, rational choice analysis can frequently explain such behavior, and can do so without complacently invoking notions of ideological mystifi-cation or irrationality. Moreover, in cases where such explanations do properly identify the underlying mechanisms through which these self-frustrating predicaments are produced and reproduced, rational choice analysis can suggest new strategies for overcoming them.

Consider, for example, the almost universally bemoaned "media circus" that emerges in response to high-profile stories or events, such as the O. J. Simpson trial, the Lewinsky-Clinton scandal, or the two Persian Gulf Wars.[97] As media critics and much of the viewing public often ruefully (and with a tone of helplessness) observe, it is common for coverage of such events to reach a "saturation level" in which all major networks are "showing exactly the same thing."[98] This, as Joseph Heath remarks, "is clearly a suboptimal outcome; if one channel is providing 24-hour live coverage of a particular story, then there is no point having the others do the same. The same applies when every news program covers exactly the same five or six stories in their evening broadcast."[99]

Although the very term "media circus" typically connotes not only the transformation of news into spectacle but also the existence of profound irrationality at the heart of that spectacle (hence the use of phrases like "feeding frenzy" to describe it), Heath contends that what is interesting about the almost ritualized lamentations of critics is not only the fact that they are circulated broadly throughout the public sphere, but also that they are frequently uttered by journalists who are themselves agents in the production of the circus they deplore. When queried about their own views, journalists will often complain that "the situation is ridiculous, that there are interesting stories being ignored, etc."[100] Such responses suggest that the predicament is not likely to be well explained by accounts that invoke "mistaken priorities" or irrationality, or by allegations of a simple failure on the part of journalists and network executives to un-derstand clearly what kind of programming would most benefit viewers. Rather, Heath argues, "The pattern persists because they are stuck in a suboptimal equilibrium. Stations compete with one another for viewers. Given a choice between a small portion of a large audience and a large portion of a small audience, it will often be in the interest of broadcasters to choose the former. When all stations reason the same way, all will provide exactly the same coverage. The result is simply a waste of one or more broadcast frequencies."[101]

In short, rather than insulting the intelligence of those who are caught in these types of predicaments, reframing them as collective action problems permits the social critic to show how actions that may be rational from the perspective of individual agents produce and reproduce outcomes that no one wants or intends. As Heath remarks,

> the mere fact that people know that a certain social change would be *in their interest* (broadly construed) does not mean that they will have an incentive to do anything about it . . . journalists may recognize that their entire profession loses credibility when [they] behave as a pack or pursue lurid stories—and so it is not in *their* interest—but it may still be in the interest of each individual reporter, each individual news organization, to do so (since it is possible to increase one's *share* of viewers even when the total *number* drops—exactly the same logic underlies "negative" campaign ads). From the outside, then, it may look as if people are confused about where their interests lie, that they are in the grip of some ideology. But upon closer examination, they turn out to be quite rational. They may even join the critical theorist in lamenting the sad consequences of their own actions.[102]

As Charles Taylor has aptly remarked, these types of analyses are both interesting and germane because they illuminate, sometimes profoundly, all-too-familiar paradoxes of social action. They do so, moreover, because many modern social institutions, as well as modes of identity and action, have developed in a manner such that people do act to some degree as atomistic individuals engaged in calculating their interest and advantage.[103] Indeed, precisely because a significant part of humanity today spends a good deal of time living and breathing the conditions that rational choice theory postulates, it provides important resources for understanding many problems of social action.

For the reasons just sketched, however, rational choice theory holds much less promise when it is conceived as a "grand" or "universal theory of human behavior,"[104] or when it is applied indiscriminately outside of those contexts in which it is most likely to provide illumination. When, for example, rational choice theorists seek to explain all, or virtually all, religious activity in terms of market logic, they invite the very errors that, on my reading above, the theory is intended to avoid. That is, when phenomena such as fundamentalism and religious participation more generally are explained in terms of an "afterlife consumption" motive, or of a desire for "religious commodities" that include "assurance and security," it becomes difficult to avoid the conclusion that the agents whose actions the theorist purports to explain are, if not irrational, then unintelligent, immature, and distinctly ill-equipped to negotiate the pressures and exigencies of modern life. As Roxanne Euben, summarizing the rational actor literature on religion, observes, "The logic of rational actor theory tends to portray fundamentalists as 'risk-averse' and too immature and unintelligent to cope with the stresses and strains of modernization and secularization . . . such analyses suggest that religious participation in general, and fundamentalism by extension, fulfills a need to belong, a need to escape the press of difficult lives, or a need to relieve the stress and uncertainty of modern life."[105] In such cases, the neglect of interpretive accounts in favor of a presumption that explanations of religious commitment must be explicable in terms of market logic (and the belief-desire model of instrumental action that animates that logic) yields a classic "tail wagging the dog" scenario, one in which the dictates of the theory lead the analyst to consider only "those aspects of the fundamentalist's so-called character—such as insecurity, immaturity, or intolerance of risk—that render fundamentalist membership and behavior intelligible to market logic. In these instances rational actor theory begins and ends with an image of Islamic fundamentalism as the refuge of the disenfranchised, those unable to cope with the challenges and insecurity of modern life. While fundamentalist action may be understood as instrumentally rational, its appeal is nevertheless rendered as a function of psychological insecurity, strain, or perceived deprivation."[106] In short, what is left unexplored are those phenomena that cannot be readily incorporated into the market logic of rational choice explanation, but that constitute the starting point of interpretive analyses, namely, the shared meanings and social imaginaries that animate members of religious communities, as well as the content and structure of religious or fundamentalist ideas, rituals, and practices.[107]

In fact, however, the dangers posed by such explanations are not singular but plural. The conviction that all behavior must be explicable in market logic terms not only yields explanations that violate interpretive principles extolled by many partisans of rational actor theories, but also fuels efforts to explain through radical redescription phenomena that would otherwise appear to defy explanation in such terms. This problem, of course, is not new. More than three decades ago, Brian Barry warned that "the constant danger of economic theories is that they can come to 'explain' everything merely by redescribing it. They then fail to be any use in predicting that one thing will happen rather than another."[108] These cautionary remarks notwithstanding, the temptation has often been difficult to resist, as ungainly terms like "afterlife consumption motive" attest.[109] And it is undoubtedly more difficult to resist if one grants economic theories epistemic priority and conceives of them as general, unifying theories of social and political life. By contrast, theories informed by the Gadamerian idea of a "fusion of horizons" are much less inclined to encourage these particular types of errors. Because such theories posit that coming to an understanding of unfamiliar actions, practices, persons, cultures, and institutions typically requires an alteration of one's own horizon, the impulse to assume that one's own language already contains the requisite concepts and categories for understanding the Other is muted considerably.

Indeed, to the extent that one assumes or asserts that rational choice theories can and should constitute a unifying paradigm for social and political inquiry, one encourages one of two serious errors: (1) the error of insisting that all social and political phenomena can and should be redescribed adequately in rational choice terms and (2) the error of excluding from investigation all social and political phenomena that may appear to resist adequate explanation in these terms (on the grounds that such phenomena lie outside the proper boundaries of social scientific explanation). There are, of course, well-known categories of action that are not in any obvious sense nonrational (unless, of course, one defines rationality a priori in economistic terms), yet cannot be brought within the purview of rational choice theory's psychological and explanatory framework. Amartya Sen, for example, has famously argued that people often act out of a sense of "commitment" that is closely related to their identities as members of a community, nation, class, sex, ethnicity, race, and the like, or their identification with various ethical or moral values.[110] Action guided by commitment, however, directly contravenes economic rationality because it involves "counterpreferential choice."[111] Where it operates (and Sen suggests that it operates quite widely), commitment supplants utility maximization by undermining the idea that more is preferable to less.

In addition to Sen's conception of commitment, a number of scholars, including some rational choice theorists, have identified alternative forms of rationality and mechanisms of action that in important ways resist integration into the instrumental model of action that lies at the center of rational choice theory. Among the candidates more or less frequently advanced are normative reasoning and expressive rationality or behavior; altruistic, moral, and norm-guided dispositions; identificatory and intrinsic motivations; and communicative and "meaning-seeking," that is, "the propensity to seek coherence and sense in the norms and other symbolic structures ... through which one lives," mechanisms of action.[112] To the extent that evidence indicates that these and other types of actions are irreducible to rational actor models of explanation—and there is abundant evidence that some of these types of actions are—rational choice theorists face a trinity of choices. First, they can attempt to preserve the goals of unification and methodological purity by excluding from the domain of social and political science phenomena that resist incorporation into the formal and instrumental models of rational choice theory. Or, second, they can try to redescribe recalcitrant forms of action in a language consistent with the dictates of rational choice theory, taking on board all of the concomitant risks outlined above. Or, third, they can embrace a more capacious and disorderly conception of the scientific enterprise, while striving to clarify the scope and limits of their own theoretical frameworks.

My own view leans heavily toward the third option. As I have argued, the first option erroneously presumes that all science must be unified science and that scientific progress demands methodological unification. In addition, it makes methodological compatibility rather than problems of political life the criterion for determining what "objects" such a science should study. The second option may well be appropriate in some circumstances, but when pressed too far is likely to distort one's understanding while reducing the theory itself to an empty tautology.[113] By contrast, the third option grants a significant if circumscribed role to rational choice analysis. Acknowledging that the application of rational choice models is likely to be fruitful only under particular conditions or in certain contexts, this approach welcomes as vital to the enterprise of political inquiry both formal theories and a variety of alternative theories that may better explain those phenomena that resist subsumption into rational choice models. Moreover, by acknowledging limitations on the application of rational choice models, this option grants high (if not the highest) priority to the task of identifying those limitations.

In addition, this third option, by attending carefully to differences of meaning both across cultures and "civilizations" and within them, lends itself to more genuinely *comparative* analysis than competing approaches. Indeed, if concepts like "pride" are very often unstable even within what is often purported to be a single (in this case, "European") culture or "civilization," then it is particularly presumptuous to assume conceptual stability and continuity across cultures. One of the distinct advantages of my approach is that, by insisting on the importance of disaggregating meanings and practices within and across cultures, it militates against the forms of "Orientalism" that Edward Said and others have so vividly brought to our attention.[114] By contrast, approaches that abandon hermeneutical commitments and modes of analysis (which are, conceived broadly, the only ones we possess for understanding meanings) shield these questions from critical scrutiny. To the degree that they do so, moreover, they subvert the possibility of truly comparative forms of political inquiry.[115]

Finally, the third option has yet another advantage over its rivals: unlike them, it possesses the resources to, if not counteract, at least mitigate tendencies within contemporary societies to view all behavior as self-interested and all action as instrumental. As I noted in chapter 4, the social sciences are distinguished from the physical sciences in one (although not only one) very important respect: the relationship between theory and practice is often circular in the former but never in the latter. That is, to the extent that social scientific theories and descriptions circulate and gain purchase throughout the societies they purport to describe and explain, they can become self-fulfilling prophecies, literally manufacturing the kind of "material," that is, the beliefs, habits of thought, patterns of behavior, and overall character or ethos, required to "confirm" the theory or description in question. Because physicists and chemists do not study self-interpreting beings—as Ian Hacking aptly remarks, "calling a quark a quark makes no difference to the quark"—this relationship has no analogue in the physical sciences.[116] And because there is no analogue, the peculiar "looping effects" that the relationship often produces also do not exist.[117] Nonetheless, this is an important if underappreciated aspect of social and political inquiry, for it demonstrates quite clearly that there are critical moral and political stakes in the production and propagation of social scientific theories, stakes that cannot typically be erased merely by stating that the theory is intended to explain rather than describe or recommend behavior, or that the assumptions animating it are only heuristic devices. In the case of economic theories like rational choice these stakes are very real indeed, for there is some empirical evidence indicating that "exposure to the self-interest model commonly used in economics alters the extent to which people behave in self-interested ways."[118] In their study of this question, Robert H. Frank, Thomas Gilovich, and Dennis T. Regan adduced evidence showing that "despite their generally higher incomes," economists are considerably less likely than professors in other disciplines to give money to charities and that they are "among the least generous in terms of their median gifts to large charities like viewer–supported television and the United Way";[119] that economics students display less concern with fairness, and exhibit more exclusively self-interested behavior in bargaining games, even when doing so is *detrimental* to their interests;[120] that "one semester's training [in an introductory micro-economics class] is accompanied by greater movement toward more cynical ('less honest') responses"[121] on honesty surveys; and that these tendencies—with the exception of the honesty surveys, which were administered only at the beginning and end of a semester-long course—become more pronounced over the course of students' college education.[122] Frank et al. conclude that "a variety of evidence suggests a large difference in the extent to which economists and noneconomists behave self-interestedly."[123]

If one agrees with Frank et al.'s claim that "in an evermore interdependent world, social cooperation has become increasingly important— and yet increasingly fragile,"[124] then the ontological arguments I have marshaled in defense of social scientific disunity might be further buttressed by moral and political considerations. Given even limited evidence that sustained exposure to the self-interest model of human behavior increases the degree to which people behave self-interestedly, it is worth asking whether a discipline unified around such a view of human motivation is the kind of discipline that political scientists, or the publics that support them, should want.[125] Indeed, one of the virtues of a disunified and pluralist conception of social and political inquiry is that by incorporating multiple models of human agency and identity into both pedagogy and research, it supplies resources for mitigating the sometimes disturbing looping effects that occur when theories of social phe-

nomena are accepted by social agents and hence become part of the social world, in the process altering the very practices and institutions they
describe.

Revitalizing Political Inquiry

In the end, of course, the fate of any proposal rests not only on its
intellectual merits, but also on its pragmatic appeal. The proposal that I
have advanced throughout this book is surely no exception to this rule.
In closing, therefore, the reader might reasonably ask whether, given the
present conflicts and cleavages within the discipline of political science,
my defense of disunified social and political inquiry is likely to appeal
either to the proponents of hegemony or to the partisans of Perestroika.
Or, rather, is it likely to be dismissed by both, with Perestroikans finding
it either too constraining (in its defense of critical pluralism rather than
laissez-faire pluralism) or too generous (in its qualified defense of quantitative and rational choice analysis), and the representatives of hegemony
finding it at once too capacious in its conception of science and too
modest in its epistemological ambitions?

Although it would clearly be disingenuous for one who rejects the
predictive criterion of social explanation to offer armchair forecasts of
one's own, a few additional words might be said about the state of current
methodological conflicts in political science. Although it is true that much
of the rhetoric fueling the recent methodological controversies pivots
around a series of intellectually untenable but mutually sustaining dichotomies, I would contend that a careful survey of these disputes reveals
a broader and more complex range of views than much of the current
debate and commentary suggests. Along with the familiar plotting and
enactment of dichotomous positions, one can detect views and voices
that are distinctly less invested in preserving binary divisions, and hence
are less inclined to interpret the current methodological disputes as
nothing more than another prescripted iteration of conflicts between the
defenders of unity and anarchy, science and antiscience, quantitative
methods and qualitative methods. Whether ecumenical or agonistic in
their conception of political inquiry, these less audible voices display an
ongoing commitment to forms of critical pluralism that sustain communication across theoretical and methodological boundaries, without
insisting that such communication presupposes something like a single,

unified "disciplinary matrix." In so doing, they enact and bring into view what I have tried to describe, namely, an image of disunified and disordered political inquiry, one that stands as an alternative to the dominant images of homogenous unification and crazy-quilt fragmentation. Significantly, those who profess and practice these commitments are not quarantined in a single field of political inquiry or on one or the other side of the standard methodological and ideological cleavages. Instead, they are scattered orthogonally across them. Thus, just as one hears Perestroikan appeals for a conception of political inquiry that affirms the value, without acquiescing to the hegemony, of statistical and formal modes of analysis, so does one find proponents of rational choice theory recommending a more epistemologically modest conception of their enterprise, one that exploits its value within certain contexts, yet abandons the grand, universalist, predictivist ambition to transform social science into social physics. It is here, I would argue, that the most promising possibilities for the revitalization of political inquiry lie.

Notes

Introduction

1. Alan Sokal, "Revelation: A Physicist Experiments with Cultural Studies," in the editors of *Lingua Franca*, eds., *The Sokal Hoax: The Sham That Shook the Academy* (Lincoln: University of Nebraska Press, 2000), pp. 49, 51.
2. Ibid.
3. Alan Sokal, "Transgressing the Boundaries: Toward a Transformative Hermeneutics of Quantum Gravity," *Social Text* 46–47 (Spring–Summer 1996): 217–252. This article is reprinted in the editors of *Lingua Franca*, eds., *The Sokal Hoax*, pp. 11–45.
4. Linda Seebach, "Scientist Takes Academia for a Ride with Parody," in the editors of *Lingua Franca*, eds., *The Sokal Hoax*, p. 72.
5. Stanley Fish, "Professor Sokal's Bad Joke," in ibid., pp. 81–84. Similar concerns were also voiced by the coeditors of *Social Text*, Bruce Robbins and Andrew Ross. See "Response: Mystery Science Theater," in ibid., p. 54–58.
6. John Omicinski, "Hoax Article Yanks Academics' Legs," in ibid., p. 94.
7. Evelyn Fox Keller, "Selected Letters to the Editors," in ibid., pp. 59–60.
8. Steven Weinberg, "Sokal's Hoax," *New York Review of Books*, August 8, 1996, p. 11.
9. Bruno Latour, "Is There Science after the Cold War?" in the editors of *Lingua Franca*, eds., *The Sokal Hoax*, pp. 123–124.
10. Janny Scott, "Postmodern Gravity Deconstructed, Slyly," in ibid., p. 76.
11. Ellen Schrecker, "The Sokal Hoax: A Forum," *Lingua Franca* 6 (July–August 1996): 61.
12. Alan Sokal and Jean Bricmont, *Fashionable Nonsense: Postmodern Intellectuals' Abuse of Science* (New York: Picador, 1999), p. 3. See also Alan D. Sokal, "What the *Social Text* Affair Does and Does Not Prove," *Critical Quarterly* 40 (Summer 1998): 6.

13. Alan D. Sokal, "Transgressing the Boundaries: An Afterword," *Philosophy and Literature* 20 (1996): 339.

14. Sokal, "Revelation: A Physicist Experiments with Cultural Studies," p. 50.

15. Sokal, "Transgressing the Boundaries: An Afterword," p. 339. Elsewhere, Sokal states that "it was my concern for leftist politics that was my *principal* motivation for writing the parody." See Sokal, "What the *Social Text* Affair Does and Does Not Prove," p. 4. Emphasis added.

16. Sokal, "Transgressing the Boundaries: An Afterword," p. 344. See also *Fashionable Nonsense,* where Sokal and Bricmont maintain that "the most serious consequences of relativism come from its application to the social sciences" (p. 207).

17. Sokal, for instance, presents his hoax as an effort to expose a lazy form of epistemic relativism that is embraced by a variety of postmodernists and feminists, as well as scholars of science and cultural studies. Yet apart from his failure to disambiguate adequately the quite different meanings and senses attached to the phrases like "physical 'reality' . . . is a social and linguistic construct" (Sokal, "Transgressing the Boundaries," p. 12; idem, "Revelation: A Physicist Experiments with Cultural Studies," p. 50; for a lucid untangling of the disparate meanings attached to and uses of the phrase "social construction," see Ian Hacking, *The Social Construction of What?* [Cambridge, MA: Harvard University Press, 1999]), Sokal often quotes and cites writers who explicitly reject the radical epistemic relativism his article purports to parody. For example, Sokal's extensive list of references includes two books and one article written by Donna Haraway. Indeed, only two other scholars, Stanley Aronowitz and Katherine Hayles, figure more prominently in his bibliography. But in an interview published, strangely enough, in *Social Text,* Haraway plainly rejects the relativist views that Sokal condemns. As Haraway remarks, "Scientific discourses . . . make claims on you, ethically, physically. The objects of these discourses . . . have a kind of materiality; they have a sort of reality that is inescapable. No scientific account escapes being story-laden, but it is equally true that stories are not all equal here. Radical relativism just won't do as a way of finding your way across and through these terrains." See Constance Penley and Andrew Ross, "Cyborgs at Large: Interview with Donna Haraway," *Social Text* 25–26 (1990): 8. Likewise, Sokal's bibliography includes three works by Sandra Harding. But, as Harding has often insisted in her writings, the animating impulse behind her use of feminist research to explore entrenched assumptions about science and scientific method is to diminish distortions and biases in science, not to show that science is so fully constructed socially that talk of distortion and bias is beside the point. In her own words: "The issue here is not so

much one of the right to claim a label [feminism] as it is of the prerequi-
sites for producing less partial and distorted descriptions, explanations,
and understandings." See Sandra Harding, "Introduction: Is There a Feminist Method?" in Sandra Harding, ed., *Feminism and Methodology: Social
Science Issues* (Bloomington: University of Indiana Press, 1987), p. 12.
This indeed is one of the suppositions that underlie her effort to develop
a notion of "strong objectivity" as an alternative to orthodox construals
of that concept. See Sandra Harding, "Strong Objectivity and Socially Situated Knowledge," in *Whose Science? Whose Knowledge? Thinking from
Women's Lives* (Ithaca, NY: Cornell University Press, 1991), pp. 138–163.
It is, of course, possible to acknowledge these views yet argue nonetheless
that writers like Haraway and Harding cannot ultimately reconcile them
with other commitments expressed in their work. Demonstrating that this
was the case, however, would require that one not only identify the tensions in Haraway's and Harding's thought; it would also entail an argument about the intractability of those tensions from within Haraway's and
Harding's frameworks of thought and their tractability from within an alternative framework. However, because Sokal's readings of Haraway and
Harding do not even acknowledge possible tensions, he is in no position
to advance arguments about them, nor does he. Finally, Elizabeth Lloyd
has noted that much work in science studies aims not to *delegitimize* science but rather to *demystify* it. Sokal, like many other critics of science
studies, often views the former rather than the latter as its principal aim.
See Elizabeth A. Lloyd, "Science and Anti-Science: Objectivity and Its Real
Enemies," in Lynn Hankinson Nelson and Jack Nelson, eds., *Feminism,
Science, and the Philosophy of Science* (Dordrecht: Kluwer Academic Publishers, 1996), pp. 217–259.

18. Sokal maintains that his primary interest is political: to combat the political dangers of shoddy "postmodern" scholarship that simultaneously
abandons scientific commitments and invokes scientific theories and concepts that at best are only vaguely understood. Yet the veracity of the
proposition that postmodern accounts of science (or, more precisely, "the
radical version of postmodernism," which Sokal states is the only version
he is criticizing) and postmodern attachments to epistemic relativism pose
a political danger would seem to depend at least in part on the empirical
issue of how pervasive and influential radical postmodernist ideas are,
particularly in those fields that Sokal regards as most seriously threatened
by these ideas, namely, history and the social sciences. On the distinction
between moderate and radical forms of postmodernism, see Sokal and
Bricmont, *Fashionable Nonsense*, p. 183. But Sokal neither undertakes nor
cites any such investigation and more recently has asserted—again,

without empirical evidence—that "viewed on a global scale, [postmodernism] is a rather marginal phenomenon"; see ibid., p. 16. More generally, if Sokal's purpose is, as he asserts, *political,* it would appear to be incumbent upon him to justify via evidence or argument the decision to focus exclusively on postmodern abuses of science while remaining silent about other, and arguably much more politically damaging, distortions of science, such as those contained in works like Richard Herrnstein and Charles Murray's best-selling book, *The Bell Curve,* which adorns what can at best be described as a questionable political agenda in the respectable clothing of scientific objectivity. In this respect, Sokal and Bricmont's claim that the question "Why do you criticize these authors and not others?" is "irrelevant to the validity or invalidity of our arguments" is convincing only as long as their aims and intentions remain exclusively cognitive rather than expressly political. See *Fashionable Nonsense,* p. 14. Once these issues enter the political arena, however, it is certainly reasonable to ask why one would devote considerable time and energy refuting allegedly false ideas of little political consequence when equally specious ideas of much greater political significance are summarily ignored. In short, if Sokal's aim is to change the world rather than to make a point, then he cannot by his own lights be content to offer, or expect his critics to accept, epistemic answers to political questions.

19. A case in point is Sokal's treatment of Bruno Latour's article, "A Relativistic Account of Einstein's Relativity." See Latour, "A Relativistic Account of Einstein's Relativity," *Social Studies of Science* 18 (1988): 3–44. This article figures in Sokal's *Social Text* parody and occupies one chapter of his coauthored book, *Fashionable Nonsense.* In that chapter, Sokal and Bricmont maintain that "Latour's interpretation of relativity . . . illustrates perfectly the problems encountered by a sociologist who aims to analyze the content of a scientific theory he does not understand very well" (p. 124). Sokal and Bricmont subsequently purport to expose a number of elementary confusions and technical errors in Latour's article, for example, Latour's allegedly confused use of the concept of "frame of reference." Yet when N. David Mermin, a specialist in theoretical theoretical physics who holds an endowed chair at Cornell University, read Latour's article, he reached strikingly different conclusions. Noting that there are "many obscure statements . . . which may well be misconstruals of elementary technical points," Mermin contended that ultimately these "are peripheral to the central issues." Moreover, he argued that "some current diatribes [against Latour] are superficial in their identifications of 'error.' " Among these are criticisms of Latour's use of the concept of frame of reference, which Mermin agrees is in some ways rather loose but nonetheless

"is irrelevant to his analogy." More generally, Mermin takes to task some of Latour's own critics for failing to articulate accurately many of the ideas they accuse Latour of misunderstanding, adding that "although Latour is not primarily interested in relativity as physics, there are passages in which he gets this aspect not only right, but eloquently so." See N. David Mermin, "What's Wrong with This Reading," *Physics Today* 50 (October 1997): 11–12. As should be clear, my intention here is not to settle but to complicate the allegations regarding Latour's "abuses of science." Sokal's charges of charlatanism clearly rest on the assumption that Latour's errors are so grievous and transparent as to be detectable by any minimally competent physicist. The fact that prominent physicists themselves disagree about the nature and significance of Latour's alleged perversions of relativity theory suggests the possibility that there may be not one but two (or more) sources of "nonsense": the first resulting from confusions and distortions attributable to the author's own deep misunderstandings, and the second resulting from a lack of interpretive nuance or sensitivity on the part of the interpreter. This latter problem is particularly acute when scholars in one field venture into the literature of another field, where literary and stylistic conventions may vary from those regnant in one's home discipline. By projecting onto those alien literatures one's "local" expectations, understandings, assumptions, and modes of reading, one may well produce an unintended but potentially serious error, that of manufacturing rather than discovering nonsense.

20. See Paul R. Gross and Norman Levitt, *Higher Superstition: The Academic Left and Its Quarrels with Science* (Baltimore: The Johns Hopkins University Press, 1994); Paul R. Gross, Norman Levitt, and Martin W. Lewis, eds., *The Flight from Science and Reason* (New York: The New York Academy of Sciences, 1996); and Noretto Koertge, ed., *A House Built on Sand: Exposing Postmodern Myths About Science* (New York: Oxford University Press, 1998). Sokal claims that the idea of a hoax came to him after reading *Higher Superstition*.

21. See Emily Eakin, "Political Scientists Leading a Revolt, Not Studying One," *New York Times*, November 4, 2000, pp. B11, B13; Kurt Jacobsen, "Unreal, Man," *Guardian*, April 3, 2001; and Jonathan Cohn, "Irrational Exuberance," *New Republic* 221 (October 25, 1999): 25–31.

22. Mr. Perestroika, "On Globalization of the APSA and APSR: A Political Science Manifesto," *Newsletter of the New Political Science Section of the APSA* 9 (February 2001): 7–8. See also the open letter—initiated by the Perestroika exchanges, drafted by Rogers Smith, and signed by 222 scholars—to the leadership and members of the American Political Science Association, "An Open Letter to the APSA Leadership and Mem-

bers" (and additional letters), *PS: Political Science & Politics* 33 (December 2000): 735–741.

23. By demanding the application of a rigorous analysis of power to debates about rigor, Perestroika's supporters were also implicitly claiming to be more attuned than their opponents to the soul of political science.

24. In a recent discussion of methodological controversies in sociology, Craig Calhoun expresses quite similar sentiments. Noting ruefully that "sociologists seem doomed to fight the *methodenstreit* again and again," he remarks that "for every practitioner of intelligent division of labor or multidimensional research, there are a dozen advocates of one against the other." See Craig Calhoun, "Explanation in Historical Sociology: Narrative, General Theory, and Historically Specific Theory," *American Journal of Sociology* 104 (November 1998): 846.

25. Perestroika, "On Globalization of the APSA and APSR," p. 7.

26. Ibid., p. 8.

27. In a recent discussion of the Perestroika controversy, an important scholar of both the history of political science and the philosophy of political inquiry, John Dryzek, bemoaned "the virtual absence of methodological argument by any side." See John Dryzek, "A Pox on Perestroika, A Hex on Hegemony: Toward a Critical Political Science," paper presented at the 2002 Annual Meeting of the American Political Science Association, Boston, MA, p. 2.

28. I use the term "postempiricist" in a deliberately broad fashion, one that encompasses the work not only of N.R. Hanson, Thomas Kuhn, and Paul Feyerabend, but also of disparate pragmatist, constructivist, and feminist accounts of natural scientific practice. While this usage obviously assimilates an extraordinarily diverse range of work, it also conveys, as I wish it to do, some of its broad commonalities—for example, its rejection of standard empiricist accounts of objectivity and scientific explanation.

29. As historians of science such as Peter Galison have noted, the principal architects of empiricist philosophy of science during the past century were trained in mathematics rather than physical sciences like physics or chemistry, and perhaps for this reason were quite uninterested in phenomena that would seem to be central to any adequate account of natural scientific inquiry, namely, experiments. Galison notes, "It is ironic that the very philosophers who called themselves logical empiricists had virtually no interest in the *conduct* of experiments." Indeed, "though they disagree among themselves on other points, none of the empiricists, inter alia, Hempel, Braithwaite, Nagel, and Popper, paid much attention to experiments." See Galison, *How Experiments End* (Chicago: University of Chicago Press, 1987), p. 8.

30. On the former, see Donald P. Green and Ian Shapiro, *Pathologies of Rational Choice: A Critique of Applications in Political Science* (New Haven, CT: Yale University Press, 1994); Jeffrey Friedman, ed., *The Rational Choice Controversy: Economic Models of Politics Reconsidered* (New Haven, CT: Yale University Press, 1996); Emily Hauptmann, *Putting Choice Before Democracy: A Critique of Rational Choice Theory* (Albany: SUNY Press, 1996); Brian Fay, *Critical Social Science: Liberation and Its Limits* (Ithaca, NY: Cornell University Press, 1987); Stephen T. Leonard, *Critical Theory in Political Practice* (Princeton, NJ: Princeton University Press, 1990); and Pauline Marie Rosenau, *Postmodernism and the Social Sciences: Insights, Inroads, and Intrusions* (Princeton, NJ: Princeton University Press, 1992). For examples of the latter approach, see Raymond Seidelman (with the assistance of Edward J. Harpham), *Disenchanted Realists: Political Science and the American Crisis, 1884–1984* (Albany: SUNY Press, 1985); and John G. Gunnell, *The Descent of Political Theory: The Genealogy of an American Vocation* (Chicago: University of Chicago Press, 1993).

31. Both historically and philosophically, the unity-of-science thesis has taken different forms and been assigned different meanings and references. It is, for example, sometimes conceived as an ontological thesis, one that denies, in principle, any ontological distinction between human beings and physical nature. At other times, it is construed as a methodological thesis, namely, as a thesis that denies, in principle, any methodological distinction between the social and natural sciences. While conceptually and philosophically distinct, most contemporary debates within the social sciences couple these two versions of the thesis. That is, those who defend the unity-of-science thesis intend typically to defend the thesis of methodological unity. They do so, however, by deriving it from a prior claim of ontological unity. By contrast, those who reject the unity-of-science thesis also aim generally to refute the thesis of methodological unification. But like their opponents, they derive their methodological thesis from an ontological one. Throughout this book, discussion of the unity-of-science thesis refers, unless otherwise noted, to a thesis of methodological unity that is grounded in a prior claim of ontological unity.

32. Georgia Warnke, "Translator's Introduction," in Karl Otto-Apel, *Understanding and Explanation: A Transcendental-Pragmatic Perspective,* trans. Georgia Warnke (Cambridge, MA: MIT Press, 1984), p. viii.

33. On these two views, see Terence Ball, "The Ambivalent Alliance: Political Science and American Democracy," in James Farr, John S. Dryzek, and Stephen T. Leonard, eds., *Political Science in History: Research Programs and Political Traditions* (New York: Cambridge University Press, 1995), pp. 41–65.

34. John Dewey, "Scientific Method," in *The Middle Works, 1899–1924*, vol. 7 (Carbondale: Southern Illinois University Press, 1979), p. 339.

35. This catalogue is not meant to imply that each commitment is the property of one and only one of these philosophical positions. To the contrary, many of them, with few or no modifications in formulation, are held and endorsed by the representatives of other currents of thought. Indeed, one of the aims of this book is to make explicit some of these less noticed points of convergence.

36. In the title of his recent book, *Historical Ontology*, Ian Hacking appropriates (with some reservations) a phrase first used by Michel Foucault. Although the manuscript of this book was completed prior to the publication of Hacking's study, his, or rather Foucault's, phrase nonetheless expresses nicely many (but not all) aspects of my approach, particularly insofar as Foucault's use of the term is meant specifically to highlight the nexus of knowledge, power, and ethics. See Ian Hacking, *Historical Ontology* (Cambridge, MA: Harvard University Press, 2002). On Foucault's earlier usage, see "What Is Enlightenment?" in Michel Foucault, *Ethics: Subjectivity and Truth*, vol. 1 of Paul Rabinow, ed., *Essential Works of Foucault 1954–84* (New York: New Press, 1997), pp. 303–320. This general interest in ontology is also displayed in Stephen White's recent book, *Sustaining Affirmation*. Like Hacking and myself, White wishes to rethink yet also affirm some forms of ontological argument and inquiry, namely, those he terms "weak ontologies." One feature that his account of weak ontology shares with my own approach is its "rooting of fundamental concepts [of ontology] in a historical context." See Stephen K. White, *Sustaining Affirmation: The Strengths of Weak Ontology* (Princeton, NJ: Princeton University Press, 2000), p. 20.

37. Pierre Bourdieu, "Fieldwork in Philosophy," in Pierre Bourdieu, *In Other Words: Essays Towards a Reflexive Sociology* (Standford, CA: Standford University Press, 1990), p. 3.

38. Pierre Bourdieu, "Une science qui dérange," in *Questions de Sociologie* (Paris: Les Éditions de Minuit, 1984), pp. 19–36.

1. Science Turned Upside Down

1. Charles Taylor, "Understanding in Human Science," *Review of Metaphysics* 34 (September 1980): 26.

2. Richard Rorty, *Consequences of Pragmatism* (Minneapolis: University of Minnesota Press, 1982), p. 199.

3. Richard Rorty, *Philosophy and the Mirror of Nature* (Princeton, NJ: Princeton University Press, 1979), p. 179.

4. Ibid., p. 7.
5. Ibid., p. 5.
6. Ibid., p. 3.
7. Ibid., p. 9.
8. Mark Okrent, "The Metaphilosophical Consequences of Pragmatism," in Avner Cohen and Marcelo Dascal, eds., *The Institution of Philosophy: A Discipline in Crisis?* (La Salle, IL: Open Court Press, 1989), p. 178.
9. See, for example, "Introduction," in Richard Rorty, *Contingency, Irony, and Solidarity* (New York: Cambridge University Press, 1989), pp. xiii–xvi.
10. For a critical discussion of the idea that language's intrinsic purpose is to operate as some "third thing," as a "medium" of either expression or representation, see Richard Rorty, "The Contingency of Language," in *Contingency, Irony, and Solidarity*, pp. 3–22.
11. Ibid., p. 3.
12. Rorty, *Philosophy and the Mirror of Nature*, p. 5.
13. Rorty, *Contingency, Irony, and Solidarity*, p. xvi.
14. Ibid.
15. Richard Rorty, "Introduction: Pragmatism as Anti-Representationalism," in John P. Murphy, *Pragmatism: From Peirce to Davidson* (Boulder, CO: Westview Press, 1990), pp. 1–6.
16. Richard Rorty, "Pragmatism, Relativism, Irrationalism," in *Consequences of Pragmatism*, pp. 162–163.
17. Ibid., p. 165.
18. Rorty, *Philosophy and the Mirror of Nature*, pp. 264, 371–373, 377–378, 389–394. For Oakeshott's original formulation, see Michael Oakeshott, "The Voice of Poetry in the Conversation of Mankind," in *Rationalism and Politics and Other Essays* (London and New York: Methuen, 1981), pp. 197–247.
19. For an explicit statement of this idea, see Richard Rorty, "Philosophy as Science, as Metaphor, and as Politics," in Cohen and Dascal, eds., *The Institution of Philosophy*, pp. 13–33.
20. Richard Bernstein, *Beyond Objectivism and Relativism: Science, Hermeneutics, and Praxis* (Philadelphia: University of Pennsylvania Press, 1983), p. 18.
21. Such an attitude is apparent both in specific discussions of pragmatism and in attacks on a wide range of "postempiricist" philosophies and histories of science. In this respect, Imre Lakatos's charge that Thomas Kuhn had reduced the problem of evaluating scientific theories to "*a matter for mob psychology*" is perhaps the best example of the profound discomfort generated by postempiricist efforts to abandon traditional correspondence theories of truth. Significantly, Lakatos's alarm was fueled not by a fear

that Kuhn's queries might produce disorder and anarchy in ongoing scientific practice—to the contrary, he assumed that scientists would proceed with blithe indifference to his claims—but by Kuhn's failure to preserve a *philosophical* foundation for scientific truth. See "Falsification and the Methodology of Scientific Research Programs," in Imre Lakatos and Alan Musgrave, eds., *Criticism and the Growth of Knowledge* (Cambridge: Cambridge University Press, 1970), p. 178. For a more recent expression of this same concern, see Barry Gower, "Chalmers on Method," *British Journal for the Philosophy of Science* 39 (1988): 59–65.

22. Rorty, *Contingency, Irony, and Solidarity,* pp. 4–5.

23. Ibid., p. 21.

24. Ibid., p. 5.

25. Ibid., p. 22.

26. Rorty, *Philosophy and the Mirror of Nature,* p. 320.

27. Ibid., p. 352.

28. Ibid., p. 321.

29. Ibid., p. 320.

30. Ibid., pp. 320–321, 343.

31. Ibid., p. 321.

32. Ibid., p. 352.

33. Richard Rorty, "Method, Social Science, and Social Hope," in *Consequences of Pragmatism,* p. 193.

34. Ibid.

35. Hubert L. Dreyfus, "Defending the Difference: The *Geistes/Naturwissenschaften* Distinction Revisited," in Academie der Wissenschaften zu Berlin (Jürgen Mittelstraß, Director), ed., *Einheit der Wissenschaften* (Berlin: Walter de Gruyter, 1991), p. 476.

36. Hubert L. Dreyfus, "Holism and Hermeneutics," *Review of Metaphysics* 34 (September 1980): 7.

37. Ibid., p. 10.

38. Dreyfus, "Defending the Difference," p. 476.

39. Ibid., p. 477.

40. Ibid.

41. See especially, Hubert L. Dreyfus, "Why Studies of Human Capacities Modeled on Ideal Natural Science Can Never Achieve Their Goal," in J. Margolis, M. Krausz, and R. M. Burian, eds., *Rationality, Relativism and the Human Sciences* (Dordrecht: Martinus Nijhoff Publishers, 1986), p. 9.

42. For an interesting effort to apply this account of skills to ethical questions, see Hubert L. Dreyfus and Stuart E. Dreyfus, "Towards a Phenomenology of Ethical Expertise," *Human Studies* 14 (October 1991): 229–250.

43. On the specific character of "equipment" and equipmental wholes, see

Martin Heidegger, *Being and Time,* trans. John Macquarrie and Edward Robinson (New York: Harper & Row Publishers, 1962), pp. 97–107.

44. Hubert L. Dreyfus, *Being-in-the-World: A Commentary on Heidegger's* Being and Time, *Division 1* (Cambridge, MA: MIT Press, 1991), p. 117.

45. Ibid., p. 118.

46. Dreyfus, "Defending the Difference," p. 482.

47. Ibid., pp. 482–483. Dreyfus's point, of course, is not that social scientific predictions are never correct. To the contrary, he states unambiguously that they frequently are. What distinguishes them, rather, is their intrinsic unreliability—they are reliable only as long as the decontextualized elements isolated and organized via the theory "happen to coincide" with events and objects picked out in everyday situations. Ibid., p. 476.

48. See especially Charles Taylor, "Interpretation and the Sciences of Man," in *Philosophy and the Human Sciences: Philosophical Papers,* vol. 2 (New York: Cambridge University Press, 1985), pp. 15–57; idem, "Understanding in Human Science," pp. 25–58; and idem, "Self-Interpreting Animals," in *Human Agency and Language: Philosophical Papers,* vol. 1 (New York: Cambridge University Press, 1985), pp. 45–76.

49. Taylor, "Understanding in Human Science," p. 31.

50. In addition, Taylor develops a weaker argument against the unity-of-science thesis. This position concedes the possibility of a predictive science of human beings under some description purged of subject-related terms, yet insists that because relations of meaning and the vocabulary of human agency form an essential part of human reality as we conceive it, attempts to eliminate them from our explanatory accounts—regardless of the predictive power of such accounts—contravene what is basic to the very notion of human action. According to Taylor, "This supposition [that our vocabulary of human action is systematically misleading] is too preposterous to be believed." See "How Is Mechanism Conceivable?" in *Human Agency and Language,* p. 169.

51. Richard Rorty, "A Reply to Dreyfus and Taylor," *Review of Metaphysics* 34 (September 1980): 46.

52. Ibid., p. 44.

53. Rorty, *Philosophy and the Mirror of Nature,* p. 354.

54. Ibid., p. 354; see also pp. 28n., 204–205, 387.

55. See especially Richard Rorty, "Introduction: Pragmatism and Philosophy," in *Consequences of Pragmatism,* pp. xliii; and idem, "Method, Social Science, and Social Hope," pp. 195–198.

56. Rorty's views on the *current* status of the human sciences are rather difficult to pin down, and at least prima facie inconsistent. Sometimes, in response to suggestions that advances in modern social science might pose

serious threats to human freedom, he maintains that the sciences of human behavior are already so far advanced that the only barriers to the Orwellian control of human beings are moral, not scientific, ones. Thus, he remarks that "the torturers and brainwashers are . . . already in as good a position to interfere with human freedom as they could wish; further scientific progress cannot improve their position." At other times, however, he offers a much more circumspect view of the matter, as when he asserts that neither hermeneuticists nor "value-free" social scientists are "very good at making . . . [accurate] predictions." See Rorty, *Philosophy and the Mirror of Nature,* p. 354; and idem, "Method, Social Science, and Social Hope," p. 196.

57. Richard Bernstein, "Philosophy and the Conversation of Mankind," in *Philosophical Profiles: Essays in a Pragmatic Mode* (Philadelphia: University of Pennsylvania Press, 1986), p. 21.

58. Chris Murphy, "Critical Notice (PMN)," *Australasian Journal of Philosophy* 59 (1981): 345.

59. Richard Rorty, "Beyond Realism and Anti-Realism," in Ludwig Nagl et al., eds., *Weiner Reihe: Themen der Philosophie,* vol. 1 (Vienna: R. Oldenbourg Verlag, 1986), pp. 103–115.

60. Rorty, *Contingency, Irony, and Solidarity,* p. 7.

61. Ibid., pp. 5–6.

62. Bas C. van Fraassen, *The Scientific Image* (Oxford: Clarendon Press, 1980).

63. Rorty, "Introduction: Pragmatism as Anti-Representationalism," p. 4.

64. Richard Rorty, "Introduction: Antirepresentationalism, Ethnocentrism, and Liberalism," in *Objectivity, Relativism, and Truth: Philosophical Papers,* vol. 1 (New York: Cambridge University Press, 1991), p. 2.

65. In addition to previous references, see Rorty's discussion of astronomy in Richard Rorty, "Just One More Species Doing Its Best," *London Review of Books,* July 25, 1991, p. 3.

66. Rorty, "Introduction: Pragmatism as Anti-Representationalism," p. 3.

67. Ibid., p. 3.

68. It might be suggested that Rorty's view is compatible with Hilary Putnam's "internal realism," a position that tries to preserve "commonsense realism" while insisting that truth and reality are internal to conceptual schemes and languages. Much of what Rorty says in *Philosophy and the Mirror of Nature,* as well as in his discussions of alternative language-games, would seem to sanction this conclusion. However, his more recent pragmatist-inspired defenses of anti-representationalism undercut even this variant of realism, implying instead that the only relevant and arbitrable questions are those about usefulness for some particular

purpose, not about ontology. For Putnam's views, see Hilary Putnam, *Meaning and the Moral Sciences* (London: Routledge and Kegan Paul, 1978), p. 125; and idem, *The Many Faces of Realism* (La Salle, IL: Open Court Publishing Company, 1987), pp. 17, 32–36. Interestingly, Putnam says in this latter work that internal realism should have been called "pragmatic realism."

69. In his discussion of Kuhn, Rorty articulates this idea by talking about the hopelessness of "providing an algorithm for theory-choice." See Rorty, *Philosophy and the Mirror of Nature*, p. 324.

70. Colin Turnbull, *The Mountain People* (New York: Simon & Schuster, 1972), p. 112. Turnbull's account of the Ik has been sharply attacked by a number of anthropologists who charge that it is hyperbolic, if not fictional. If even partly true, however, these practices, like other forms of extreme and seemingly pointless cruelty, stretch to the limit one's capacity to locate appropriate terms, categories, and analogies for describing and understanding them. For an account of the controversies provoked by Turnbull's book, see Roy Richard Grinker, *In the Arms of Africa: The Life of Colin M. Turnbull* (New York: St. Martin's Press, 2000).

71. Ian Hacking, *Representing and Intervening: Introductory Topics in the Philosophy of Natural Science* (Cambridge: Cambridge University Press, 1988), pp. 69–72.

72. As I suggest below, *whether* this is possible—and here it is worth examining Turnbull's own attempts to make sense of the Ik's behavior—cannot be determined by philosophical fiat, but only by an examination of specific cases. In scientific discourse, Hacking identifies two "linguistic correlates" of dissociative incommensurability: (1) that large numbers of statements are not even "among our candidates for truth or falsehood," and (2) that "forgotten styles of reasoning are central" to the form of thought in question. If these two conditions hold, one has a case of dissociation. See ibid., p. 71.

73. Ibid., p. 71.

74. Thomas Kuhn, "Objectivity, Value Judgment, and Theory Choice," in *The Essential Tension: Selected Studies in Scientific Tradition and Change* (Chicago: University of Chicago Press, 1977), p. 324. For a much more detailed examination of this matter, see Kuhn's classic *The Copernican Revolution: Planetary Astronomy in the Development of Western Thought* (Cambridge, MA: Harvard University Press, 1957).

75. Thomas Kuhn, *The Structure of Scientific Revolutions* (Chicago: University of Chicago Press, 1970), p. 200. As I will discuss in more detail below, the notion of "an algorithm for theory-choice" is pivotal to Rorty's narrative about incommensurability, representationalism, choice, and change in the

natural sciences. For his most complete discussion of this phrase and its relation to these issues, see Rorty, *Philosophy and the Mirror of Nature*, pp. 332–356.

76. Kuhn, *The Essential Tension*, pp. 331–332.

77. Ibid., p. 332.

78. Kuhn, *The Copernican Revolution*, p. 225.

79. Kuhn, *The Essential Tension*, p. 332. In this essay, Kuhn argues for a distinction between criteria that function as rules, on the one hand, and criteria that function as maxims, norms, or values, on the other. The former, he says, operate mechanically as algorithms and therefore *determine* choice, whereas the latter only influence it. Criteria that function as maxims, norms, or values thus permit disagreement, yet "they do specify a great deal: what each scientist must consider in reaching a decision, what he may and may not consider relevant, and what he can legitimately be required to report as the basis for the choice he made" (p. 331). Although Kuhn's language here is perhaps too subjectivistic—these "values" are more adequately understood as communally established scientific practices, or shared patterns of scientific behavior, rather than individual values—it does possess the virtue of preserving a distinction between genuine disagreement and incommensurability or inarbitrability. Conversely, Rorty's account of natural science and language-games assumes implicitly that the absence of criteria operating as rules (or algorithms) that dictate choice amounts to the absence of comparability or choice altogether. Among other things, this view has the disturbing consequence of eradicating the distinction—one that Kuhn's account, as well as my own, seeks to preserve—between legitimate disagreement and incommensurability or inarbitrability. For Kuhn's remarks, see ibid., pp. 330–332.

80. Rorty vacillates periodically between a formal and "philosophical" definition of incommensurability, one in which commensurability requires something like Kuhn's "algorithm" that dictates "rational, unanimous choice," and a pragmatic definition, where commensurability implies only particular shared understandings about what sorts of evidence and procedures might be needed to resolve some conflict. This tension is apparent in *Philosophy and the Mirror of Nature*, where he defines commensurability as follows:

> By "commensurable" I mean able to be brought under a set of rules which will tell us how rational agreement can be reached on what would settle the issue on every point where statements seem to conflict. These rules tell us how to construct an ideal situation, in which all residual disagreements will be seen to be "noncognitive" or merely verbal, or else temporary—capable of being resolved by doing something further. What matters is that there should be agreement about

what would have to be done if a resolution *were* to be achieved. In the meantime, the interlocutors can agree to differ—being satisfied of each other's rationality the while.

Notice that Rorty begins with the demand for an explicit set of rules that constitute a context-free definition of "rational agreement," one that would permit a point-by-point comparison of competing theories or vocabularies, and that could in principle resolve all epistemic conflicts. But two sentences later he loosens this definition considerably by suggesting that commensurability is merely a matter of local agreement, and that incommensurability is simply the failure of those "parties to a controversy" to "find a way of agreeing on what would settle the issue." In general, Rorty privileges the former definition, and therefore attacks the goal of commensuration on the grounds that it represents a return to traditional, epistemology-centered philosophy (see his comments immediately following the above statement). Additionally, this privileging is evident in his frequent and previously noted claims that there is never any common ground for comparing alternative language-games or vocabularies-as-wholes. After all, if Rorty's definition were based on agreement rather than the existence of an algorithm, it would (1) undercut his claims about scientific change, since clearly there are conflicts between language-games and vocabularies-as-wholes that do get settled, and from which we cannot imagine looking back (How can we today even begin to seriously advance arguments in support of Ptolemy's geocentric vocabulary? Can we really imagine recovering such a view?); and (2) be demonstrable only on a case-by-case basis, and thus could not be stated as a general principle. Finally, Rorty's privileging of the formal definition of commensurability is evinced in his discussion of Kuhn's views on the subject. Here he criticizes Kuhn for not being content to show merely that natural science has no "algorithm for choice among scientific theories"—thus implying that such a standard is the crucial one. See Rorty, *Philosophy and the Mirror of Nature,* pp. 316, 322–333.

81. Kuhn, *The Essential Tension,* p. 339.

82. Ibid.

83. In a similar vein, Dudley Shapere has argued that even in those cases where competing or successive theories contain radically different conceptual structures, there is nevertheless enough unity of meaning to permit theory comparison. See Dudley Shapere, "Meaning and Scientific Change" in Ian Hacking, ed., *Scientific Revolutions* (New York: Oxford University Press, 1985), pp. 28–59.

84. Peter Galison, *Image and Logic: A Material Culture of Microphysics* (Chicago: University of Chicago Press, 1997), p. 781, 844.

85. Ibid., pp. 783, 797–798.

86. Peter Galison, "The Trading Zone: The Coordination of Action and Belief," preprint for TECH-KNOW Workshops on Places of Knowledge, Their Technologies and Economies, UCLA Center for Cultural History of Science and Technology, Los Angeles, May 1989, p. 17. As Galison points out, the subcultures of theory and experiment satisfy both Kuhn's and Feyerabend's criteria for identifying incommensurable belief systems or theories. See also ibid., p. 15; and idem, *Image and Logic*, p. 783.
87. Ibid.
88. Kuhn, *The Structure of Scientific Revolutions*, esp. ch. 10. Also quoted in Galison, "The Trading Zone," p. 18.
89. Galison, "The Trading Zone," p. 18; and idem, *Image and Logic*, p. 838.
90. Ibid., p. 803.
91. Ibid., p. 46.
92. Ibid., pp. 46–47, 803–844.
93. Ibid., p. 803.
94. Peter Galison, "Trading Zone: Coordinating Action and Belief," in Mario Biagioli, ed., *The Science Studies Reader* (New York: Routledge, 1999), p. 146.
95. On some of the difficulties involved in locating Rorty's stance on particular controversies and transitions in the history of science, see fn. 81. In addition to the considerations adumbrated there, it should be noted that, although Rorty sometimes quibbles with Kuhnian formulations of incommensurability, and in particular with efforts to focus on "sameness of meaning" as the crucial gauge of incommensurability, there is no evidence that his standard is more conservative than Kuhn's when applied to specific cases of scientific change (although here too evaluation is difficult, because Rorty discusses almost no transitions other than the shift from Ptolemiac to Copernican astronomy—where his position is *more* radical than those of both Kuhn and Feyerabend, who either avoid or openly reject the label of incommensurability in this case—and from Aristotelian to Galilean and Newtonian physics). To the contrary, he invokes Kuhn regularly in both his claims about alternative language-games and vocabularies and in his defense of a nonrealist construal of natural science. See, for example, Rorty, *Contingency, Irony, and Solidarity*, pp. 6, 20, as well as the passages cited in fn. 81. On Kuhn and Feyerabend, see Kuhn, *The Essential Tension*, p. 332; and Paul Feyerabend, *Against Method: Outline of an Anarchistic Theory of Knowledge* (London: Verso, 1978), p. 114.
96. Galison, *Image and Logic*, pp. 810–812.
97. Ibid., p. 812.
98. Ibid.
99. Ibid.

100. Ibid.

101. In a fascinating analysis, Galison draws on recent work in anthropological linguistics to describe the development of various "pidgens" and "creoles" that "characterize the border zones between different theoretical, experimental, and engineering cultures." These pidgens and creoles enable members of different subcultures to communicate, collaborate, and "trade" information in the absence of "a full blown translation." See Galison, *Image and Logic,* pp. 48–51, 769–770, 831–837.

102. For an interesting discussion of incommensurability that reaches similar conclusions about the necessary role of disunity in the process of scientific and cognitive advance, see Mario Biagioli, "The Anthropology of Incommensurability," *Studies in the History and Philosophy of Science* 21 (1990): 207–208.

103. None of this implies that trading zones establish themselves *automatically*. In fact, as Mario Biagioli points out, there are often strategic reasons for avoiding communication. However, there are also powerful forces operating in the other direction, namely, the survival of the discipline as a whole (the broader "culture" of physics, chemistry, and so on) depends in large degree on communication and collaboration among the different subcultures that constitute it. Consequently, if the felt need for communication and collaboration is sufficiently strong—if important conflicts or issues do not simply disappear, but persist—then one would expect that trading zones would emerge *eventually*. When and how this happens is, of course, a matter for empirical investigation. See ibid., pp. 183–209.

104. Galison, *Image and Logic,* p. 816.

105. As I have noted, Rorty never questions the independent existence of entities and causal processes, only the representationalist and realist idea that there are better and worse representations of those entities and processes. See, for example, "Just One More Species Doing Its Best," p. 3. For an example of a "strong" social constructivist account of science, see Steven Woolgar, *Science: The Very Idea* (London and New York: Tavistock Publications, 1988). In general, one should avoid the temptation to view "constructivism" as a single, unified school of thought, and instead distinguish between "strong" and "weak" (or "constrained" and "unconstrained") variants of it. The former, represented by Woolgar, David Bloor, Harry Collins, Andrew Pickering, and others, argues that the theoretical frameworks and social practices that are requisite for the production of scientific knowledge—the constructional work of scientists—so thoroughly shape the processes of producing and interpreting data that the content of scientific activity—that is, the establishment, definition, and study of theoretical entities and their properties, relations, and causal

powers—has no stability across transformations of those frameworks or
practices. The latter, exemplified by writers such as Peter Galison and Ian
Hacking, agree that theoretical constructs and background practices are
necessary features of the production of all scientific knowledge, and that
"there are no original, pure, and unblemished data." See Galison, *Image
and Logic,* pp. 543–544. They reject, however, the strong constructivist
claim that the absence of such bedrock data entails that "the physics conclusions drawn from the experiment rest on a bottomless and shifting sea
of sand." ibid., p. 544. Obviously this latter position leaves room for
some version of realism, whereas the former does not. For a fuller discussion of these issues. see ibid., pp. 540–545.

106. Rorty, *Contingency, Irony, and Solidarity,* p. 6.
107. Ibid., p. 17.
108. As Rorty puts it, "To say that astrology is out of touch with reality
cannot *explain* why astrology is useless; it merely restates that fact in misleading representationalist terms." See "Introduction: Pragmatism as Anti-
Representationalism," p. 3.
109. See especially, Rorty, "Is Natural Science a Natural Kind?"; idem, "Beyond
Realism and Anti-Realism"; and idem, "Introduction: Antirepresentationalism, Ethnocentrism and Liberalism."
110. Rorty, "Introduction: Pragmatism as Anti-Representationalism," p. 3; and
idem, "Introduction: Antirepresentationalism, Ethnocentrism, and Liberalism," p. 5.
111. Rorty, "Beyond Realism and Anti-Realism," p. 111.
112. For an interesting discussion of a case where ontological agnosticism contributed to progress in natural science, see the discussion of electrody-
namics in Richard Miller, *Fact and Method: Explanation, Confirmation
and Reality in the Natural and Social Sciences* (Princeton, NJ: Princeton
University Press, 1987), pp. 448–453.
113. William Riker, *The Theory of Political Coalitions* (New Haven, CT: Yale
University Press, 1962), p. 3.
114. David Easton, *The Political System: An Inquiry into the State of Political
Science* (New York: Knopf, 1953), p. 58. See also idem, *A Framework for
Political Analysis* (Englewood Cliffs, NJ: Prentice-Hall, 1965), p. 8.
115. On current disciplinary understandings of "political methodology," and in
particular on the urge to conflate questions of method with questions of
formal and quantitative methods, see both the journal of the same name,
Political Methodology, and the descriptions of the field found in the "Calls
for Papers" for the annual meetings of the American Political Science Association. On journals that reflect scientistic aspirations, see not only the
above-mentioned *Political Methodology* but also *Political Behavior,* as well
as articles on politics contained in interdisciplinary journals such as the

American Behavioral Scientist. On the institutionalization of efforts to transform political science into a "hard" science by rooting it in a science of biology, note the existence of professional organizations such as the Association for Politics and the Life Sciences, as well as the association's journal, *Politics and the Life Sciences.* For a small sampling of work in this domain, see Douglas Madson, "A Biochemical Property Related to Power-Seeking in Humans," *American Political Science Review* 79 (1985): 448–457; Roger Masters, *The Nature of Politics* (New Haven, CT: Yale University Press, 1989); idem, "Evolutionary Biology and Political Theory," *American Political Science Review* 84 (1990): 195–210; Elliott White, ed., *Sociobiology and Human Politics* (Lexington, MA: Lexington Books, 1981); and James Q. Wilson and Richard D. Herrnstein, *Crime and Human Nature* (New York: Simon & Schuster, 1985). For an excellent discussion of how images of natural scientific method continue to shape the practice of political science, see John G. Gunnell, *Between Philosophy and Politics: The Alienation of Political Theory* (Amherst: University of Massachusetts Press, 1986), ch. 2.

116. Rorty himself makes arguments of this kind when he says, for instance, that "there are lots of things you want to do with human beings for which descriptions of them in nonevaluative, 'inhuman' terms are very useful; there are others (e.g., thinking of them as your fellow citizens) in which such descriptions are not"; or when he states that "predictions will do 'policymaking' no good if they are not phrased in the terms in which the policy can be formulated." See "Method, Social Science, and Social Hope," pp. 196–197.

117. Rorty, *Contingency, Irony, and Solidarity,* p. 3.

2. In Defense of Disunity

1. Richard Rorty, "Nineteenth-Century Idealism and Twentieth-Century Textualism," in *Consequences of Pragmatism* (Minneapolis: University of Minnesota Press, 1982), p. 153.

2. Richard Rorty, "Science as Solidarity," in *Objectivity, Relativism, and Truth: Philosophical Papers,* vol. 1 (New York: Cambridge University Press, 1991), p. 40.

3. Ibid.

4. Richard Rorty, "Method, Social Science, and Social Hope," in *Consequences of Pragmatism,* p. 195.

5. Carl Hempel, "The Function of General Laws in History," in *Aspects of Scientific Explanation, and Other Essays in the Philosophy of Science* (New York: Free Press, 1965), p. 234.

6. Ibid., pp. 234, 239.

7. Charles Taylor, "Interpretation and the Sciences of Man," in *Philosophy and the Human Sciences: Philosophical Papers,* vol. 2 (New York: Cambridge University Press, 1985), p. 56.
8. Ibid.
9. Ibid.
10. Hubert Dreyfus, "Why Studies of Human Capacities Modeled on Ideal Natural Science Can Never Achieve Their Goal," in J. Margolis, M. Krausz, and R. M. Burian, eds., *Rationality, Relativism, and the Human Sciences* (Dordrecht, Boston, and Lancaster, UK: Martinus Nijhoff Publishers, 1986), p. 16.
11. Rorty, "Method, Social Science, and Social Hope," p. 196.
12. Ibid.
13. Ibid., p. 197.
14. Ibid.
15. Ibid.
16. Ibid.
17. Ibid.
18. Richard Rorty, "Method and Morality," in Norma Haan, Robert N. Bellah, Paul Rabinow, and William M. Sullivan, eds., *Social Science as Moral Inquiry* (New York: Columbia University Press, 1983), p. 163.
19. Rorty, "Method, Social Science, and Social Hope," p. 198.
20. Ibid.
21. Ibid.
22. Ibid.
23. Richard Rorty, *Contingency, Irony, and Solidarity* (New York: Cambridge University Press, 1989), p. 35.
24. Ibid., p. 43.
25. Rorty, "Method, Social Science, and Social Hope," p. 198.
26. Ibid.
27. Ibid., p. 198–199.
28. Ibid., p. 198.
29. Ibid., p. 199.
30. Ibid.
31. Ibid., p. 200.
32. Winch has similarly been accused of committing this "reproductive fallacy." See Richard Rudner, *Philosophy of Social Science* (Englewood Cliffs, NJ: Prentice-Hall, 1966), p. 83. Although these charges are not entirely unwarranted, they derive in part from the practice of isolating specific passages in his work while neglecting others. As Hanna Pitkin has suggested, Winch is perhaps best understood not simply as holding the radically subjectivistic and "patently false" view of privileged access but as

equivocating between some variant of this view and a more tempered position, one whereby "actions can be explained in terms unintelligible to the actors, but only if those terms are translatable into the actors' own." See Hanna Fenichel Pitkin, *Wittgenstein and Justice* (Berkeley and Los Angeles: University of California Press, 1972), pp. 251, 254.

33. Richard Rorty, *Philosophy and the Mirror of Nature* (Princeton, NJ: Princeton University Press, 1979), p. 349.

34. Ibid.

35. Ibid.

36. Rorty, "Method and Morality," pp. 169–170.

37. Ibid., p. 170.

38. Rorty, "Pragmatism, Relativism, Irrationalism," in *Consequences of Pragmatism*, p. 164; idem, "Solidarity or Objectivity?" in *Objectivity, Relativism, and Truth*, p. 27; and idem, "Science as Solidarity," pp. 41–42.

39. Although Rorty invariably suggests that a Galilean vocabulary is more useful for prediction and control, whereas a hermeneutical one is more appropriate for moral deliberation, he refuses to rule out the possibility that these diverse aims might someday be synthesized under a single vocabulary "that contains no hint of a descriptive-normative distinction." See Rorty, "Method and Morality," p. 164.

40. At first glance this claim may seem surprising, given both the general neglect of Rorty's work by mainstream social and political scientists and the tendency to associate his thought, fairly or not, with postmodernism and promiscuous relativism. If, however, one attends to the rhetoric, structure, and substance of Rorty's views rather than received interpretations of them, it becomes evident that they closely resemble widely held views within political science and parallel strikingly those of highly influential research programs in the social sciences. Indeed, views curiously symmetrical to Rorty's are among the dominant ones within political science today. To see this connection, one need only recall Rorty's recommendation that social scientists adopt a stance of benign neglect toward ontological questions and turn instead to issues about the "usefulness" of one or another vocabulary for advancing particular sorts of inquiries. This view, which often scandalizes Rorty's foundationalist critics, is echoed not only by some methodological pluralists but also by many proponents of "positive" economics and rational choice theory. Like Rorty, rational actor theorists aim to undercut realist and ontological criticisms—namely, of the "unrealistic" assumptions of microeconomic theories—on the ground that such critiques are irrelevant to any appraisal of their theories and hypotheses. Thus, the Nobel laureate Milton Friedman, whose essay, "The Methodology of Positive Economics," in *Essays in Positive Economics*

(Chicago: University of Chicago Press, 1953), pp. 3–43, is one of the most widely cited and reprinted in all of social science—Joseph Agassi, for instance, terms it "the official view of the profession" in "Testability and Tautology in Economics," *Philosophy of the Social Sciences* 1 (1971): 62— joins Rorty in defending a strict instrumentalist account of theory choice, one in which the appropriate criterion of choice is "usefulness" or, in Friedman's words, what "works." It is true, of course, that Friedman and Rorty diverge on the question of how usefulness "for the purpose in hand" should be defined. See Friedman, "The Methodology of Positive Economics," p. 15. For Friedman, it is to be defined exclusively in terms of prediction, whereas Rorty invariably distinguishes between two distinct purposes at hand, only one of which embraces prediction as the criterion of adequacy. This, moreover, points to a further difference between Friedman and Rorty. Insofar as the former links his account of theory-choice exclusively to the criterion of prediction, he embraces what might be called "classical" naturalism, whereas Rorty wants to elide what he sees as the metaphysical impulses implicit in this position and to supplant it with a "new," postmetaphysical, pragmatic naturalism. Yet considering the numerous criticisms of Friedman's predictivist criterion, as well as recent work in the history and philosophy of science, most of which is deeply critical of the metaphysics of classical naturalism, one might argue that Rorty's pragmatic naturalism not only shares much in common with familiar defenses of microeconomic and rational choice theory but also is a more philosophically sound defense of them. In this regard, it is perhaps significant that two proponents of rational choice theory, Jack Knight and James Johnson, have recently sketched similarities between pragmatic inquiry and rational choice analysis and have sought to identify specific contributions of rational choice theory within the framework of a pragmatist, though only partially Rortian, conception of inquiry. See "Inquiry into Democracy: What Might a Pragmatist Make of Rational Choice Theories?" *American Journal of Political Science* 43 (April 1999): 566–589. For two of the most effective critical assessments of Friedman's methodology, see Alexander Rosenberg, "Friedman's 'Methodology' for Economics: A Critical Examination," *Philosophy of the Social Sciences* 2 (March 1972): 15– 29, reprinted in *Microeconomic Laws* (Pittsburgh: University of Pittsburgh Press, 1976), pp. 155–170, and *Economics—Mathematical Politics or Science of Diminishing Returns?* (Chicago: University of Chicago Press, 1992), pp. 56–62. For an analysis of Friedman's work that argues that there are important similarities between his conception of positive economics and Dewey's pragmatism, see Abraham Hirsch and Neil de March, *Milton Friedman: Economics in Theory and Practice* (Ann Arbor: University of

Michigan Press, 1990). Interestingly, the authors quote private correspondence between Friedman and Donald McCloskey in which the former claims that "my own methodological views are almost identical with those of John Dewey" (p. 6). Unfortunately, a full discussion of these complex relationships is beyond the scope of this book.

Apart from these perhaps surprising family resemblances, there are other reasons for thinking that Rorty's views are not nearly as marginal, or radical in their consequences, as they may initially appear. To fully grasp this point, it is important to distinguish between Rorty's redescription of the *erklären/verstehen* controversy, which is indeed philosophically radical, and his own understanding of the consequences of embracing and deploying that redescription, which is mildly reformist. Regarding the latter, consider that although Rorty's postmetaphysical naturalism is designed to weaken current hierarchies of prestige among and within natural science, social science, and the humanities, it also provides a rationale for leaving in place one of the most fundamental oppositions in all of social and political science, namely, the opposition between "normative" and "empirical" or "predictive" theories. As I have remarked above, Rorty's redescription of disputes between Galilean and hermeneutical conceptions of social science casts this quarrel as a fruitless and anachronistic metaphysical debate that could be circumvented by simply conceding that some theories are useful for the purposes of prediction and control, whereas others are useful for informing questions of moral identity, moral conduct, and what "we" should do. See Rorty, "Method, Social Science, and Social Hope"; and idem, *Achieving Our Country: Leftist Thought in Twentieth-Century America* (Cambridge, MA: Harvard University Press, 1998), pp. 13, 19. If adopted, this redescription might not only have the effect of entrenching, albeit postmetaphysically, long-standing theoretical and disciplinary divisions but also might encourage normative theorists to neglect empirical investigations, while shielding empirical inquiries from examination of the normative commitments that dictate and influence them.

41. Rorty, "Method, Social Science, and Social Hope," p. 200.
42. Ibid.
43. Taylor, "Rationality," in *Philosophy and the Human Sciences,* p. 140. Emphasis added.
44. Taylor, "Interpretation and the Sciences of Man," pp. 15–57.
45. Ibid., pp. 32–34.
46. Ibid., p. 32.
47. Ibid., p. 33.
48. Rorty, "Method, Social Science, and Social Hope," p. 200.

49. Taylor, "Interpretation and the Sciences of Man," p. 36.
50. Ibid.
51. Charles Taylor, *Sources of the Self: The Making of the Modern Identity* (Cambridge, MA: Harvard University Press, 1989), p. 15.
52. As Taylor explains, "The meanings and norms implicit in these practices are not just in the minds of the actors but are out there in the practices themselves." See "Interpretation and the Sciences of Man," p. 36.
53. Charles Taylor, "How Is Mechanism Conceivable?" in *Human Agency and Language: Philosophical Papers,* vol. 1 (New York: Cambridge University Press, 1985), p. 178. See also Taylor's strong protest against this interpretation of his work in "The Hermeneutics of Conflict," in James Tully, ed., *Meaning and Context: Quentin Skinner and His Critics* (Princeton, NJ: Princeton University Press, 1988), p. 228.
54. In the essay "Freedom, Cruelty, and Truth: Rorty versus Orwell," James Conant underscores the stakes of these issues. In an analysis of Rorty's interpretation of George Orwell, Conant argues not only that Rorty systematically misreads Orwell—in Conant's words, "There is a fairly literal sense in which Rorty is *unable to read* Orwell"—but also that this misreading conceals from him the way in which Orwell's views constitute an attack on Rorty's conviction that there is, in Conant's phrase, a *"congenial fit"* between, on the one hand, his views regarding language, truth, and anti-representationalism and, on the other hand, democratic politics. Although Rorty would surely be unmoved by the former criticism, the latter, by his own lights, cannot be so easily ignored. Indeed, Conant argues, one unintended consequence of Rorty's misreading is a failure to see how his own philosophical views may seriously jeopardize things he cares, and thinks we should care, deeply about, that is, liberalism and democracy. See "Freedom, Cruelty, and Truth: Rorty versus Orwell," in Robert B. Brandom, ed., *Rorty and His Critics* (Oxford: Blackwell, 2000), pp. 269, 316n3.

  Similar problems emerge in Rorty's most recent book, *Achieving Our Country*. In this work he argues that the academic Left's growing infatuation with "High Theory" and cultural politics has reduced it, and the American Left generally, to the role of mere spectator on the national political stage. Simultaneously demoralized by its own sense of national self-disgust, paralyzed by its own theoretical analyses, and preoccupied with nebulous and unattainable movements rather than finite campaigns to improve the economic condition of the poor and vulnerable, the Left has made itself politically moribund. Further discussion of the complicated political issues raised by Rorty in this book requires a lengthier treatment than can be given here. Suffice to say, for our purposes, Rorty's neglect of the contextual and interpretive considerations that Taylor emphasizes often works to the detriment of his own best aims and arguments. By omitting any analysis of the institutional factors and pressures that shape and constrain academic production, as well as the complex relationships between the academy, the national media, and other political forces, Rorty elides central questions about the relationship between institutional structures and politics.

55. Ibid., p. 36.
56. Joseph Rouse, "Interpretation in Natural and Human Science," in David R. Hiley, James F. Bohman, and Richard Shusterman, eds., *The Interpretive Turn: Philosophy, Science, Culture* (Ithaca, NY, and London: Cornell University Press, 1991), p. 46.
57. Taylor, "Interpretation and the Sciences of Man," pp. 36–40, 46–52.
58. Rorty, "Method, Social Science, and Social Hope," p. 202.
59. Rorty, *Philosophy and the Mirror of Nature*, p. 349.
60. By reliable I mean not only stable but also conceptually sound. A good example of conceptual confusion is offered by Hubert Dreyfus, who recalls the "Stanford psychologist who announced that . . . the concept of talkativeness is unfounded. If you count the number of words uttered by an individual in a day, the would-be theorist explained, you find that there is no significant difference in the quantity of words uttered by so-called normal and by so-called talkative people." As Dreyfus rightly replies, "It never occurred to this objective psychologist that what makes a person count as talkative may be the meaning of what is said and the situation in which it is said. Talkative people presumably say little of importance and say it during other people's lectures, at funerals, and so forth. The general agreement among participants in the everyday world as to who is talkative is no illusion. Rather the sort of data collection appropriate to the natural sciences . . . is simply inappropriate to the study of human beings' understandings of themselves and other human beings." See Hubert Dreyfus, "Defending the Difference: The *Geistes/Naturwissenschaften* Distinction Revisited," in Academie der Wissenschaften zu Berlin (Jürgen Mittelstraβ, Director), *Einheit der Wissenschaften* (Berlin and New York: Walter de Gruyter, 1991), pp. 476–477.
61. Thomas Kuhn has offered a vivid account of the epistemic and pragmatic indispensability of internal understanding. He describes how, approaching Aristotle's writings on physical theory from the standpoint of Newtonian mechanics, he initially saw Aristotle as "not only ignorant of mechanics, but a dreadfully bad physical scientist as well. About motion, in particular, his writings seemed to me full of egregious errors, both of logic and of observation." Noting that he "could easily believe that Aristotle had

stumbled, but not that, on entering physics, he had totally collapsed," he finally asked whether "perhaps his words had not always meant to him and his contemporaries quite what they meant to me and mine." Upon doing so, Kuhn found that "suddenly the fragments in my head sorted themselves out in a new way, and fell into place together. My jaw dropped, for all at once Aristotle seemed a very good physicist indeed, but of a sort I'd never dreamed possible. Now I could understand why he had said what he'd said, and what his authority had been. Statements that had previously seemed egregious mistakes, now seemed at worst near misses within a powerful and generally successful tradition." See Thomas Kuhn, "What Are Scientific Revolutions?" in L. Krüger, L. J. Daston, and Michael Heidelberger, eds., *The Probabilistic Revolution*, vol. 1 of *Ideas in History* (Cambridge, MA: MIT Press, 1987), p. 9.

62. Kenneth Waltz, *Theory of International Politics* (Reading, MA: Addison-Wesley, 1979), p. 69.

63. David Easton, *A Systems Analysis of Political Life* (Chicago: University of Chicago Press, 1979), p. 14.

64. Rorty, "Method, Social Science, and Social Hope," p. 197.

65. See, for example, David Easton's 1969 presidential address to the American Political Science Association. In acknowledging the failures of behavioral political science, Easton offered a list of "continuing conditions entirely unpredicted by political science, behavioral or otherwise," and proposed that "the search for an answer as to how we as political scientists have proved so disappointingly ineffectual in anticipating the world of the 1960's has contributed significantly to the birth of the post-behavioral revolution" (p. 1053). David Easton, "The New Revolution in Political Science," *American Political Science Review* 63 (December 1969): 1051–1061. For a more recent and general statement, see William H. Riker, "Political Science and Rational Choice," in James E. Alt and Kenneth A. Shepsle, eds., *Perspectives on Positive Political Economy* (New York: Cambridge University Press, 1990), p. 163. In this essay, Riker suggests "that the rate of successful theorizing seems to have picked up in the last two decades" (p. 180), but he provides no empirical support for his assertion. By contrast, Alasdair MacIntyre offers a much less sanguine assessment of the predictive achievements of contemporary social science. Citing studies done during the mid-1970s, he writes that "no economist predicted 'stagflation' before it occurred, the writings of monetary theorists have signally failed to predict the rates of inflation correctly (Levy, 1975) and D.J.C. Smyth and J.C.K. Ash have shown that the forecasts produced on the basis of the most sophisticated economic theory for OECD since 1967 have produced less successful predictions than would

have been arrived at by using the commonsense, or as they say, naive methods of forecasting rates of growth by taking the average rate of growth for the last ten years as a guide or [sic] rates of inflation by assuming that the next six months will resemble the last six months." See Alasdair MacIntyre, "The Character of Generalizations in Social Science and their Lack of Predictive Power," in *After Virtue: A Study in Moral Theory* (Notre Dame, IN: University of Notre Dame Press, 1981), p. 85. These findings are further supported by more recent assessments. A seven-year study (1987–1994) of economic forecasts among 34 United Kingdom forecasting groups—"including all the most quoted forecasters"—revealed both that economic forecasters "all say more or less the same thing at the same time" and that their forecasts "are almost always wrong." As John Kay writes, "It is clear from the analysis that there is a consensus forecast, which most forecasters cluster around—to such a degree that it is barely worth distinguishing between one estimate and another. Yet the consensus forecast failed to predict any of the most important developments in the economy over the past seven years—the strength and resilience of the 1980s consumer spending boom, the depth and persistence of the 1990s recession, or the dramatic and continuing decline in inflation since 1991." See John Kay, "Cracks in the Crystal Ball," *Financial Times,* September 29, 1995, p. 19. In political science, Donald Green and Ian Shapiro have offered an equally critical assessment of work in rational choice theory. Noting that "a syndrome of fundamental and recurring" methodological errors makes any rigorous evaluation of current rational choice theories highly problematical in the first place, the authors observe that "in those rare cases when appropriate tests are appropriately conducted the results seldom sustain any novel or counterintuitive propositions." This book has been highly controversial. Yet among its critics, few have attacked Green and Shapiro's claims about the lack of predictive success and adequate testing of rational choice theories. Instead they have focused on other features of the argument. See Donald Green and Ian Shapiro, *Pathologies of Rational Choice Theory: A Critique of Applications in Political Science* (New Haven, CT: Yale University Press, 1994), pp. 33, 34n1. For a collection of primarily critical essays on Green and Shapiro's book, see Jeffrey Friedman, ed., *The Rational Choice Controversy: Economic Models of Politics Reconsidered* (New Haven, CT: Yale University Press, 1996). Also, see Ronald Rogowski's review of three eminent writers' (Robert Gilpin, Douglass C. North, and Mancur Olson) efforts to apply rational choice theories to the study of international politics and economic growth. Especially in his analysis of Olson's work, Rogowski offers a lengthy list of cases that contravene directly the predictions generated by Olson's deductive model, calling the model "calamitously wrong in many of its implications." See Rogowski, "Structure, Growth, and Power: Three Rationalist Accounts," *International Organization* 37 (Autumn 1983): 713. For a discussion of some of these issues in the field of economics, see Tony Lawson, *Economics and Reality* (New York: Routledge, 1997); and Alexander Rosenberg, *Economics,* ch. 3. Discussing economists' failure to locate universal laws that yield accurate predictions of economic behavior, Lawson remarks that "the most telling point against this econometrics project is the *ex posteriori* result that significant invariant event regularities, whether of a probabilistic kind or otherwise, have yet to be uncovered in economics, despite the resources continually allocated to their pursuit . . . Econometricians continually puzzle over why it is that 'estimated relationships' repeatedly 'break down,' usually as soon as new observations become available" (p. 70). In the final analysis, perhaps the best way to articulate the distinction between the social and natural sciences is simply to note that even in the most "advanced" social sciences, for example, economics, there remain heated debates about whether any notable improvements in predictive success have occurred during the past century—as Alexander Rosenburg notes, "It is easy to pile up Nobel laureates on either side of the question of whether economics has met the test of empirical progress" (p. 98). By contrast, there is no parallel dispute among physicists about whether work in thermodynamics is predictively more successful than it was a century ago.

66. John Stuart Mill, "Inaugural Address Delivered to the University of St. Andrews," in *The Collected Works of John Stuart Mill,* vol. 21 (Toronto: University of Toronto Press, 1984), p. 241.

67. Although Mill is often viewed as a proto-positivist, see, for example, his vocal criticisms of Jeremy Bentham's massive "one-sidedness," especially as evidenced in Bentham's understanding of the universal "Springs of Action" in human beings. Also note the remarks in his methodological writings on the severe limitations of a pure science of political economy, and particularly the consequences of failing to include "ethological considerations" (*Logic,* p. 94), that is, considerations about the formation and transformation of character, in the axioms of political economy. In these respects Mill's assessment of universalizing theory in social science closely resembles the positions developed by hermeneuticists like Taylor and Dreyfus. John Stuart Mill, "Bentham," in *Essays on Politics and Culture* (Garden City, NY: Anchor Books, 1963), pp. 77–120; and idem, *The Logic of the Moral Sciences* (La Salle, IL: Open Court, 1988).

68. Rorty frequently suggests that Taylor's position is based on either epistemologically foundationalist or a priori ontological assumptions, or both.

For example, in "A Reply to Dreyfus and Taylor," Rorty criticizes Taylor's distinction between subject-related and subject-independent properties as a return to foundationalist notions of correspondence to absolute reality. See "A Reply to Dreyfus and Taylor," *Review of Metaphysics* 34 (September 1980): 39–46. Similarly, in "Method, Social Science, and Social Hope," he concludes his attack against Taylor's views on internal understanding with the claim that "I have been arguing . . . that the notion that we know *a priori* that nature and man are distinct sorts of objects is a mistake. It is a confusion between ontology and morals." See Rorty, "Method, Social Science, and Social Hope," p. 203. Presumably this censure of a priori ontology is directed at Taylor—if not hermeneutical social science generally—since Taylor's ideas are the principal source of criticism in the section in question. In neither discussion does Rorty consider the possibility that epistemic principles and ontological distinctions might be adduced a posteriori, as conclusions reached from an examination of the histories of scientific inquiries.

69. Rorty, *Philosophy and the Mirror of Nature,* p. 6.
70. There is, I would argue, little if any historical evidence to suggest that internal understanding should be a precondition of inquiries in the physical sciences, and it may or may not be appropriate in various branches of biology, depending upon the branch in question.
71. I borrow the phrase "fortunes of inquiry" from Nicholas Jardine's interesting book of the same name. Although confined exclusively to a discussion of truth and justification in natural science, Jardine's attempt to exploit history "as a source of standards against which to test the reliabilities of methods of theory assessment" is in many ways similar to the position outlined above. See Nicholas Jardine, *The Fortunes of Inquiry* (New York: Oxford University Press, 1986), p. 108.
72. Rorty, "Method, Social Science, and Social Hope," p. 199.
73. Thomas Kuhn, *The Structure of Scientific Revolutions,* p. 111.
74. Charles Taylor, "Understanding in Human Science," *Review of Metaphysics* 34 (September 1980): 3–23; Hubert Dreyfus, "Defending the Difference"; and idem, *Being-in-the-World: A Commentary on Heidegger's* Being and Time, *Division 1* (Cambridge, MA: MIT Press, 1991), pp. 198–208. A similar, though much less fully developed, argument is made by Anthony Giddens. See Anthony Giddens, *Profiles and Critiques in Social Theory* (Berkeley and Los Angeles: University of California Press, 1982), pp. 7–8, 11–14.
75. Dreyfus, *Being-in-the-World,* p. 265. For Taylor's views, see his discussion of the inseparability of language and social reality in "Interpretation and the Sciences of Man," p. 33.

76. Peter Galison, *How Experiments End* (Chicago: University of Chicago Press, 1987), p. 254.
77. Dreyfus, *Being-in-the-World,* p. 203.
78. As Galison notes, physical scientists place a premium on the "stability of the phenomena"—the continual appearance of an effect in spite of changes in various features of experimental conditions, for example, samples, apparatus, data analysis, test substance, or temperature—when determining the existence or nonexistence of some effect or theoretical entity. When effects remain despite numerous variations in conditions, even longstanding and deeply held beliefs must sometimes be revised, as in the case of physicist David Cline, whose brief confession in a memorandum— "At present I do not know how to make this effect go away"—signaled the end of "his career-long commitment to the nonexistence of neutral currents." See Galison, *How Experiments End,* p. 258, 260.
79. Sandra Harding, "After the Neutrality Ideal: Science, Politics, and 'Strong Objectivity,' " *Social Research* 59 (Fall 1992): 574–575.
80. Richard Ashcraft, "Liberal Political Theory and Working-Class Radicalism in Nineteenth Century England," *Political Theory* 21 (May 1993): 266.
81. For detailed accounts of problems besetting research in artificial intelligence, see Hubert L. Dreyfus, *What Computers Still Can't Do: A Critique of Artificial Reason* (Cambridge, MA: MIT Press, 1992); and Hubert L. Dreyfus and Stuart E. Dreyfus, with Tom Athanasiou, *Mind over Machine: The Power of Human Intuition and Expertise in the Era of the Computer* (New York: Free Press, 1988).
82. Green and Shapiro, *Pathologies of Rational Choice Theory.*
83. See fn. 65.
84. Richard Rorty, "A Reply to Dreyfus and Taylor," p. 46.
85. Ibid., p. 41.
86. Ibid., p. 46.
87. Rorty never says explicitly that the repeated failures of a particular methodological strategy or research program are an inadequate basis for doubting the possibility of its future success. Nevertheless, it is difficult, if not impossible, to understand how else Rorty can concede, on the one hand, that "the last fifty years of research in the social sciences have not notably increased our predictive abilities," yet still maintain, on the other hand, that a methodological strategy like Skinnerian behaviorism probably "*does* work," or that "physicalism is probably right in saying that we shall someday be able, 'in principle,' to predict every movement of a person's body (including those of his larynx and his writing hand) by reference to the microstructures within his body." See Rorty, "Method, Social Science, and Social Hope," p. 197; idem, "Rorty, Taylor, and Dreyfus: A Discussion," p. 50; and idem, *Philosophy and the Mirror of Nature,* p. 354. In the

case of Skinner's behaviorism in particular, Rorty's optimism is explicable only if one also attributes to him a deeply skeptical attitude regarding the possibility of using history as a ground for adjudicating philosophical and methodological disputes. As I have argued throughout, however, this stance is entirely incongruent with Rorty's pragmatist commitments.

88. For a brief description of what this "stabilization" involves, see fn. 78.

89. Of course, I am not implying that the abandonment of alchemy is scientifically unwarranted but simply that the sort of strong, in principle proof that Rorty demands of his opponents is rarely if ever the basis upon which theories or research programs are abandoned. If it were, alchemists would still be competing with chemists for research grants.

90. See, for example, John Dewey, *Experience and Nature* (New York: Dover Publications, 1958); idem, "The Subject Matter of Metaphysical Inquiry," in Richard Bernstein, ed., *John Dewey on Experience, Nature and Freedom* (New York: The Liberal Arts Press, 1960); William James, "What Pragmatism Means," in *Pragmatism: A New Name for Some Old Ways of Thinking* (New York: Longmans, Green, and Co., 1907), pp. 45, 51–53; Charles Sanders , "The Approach to Metaphysics," in *Philosophical Writings of Peirce* (New York: Dover Publications, 1955); and John E. Smith, "Pragmatism and Metaphysics," in *Purpose and Thought* (Chicago: University of Chicago Press, 1978), pp. 119–158.

91. Rorty, "Method, Social Science, and Social Hope," p. 198.

92. Rorty, "Method and Morality," p. 164.

93. Rorty, "Method, Social Science, and Social Hope," p. 198.

94. See Dreyfus, *Being-in-the-World*, p. 264.

95. Taylor, *Sources of the Self*, pp. 68–69.

96. Taylor, "How Is Mechanism Conceivable?" p. 178.

3. The Politics of Redescription

1. Richard Rorty, "Method, Social Science, and Social Hope," in *Consequences of Pragmatism* (Minneapolis: University of Minnesota, 1983), pp. 203–204.

2. Ibid., p. 204.

3. Ibid., p. 203.

4. Richard Rorty, *Contingency, Irony, and Solidarity* (New York: Cambridge University Press, 1989), p. xvi.

5. Richard Rorty, "The Contingency of Community," *London Review of Books,* July 24, 1986, 13.

6. Richard Rorty, "Pragmatism, Relativism, and Irrationalism," in *Consequences of Pragmatism*, p. 166.

7. Rorty describes his desired polity as both "postmodernist bourgeois liber-

alism" and, more recently, as a "liberal utopia." See Richard Rorty, "Post-modernist Bougeois Liberalism," in *Objectivity, Relativism and Truth: Philosophical Papers*, vol. 1 (New York: Cambridge University Press, 1991), pp. 197–202. In a subsequent essay, however, he expresses regret about his use of the term "postmodern" (which, following Jean-François Lyotard, he defines as "distrust of metanarratives"), primarily because it is now "so over-used that it is causing more trouble than it is worth." See Richard Rorty, *Essays on Heidegger and Others: Philosophical Papers*, vol. 1 (New York: Cambridge University Press, 1991), p. 1.

8. Rorty, *Contingency, Irony, and Solidarity*, p. 9.

9. Ibid., p. 8.

10. Ibid., p. 9.

11. Ibid.

12. Ibid.

13. Ibid., p. 99.

14. Richard Rorty, "Truth and Freedom: A Reply to Thomas McCarthy," *Critical Inquiry* 16 (Spring 1990): 638–639.

15. Rorty, *Contingency, Irony, and Solidarity*, p. 9.

16. Ibid., p. 44.

17. John McCumber, "Reconnecting Rorty: The Situation of Discourse in Richard Rorty's *Contingency, Irony, and Solidarity*," *Diacritics* 20 (Summer 1990): 8.

18. See chapter 1. It should be noted that if, pace Rorty, it is not always impossible to argue for or against the introduction of a new vocabulary, then the crucial question becomes one of deciding when, in the course of an ongoing exchange, it may become unreasonable or absurd to continue arguing. As Jacques Bouveresse has rightly stated: "Il n'est pas contestable qu'il arrive en philosophie, comme d'ailleurs également dans n'importe quelle autre entreprise intellectuelle, un moment où il est déraisonnable et absurd de vouloir continuer à argumenter ... Mais la difficulté est, comme toujours, de reconnaître le point où l'on doit s'arrêter." [It is undeniable that a moment comes in philosophy, as in any other intellectual undertaking, when it is unreasonable and absurd to want to continue arguing ... The problem, as always, is recognizing exactly when one should call a halt to it.] See Jacques Bouveresse, "Sur Quelques conséquences indésirables du pragmatisme," in Jean-Pierre Cometti, ed., *Lire Rorty* (Combas, France: Editions de l'éclat, 1992), p. 47.

19. Rorty, *Contingency, Irony, and Solidarity*, p. xiv.

20. Ibid., p. xv.

21. Ibid., pp. xiii, xv.

22. Ibid., p. xiii.

23. Ibid., pp. xiii, xvi.

24. Ibid., p. xiii.

25. Harold Bloom, *The Anxiety of Influence* (Oxford: Oxford University Press, 1973), p. 80, quoted in Rorty, *Contingency, Irony, and Solidarity*, p. 46.

26. Ibid., p. xiv.

27. Ibid.

28. Ibid.

29. Ibid., xv. On Shklar's definition of "liberal," see Judith Shklar, *Ordinary Vices* (Cambridge, MA: Harvard University Press, 1984), p. 8; and idem, "The Liberalism of Fear," in Nancy L. Rosenblum, ed., *Liberalism and the Moral Life* (Cambridge, MA: Harvard University Press, 1989), pp. 21–38.

30. Rorty, *Contingency, Irony, and Solidarity*, p. xv.

31. Ibid.

32. Ibid.

33. Ibid.

34. Ibid.

35. Ibid.

36. Ibid.

37. Ibid.

38. Ibid., p. 68.

39. Ibid., pp. xiv–xv, 68.

40. Ibid., p. 73; and idem, "Heidegger, Contingency, and Pragmatism," in Hubert L. Dreyfus and Harrison Hall, eds., *Heidegger: A Critical Reader* (Cambridge, MA: Basil Blackwell, 1992), p. 216.

41. Rorty, *Contingency, Irony, and Solidarity*, p. 68.

42. Ibid., pp. xv, 68.

43. Ibid., p. 61.

44. Ibid., p. 73.

45. Ibid., pp. 83, 120.

46. Ibid., p. 65.

47. Ibid., p. 68.

48. Ibid., pp. 65, 83.

49. Ibid., p. xiv.

50. Ibid.

51. Ibid., pp. 59–60.

52. Ibid., pp. 197; and idem, "Solidarity or Objectivity?" and "Cosmopolitanism without Emancipation: A Response to Jean-François Lyotard," in *Objectivity, Relativism, and Truth: Philosophical Papers,* vol. 1 (New York: Cambridge University Press, 1991), pp. 29, 212.

53. Rorty, "Solidarity or Objectivity?" p. 29; and idem, *Contingency, Irony, and Solidarity*, p. xv. As Rorty explains, humiliation is a particularly dev-

astating form of nonphysical cruelty, one that is tied closely to the ironist's preoccupation with redescription. Here, too, Rorty borrows from
Judith Shklar's discussion in *Ordinary Vices*. For his account of humiliation and especially his reasons for thinking that irony and redescription
must be kept private (in part because they have the potential of humili-
ating others), see *Contingency, Irony, and Solidarity,* p. 90.

54. Ibid., p. 68; and idem, "Solidarity or Objectivity?" p. 29.

55. Although Rorty himself never appeals to such arguments, nonfoundation-
alists have also sought to answer the charge of relativism by pointing out
that today many of the tenets of liberal democracy are almost universally
accepted as principles of political legitimation, even if they are violated
frequently in practice. This, they claim, makes the charge of radical relativism moot as a practical issue. See, for example, Charles Taylor, "The Politics
of Recognition," in Amy Gutmann, ed., *Multiculturalism and "The Politics
of Recognition"* (Princeton, NJ: Princeton University Press, 1992), p. 38.

56. Rorty, "The Priority of Democracy to Philosophy," in *Objectivity, Relativism, and Truth,* pp. 175–196.

57. Rorty, *Contingency, Irony, and Solidarity,* pp. 63.

58. Ibid.; idem, "Truth and Freedom," pp. 633–643; and idem, "De Man and
the Cultural Left," in *Essays on Heidegger and Others: Philosophical Papers,*
vol. 2 (New York: Cambridge University Press, 1991), pp. 129–139.

59. Rorty, *Contingency, Irony, and Solidarity,* pp. 66–67.

60. Jürgen Habermas, *The Philosophical Discourse of Modernity: Twelve Lectures* (Cambridge, MA: MIT Press, 1987).

61. Rorty, *Contingency, Irony, and Solidarity,* p. 65.

62. Ibid., p. 84.

63. Ibid., p. xiv.

64. Richard Rorty, "The Contingency of Selfhood," *London Review of Books,*
May 8, 1986, 12.

65. Richard Rorty, "On Ethnocentrism: A Reply to Clifford Geertz," in *Objectivity, Relativism, and Truth,* p. 210.

66. Rorty, "Pragmatism, Relativism, and Irrationalism," p. 166.

67. See Ronald Dworkin, *Taking Rights Seriously* (Cambridge, MA: Harvard
University Press, 1977); Robert Nozick, *Anarchy, State and Utopia* (New
York: Basic Books, 1974); and John Rawls, *A Theory of Justice* (Cam-
bridge, MA: Harvard University Press, 1971).

68. Richard Rorty, "Posties," *London Review of Books,* September 3, 1987, 11.

69. The first three chapters of *Contingency, Irony, and Solidarity* are entitled
"The Contingency of Language," "The Contingency of Selfhood," and
"The Contingency of a Liberal Community."

70. Hubert L. Dreyfus and Harrison Hall, "Introduction," in Dreyfus and Hall, eds., *Heidegger*, p. 18.
71. Rorty, *Contingency, Irony, and Solidarity*, p. xiii.
72. Ibid., p. 37.
73. Rorty, "Method, Social Science, and Social Hope," p. 193.
74. Rorty, *Contingency, Irony, and Solidarity*, p. 68.
75. Ibid., p. 17; and idem, "The Contingency of Selfhood," p. 12.
76. Rorty, *Contingency, Irony, and Solidarity*, pp. 23–26, 141. For an even more explicit link between contingency and "chance events," see the "possible world" sketch of Heidegger's life in Richard Rorty, "Diary," *London Review of Books*, February 8, 1990, 21.
77. This dichotomy between voluntarism and determinism has a corollary in Rorty's attempt to defend (1) the physicalist idea that "one day we will be able, 'in principle,' to predict every movement of a person's body . . . by reference to the microstructures within his body": and (2) the existentialist commitment to the idea of radical freedom. See Rorty, *Philosophy and the Mirror of Nature*, pp. 354, 376–379. Interestingly, Rorty's effort to preserve both freedom and determinism by claiming that these are different descriptions of a single event or bodily movement is remarkably similar to Kant's attempt to reconcile moral freedom and natural necessity by viewing them as both true under different aspects of reality. See Roy Bhaskar, "Rorty, Realism and the Idea of Freedom," in *Reclaiming Reality* (London: Verso. 1989), pp. 164–165.
78. For a relevant discussion of this issue from the standpoint of art history, see Rozsica Parker and Griselda Pollock, *Old Mistresses* (New York: Pantheon Books, 1981). In political theory, writers such as Carole Pateman have appropriately asked, "Why is Paine's reply to Burke's polemic against the French revolution studied, but not Mary Wollstonecraft's earlier reply? Why have the early socialists, who were concerned with relations between the sexes and new modes of household organization, been dismissed as 'utopian'? Why, more generally, are none of the feminist theorists' writings from the seventeenth century onward discussed, when the most minor male figures are given their due?" See Carole Pateman, "Introduction: The Theoretical Subversiveness of Feminism," in Carole Pateman and Elizabeth Gross, eds., *Feminist Challenges: Social and Political Theory* (Boston: Northeastern University Press, 1986), pp. 2–3.
79. Rorty, *Contingency, Irony, and Solidarity*, p. 42.
80. Ibid., p. 141.
81. Ibid.
82. Ibid.

83. Ibid., p. xvi; and idem, "Habermas and Lyotard on Postmodernity," in *Essays on Heidegger and Others,* p. 175.
84. Rorty, *Contingency, Irony, and Solidarity,* p. 191.
85. Rorty, *Philosophy and the Mirror of Nature,* p. 362n7.
86. Bhaskar, "Rorty, Realism and the Idea of Freedom," pp. 176–177.
87. Pierre Bourdieu, *Homo Academicus,* trans. Peter Collier (Stanford, CA: Stanford University Press, 1988), pp. 194–225.
88. Ibid., p. 197.
89. Ibid., pp. 198–199.
90. Ibid., p. 199.
91. Ibid.
92. Ibid., p. 200.
93. Ibid., pp. 207–208.
94. Ibid., p. 205.
95. Ibid.
96. Ibid., pp. 207–208.
97. Ibid., p. 206; see also p. 208.
98. Carole Pateman, "Feminist Critiques of the Public/Private Dichotomy, in *The Disorder of Women,* pp. 121–122.
99. Ibid., p. 120.
100. It should be emphasized that Rorty's intent is not to preserve patriarchical or sexist social relations or modes of behavior. On his account, cruelty is by definition a public affair, whether it occurs in the home, workplace, or anywhere else. Nevertheless, his failure to examine the ways in which the public/private distinction has operated historically as a bulwark against not only sexual (and hence civic) equality but also against gays, lesbians, and other minorities raises the question of whether his version of the distinction (which in its formal features is almost identical to the classical distinction) is the most useful tool for advancing the ideals of liberal democracy. Given the historical record, it would seem incumbent on Rorty to show how his construal of the distinction would operate in practice to reduce sexual and gender inequalities and to explain why this construal would be more useful than alternative versions proposed by recent feminist writers. One model for such an undertaking might be Will Kymlicka's recent attempts to apply an interpretation of liberalism to current conflicts regarding the rights of minority cultures. See Will Kymlicka, *Liberalism, Community, and Culture* (New York: Oxford University Press, 1991); and idem, *Multicultural Citizenship* (Oxford: Oxford University Press, 1995).
101. Pateman, "Feminist Critiques of the Public/Private Dichotomy," p. 131.
102. Ibid., p. 136.

103. Rorty, *Contingency, Irony, and Solidarity,* p. 182.

104. In his writings, Cornel West makes similar criticisms of Rorty. West contends, for example, that Rorty embraces "an aestheticized version of historicism in which the provisional and variable are celebrated at the expense of highlighting who gains, loses or bears what costs"; and that he offers " 'thin' historical narratives which rarely dip into the complex world of politics and culture." See Cornel West, *Keeping Faith: Philosophy and Race in America* (New York: Routledge, 1993), pp. 23, 127; and idem, *Prophetic Thought in Postmodern Times* (Monroe, ME: Common Courage, 1993), p. 177. Although the preceding analysis strongly underscores these remarks, I would perhaps differ with West on two issues. First, West implies that Rorty's errors are chiefly (contingent) ones of omission, that is, that he neglects thick, politically engaged historical description and fails to articulate the social and political implications of specific social practices and institutional arrangements (for hints of stronger objections, see *Prophetic Thought in Postmodern Times,* p. 177). I argue, however, that Rorty not only fails to engage in detailed social and historical analysis but also lacks the conceptual resources for such analysis. At a minimum, such an undertaking would require, if not a theory in Rorty's sense, at least a satisfactory (or prudent and plausible) account or (re)description of power and power relations, something Rorty (like the classical pragmatists) not only omits but also cannot develop without revising considerably his understanding of contingency. Secondly, West, like other critics, accents the celebratory aspects of Rorty's narrative, criticizing it for its inattentiveness to the everyday miseries and cruelties that punctuate the lives of so many Americans. I would maintain, however, that such criticisms are incomplete, for they overlook the fact that Rorty's narratives contain both an effusive optimism *and* a deep and often fatalistic pessimism. Indeed, I take it that any adequate assessment of Rorty's political thought must account for the disconcerting shifts between these binary poles.

105. Rorty, *Contingency, Irony, and Solidarity,* p. xiv.

106. The following sketch of ideological conflict is indebted to Jeff King's discussion. See Jeff King, "Ontology, Reflexivity & Policy: Toward a Post-Cartesian Politics," paper presented at the annual meeting of the New York State Political Science Association, Albany, 1990, pp. 8–9. Although King's analysis accents the "the problem of the mutual intrusion or colonization of the public and private spheres" (p. 7), my concern below is to show the practical limitations of Rorty's redescriptive efforts, as well as his conceptual inability to deal with concrete social problems.

107. Rorty, *Contingency, Irony, and Solidarity,* pp. 60, 67.

108. Ibid., pp. 63, 66–67.

109. For some recent efforts to discuss difficult and controversial issues of educational reform, see Amy Gutmann, *Democratic Education* (Princeton, NJ: Princeton University Press, 1987; and Benjamin Barber, *An Aristocracy of Everyone: The Politics of Education and the Future of America* (New York: Ballantine Books, 1992).

110. Richard Rorty, "Education, Socialization, and Individuation," *Liberal Education* 75 (September–October 1989): 2–9.

111. Ibid., p. 7; and idem, "Truth and Freedom," p. 642. The claim that current social ills in the United States are due primarily to an increasingly greedy middle class is a recurring theme in Rorty's work over the past two decades. See Rorty, "Truth and Freedom," p. 642; and idem, "Introduction: Antirepresentationalism, Ethnocentrism, and Liberalism," in *Objectivity, Relativism, and Truth*, p. 15n29.

112. Rorty, "Truth and Freedom," p. 642.

113. Ibid., p. 643.

4. Reclaiming the Language of Emancipation

1. See Roy Bhaskar, *A Realist Theory of Science*, 2nd ed. (London: Harvester Wheatsheaf, 1978), *The Possibility of Naturalism: A Philosophical Critique of the Contemporary Human Sciences* (Brighton, UK: Harvester Press, 1979), *Scientific Realism and Human Emancipation* (London: Verso, 1986), *Reclaiming Reality: A Critical Introduction to Contemporary Philosophy* (London: Verso, 1989), *Philosophy and the Idea of Freedom* (Oxford: Basil Blackwell, 1991), *Dialectic: The Pulse of Freedom* (New York: Verso, 1993), and *Plato, Etc.: The Problems of Philosophy and Their Resolution* (New York: Verso, 1994); Richard Boyd, "The Current Status of Scientific Realism," in Jarrett Leplin, ed., *Scientific Realism* (Berkeley and Los Angeles: University of California Press, 1984), pp. 41–82, and "What Realism Implies and What It Does Not," *Dialectica* 43 (1983): 5–29; Rom Harré, *Social Being: A Theory for Social Psychology* (Oxford: Basil Blackwell, 1979) and *Varieties of Realism* (Oxford: Basil Blackwell, 1986); Jeffrey Isaac, *Power and Marxist Theory: A Realist View* (Ithaca, NY: Cornell University Press, 1987), "Realism and Social Scientific Theory: A Comment on Porpora," *Journal for the Theory of Social Behavior* 13 (1983): 301–308, "After Empiricism: The Realist Alternative," in Terence Ball, ed., *Idioms of Inquiry: Critique and Renewal in Political Science* (Albany: State University of New York Press, 1987), pp. 187–205, "Beyond the Three Faces of Power: A Realist Critique," *Polity* 20 (Fall 1987): 4–31, and "Realism and Reality: Some Realistic Reconsiderations," *Journal for the Theory of Social*

Behavior 20 (March 1990): 1–31; Ian Shapiro, *Political Criticism* (Berkeley and Los Angeles: University of California Press, 1990) and "Realism in the Study of the History of Ideas," *History of Political Thought* 3 (Winter 1982): 535–578; Ian Shapiro and Alexander Wendt, "The Difference that Realism Makes: Social Science and the Politics of Consent," *Politics and Society* 20 (June 1992): 197–223; Alexander Wendt and Ian Shapiro, "The Misunderstood Promise of Realist Social Theory," in Kristen Renwick Monroe, ed., *Contemporary Empirical Political Theory* (Berkeley and Los Angeles: University of California Press, 1997), pp. 166–187; Alexander Wendt, *Social Theory of International Politics* (New York: Cambridge University Press, 1999); Tony Lawson, *Economics and Reality* (London: Routledge, 1997); Margaret Archer, *Realist Social Theory: The Morphogenetic Approach* (New York: Cambridge University Press, 1995); Derek Layder, *The Realist Image in Social Science* (London: MacMillan Press, 1990); William Outhwaite, *New Philosophies of Social Science: Realism, Hermeneutics, and Critical Theory* (New York: St. Martin's Press, 1987) and "Realism, Naturalism and Social Behavior," *Journal for the Theory of Social Behavior* 20 (December 1990): 365–377; Andrew Sayer, *Method in Social Science: A Realist Approach*, 2nd ed. (London: Routledge, 1992) and *Realism and Social Science* (Thousand Oaks, CA: Sage Publications, 2000).

2. Bhaskar, *The Possibility of Naturalism*, p. 1.

3. Bhaskar, *Scientific Realism and Human Emancipation* (London: Verso, 1986), p. 5. As I shall discuss below, this minimal definition does not in itself distinguish realism from Rorty's nonrealist pragmatism. Rorty states explicitly that there is a world "out there," that "it is not our creation," and that "most things in space and time are the effects of causes which do not include human mental states" (pp. 4–5). What ultimately differentiates Rorty from his realist opponents is not a set of beliefs about the existence of objects and causal processes operating independently of scientists and their activities, but disparate understandings of the relationship between language, truth, and that independent reality. See *Contingency, Irony, and Solidarity* (New York: Cambridge University Press, 1989), as well as my discussion of these issues in chapter 3.

4. I should emphasize that the foregoing distinction between Winch's view of social scientific inquiry and those of contemporary realists applies primarily to his formulations in the first edition (1958) of *The Idea of a Social Science and Its Relation to Philosophy*. In his "Preface to the Second Edition" of this volume, Winch reconsiders questions of causality and articulates a position that is very close to that of present-day realists.

5. Michael Walzer, "Liberalism and the Art of Separation," *Political Theory* 12 (August 1984): 315–330.

6. Bhaskar, *The Possibility of Naturalism*, p. 57.

7. Bhaskar alludes to something like this argument when, in an analysis of Paul Feyerabend's defense of methodological anarchism, he states briefly that "without realism, fallibilism collapses into dadaism." See *Scientific Realism and Human Emancipation*, p. 61.

8. Shapiro, *Political Criticism*, pp. 295–296.

9. In this respect, the discussion up to this point requires qualification. As a way of accenting some of the most common and distinctive features of realist social theory, I have often spoken of it as if it were a tightly unified school of thought. As I shall argue below, these affinities do not preclude the existence of significant differences of opinion regarding the central presuppositions and implications of social scientific realism.

10. Although an exhaustive discussion of the salient similarities and differences between these positions is beyond the purview of this chapter, it may nonetheless be useful to indicate very broadly what some of these terms denote. "Internal realism," a term coined by Hilary Putnam, is also variously labeled "realism with a small 'r'" and, more recently, "pragmatic realism." These expressions designate a species of realism that aims to vindicate both commonsense realism—that is, our ordinary beliefs about the existence of "middle-sized material objects" like tables and chairs, and their properties, for example, solidity—and scientific knowledge, yet eschews the scientistic commitments often associated with metaphysical realism, particularly those forms of metaphysical realism that endorse the idea of "convergence" on a single privileged description, language, or account of reality, that is, the idea of "One True Image" or a "God's Eye View" of the world. See *Reason, Truth and History* (New York: Cambridge University Press, 1981), p. 49. Importantly, Putnam holds that internal realism is compatible with conceptual relativity, but irreconcilable with the notion of a "thing-in-itself" (and the corollary idea of "intrinsic properties"), an idea that, he avers, "makes no sense." See *The Many Faces of Realism* (La Salle, IL: Open Court, 1987), pp. 3, 17, 36. As a result, claims about reality, Putnam submits, are always and unavoidably internal to particular descriptions, languages, conceptual schemes, or systems of representation. Hence his simultaneously Kantian and Hegelian claim that "the mind and the world jointly make up the mind and the world." See *Reason, Truth and History*, p. xi. By contrast, "external realism" stipulates that "the world (or, alternatively, reality or the universe) exists independently of our representations of it." See John Searle, *The Construction of Social Reality* (New York: Free Press, 1995), p. 150. According to Searle, this more robust conception of realism is also entirely consistent with the thesis of conceptual relativity. Consequently, Searle at-

tacks what he sees as Putnam's misplaced effort to carve out a position, internal realism, "halfway between external realism . . . and out-and-out antirealism" (ibid., p. 164; see also pp. 174–175). "Metaphysical realism," the stronger versions of which are often negative contrast terms for softer variants of realism, is defined in a number of subtly distinct ways. Sometimes it is conceived in a manner that largely mirrors Searle's definition of external realism as (1) the view that reality exists independently of our experience or knowledge of it. Sometimes it is conceived more broadly as (2) entailing a belief in the existence of "real objects" that "have properties and enter into relations independently of the concepts with which we understand them or of the language with which we describe them." See Panayot Butchvarov, "Metaphysical Realism," in Robert Audi, ed., *The Cambridge Dictionary of Philosophy* (New York: Cambridge University Press, 1995), p. 488. At still other times, it is held to encompass more highly controversial theses such as the idea that (3) there is one and only "one true account of . . . independent reality" (See Hubert L. Dreyfus, "Heidegger's Hermeneutic Realism," in David Hiley, James Bohman, and Richard Schusterman, eds., *The Interpretive Turn: Philosophy, Science, Culture* [Ithaca, NY: Cornell University Press, 1991], p. 28), one best conceptual scheme, theory, or vocabulary for describing reality, or, in Putnam's famous phrase, a single "God's Eye point of view." A fourth conception of realism, and the view that will comprise the principal subject matter of this chapter, is equally slippery. "Scientific realism"—a term that is often closely affiliated with "transcendental realism," "critical realism," and "relational realism" (Margaret R. Somers, " 'We're No Angels': Realism, Rational Choice, and Relationality in Social Science," *American Journal of Sociology* 104 [November 1998]: 722–784)—is defined by Roy Bhaskar as "the theory that the objects of scientific inquiry exist and act, for the most part, quite independently of scientists and their activity." See *Scientific Realism and Human Emancipation*, p. 5. Although this minimal definition does not logically entail specific commitments about the existence of *unobservable* entities, the overwhelming majority of scientific realists do in fact hold such commitments (in addition to Bhaskar, see Somers, " 'We're No Angels,' " and Wendt and Shapiro, "The Misunderstood Promise of Realist Social Theory") and some, such as Michael Devitt, construe scientific realism in such a way as to make claims about the existence of unobservables internal to it. See *Realism and Truth* (Princeton, NJ: Princeton University Press, 1984), p. 104; and Richard R. Boyd, "The Current Status of Scientific Realism." Similarly, there is much disagreement about whether scientific realism entails or is identical with some version of the correspondence theory of truth. Searle, for instance, denies any intrinsic link between realism and correspondence theory, arguing that scientific realism is a theory of ontology rather than a semantic theory and thus is "strictly speaking . . . consistent with any theory of truth." See *The Construction of Social Reality*, p. 154. By contrast, Brian Fay, qualifying himself ever so slightly, maintains that "a realist ontology . . . almost requires a correspondence conception of truth." See Fay, "*Critical* Realism?" *Journal of the Theory of Social Behavior* 20 (March 1990): 34. Others, such as Joseph Rouse and Michael Devitt, are less hesitant and posit categorically that realism presupposes or implies a correspondence theory of truth. See Joseph Rouse, *Knowledge and Power: Toward a Political Philosophy of Natural Science* (Ithaca, NY: Cornell University Press, 1987), p. 127; and Michael Devitt, *Realism and Truth,* ch. 7. Finally, it should be added that all of these species of realism differ substantially from the meanings attached to realism and neorealism in the fields of international relations and political theory, and in ordinary political discourse. For useful if partial inventories of several "characteristically realist theses," see James Conant's essay, "Freedom, Cruelty and Truth: Rorty versus Orwell," in Robert B. Brandom, ed., *Rorty and His Critics* (Oxford: Blackwell, 2000), pp. 268–342; and Jarrett Leplin, "Introduction," in Leplin, ed., *Scientific Realism,* pp. 1–2.

11. Ibid., p. 1.

12. Even here, of course, there is considerably more heterogeneity than these singular terms might appear to suggest. See, for example, Hilary Putnam, "Three Kinds of Scientific Realism," *The Philosophical Quarterly* 32 (July 1982): 195–200.

13. Wendt and Shapiro, "The Misunderstood Promise of Realist Social Theory," p. 179. Wendt and Shapiro are not alone in their assessment. Jeffrey Isaac also claims that "Bhaskar's *A Realist Theory of Science* (1975) and *The Possibility of Naturalism* (1979) are, arguably, the two central works of scientific realism," a judgment that in turn accords with Ruth Lane's characterization of *A Realist Theory of Science* as a "now classic exposition." Michael Sprinker, in a review essay, underscores these appraisals, while adding that Bhaskar's more recent collection of essays, *Reclaiming Reality,* "contains, among other riches, perhaps the finest brief historical and methodological assessment in English of the major issues of Marxist philosophy." In another review essay, Peter Baehr asserts that "critical realism is an immensely intelligent and challenging development in the philosophy of social science" and that "the major stimulus to realist thinking since 1975 has been due to the books, articles and lectures of Roy Bhaskar." Finally, Craig Calhoun, remarking on debates about realism in sociology, maintains that Bhaskar "is the philosophical realist

who has probably had the most influential engagement with sociology." See Isaac, "Realism and Reality: Some Realistic Reconsiderations," p. 14; Ruth Lane, "Positivism, Scientific Realism and Political Science: Recent Developments in the Philosophy of Science," *Journal of Theoretical Politics* 8 (July 1996): 366; Michael Sprinker, "The Royal Road: Marxism and the Philosophy of Science," *New Left Review* 191 (January–February 1992): 123; Peter Baehr, "Review Article: Critical Realism, Cautionary Realism," *The Sociological Review* 38 (November 1990): 765, 770; and Craig Calhoun, "Explanation in Historical Sociology: Narrative, General Theory, and Historically Specific Theory," *American Journal of Sociology* 104 (November 1998): 847.

14. Andrew Collier, *Critical Realism: An Introduction to Roy Bhaskar's Philosophy* (London and New York: Verso, 1994), p. ix.

15. Bhaskar, *Reclaiming Reality*, p. vii.

16. Bhaskar, *Plato Etc.*, p. 16.

17. Bhaskar, *A Realist Theory of Science*, p. 24.

18. Ibid.

19. In a trivial sense, of course, the standards of evaluation and comparison of competing explanations, theories, research programs, and the like must remain local. Because philosophers have neither the power nor any special legal or institutional authority to impose epistemic criteria on those working in particular sciences, the prevailing criteria and standards within scientific communities will be the ones accepted by the members of those communities or by specific dominant groups within them. Bhaskar does want to insist, however, that philosophical analysis of scientific practices, norms, and concepts can at times show them to be incoherent or inappropriate, and therefore unscientific or even ideological. Importantly, the validity of these arguments and conclusions does not rest wholly on their acceptance by members of the scientific community in question. Holding otherwise would entail that the criterion of epistemic or explanatory adequacy within a particular discipline or relevant community is nothing more than a matter of consensus among that discipline's or community's members at any given time. Although Bhaskar tends to assume rather than show that this view cannot be coherently sustained, there are certainly some good reasons for being wary of it. Apart from the well-known epistemological objections to this stance, it might be noted that it is also historically and politically suspect. It has been well documented, for instance, that appeals to local authority on the part of scientific and other specialized or "relevant" communities have often constituted the principal justification for excluding not just philosophers but also the public from their deliberations. These exclusions, moreover, have often

impeded rather than advanced the quest for knowledge and under-
standing. For a recent study of such a struggle, see Steven Epstein, *Impure
Science: AIDS, Activism, and the Politics of Knowledge* (Berkeley and Los
Angeles: University of California Press, 1996).

20. Bhaskar traces this approach to philosophy, which bears strong resemblances to contemporary hermeneutical approaches, to Aristotle's "apor-
etic method" and what is more commonly called immanent critique. See
Plato Etc., p. 8.

21. Bhaskar's conception of philosophy and the philosophy of science is often
quite difficult to pin down, due to his rather elastic characterizations of
them. On the one hand, his official position, stated in *Reclaiming Reality*
and elsewhere, is that "philosophy distinguishes itself from science by its
method, and more generally by the kinds of considerations and arguments
it deploys, which are transcendental in Kant's sense" (p. 14). On the other
hand, Bhaskar's metaphorical images of philosophy as underlaborer and
midwife suggest a more variegated, if also less precise, understanding of
the philosophical enterprise. This latter conception, for instance, might
include what is sometimes called *articulation*, that is, the activity of
making explicit meanings that are implicit in some practice or concept,
and at times appears also to incorporate a "*Socratic/Nietzschean*" dimension. On this broader construal, one might also consider AIDS activists'
demands for accelerating clinical trials, expediting the approval of new
drugs, and enlarging access to new treatments as "philosophical" (as well
as political) critiques of existing medical and scientific practice. On
Bhaskar's conception of philosophy and the philosophy of science, see *A
Realist Theory of Science*, pp. 21–24, 259–262; "Realism in the Natural Sciences," in *Reclaiming Reality*, pp. 14–15; *Scientific Realism and Human
Emancipation*, pp. 10–23; *The Possibility of Naturalism*, pp. 5–11; and
Plato, Etc., pp. 214–215. For an excellent discussion of the epistemological
and political issues raised by the interactions between activist groups and
biomedical institutions, and of the ways in which these interactions
changed the attitudes of researchers and activists, see Epstein, *Impure Science*.

22. Bhaskar, *Reclaiming Reality*, p. 24.

23. Ibid., pp. vii, 24, 182, 208n32. Bhaskar's tendency to favor the image of
underlaborer over that of the midwife may appear to signal a shift from a
more feminine conception of the philosophical enterprise to one that is
more gender-neutral. This interpretation is persuasive, however, only if
one first accepts the assumption that the category of labor is gender neutral. Seen historically and politically, this is at best contestable.

24. John Locke, *An Essay Concerning Human Understanding* (London: Oxford
University Press, 1934), p. 7.

25. Bhaskar, *Reclaiming Reality*, p. vii.
26. Ibid., p. 2.
27. Ibid.
28. Immanuel Kant, *Critique of Pure Reason,* trans. by Norman Kemp-Smith (New York: St. Martin's Press, 1961), p. 135 (A 105).
29. It goes without saying that Kant's arguments have not escaped challenge. My objective, however, is not to establish the validity of Kant's views but rather to illustrate the mode of argument he employs and the source of its appeal to a variety of thinkers, Bhaskar included.
30. Peter Galison, *How Experiments End* (Chicago and London: University of Chicago Press, 1987), p. 8. This claim has also been made more broadly about the dominant currents in the philosophy of science. As Ian Hacking has asserted, "Philosophers of science constantly discuss theories and representations of reality, but say almost nothing about experiment, technology, or the use of knowledge to alter the world." See Ian Hacking, *Representing and Intervening: Introductory Topics in the Philosophy of Natural Science* (New York: Cambridge University Press, 1983), p. 149.
31. As I have indicated, Bhaskar is interested in deriving ontological conclusions from a transcendental analysis of the activity of experiment. It is unfortunate, however, that he neglects the important work of "experimental realists" such as Ian Hacking and Galison. At a minimum, engagement with this scholarship would buttress his own transcendental arguments, providing a detailed, on-the-ground, empirical defense of realism to complement his own highly abstract transcendental approach. Moreover, given the well-known tendency of transcendental arguments to intensify rather than foreclose debate—as Charles Taylor has aptly remarked, they paradoxically "articulate a grasp of the point of our activity which we cannot but have, and their formulations aspire to self-evidence; and yet they must articulate what is most difficult for us to articulate, and hence are open to endless debate" (p. 33)—it would seem philosophically and pragmatically wise to proceed from both ends of the problem. See Charles Taylor, "The Validity of Transcendental Arguments," in *Philosophical Arguments* (Cambridge, MA: Harvard University Press, 1995), pp. 20–33. A practice-based account of realism, one that supplied sociological and historical depth and provided something like a microfoundation for his transcendental arguments, would help counter the weaknesses endemic to Bhaskar's philosophical approach. Indeed, I would argue that Bhaskar's failure to avail himself of these resources has helped fuel charges that his putatively more "modest" conception of philosophy remains committed—despite protestations to the contrary—to an outdated foundationalist view of "philosophy as the 'Queen of the Sciences.'" See R. Albury, G. Payne, and W. Suchting, "Naturalism and the

Human Sciences," *Economy and Society* 10 (August 1981): 370. Perhaps one of the reasons for Bhaskar's failure to mine these resources is his animosity toward all forms of pragmatism, which he views as insufficiently committed to the realist ontology he advocates. Having conceived of pragmatism as necessarily anti-realist, he cannot help but overlook the ways in which realist commitments in science are established in and through scientific inquiry itself.

32. Bhaskar, *The Possibility of Naturalism,* p. 11.
33. Bhaskar, *A Realist Theory of Science,* p. 21. Emphasis in original.
34. Ibid., p. 17; and idem, *The Possibility of Naturalism,* p. 14.
35. Bhaskar, *A Realist Theory of Science,* p. 21.
36. Ibid., p. 31.
37. Norwood Russell Hanson, *Patterns of Discovery: An Inquiry into the Conceptual Foundations of Science* (New York: Cambridge University Press, 1965), p. 182.
38. Ibid., p. 4.
39. Bhaskar, *A Realist Theory of Science,* p. 33.
40. Ibid.
41. Bhaskar, "Realism in the Natural Sciences," in *Reclaiming Reality,* pp. 15–16; and idem, *The Possibility of Naturalism,* p. 12.
42. Bhaskar, "Realism in the Natural Sciences," p. 15.
43. Bhaskar, *A Realist Theory of Science,* p. 261.
44. Baskar, *Plato, Etc.,* p. 259.
45. In holding that experimental activity presupposes or "must assume" the endurance and operation of causal laws even in open systems, it should again be emphasized that Bhaskar is not making a psychological claim about what experimental scientists must necessarily believe. Rather, he is making a transcendental one about what the world must be like in order for the practice of experimentation to be intelligible. Bhaskar maintains that in the absence of presuppositions regarding what he calls the "transfactual activity of laws," the diverse practices of experimentation would be incoherent.
46. Collier, *Critical Realism,* p. 36.
47. Bhaskar, *A Realist Theory of Science,* p. 51.
48. There are in fact two distinct variants of the empiricism Bhaskar attacks. One is the empiricism of Bishop Berkeley, who, by making perception the criterion of existence, reduces reality to the realm of the empirical. Although this view may on the face of it appear deeply misconceived, it is not without its champions in the social sciences. Nelson Polsby, for instance, articulates a position virtually indistinguishable from Berkeley's when he proclaims, "My idea of a theory . . . is that it exists primarily for the purpose of facilitating the storage of information about objects of em-

pirical inquiry, and for producing knowledge . . . about a world that has some existence independent and apart from the language in which scholars palaver." See *Community Power and Political Theory,* 2nd ed. (New Haven, CT: Yale University Press, 1980), p. 233, quoted in Isaac, *Power and Marxist Theory,* p. 46. The other and more common variant assumes a two-tiered account of reality, one that includes in its ontology events as well as experiences.

49. Bhaskar, *Plato, Etc.,* p. 259. Bhaskar believes that this ontological flattening of reality, which he labels "empirical realism," is characteristic not only of empiricism, but also of idealism and hermeneutics. All three schools, he asserts, reject the realist commitment to ontological depth, and thus are incapable of sustaining a convincing, or even intelligible, account of science. In a later section I will challenge some of these remarks.

50. Bhaskar, *A Realist Theory of Science,* p. 14.

51. Bhaskar, *The Possibility of Naturalism,* p. 24.

52. Bhaskar, *A Realist Theory of Science,* p. 14.

53. Ibid., p. 111.

54. On these issues, see Peter Manicas, *A History and Philosophy of the Social Sciences* (New York: Blackwell, 1987), pp. 15–20.

55. Bhaskar, *Dialectic,* p. 397.

56. For an interesting discussion of another of Polanyi's examples, see Ian Shapiro, *Political Criticism,* pp. 239–242. It should be added that, although Polanyi offers perhaps the most fully developed account of the doctrine of emergence, the doctrine itself is not a new one. Émile Durkheim, who is often cited as the originator of this notion in the social sciences, articulated an interestingly similar account at the end of the nineteenth century. See "Individual and Collective Representations," in *Sociology and Philosophy,* trans. D. F. Pocock (New York: Free Press, 1974), pp. 1–34.

57. Michael Polanyi, *The Tacit Dimension* (Garden City, NY: Anchor Books, 1967), p. 35.

58. Ibid., p. 36. In his discussion of emergence, Bhaskar refers not only to "dual control," but also to "multiple control." For Bhaskar's discussions of emergence, see *A Realist Theory of Science,* pp. 109ff; idem, *The Possibility of Naturalism,* pp. 125–126; idem, *Scientific Realism and Human Emancipation,* pp. 104–113; and idem, *Plato Etc.,* p. 75.

59. Bhaskar, "Scientific Explanation and Human Emancipation," in *Reclaiming Reality,* p. 114.

60. Ibid.

61. Ibid., p. 183.

62. Bhaskar, "Feyerabend and Bachelard: Two Philosophies of Science," in *Reclaiming Reality,* p. 40.

63. Bhaskar, *A Realist Theory of Science,* p. 17.

64. Ibid, p. 21.
65. See, for example, Robert Dahl, "The Behavioral Approach in Political Science: Epitaph for a Monument to a Successful Protest," *American Political Science Review* 55 (December 1961): 764.
66. Bhaskar, *The Possibility of Naturalism*, p. 15; see also idem, *Scientific Realism and Human Emancipation*, p. 61.
67. Bhaskar, *The Possibility of Naturalism*, p. 15.
68. Karl Marx, *Capital: A Critique of Political Economy*, vol. 3 (New York: International Publishers, 1967), p. 817.
69. Bhaskar, *The Possibility of Naturalism*, pp. 17, 24. See also Bhaskar, "On the Possibility of Social Scientific Knowledge and the Limits of Naturalism," in *Reclaiming Reality*, p. 69; and idem, "Realism in the Natural Sciences," p. 20.
70. Bhaskar, *The Possibility of Naturalism*, p. 203. Emphasis in original.
71. Ibid., pp. 57, 205.
72. Ibid., pp. 48–49.
73. For a series of interesting criticisms of Bhaskar's formulations, see Ted Benton, "Realism and Social Science: Some Comments on Roy Bhaskar's 'The Possibility of Naturalism,' " in Margaret Archer et al., *Critical Realism*, pp. 304–307; and Andrew Collier, *Critical Realism*, pp. 244–248. For an effort to qualify and partially reconstruct these same formulations, see William Outhwaite, *New Philosophies of Social Science: Realism, Hermeneutics and Critical Theory* (New York: St. Martin's Press, 1987), pp. 53–55.
74. This, of course, is not to say that the relationship between language and human reality is one of identity, such that language is fully constitutive of human reality. Rather, we should conceive of the relationship as one of mutual dependence.
75. Roy Bhaskar, "General Introduction," in Margaret Archer et al., eds., *Critical Realism*, p. xvii.
76. The above characterization of this relationship as "circular," as well as the subsequent remarks about the significance of this circularity, are mine, not Bhaskar's. They are, however, important, if underappreciated, consequences of the relational limit on naturalism.
77. Roy Bhaskar, "General Introduction," p. xvii; see also idem, *The Possibility of Naturalism*, p. 60. Although stressing this causal interdependency, Bhaskar also emphasizes the importance of distinguishing it from what he calls "existential intransitivity." This latter term, which refers to the irreducibility of the existence of an object to the processes through which it is produced, is intended to limit ontological relativism by separating the process of production of an object from its ontological status once it is produced. Ibid.

78. Bhaskar, *The Possibility of Naturalism*, p. 60.

79. Bhaskar, "Scientific Explanation and Human Emancipation," in *Reclaiming Reality*, p. 104.

80. Contrary to Bhaskar's claims, it is not at all clear that *all* social objects and concepts are necessarily value impregnated in the sense that they defy description in neutral terms. Economics, for instance, does describe some phenomena in terms of "neutral" social laws. However, if the social sciences are understood pragmatically as sciences of practical action, as this study presumes, then the question becomes: how important are any such neutral definitions or laws likely to be in deliberating about proposals for social or political reform? Even if one could do what has yet to be done, namely, articulate neutral definitions of concepts such as equality, democracy, community, risk, culture, and the like, would they prove at all adequate for their purpose? And even if one thinks they would, would *that* answer be neutral?

81. For a discussion of the ways in which earlier disputes about the nature of political inquiry were structured around "a powerful and widely held consensus on a distinction between facts and values" (p. 516), see Richard Ashcraft, "One Step Backward, Two Steps Forward: Reflections upon Contemporary Political Theory," in John S. Nelson, ed., *What Should Political Theory Be Now?* (Albany: State University of New York Press, 1983), pp. 515–548.

82. Bhaskar, "Scientific Explanation and Human Emancipation," in *Reclaiming Reality*, p. 101; see also idem, *Scientific Realism and Human Emancipation*, p. 184. In Bhaskar's nomenclature, S refers to an "object(s)" (that explains, or is the source of, the false belief P), for example, a psychological mechanism, social structure, or system of social relations, and CP stands for *ceteris paribus*.

83. Although I will have more to say about the limitations of Bhaskar's philosophical abstractions in the following section, his ritual invocation of the *ceteris paribus* clause often insulates his position from what would otherwise appear to be valid criticism or even decisive refutation. For instance, Bhaskar's brisk deduction from fact to value to action—that is, his claim that the identification of an object or source of false belief logically entails, *ceteris paribus*, both a negative evaluation of it and action directed at its removal—neglects the fact that any proposal to remove a source of distortion, "rationalization," or "ideological mystification" (*Reclaiming Reality*, p. 107) should consider not only isolated and discrete relationships of causality but also more broadly the range of causal relationships in which that object is embedded (*especially* if that object is as pervasive and large scale as an institution, social structure, or "system of social rela-

tions"). More specifically, one must consider the possibility that a source of false belief, as well as the belief itself, may be productive as well as debilitating, and thus its removal may yield differential consequences, many of which may not be entirely or even primarily liberating. In addition, one must investigate the matrix of causal tendencies likely to be activated by any proposed action to remove a source of false belief. Finally, one must compare the implications of various actions or inactions. To take an example, much of the rhetoric of the American civil rights movement appealed to the Declaration of Independence as a source of moral and political authority. Conceived as historical propositions about the meaning of the Declaration of Independence, these appeals were at best highly dubious. The mere fact that Jefferson's moral condemnation of the British Crown's involvement in slave trade was removed from the final version of the document provides strong evidence supporting the view that it was not the signatories' intent to found a new nation based on principles of racial equality. Yet, as a way of constructing a national narrative that might foster meaningful and concrete steps toward such equality without inducing racial war or national dissolution, this appeal was ingenious. Would the civil rights movement have been more or less effective in realizing its aims if it had jettisoned these appeals as cognitive errors, historical fictions, or ideological distortions? I cannot answer this question definitively. The point, however, is that neither can Bhaskar. But if Bhaskar cannot answer such questions definitively—or, to put the matter more precisely, cannot establish convincingly that removing these distortions from the rhetoric and vocabulary of the civil rights movement would have initiated causal tendencies that in the long run would have issued in greater racial equality—then one of two possibilities remains. Either his claim that there is a relationship of entailment between the identification of a source of false belief and a commitment to action aimed at removing it is unsubstantiated and must be revised or abandoned, or the considerations I have just raised must be reintroduced in such a way as to save the entailment claim. This, I would argue, is precisely the function of Bhaskar's *ceteris paribus* clause, as well as phrases such as "action rationally directed." These clauses enable him to defend his formal and categorical claim by providing a net that contains and assimilates all of the complex contextual considerations that are central to almost any concrete question of social or political action. If, however, these considerations are not really eliminated but are instead inconspicuously relocated in *en passant* phrases, then it is not clear what epistemic or practical purpose the categorical claim serves. Nor is it clear what purpose the major if implicit premise of his argument, namely, that truth is always the highest good, serves if it too must be qualified—but *not,* one should emphasize, eviscerated—in a similar manner. Indeed, it is Bhaskar's tendency to shift as necessity dictates between formal and contextual registers that encourages critics such as John Gunnell to characterize critical realism as "a very porous position" and Bhaskar's work in particular as inhabiting "a discursive demimonde." See John G. Gunnell, *The Orders of Discourse: Philosophy, Social Science, and Politics* (New York: Rowman & Littlefield Publishers, 1998), pp. 151, 152. For similar but not identical observations about the role of *ceteris paribus* clauses in Bhaskar's model of explanatory critique, see Sayer, *Realism and Social Science,* pp. 164–165.

84. Isaac, "Realism and Reality: Some Realistic Reconsiderations," p. 22.
85. I emphasize the *lineage* of hostility to distinguish the appropriations of Frankfurt School critical theory from the work of its members, much of which sought to unite philosophical reflection and empirical research. In this respect, critical realism might be conceived as an effort, broadly speaking, to recover a mode of critical social theory that has been distorted or misunderstood by some of its most enthusiastic advocates.
86. On this issue, see Shapiro and Wendt, "The Misunderstood Promise of Realist Social Theory," pp. 171, 174–175. It might be noted that in his effort to revive the language of interest, Bhaskar's normative project broadly converges, though is not identical, with that of scholars such as Martha Nussbaum and Amartya Sen. See Martha C. Nussbaum and Amartya K. Sen, ed., *The Quality of Life* (New York: Oxford University Press, 1993); Amartya Sen, "The Equality of What?" in S. M. McMurrin, ed., *Liberty, Equality, and Law: Selected Tanner Lectures on Moral Philosophy* (Cambridge: Cambridge University Press, 1987), pp. 137–162; and Lawrence Hamilton, "A Theory of True Interests in the Work of Amartya Sen," *Government and Opposition* 34, no. 4 (1999): 516–546.
87. For discussions of contemporary critical theory, see Craig Calhoun, *Critical Social Theory: Culture, History, and the Challenge of Difference* (Cambridge, MA: Blackwell, 1995); Brian Fay, *Critical Social Science* (Ithaca, NY: Cornell University Press, 1987); Stephen T. Leonard, *Critical Theory in Political Practice* (Princeton, NJ: Princeton University Press, 1990); and Thomas McCarthy and David Cousins Hoy, *Critical Theory* (Cambridge, MA: Blackwell, 1994).
88. Bhaskar, *The Possibility of Naturalism,* pp. 25–26.
89. Ibid., pp. 2, 28, 169.
90. Ibid., pp. 2, 22. See also Bhaskar, *Scientific Realism and Human Emancipation,* p. 120; and idem, *Plato Etc.,* pp. 91, 200.
91. The claim that the champions of hermeneutics either discount radically

the significance of causal explanations of social phenomena or reject the very possibility or appropriateness of developing such explanations is quite common; in many respects it has become the disciplinary common sense of both social scientists and mainstream philosophy of social science. In an essay on Charles Taylor's philosophy of social science, for instance, Michael Martin correctly observes, first, that Taylor opposes empiricist conceptions of causality and, second, that "some of Taylor's own descriptions of the meaning of concepts in the social sciences implicitly assume causality." However, rather than taking these twin observations as provisional evidence of a distinctive conception of causation—one that might be quite unlike standard empiricist views—Martin concludes that "the most plausible reading is that he thinks causality is unimportant." See Michael Martin, "Taylor on Interpretation and the Sciences of Man," in Michael Martin and Lee C. McIntyre, eds., *Readings in the Philosophy of Social Science* (Cambridge, MA: MIT Press, 1994), pp. 263–264. Even more strongly, Daniel Little, in a widely used text for courses in the philosophy of social science, asserts that writers such as Taylor advocate a hermeneutical and anti-naturalistic conception of social science, one that joins the view that "social phenomena can only be explained through a hermeneutic unpacking of the meanings that constitute them" with a belief that "causal explanation has no legitimate role in social science." See Daniel Little, *Varieties of Social Explanation: An Introduction to the Philosophy of Social Science* (Boulder, CO: Westview Press, 1991), p. 233, see also p. 235. Similarly, Alexander Wendt and Ian Shapiro maintain that "what divided interpretivists from behaviorists was the possibility of a causal social science." See Wendt and Shapiro, "The Misunderstood Promise of Realist Social Theory," p. 170. See also Isaac, *Power in Marxist Theory,* pp. 55–56; and Brian Fay, *Social Theory and Political Practice* (London: George Allen & Unwin, 1975), pp. 83–85. Finally, Edgar Kiser and Michael Hechter argue that those forms of historicism that draw on "phenomenologist and hermeneutic philosophy" clearly decouple "interpretative understanding" and causal analysis, believing as these historicists putatively do that "the detached objectivity that is often assumed to be necessary for causal analysis is unattainable." See "The Role of General Theory in Comparative-Historical Sociology," *American Journal of Sociology* 97 (July 1991): 10–11. As I shall argue below, these accounts, by linking hermeneutics to a profoundly anti-causal conception of social inquiry, fundamentally distort Taylor's views and also, like Bhaskar's account, mistakenly assimilate all of hermeneutical thought to a single position.

92. Bhaskar, *The Possibility of Naturalism,* p. 3. Although this indictment as

well as the preceding ones are issued specifically against the views of Peter Winch, Bhaskar's discussion of Winch occurs in the context of a more general critical analysis of what he rather sweepingly refers to as "the anti-naturalist tradition" and "the hermeneutical tradition." In his discussion, Winch's *The Idea of a Social Science* is introduced as an example of errors characteristic of these widely overlapping traditions. As I shall discuss below, Bhaskar's failure to acknowledge and attend to the diversity of views within these "traditions" contributes substantially to his miscasting, first, of the relationship between hermeneutics and positivism, and, second, of the relationship between hermeneutics and critical realism.

93. Bhaskar, *The Possibility of Naturalism,* pp. 28, 157.

94. Ibid., pp. 195–203.

95. Charles Taylor, "Rorty in the Epistemological Tradition," in Alan Malachowski, ed., *Reading Rorty: Critical Responses to* Philosophy and the Mirror of Nature *(and Beyond)* (Cambridge, MA: Basil Blackwell, 1990), p. 258.

96. Ibid., p. 269. It is perhaps worth noting that although Bhaskar often contrasts the allegedly Humean ontology of hermeneutical writers to his own more Kantian approach to ontological questions, Taylor, in a critical analysis of Humean empiricism, foregrounds Kant as the crucial figure who first demonstrates "the incoherence of the Humean picture." See Taylor, "Overcoming Epistemology," in *Philosophical Arguments* (Cambridge, MA: Harvard University Press, 1995), p. 10; see also idem, "Lichtung or Lebensform: Parallels between Heidegger and Wittgenstein," in *Philosophical Arguments,* pp. 71–72. This is not to say that Taylor is a thoroughgoing Kantian—he, like Bhaskar, expressly rejects important aspects of Kant's thought—but it does suggest that Bhaskar's sharp contrast between hermeneutical and critical realist understandings of natural science and empiricism rests on a flattening of hermeneutics that obscures at least as much as it clarifies.

97. Hubert L. Dreyfus, *Being-in-the-World: A Commentary on Heidegger's* Being and Time, *Division I* (Cambridge, MA: MIT Press, 1991), pp., 254, 258, 261. See also idem, "Heidegger's Hermeneutic Realism," in Hiley, Bohman, and Schusterman, eds., *The Interpretive Turn,* pp. 25–41; and idem, "Defending the Difference: The Geistes/Naturwissenschaften Distinction Revisited," in Academie der Wissenschaften zu Berlin (Jürgen Mittelstraß, Director), *Einheit der Wissenschaften* (Berlin and New York: Walter de Gruyter, 1991), p. 469.

98. Dreyfus, "Heidegger's Hermeneutic Realism," p. 35.

99. Ibid. p. 37. See also Dreyfus, "Defending the Difference," p. 472; and Hubert L. Dreyfus and Charles Spinosa, "Coping with Things-in-

Themselves: A Practice-Based Phenomenological Argument for Realism,"
Inquiry 42 (March 1999): 49–78.

100. Dreyfus, "Heidegger's Hermeneutic Realism," p. 38.

101. Dreyfus, "Defending the Difference," p. 474.

102. Because Dreyfus's arguments are primarily intended to challenge and develop an alternative to contemporary forms of anti-realism that seek to
undermine the worship of natural science "by denying that it discovers
anything at all" ("Defending the Difference," p. 466), his defense of hermeneutic and plural realism is less preoccupied with positivist distinctions
between observables and unobservables than with establishing the coherence of the idea that "science can in principle give us access to the func-
tional components of the universe as they are in themselves in distinction
from how they appear to us on the basis of our quotidian concerns or
sensory capacities." See Dreyfus and Spinosa, "Coping with Things-in-
Themselves," p. 50. Nonetheless, a number of passages (including the previous one) makes it quite clear that Dreyfus's realism is not an empirical
realism that denies the thesis of ontological depth and adheres to the
dictum that all unobservables must be expelled from the precincts of scientific investigation. This reading has also been confirmed in conversations with Dreyfus.

103. Dreyfus and Spinosa, "Coping with Things-in-Themselves," p. 50; and
Dreyfus, *Being-in-the-World*, p. 256. To observe just how closely Dreyfus's
and Bhaskar's views converge on questions of natural scientific ontology,
one might compare the above quotations, as well as others—for example,
"making sense of reality as independent is something we do, but what
there independently is does not depend on us" (Dreyfus, "Heidegger's
Hermeneutic Realism," p. 31)—with Bhaskar's own remark in *A Realist
Theory of Science* that "perception gives us access to things and experimental activity access to structures that exist independently of us" (p. 9).

104. I have already noted the frequency with which critics of hermeneutics erroneously claim that writers such as Taylor jettison the very idea that
human activity can or should be explained causally. I should add that it
is, if anything, even more common for critics to fail to notice the claim
that I advance below, namely, the claim that hermeneutic resistance to the
naturalist thesis is itself grounded in a (non-Humean) theory of causation, one that grants causal efficacy to meanings. Although it is beyond
the scope of the present study to explore in detail the sources of this misconception, it should be noted that Taylor himself states quite explicitly
that meanings are causally efficacious. Distinguishing his own views of
"the way our practices shape our lives, the way they change in history,
the way this change, or resistance to change, can figure in our moral and

political striving" from those of Derrida and Foucault, Taylor writes that "while they are aware of the *results* in terms of meaning, they seem to want to deny meaning any *causal* role in bringing the fateful changes about" (emphasis in original). See Taylor, "What's Wrong with Foundationalism? Knowledge, Agency, and World," in Mark Wrathall and Jeff Malpas, eds., *Heidegger, Coping, and Cognitive Science: Essays in Honor of Hubert Dreyfus,* vol. 2 (Cambridge, MA: MIT Press, 2000), p. 123.

105. The following remarks about causation draw in part on a presentation by and conversations with Charles Taylor during the 1998 NEH Summer Institute on the Philosophy of Social Science. I do not know, however, whether he would agree with this account in its entirety.

106. Charles Taylor, "Relations between Cause and Action," in *The Seventh Inter-American Congress of Philosophy, Proceedings of the Congress,* vol. 1 (Quebec: Les Presses de l'Université Laval, 1967), p. 245.

107. As Taylor explains, this dualistic understanding of causal and action explanations posits, on the one hand, that causal explanations tell us how movements come about through antecedent physiological causes, and, on the other hand, that action explanations tell us something radically different, for example, they make actions "more comprehensible" by redescribing them or "putting them in a different light." See Charles Taylor, "Explaining Action," *Inquiry* 13 (1970): 56–57; and idem, "Relations between Cause and Action," p. 247. Taylor's construal, by contrast, aims to undercut this dualism.

108. Taylor, "Explaining Action," p. 57.

109. Ibid., p. 59.

110. David Hume, *Treatise of Human Nature,* 2nd ed., ed. L. A. Selby-Bigge and rev. P. H. Nidditch (Oxford: Clarendon Press, 1978), pp. 76–77, 87, 93–94, 170. These issues are also discussed in Hume's *Enquiry.* See *An Enquiry Concerning Human Understanding and A Letter from a Gentleman to His Friend in Edinburgh* (Indianapolis: Hackett Publishing Co., 1977).

111. The theory is evident, for instance, in the "positive economics" of writers like Milton Friedman and in textbooks such as *Designing Social Inquiry,* an influential exploration of descriptive and causal inference in social inquiry authored by three eminent political scientists. See Milton Friedman, "The Methodology of Positive Economics," in *Essays in Positive Economics* (Chicago: University of Chicago Press, 1953), pp. 3–43; and Gary King, Robert O. Keohane, and Sidney Verba, *Designing Social Inquiry: Scientific Inference in Qualitative Research* (Princeton, NJ: Princeton University Press, 1994). For a discussion of the largely Humean view of causation implicit in King, Keohane, and Verba's book, see George Steinmetz, "Critical Realism and Historical Sociology: A Review Article," *Comparative*

Studies in Society and History 40 (January 1998): 172n7. I emphasize that this position is *largely* Humean because, unlike Hume, the authors do not rule out in principle the use of unobservable concepts. Their analysis of the issue, however, reveals that the ghost of Hume is never far in the background. The authors begin by stating correctly, if trivially, that "we should choose observable, rather than unobservable, concepts whenever possible" (p. 109). They then proceed, also correctly if rather curiously, to insist that unobservable concepts can be a "hindrance" to the evaluation of theories and hypotheses "unless they can be defined in such a way that they, or at least their implications, can be observed and measured" (ibid.). It is not clear to whom these comments are addressed, since realism, at least, has never entailed that observable phenomena play no role in scientific explanation. The heart of critical and scientific realism is its commitment to transdiction—that is, to the legitimacy of inferring from experience and/or observation to what may in principle be beyond experience and/or observation. Why the authors accent so strongly a point on which there is no disagreement—neither hermeneuticists nor intentionalists nor structuralists argue that no noncircular empirical evidence is required to support claims of unobservables—remains a mystery.

112. Barry Stroud, *Hume* (London: Routledge and Kegan Paul, 1978), pp. 57–67.

113. These examples are borrowed from Douglas Gasking, "Causation and Recipes," *Mind* 64 (October 1955): 482.

114. Richard W. Miller, *Fact and Method: Explanation, Confirmation and Reality in the Natural and the Social Sciences* (Princeton, NJ: Princeton University Press, 1987), p. 82.

115. Ibid., p. 79.

116. The priority claim being made here is both ontological and explanatory. That is, I am arguing that the primitive meaning of causation is ontologically prior to second-order conceptions because it is only on the basis of the former that we extend the meaning of causation to include our second-order conceptions. The primitive conception also, however, claims explanatory priority, since starting from it we can account for and render intelligible the second-order conception, but not vice versa. Regarding this latter point, Karl Otto-Apel has argued persuasively that standard Humean and deductive-nomological models of causal explanation presuppose a capacity to manipulate chains of events and this, by providing the basis of our understanding of the connection between events, constitutes the transcendental-pragmatic ground of the concept of causation. However, precisely because this experimental action that forms the ground of the concept of causation cannot be analyzed in terms of a deductive-nomological account of causation without abrogating the very concept of

causality itself, the deductive-nomological account cannot possibly be complete. As Apel writes, "If we wish to understand an experimental interventionist action as such, we cannot objectify it as an observable nexus of events in the external world. If we could, we would of course again confront the Humean problem, and would be unable to infer a causal necessity from the conjunction of phenomena observed." See *Understanding and Explanation: A Transcendental-Pragmatic Perspective*, trans. Georgia Warnke (Cambridge, MA: MIT Press, 1984), p. 60.

117. Perhaps the most influential philosophical proponent of a counterfactual conception of causation is David Lewis. See *Counterfactuals* (Cambridge, MA: Harvard University Press, 1973); and idem, "Causation," in Ernest Sosa, ed., *Causation and Conditionals* (London: Oxford University Press, 1975), pp. 180–191. For an account of the role of singular causal statements in historical explanation, see William Dray, *Laws and Explanation in History* (Oxford: Oxford University Press, 1957).

118. Joshua Cohen and Joel Rogers, *Rules of the Game: American Politics and the Central American Movement* (Boston: South End Press, 1986), ch. 1.

119. Carl G. Hempel, "The Function of General Laws in History," in *Aspects of Scientific Explanation and Other Essays in the Philosophy of Science* (New York: Free Press, 1965), p. 238.

120. Steven Lukes, "Methodological Individualism Reconsidered," in *Essays in Social Theory* (New York: Columbia University Press, 1977), p. 184.

121. Advocates of radical and participatory democracy, for instance, share Cohen and Rogers's concerns about the low levels of political participation in the United States. Unlike Cohen and Rogers, however, they argue that local political initiatives and action operate as the school in which citizens become educated and committed participants in political affairs. For this reason, they are in general much less critical of the institutional structures of federalism than are Cohen and Rogers—indeed, they often view it as facilitating rather than impeding democratic participation. If this argument is sound, it would not only suggest that federalism is much less central to the explanation of American exceptionalism than Cohen and Rogers believe, but would also imply that Cohen and Rogers infer without adequate warrant a link between participation and centralization of power. On the Hartz thesis, see Louis Hartz, *The Liberal Tradition in America: An Interpretation of American Political Thought since the Revolution* (New York: Harcourt Brace Jovanovich, 1955).

122. Philip Gaspar, "Explanation and Scientific Realism," in Dudley Knowles, ed., *Explanation and Its Limits* (New York: Cambridge University Press, 1990), p. 288.

123. John Gaventa, *Power and Powerlessness: Quiescence and Rebellion in an*

Appalachian Mining Valley (Urbana and Chicago: University of Illinois Press, 1982). The status of Gaventa's book within political and social science is indicated by the large number of awards it has received: the Woodrow Wilson Foundation Book Award (of the American Political Science Association), the V. O. Key Book Award (of the Southern Political Science Association), the Lillian Smith Book Award (of the Southern Regional Council), and the W. D. Weatherford Book Award. It was also runner-up in the competition for the Robert F. Kennedy Book Award.

124. Ibid., p. 3.
125. See Steven Lukes, *Power: A Radical View* (London and Basingstoke, UK: Macmillan, 1974).
126. Gaventa, *Power and Powerlessness,* pp. 47–121.
127. Ibid., pp. 26, 28, 76. Emphasis added.
128. As Richard Miller observes, acceptable explanations in both the natural and social sciences often lack the generality demanded by nomological models of causation. He cites, for instance, Charles Tilly's explanation of the 1793 counterrevolutionary uprising in the Vendée region of France. As Miller summarizes, Tilly attributed the uprising to the clergy's deep uneasiness with an increasingly anticlerical government. Exploiting its unique monopoly of access to the outside world, the clergy was able to mobilize the peasants in support of its own interests; hence, the ironic consequence of a royalist uprising fueled by a peasant rebellion. In his analysis of this account, Miller emphasizes that the adequacy of Tilly's explanation need not and, presumably, does not rest on its causal claims being cast in nomological form. As Miller submits, "Sketching a general description of the difference between societies obeying this law of clerical power and those that don't is not a job he [Tilly] needs to perform . . . If in tenth-century Japan the clergy dominated peasant access to the outside world, but could not get peasants to conform to their political interests, this is not a fact he needs to explain away before he can ask us to accept his explanation of the Vendée uprising." See Miller, "Fact and Method in the Social Sciences," in Daniel R. Sabia and Jerald T. Wallulis, eds., *Changing Social Science: Critical Theory and Other Critical Perspectives* (Albany: State University of New York Press, 1983), p. 89. The point here is that what constitutes a relevant counterfactual depends on judgments of comparative similarity. Although these judgments are not strictly rule-governed, neither are they arbitrary or subjective. In the hypothetical case of tenth-century Japan, for example, Miller asserts that "no working historian would take this as an admission of defeat, in the dispute over the Vendean uprising." See Miller, *Fact and Method,* p. 52. For a more formal discussion of comparative similarity and its role in counterfactual analyses of causation, see David Lewis, "Causation," pp. 183–184.

129. See Shapiro and Wendt, "The Difference that Realism Makes," pp. 214–218.

130. Ibid., p. 215.

131. Focusing on the nature and role of causation in historical explanation, William Dray has noted that when we ask for the cause of an event, say, of World War II, it is not always clear what we mean by "cause" and hence what question we are inviting our interlocutor to answer. Sometimes, for instance, the question may be motivated by an effort to assign blame or responsibility for an event, while at other times it may be prompted by a desire to identify the specific act(s) (or nonacts) that led immediately to its occurrence. Sometimes our causal explanation may seek to answer questions about *how* something was possible, while at other times it may answer any number of distinct *why* questions. Similarly, Dray maintains that there are three distinct ways in which a putative causal connection might be argued for: "by reference to manipulative experience, by reference to a logical connexion in terms of some general theory, or by reference to other conditions in a determinate situation which allow the judgment that a certain condition was crucial" (pp. 105–106). What this suggests is that the concept of causality is structurally complex and layered, the product of a long historical process of accretion and transformation. Conceptions of causation that flatten or otherwise deny this complexity are likely to occasion as many problems as they eliminate. See Dray, *Laws and Explanation in History*. For a similar analysis of the ways in which what counts as an *explanation* varies depending upon the nature of the question being posed, see Alan Garfinkel, *Forms of Explanation: Rethinking the Questions in Social Theory* (New Haven, CT: Yale University Press, 1981).

132. For a review of some of these difficulties, see Michael Tooley, "Laws and Causal Relations," in Peter A. French, Theodore E. Uehling, Jr., and Howard K. Wettstein, eds., *Midwest Studies in Philosophy, Volume IX, Causation and Causal Theories* (Minneapolis: University of Minnesota Press, 1984), pp. 93–112; and James Bohman, *New Philosophy of Social Science: Problems of Indeterminacy* (Cambridge, MA: MIT Press, 1991), pp. 18–30.

133. Peter Winch, who is often the target of Bhaskar's criticisms, is a more complicated case. In the first edition of *The Idea of a Social Science,* Winch expressed reservations regarding the Humean account of causation, but did so only briefly (see ch. 5, sec. 1). Indeed, in the 1990 "Preface to the Second Edition," Winch acknowledged his earlier failure to undertake any "serious investigation of the notion of cause" and noted that rather than denying the possibility of explaining human behavior in causal terms, he "should have been saying that our understanding of

human behavior is not elucidated by anything like the account given of 'cause' by Hume." See Winch, *The Idea of a Social Science and Its Relation to Philosophy*, 2nd ed. (London: Routledge, 1900), p. xii. Whatever Winch's intentions, it is clear that there is textual evidence supporting the proposition that Winch, in the first edition of *The Idea of a Social Science*, accepted rather uncritically a Humean conception of causation—for example, ch. 3, sec. 5 ("The Investigation of Regularities"), contrasts explanations of human behavior with "causal generalizations," "empirical generalizations," "uniformities," and the like, all of which seem to presume a Humean construal of causation—and that Bhaskar and many other critics interpreted him as holding such a view of causality. Thus, it may well be the case that Winch's earlier but not later accounts of the relationship between human conduct and causal explanation are vulnerable to Bhaskar's attacks. This, however, does not undermine the status (although it may affect the scope) of the above criticisms of Bhaskar. As I have stressed, my account of hermeneutics does not aim to represent an entire "tradition" or school of thought. Rather, it seeks to interpret the work of some central figures associated with that tradition and to advance arguments about how we might most profitably conceive of their work. In this regard, my argument is delimited to the claim that Bhaskar often consolidates distinctive positions within hermeneutical thought into the views of individuals who are deemed to be representative of the "tradition" in toto. By contrast, my interpretation of hermeneutics is designed to show that it possesses more diversity and a richer variety of intellectual resources than Bhaskar's account presumes.

134. Bhaskar, *The Possibility of Naturalism*, p. 170.
135. Ibid., p. 171.
136. Brian Fay, "Winch's Philosophical Bearings," *History of the Human Sciences* 13 (February 2000): 53.
137. Bhaskar, *The Possibility of Naturalism*, p. 171.
138. Ibid., pp. 173–175, 198–199. Bhaskar is neither the only nor the first writer to accuse Winch of embracing some form of conceptual or linguistic idealism. See also I. C. Jarvie, "Understanding and Explanation in Sociology and Social Anthropology," in Robert Borger and Frank Cioffi, eds., *Explanation in the Behavioural Sciences* (New York: Cambridge University Press, 1970), pp. 236, 246; Ernest Gellner, "The New Idealism," in Imre Lakatos and Alan Musgrave, eds., *Problems in the Philosophy of Science, Proceedings of the International Colloquium*, vol. 3 (Amsterdam: North-Holland Publishing Co., 1968), pp. 377–406; Anthony Giddens, *Central Problems in Social Theory: Action, Structure and Contradiction in Social Analysis* (Berkeley and Los Angeles: University of California Press, 1979),

p. 265n59; Bohman, *New Philosophy of Social Science,* p. 63; and Fay, "Winch's Philosophical Bearings," p. 56. Others have made similar charges against Gadamer, Heidegger, and hermeneutic thought more generally. See Jürgen Habermas, *On the Logic of the Social Sciences,* trans. Shierry Weber Nicholsen and Jerry A. Stark (Cambridge, MA: MIT Press, 1988), pp. 173–174; and Cristina Lafont, *The Linguistic Turn in Hermeneutic Philosophy,* trans. José Medina (Cambridge, MA: MIT Press, 1999), ch. 3.

139. Winch, *The Idea of a Social Science and Its Relation to Philosophy,* p. 102.

140. Ibid., p. 103.

141. Ludwig Wittgenstein, *Philosophical Investigations,* trans. G. E. M. Anscombe (New York: Macmillan, 1953), par. 124.

142. Bhaskar, *The Possibility of Naturalism,* p. 198. Although I would grant that Bhaskar's reading is not only plausible but is also the predominant one, both within *The Idea of a Social Science* and among Winch's writings as a whole there remain a number of statements and passages that militate strongly against such readings. The result is a corpus of work that contains deep and perplexing tensions and ambiguities. These are in turn reflected in interpretive disputes regarding the meaning of his texts and the philosophical and practical implications of his views. Very broadly, one can discern three positions: (1) some critics adopt interpretations similar to Bhaskar's, (2) others hold a highly qualified and ambivalent view of Winch as oscillating uneasily between some variant of conceptual idealism and a softer position in which the fit between concepts and reality is much looser, and (3) still others view him as ultimately repudiating any allegiance to conceptual idealism. For a sampling of writers who hold the first position, see fn. 137. For some examples of writers who defend the second or third positions, see Hanna Fenichel Pitkin, *Wittgenstein and Justice: On the Significance of Ludwig Wittgenstein for Social and Political Theory* (Berkeley, Los Angeles, and London: University of California Press, 1972), pp. 243–263; Fred R. Dallmayr, "Hermeneutics and Historicism: Reflections on Winch, Apel, and Vico," in *Beyond Dogma and Despair: Toward a Critical Phenomenology of Politics* (Notre Dame, IN: University of Notre Dame Press, 1981), pp. 139–155; John Horton, "Relativism, Reality and Philosophy," *History of the Human Sciences* 13 (February 2000): 21–25; Fay, "Winch's Philosophical Bearings," p. 56; and Nigel Pleasants, "Winch, Wittgenstein and the Idea of Critical Social Theory," *History of the Human Sciences* 13 (February 2000): 80–84.

143. Winch, *The Idea of a Social Science and Its Relation to Philosophy,* p. 102.

144. The reference to Azande witchcraft alludes to Winch's controversial critique of E. E. Evans-Pritchard's *Witchcraft, Oracles and Magic among the Azande.* See "Understanding a Primitive Society," in Brian Wilson, ed.,

Rationality (Oxford: Blackwell, 1970), pp. 78–111. For a recent discussion of Islamic fundamentalism from a hermeneutical perspective, see Roxanne L. Euben, *Enemy in the Mirror: Islamic Fundamentalism and the Limits of Western Rationalism* (Princeton, NJ: Princeton University Press, 1999).

145. I would maintain that Quentin Skinner holds a similar view about the value of studying hermeneutically the history of ideas and classic texts. Turning on its head the notion that such investigations have no practical or critical purchase because they explore outmoded metaphysical ideas, Skinner replies that the practical value of such studies lies in their capacity to unsettle our own certitudes about the superiority of present arrangements, the timelessness of present truths, and the naturalness and necessity of what today is most taken for granted. As Skinner writes, "The allegation that the history of ideas consists of nothing more than 'outworn metaphysical notions' . . . would then come to be seen as the very reason for regarding such histories as indispensably 'relevant', not because crude 'lessons' can be picked out from them, but because the history itself provides a lesson in self-knowledge. To demand from the history of thought a solution to our own immediate problems is thus to commit not merely a methodological fallacy, but something like a moral error. But to learn from the past—and we cannot otherwise learn at all—the distinction between what is necessary and what is the product merely of our own contingent arrangements, is to learn the key to self-awareness itself." See "Meaning and Understanding in the History of Ideas," in James Tully, ed., *Meaning and Context: Quentin Skinner and His Critics* (Princeton, NJ: Princeton University Press, 1988), p. 67.

146. Bhaskar, *The Possibility of Naturalism,* p. 202.

147. Admittedly, all efforts to differentiate distinct strands of thought within a tradition are problematic, given that some conflicts in aims, premises, and points of view exist among all, or almost all, members of any tradition. How narrowly or broadly one conceives of traditions is therefore partly a matter of judgment and intent, depending both on substantive and pragmatic considerations. In Bhaskar's case I would argue that the failure to disaggregate viewpoints within hermeneutics (or to ask whether or in what sense the various thinkers he consolidates under the term "tradition" are in fact part of one) fails the pragmatic test, since his subsumption of hermeneutics to a particular interpretation of Winch (and, to a lesser degree, Gadamer) leads him to engage in a series of mock battles that ultimately obscure important convergences between hermeneutical thinkers and critical realism and thus undercut his ambition to transform not just the philosophy of social inquiry but also social inquiry itself. In his more recent work, Bhaskar acknowledges one important fissure within

hermeneutical thought, that between "neo-Kantians, such as Weber and Habermas, who seek to synthesize positivist and hermeneutical principles, and dualists (or Vichians), such as the Wittgensteinian Winch and the Heidegerrian Gadamer, who deny positivism any applicability in the human domain" (*Plato Etc.*, p. 200). Even this more discriminating conception of hermeneutics, however, fails to attend adequately to the wide diversity of positions within these two categories (as well as those that defy easy location within either) and, more importantly, to the scope of underlying agreement between Bhaskar's conception of critical realism and some hermeneutical views.

148. Bhaskar, *Plato Etc.*, p. xi.

149. The tendency to regard internal understanding as the terminus rather than the starting point of any hermeneutical or interpretive investigation is quite pronounced. In addition to well-known philosophers such as Rorty and Bhaskar, many political theorists and social scientists subscribe to this view. In an otherwise excellent book, for instance, Timothy Kaufman-Osborn maintains that Taylor exhibits just this tendency. See *Politics/Sense/Experience: A Pragmatic Inquiry into the Promise of Democracy* (Ithaca, NY: Cornell University Press, 1991), p. 239. See also Rudra Sil, "The Division of Labor in Social Science Research: Unified Methodology or 'Organic Solidarity'?" *Polity* 32 (Summer 2000): 522.

150. As Taylor has argued, even scientific accounts that purport to bypass agents' own understandings are self-defeating because their objective cannot be achieved without surrendering the very claim to explain the phenomena under investigation. So, for example, functionalist theories that purport to explain religious practices in terms of their socially integrative function find themselves on the horns of a dilemma. Either they yield banal and insignificant truisms to the effect that disruptive religions are unlikely to persist for long, or they prove incapable of explaining "the kind of religion we see here, why there is this kind of ritual, that form of hierarchy, that type of fervour, these modes of blessedness, etc." In short, they either fail to explain in any meaningful sense the phenomena they investigate, or they generate explanations of such narrow explanatory scope as to be all but useless for most practical purposes. Moreover, in order for functionalist theories of this type to expand their explanatory scope, they must, as Taylor emphasizes, first identify what needs to be explained, which itself requires a prior understanding of the agents' understanding. This, however, subverts the original intention of circumventing agents' own understandings. See Taylor, "Understanding and Explanation in the *Geisteswissenschaften*," in Stephen H. Holtzman and Christopher Leich, eds., *Wittgenstein: To Follow a Rule* (London, Boston, and Henley,

UK: Routledge, Kegan and Paul, 1981), pp. 195–196; and idem, "Understanding and Ethnocentricity," in *Philosophy and the Human Sciences: Philosophical Papers,* vol. 2 (New York: Cambridge University Press, 1985), pp. 121–123.

151. See Charles Taylor, "Understanding and Explanation in the *Geisteswissenschaften,*" p. 206–207.

152. Charles Taylor, "Interpretation and the Sciences of Man," in *Philosophy and the Human Sciences: Philosophical Papers,* vol. 2 (New York: Cambridge University Press, 1985), p. 26.

153. Bhaskar, *The Possibility of Naturalism,* p. 171.

154. Taylor, "Understanding and Explanation in the *Geisteswissenschaften,*" p. 191.

155. Philip Petit, "Reply: Evaluative 'Realism' and Interpretation," in Stephen H. Holtzman and Christopher Leich, eds., *Wittgenstein: To Follow a Rule* (London: Routledge, Kegan and Paul, 1981), pp. 211–245; and Taylor, "Understanding and Explanation in the *Geisteswissenschaften,*" p. 200.

156. Taylor, "Understanding and Explanation in the *Geisteswissenschaften,*" p. 191.

157. Ibid., p. 192.

158. Taylor, "Understanding and Ethnocentricity," pp. 116, 118.

159. Bhaskar, *The Possibility of Naturalism,* p. 3.

160. Ibid., p. 57.

161. Taylor, "Interpretation and the Sciences of Man," p. 55. Importantly, Taylor disagrees with Bhaskar's claim that the open-systems problem constitutes the exclusive or even the primary impediment to the development of a predictive science of the social world. Rather, he argues that there are three distinct reasons why "exact prediction is radically impossible": (1) the open-systems problem; (2) the data of social inquiry must include interpretations, but these interpretations cannot be "measured" with anything like the degree of precision that one finds in sciences based on brute data; and (3) the self-defining nature of human beings—which implies that conceptual change alters human reality—vitiates one necessary condition of exact prediction, namely, "conceptual unity," the ability to bring "past and future" under "the same conceptual net" and thus "to understand the states of the latter as some function of the states of the former" (ibid., pp. 55–56). Of these reasons, Taylor maintains that the open-systems problem is the least, and the problem of conceptual unity the most, fundamental. Although a full discussion of this issue would require a more extended treatment than is possible here, I believe there are strong reasons for preferring Taylor's view. Not the least of these is the fact that scholars in some areas of physics, for example, chaos theory, also

encounter the open-systems predicament, but this does not necessarily prevent them from discovering empirical regularities. See James Gleick, *Chaos: Making a New Science* (New York: Viking Press, 1987).

162. Bhaskar, *The Possibility of Naturalism*, p. 27. As Taylor himself states, "We cannot measure such sciences against the requirements of a science of verification: we cannot judge them by their predictive capacity." See "Interpretation and the Sciences of Man," p. 57.

163. Wendt and Shapiro, "The Misunderstood Promise of Realist Social Theory," pp. 169, 171.

164. Bhaskar, *The Possibility of Naturalism*, p. 157.

165. Isaac, *Power and Marxist Theory*, p. 55 (emphasis added). I should add that it is not only realists who assert that the proponents of hermeneutical and interpretive approaches are committed to an anti-scientific conception of inquiry. See also Sil, "The Division of Labor in Social Science Research: Unified Methodology or 'Organic Solidarity'?" p. 522.

166. Peter Galison, *Image and Logic: A Material Culture of Microphysics* (Chicago: University of Chicago Press, 1997), p. 844. For further work on the topic of disunity within the natural sciences, see Peter Galison and David J. Stump, eds., *The Disunity of Science: Boundaries, Contexts, and Power* (Stanford, CA: Stanford University Press, 1996); and John Dupré, *The Disorder of Things: Metaphysical Foundations of the Disunity of Science* (Cambridge: MA: Harvard University Press, 1993).

167. See Ruth Lane, "Positivism, Scientific Realism and Political Science," *Journal of Theoretical Politics* 8 (July 1996): 361–382.

5. Sciences That Disturb

1. Ludwig Wittgenstein, *Wittgenstein's Lectures: Cambridge, 1930–32*, ed. Desmond Lee (Totowa, NJ: Rowman & Littlefield, 1980), p. 26.

2. Loïc J. D. Wacquant, "Bourdieu in America: Notes on the Transatlantic Importation of Social Theory," in Craig Calhoun, Edward LiPuma, and Moishe Postone, eds., *Bourdieu: Critical Perspectives* (Chicago: University of Chicago Press, 1993), p. 236.

3. For discussions of the cleavages characteristic of postwar political theory and science in the United States, see John G. Gunnell, *Between Philosophy and Politics: The Alienation of Political Theory* (Amherst: University of Massachusetts Press, 1986); idem, *The Descent of Political Theory: The Genealogy of an American Vocation* (Chicago: University of Chicago Press, 1993); David M. Ricci, *The Tragedy of Political Science: Politics, Scholarship, and Democracy* (New Haven, CT: Yale University Press, 1984); Raymond Seidelman (with the assistance of Edward J. Harpham), *Disen-*

chanted Realists: Politics, Science, and the American Crisis, 1884–1984 (Albany: State University of New York Press, 1985); and Richard Ashcraft, "One Step Backward, Two Steps Forward: Reflections on Contemporary Political Theory," in John S. Nelson, ed., *What Should Political Theory Be Now?* (Albany: State University of New York Press, 1983), pp. 515–549.

4. Pierre Bourdieu, *Outline of a Theory of Practice,* trans. Richard Nice (New York: Cambridge University Press, 1979), p. 168.

5. Pierre Bourdieu, *The Logic of Practice,* trans. Richard Nice (Stanford, CA: Stanford University Press, 1990), p. 1. See also Pierre Bourdieu, *Language and Symbolic Power,* trans. Gino Raymond and Matthew Adamson (Cambridge, MA: Harvard University Press, 1991), p. 163.

6. Axel Honneth, Hermann Kocyba, and Bernd Schwibs, "The Struggle for Symbolic Order: An Interview with Pierre Bourdieu," *Theory, Culture and Society* 3 (1986): 38.

7. Ibid.

8. Bourdieu himself emphasizes the import of this recursive turn, asserting that the progress of knowledge "requires one to return persistently to the same objects . . . each doubling-back is another opportunity to objectify more completely one's objective and subjective relation to the object." See Bourdieu, *The Logic of Practice,* p. 1; see also idem, *Pascalian Meditations,* trans. Richard Nice (Stanford, CA: Stanford University Press, 2000), p. 8. In this regard, it should not be surprising that Bourdieu's two most important theoretical statements, *Outline of a Theory of Practice* and *The Logic of Practice,* are both self-conscious attempts to rethink—twenty years later—the assumptions (which he characterizes as those of a "blissful structuralist;" see Bourdieu, *The Logic of Practice,* p. 9) informing his early ethnographic writings.

9. Ibid., p. 2.

10. Ibid. Bourdieu acknowledges that his early writings on Algeria "owe much to the emotional context in which they were written" (ibid.). For his description of his work as "a very self-conscious 'epistemological experiment,'" see Pierre Bourdieu and Loïc J. D. Wacquant, *An Invitation to Reflexive Sociology* (Chicago: University of Chicago Press, 1992), p. 67.

11. Pierre Bourdieu, *Algeria 1960,* trans. Richard Nice (New York: Cambridge University Press, 1979), p. vii.

12. Bourdieu, *The Logic of Practice,* p. 25.

13. Pierre Bourdieu, *In Other Words,* trans. Matthew Adamson (Stanford, CA: Stanford University Press, 1990), p. 124; and idem, *The Logic of Practice,* p. 25.

14. Bourdieu, *In Other Words,* p. 125.

15. It should be emphasized that, although Bourdieu does not distinguish be-

tween different types of subjectivism, his examples suggest that there are at least two distinct and sometimes conflicting variants. One is what might be called "phenomenological subjectivism." This form of subjectivism is exemplified by phenomenological sociologists such as Alfred Schütz and Harold Garfinkel, and is characterized by a concern with agents' "primary," "lived," or "taken-for-granted" experience of the social world (it is thus committed to the first of the three forms of privilege that I outline below). The other type of subjectivism is methodological individualism. This is epitomized by behavioralism, rational actor theorists like Jon Elster, and contract theorists such as John Rawls, and is distinguished principally by its commitment to the idea that individual acts and choices are the basic unit of all social analysis and explanation (it thus embraces the second and third of the privileges outlined below). Importantly, these two variants are grounded in quite different social ontologies, with phenomenological subjectivism based on a holist ontology and methodological individualism grounded in an atomist ontology. In spite of these sometimes considerable differences, the two forms of subjectivism converge in their failure to explore adequately the ways that objective conditions and structural constraints shape and make possible agents' primary experience and conscious choices. It might be added that some writers, like Sartre, periodically slide between these two variants.

16. Bourdieu, *The Logic of Practice*, pp. 43–44.
17. Pierre Bourdieu (with the collaboration of Monique de Saint Martin), *The State Nobility: Elite Schools in the Field of Power*, trans. Lauretta C. Clough (Stanford, CA: Stanford University Press, 1996), p. 29.
18. Bourdieu, *The Logic of Practice*, p. 25.
19. Bourdieu, *In Other Words*, p. 126.
20. Bourdieu, *Language and Symbolic Power*, p. 149; and idem, *The Logic of Practice*, p. 43.
21. Bourdieu, *The Logic of Practice*, pp. 45–46.
22. Ibid., p. 46.
23. Pierre Bourdieu, Jean-Claude Chamboredon, and Jean-Claude Passeron, *The Craft of Sociology: Epistemological Preliminaries*, trans. Richard Nice (Berlin and New York: Walter de Gruyter, 1991) pp. 109, 16–18, 111.
24. Bourdieu, *The Logic of Practice*, p. 33.
25. As Hubert Dreyfus rightly points out, the bypassing of phenomenological and subjective factors would not be a valid objection on general scientific grounds simply because the natural sciences quite "legitimately abstract from subject-relative properties." See *Being-in-the-World: A Commentary on Heidegger's* Being and Time, *Division 1* (Cambridge, MA: MIT Press, 1991), p. 204.

26. Bourdieu, *The Logic of Practice*, p. 105.
27. Ibid.
28. Ibid.
29. Honneth, Kocyba, and Schwibs, "The Struggle for Symbolic Order: An Interview with Pierre Bourdieu," p. 41.
30. Bourdieu emphasizes that in Kabylia, the dialectic of gift exchange is tightly intertwined with (at one point he claims that it is "the motor of the whole dialectic") the exchange of honor, an exchange that, he points out, implies a recognition of rough equality in honor among the participants. Thus, offering a gift to someone of greater honor risks either dishonoring oneself through a refusal or increasing one's own honor through acceptance. Likewise, offering a gift to, or accepting a gift from, someone of distinctly less honor casts dishonor on oneself. See Bourdieu, *The Logic of Practice*, pp. 100, 103.
31. Ibid., pp. 106–107.
32. Bourdieu, *Outline of Theory of Practice*, pp. 189–190; and idem, *The Logic of Practice*, p. 129.
33. Ibid., p. 126. Although my discussion of misrecognition foregrounds the inadequacies of objectivist accounts of social conduct that abstract from agents' subjective representations, it would be a mistake to infer from this that misrecognition is a fully subjective phenomenon, that is, an error at the level of the individual subject responding to objective social conditions. Because, as noted, Bourdieu's aim is to attack both sides of the subject/object divide, misrecognition must be understood as the joint product of an "agreement," or homologous relationship, between mental structures (adjusted to the objective world from which they emerge) and social structures. See Bourdieu, *The State Nobility*, pp. 4–5.
34. Bourdieu, *The Logic of Practice*, p. 127.
35. Ibid.
36. Ibid., p. 126.
37. Bourdieu's use of terms like "misrecognition" and "symbolic violence" might initially seem like a variant of ideology critique in slightly different dress. Although it is true that Bourdieu, like the proponents of ideology critique, is interested in bringing to light unjust institutions or relations of power that have become naturalized, he generally avoids the term "ideology." In a conversation with Terry Eagleton, he remarks that the word "ideology" "has very often been misused, or used in a vague manner. It seems to convey a sort of discredit. To describe a statement as ideological is very often an insult, so that this ascription itself becomes an instrument of symbolic domination. I have tried to substitute concepts like 'symbolic domination' or 'symbolic power' or 'symbolic violence' for the

concept of ideology in order to control some of the uses, or abuses, to which it is subject. I try to make visible an unperceived form of everyday violence." See Pierre Bourdieu and Terry Eagleton, "Doxa and Common Life," *New Left Review* 191 (January–February 1992): 111–112.

38. Bourdieu, *Language and Symbolic Power*, p. 52. See also Pierre Bourdieu and Luc Boltanski, "Le fétichisme de la langue," *Actes de la recherche en sciences sociales* 4 (July 1975): 2–32.

39. Bourdieu is not of course denying that language and symbols are often manipulated in cynical and self-conscious ways. Rather, his concept of symbolic violence is meant only to locate a form of domination and violence that does not conform to this pattern.

40. Bourdieu, *In Other Words*, p. 190.

41. Bourdieu, *The Logic of Practice*, p. 53.

42. Honneth, Kocyba, and Schwibs, "The Struggle for Symbolic Order: An Interview with Pierre Bourdieu," p. 42. For Bourdieu, the term "disposition" is employed specifically because of its rather rich semantic content. As he explains, "The word disposition seems particularly suited to express what is covered by the concept of habitus (defined as a system of dispositions). It expresses first the *result of an organizing action*, with a meaning close to that of words such as structure; it also designates a *way of being*, a *habitual state* (especially of the body) and, in particular, a *predisposition, tendency, propensity,* or *inclination*" (*Outline of a Theory of Practice,* p. 214). Emphasis in original.

43. Bourdieu, *Outline of a Theory of Practice,* pp. 76, 25.

44. Bourdieu, *The Logic of Practice,* pp. 56, 69.

45. Ibid., p. 54.

46. Bourdieu, *In Other Words,* p. 194; see also pp. 11–12.

47. Bourdieu and Wacquant, *An Invitation to Reflexive Sociology,* p. 97.

48. Pierre Bourdieu, "Champs de pouvoir, champs intellectuel et habitus de classe," *Scolies* 1 (1971): 161. The translation is mine.

49. Pierre Bourdieu, *The Field of Cultural Production: Essays in Art and Literature* (New York: Columbia University Press, 1993), p. 163.

50. Bourdieu, *In Other Words,* pp. 194–195.

51. For a sampling of local and internalist accounts of science, see Harry Collins, *Changing Order: Replication and Induction in Scientific Practice* (London: Sage, 1985); Bruno Latour and Steve Woolgar, *Laboratory Life: The Social Construction of Scientific Facts* (Princeton, NJ: Princeton University Press, 1986); and Andrew Pickering, *Constructing Quarks: A Sociological History of Particle Physics* (Chicago: University of Chicago Press, 1984). On externalist approaches, see Margaret Jacob, *The Newtonians and the English Revolution, 1689–1720* (Ithaca, NY: Cornell University

Press, 1976); and Robert M. Young, *Darwin's Metaphor: Nature's Place in Victorian Culture* (Cambridge: Cambridge University Press, 1985).

52. Bourdieu, *The Logic of Practice,* p. 50.

53. Ibid., p. 290.

54. Pierre Bourdieu, "The Forms of Capital," in John G. Richardson, ed., *Handbook of Theory and Research for the Sociology of Education* (Westport, CT: Greenwood Press, 1986), p. 243.

55. Bourdieu repeatedly emphasizes the significance of these "ordinary" and "unremarkable" gestures and interactions. In an early discussion of the subtle manner in which the French educational system contributes to social and cultural reproduction, Bourdieu and Jean-Claude Passeron wrote, "Everything that is referred to as culture is at stake in the 'trifling' nuances which separate cutivated allusion from scholastic commentary or, more subtly, the different significations of acquiescence by interjection and mimicry." See Pierre Bourdieu and Jean-Claude Passeron, *Reproduction in Education, Society and Culture,* 2nd ed., trans. Richard Nice (Beverly Hills, CA: Sage Publications, 1994), p. 134n17.

56. Within political theory, participatory democrats and feminist theorists explore issues regarding the quality of everyday life and control over everyday affairs. Benjamin Barber, for example, argues that "the theory of strong democracy . . . envisions politics not as a way of life but as a way of living." See *Strong Democracy: Participatory Politics for a New Age* (Berkeley and Los Angeles: University of California Press, 1984), p. 118. Anne Phillips, discussing convergences between feminists and participatory democrats, observes that "Democracy was no longer thought of in terms of a (rather feeble) mechanism for controlling government, but as popular control in everyday life." See *Engendering Democracy* (University Park: Pennsylvania State University Press, 1991), p. 11. Similarly, many of the 1989 revolutions in Eastern and Central Europe originated not from within formal political institutions, but from transformations of conduct and relations in civil society and everyday life. See Václav Havel, "The Power of the Powerless," in John Keane, ed., *The Power of the Powerless,* trans. Paul Wilson (Armonk, NY: M. E. Sharpe, Inc., 1985), 23–96; and Jonathan Schell, "Introduction," in Adam Michnik, *Letters from Prison and Other Essays,* trans. Maya Latynski (Berkeley and Los Angeles: University of California Press, 1985), pp. xvii–xlii. Finally, poststructuralists who accent the diffuse, fluid, and "capillary" operations of power also investigate the politics of everyday life. See Michel Foucault, *Discipline and Punish,* trans. Alan Sheridan (New York: Vintage, 1979); and idem, *The History of Sexuality,* vol. 1, trans. Robert Hurley (New York: Vintage, 1980).

57. In some respects, rational choice theorists are attentive to social relations

in spheres commonly thought to be private and therefore nonpolitical. Writers such as Richard Posner and Gary Becker, for example, have applied rational choice models to a wide range of relationships that are usually thought to be private or nonpolitical, for example, family and sexual relations. However, if Bourdieu's criticisms of subjectivism, his accent on the symbolic aspects of social existence, and his claims about the role that a nonconscious, embodied practical sense plays in everyday life are correct, then rational choice models must necessarily remain blind to many of the power relations operating in these putatively personal and private domains. For some of Bourdieu's specific criticisms of rational actor theories, see *The Logic of Practice*, pp. 46–50. For a brief discussion of the ways in which liberal democratic and civic republican traditions rigidly separate and oppose politics and everyday life, see Phillips, *Engendering Democracy*, ch. 2.

58. Ian Shapiro, *Political Criticism* (Berkeley: University of California Press, 1990), p. 275.
59. Maurice Merleau-Ponty, *The Phenomenology of Perception,* trans. Colin Smith (London and Aylesbury, UK: Routledge and Kegan Paul, 1962), p. 198.
60. Bourdieu, *The Logic of Practice,* p. 73.
61. Wacquant and Bourdieu, *An Invitation to Reflexive Sociology,* p. 172.
62. In addition to the enormous literatures specifically on issues of sexual harassment, domestic violence, and reproductive politics, see Judith Butler, *Bodies That Matter: On the Discursive Limits of Sex* (New York: Routledge, 1993); Foucault, *Discipline and Punish;* idem, *The History of Sexuality,* vol. 1; Donna J. Haraway, *Simians, Cyborgs, and Women: The Reinvention of Nature* (New York: Routledge, 1991); Carole Pateman, *The Sexual Contract* (Stanford, CA: Stanford University Press, 1988); Elaine Scarry, *The Body in Pain: The Making and Unmaking of the World* (New York: Oxford University Press, 1985); and Iris Marion Young, *Justice and the Politics of Difference* (Princeton, NJ: Princeton University Press, 1990), ch. 5.
63. To see how Bourdieu's ideas regarding embodiment and power might extend and clarify the insights of other social and political theorists, we might look to Iris Marion Young's interesting reflections on the politics of difference. In *Justice and the Politics of Difference,* she argues that although "explicit discrimination and exclusion are forbidden by the formal rules of our society," "unconscious racism, sexism, homophobia, ageism, and ableism" still significantly shape many everyday encounters. In particular, she maintains that "mundane signs of systemic oppression" can be discerned in "bodily reactions" such as "avoidance, aversion, expressions of nervousness, condescension, and stereotyping." For those who are subject

to such reactions, "The whole encounter often painfully fills their discursive consciousness ... [It] throws them back onto their group identity, making them feel noticed, marked, or conversely invisible, not taken seriously, or worse, demeaned" (see Young, *Justice and the Politics of Difference,* pp. 132–134). Although there are interesting family resemblances between these remarks and Bourdieu's evocation of the intricate ways in which class, sex, race, and other embodied differences structure interactions in everyday life, her account of how these interactions operate draws not from Bourdieu—whom she cites once, but does not discuss—but from Anthony Giddens's concept of "practical consciousness." Unfortunately, unlike Bourdieu's detailed theoretical and empirical descriptions of habitus, field, capital, symbolic violence, and symbolic domination, Giddens's treatment of practical consciousness is almost entirely abstract, comprising only a few pages of mostly theoretical discussion. As a consequence, Young's own description of the manner in which embodied comportment reveals and sustains social hierarchies and exclusions is never articulated as convincingly or concretely as it could have been if she had drawn on Bourdieu's much richer theoretical and empirical studies.

64. As Carole Pateman correctly observes, Rawls is a complicated case because, on the one hand, his "agents" in the original position are fully disembodied reasoners and choosers, but, on the other hand, he regularly introduces embodied, gendered beings into his argument. Thus, "Rawls' participants in the original contract are, simultaneously, mere reasoning entities, and 'heads of families', or men who represent their wives." See Pateman, *The Sexual Contract,* p. 43.

65. For an illuminating discussion and critique of Bourdieu's theory of symbolic capital, see Hubert Dreyfus and Paul Rabinow, "Can There Be a Science of Existential Structure and Social Meaning?" in Calhoun, LiPuma, and Postone, eds., *Bourdieu,* pp. 35–44. In his response to this essay, Bourdieu says cautiously that "I might be tempted to accept the interpretation put forth by Dreyfus and Rabinow, if only because it has the virtue of recording the fact (in my eyes essential) that I intend to break with the philosophy of action which haunts the unconscious of most sociologists." See "Concluding Remarks: For a Sociogenetic Understanding of Intellectual Works," in ibid., p. 273.

66. For a discussion of these themes, see J. Peter Euben, "Creatures of a Day: Thought and Action in Thucydides," in Terence Ball, ed., *Political Theory and Praxis* (Minneapolis: University of Minnesota Press, 1977), pp. 28–56.

67. Hannah Arendt, *The Human Condition* (Chicago: University of Chicago Press, 1958), p. 26.

68. Ibid., pp. 178–179.

69. Ibid., p. 176.

70. Ibid.

71. Ibid., p. 200.

72. Ibid.

73. "Des conditions principales d'une communication 'non violente.' " See Pierre Bourdieu et al., *La Misère du monde* (Paris: Éditions de Seuil, 1993), p. 905.

74. Although Bourdieu himself never makes the point, the one-sided accent on the communicative and integrative functions of language and symbolism is also characteristic of much work in political science, particularly the literature on political culture. See, for example, Donald J. Devine, *The Political Subculture of the United States: The Influence of Member Values on Regime Change* (Boston: Little, Brown and Co., 1972); and Gabriel A. Almond and G. Bingham Powell, Jr., *Comparative Politics: A Developmental Approach* (Boston: Little, Brown and Co., 1966).

75. Pierre Bourdieu, "The Economics of Linguistic Exchanges," *Social Science Information* 16(6): 660.

76. Bourdieu, *Language and Symbolic Power,* pp. 86–87.

77. Bourdieu, "The Economics of Linguistic Exchanges," p. 654.

78. Ibid., p. 656.

79. In mapping these options, I do not intend to imply that agents consciously or intentionally "decide" or "choose" between them. As the preceding discussion of the habitus suggests, agents' dispositions to act in one way or another are typically neither arbitrary nor the result of conscious, systematic calculation.

80. Bourdieu, "The Economics of Linguistic Exchanges," p. 664.

81. Bourdieu, *Language and Symbolic Power,* p. 129; and idem, "The Economics of Linguistic Exchanges," p. 663.

82. Ibid., p. 655.

83. Bourdieu notes, for example, that among working-class French males the adoption of an articulatory style characteristic of the dominant classes is often perceived as both a betrayal of one's social identity ("docility toward the dominant is also disloyalty toward the dominated, a disavowal of one's 'own flesh and blood' ") and a negation of one's sexual identity (since such styles of speech are frequently considered effeminate). The result of these restrictive demands from above and below is an existential paradox in which, on the one hand, one's speech is recognized only on the condition that one negates one's class and perhaps one's sexual identity, and, on the other hand, one's class identity is maintained only at the cost of social recognition or mobility and a more permeable, less aggressively masculinist conception of sexual identity. In a rather different

manner, Beate Krais has used Bourdieu's theoretical framework to explore symbolic violence in gender relations, suggesting implicitly that, even in those linguistic markets where more censored (and therefore feminine) modes of speech are authorized, women's speech often remains unrecognized. Summarizing studies done in recent years on the symbolic aspects of gender relations in academic settings, she holds that "in university courses, as well as in meetings and conferences, it has been observed that women are regularly overlooked when they wish to make a point; they are interrupted when they speak; male speakers refer to contributions of other male speakers, but not those of women; if a woman has said something that seems interesting to a male speaker, he refers to this by attributing it to a male participant; nonverbal, reinforcing communication behavior of men is addressed to men, but not to women; and so on." See ibid., p. 667; and Beate Krais, "Gender and Symbolic Violence: Female Oppression in Light of Pierre Bourdieu's Theory of Social Practice," in Calhoun, LiPuma, and Postone, eds., *Bourdieu,* p. 173.

84. Bourdieu holds "that each field draws the dividing line between the sayable and the unsayable (or unnameable) which defines its specificity. In other words, the form and content of discourse depend on the capacity to express the expressive interests attached to a position within the limits of the constraints of the censorship that is imposed on the occupant of the position, i.e., the required *formality*" (see Bourdieu, "The Economics of Linguistic Exchanges," p. 657).

85. Bourdieu, *Language and Symbolic Power,* pp. 68–69.

86. Ibid., p. 55.

87. Ibid., p. 51. This account also suggests an important limitation in Jürgen Habermas's effort to ground normative justification in a proceduralist discourse ethics. Though Habermas unquestionably shares Bourdieu's ideal of a "non-violent communication," and in fact seeks to spell out what he claims are inescapable presuppositions implicit in any such communication, his enumeration of "the three levels of presuppositions of argument" (p. 87) fails to identify the specifically symbolic violences that Bourdieu describes in this passage. Particularly at the third level of analysis, that is, the analysis "at the rhetorical level of processes" (ibid.), Habermas—borrowing heavily from the work of a sympathetic critic, Robert Alexy—adumbrates rules that focus either positively on all subjects being *permitted to* speak, assert, question, participate, and so forth, or negatively on speakers not being coercively *prevented from* exercising these positive rights. Bourdieu's account of symbolic violence points to a lacuna in these rules, for the exclusions from discourse, or the failure to be heard or taken seriously even when one is allowed to participate, lies neither in

formal exclusion nor in repression or coercion, whether internal or external. Rather, it lies in a relationship between the situations of embodied persons, one that may exist and exclude in the absence of any intention or juridical proscription. See Jürgen Habermas, "Discourse Ethics: Notes on a Program of Philosophical Justification," in *Moral Consciousness and Communicative Action,* trans. Christain Lenhardt and Shierry Weber Nicholson (Cambridge, MA: MIT Press, 1990), pp. 43–115.

88. In this respect it contains close affinities with what Steven Lukes calls "the one-dimensional view of power." Like that view of power, the one-dimensional view of violence limits the scientific scope of the term to acts involving directly observable, manifest conflict. See Steven Lukes, *Power: A Radical View* (London and Basingstoke, UK: Macmillan, 1984), pp. 11–15.

89. Max Weber, "Politics as a Vocation," in H. H. Gerth and C. Wright Mills, trans. and eds., *From Max Weber: Essays in Sociology* (New York: Oxford University Press, 1978), p. 78.

90. Hannah Arendt, "On Violence," in *Crises of the Republic* (New York: Harcourt Brace Jovanovich, 1972), p. 144.

91. Although neither identical to nor as fully developed as Bourdieu's conception of symbolic violence, Jürgen Habermas's notion of "structural violence" bears some interesting resemblances to it. See "Hannah Arendt's Communications Concept of Power," in Steven Lukes, ed., *Power* (Oxford: Basil Blackwell, 1986), p. 88.

92. Bourdieu, *The State Nobility,* pp. 52, 23.

93. Many years ago, Bourdieu and Jean-Claude Passeron called attention to the one of the Gordian knots at the heart of the French educational system. Arguing that the educational system presupposed yet failed to provide what was essential for success in it, they wrote that "the system demands uniformly of all its students that they should have what it does not give, i.e., the relation to language and culture exclusively produced by a particular mode of inculcation." See Bourdieu and Passeron, *Reproduction in Education, Society and Culture,* p. 128. Bourdieu's own suggestions for overcoming these inequities are outlined in "Propositions pour L'Ensignement de L'Avenir," a report responding to President François Mitterrand's 1985 request to the Collège de France for guidelines of democratic educational reform. In this report Bourdieu plots a complex course that aims simultaneously at a more equitable and universal diffusion of those "common" competences and skills requisite for active and informed democratic citizenship, autonomy, and occupational success, and a recognition of cultural pluralism and a plurality of competences. In this respect, Bourdieu repudiates the temptation—common in many

American debates about educational reform—*either* to combat social, cultural, and other hierarchies and inequities solely through a more equitable distribution of those competences and forms of knowledge most prized by the dominant powers, groups, and institutions, *or* to do so exclusively through a pedagogy that embraces a plurality of competences as deserving of equal respect and recognition. Although these recommendations are directed specifically at French educational institutions, and thus may appear at times less than radical to those unfamiliar with the French educational establishment, they nonetheless illustrate Bourdieu's efforts to counteract the injuries and insults produced by them. To take one example, Bourdieu proposes a series of structural and pedagogical reforms designed to make rigid career trajectories more flexible by easing students' movement between specific tracks or "channels," by permitting them to combine apprenticeships associated with distinct channels, by enabling choices regarding specialization to be made more gradually, by multiplying opportunities to pursue and reassess educational choices, and by recognizing a plurality of forms of excellence. The general ambition of these proposals is to mitigate the negative effects of particular "scholarly verdicts," first, by providing more options and flexibility in making educational (and hence occupational) decisions, and, second, by undercutting—by granting equal recognition to all competences—the effects of consecration and stigmatization that result from a hierarchized system of educational achievement in which some degrees and titles are much more valued than others.

94. Hanna Fenichel Pitkin and Sara M. Shumer, "On Participation," *Democracy* 2 (Fall 1982): 43.

95. Larry L. Kiser and Elinor Ostrom, "The Three Worlds of Action: A Metatheoretical Synthesis of Institutional Approaches," in Elinor Ostrom, ed., *Strategies of Political Inquiry* (Beverly Hills, CA: Sage Publications, 1982), p. 179.

96. Even many of those approaches that expand their conception of rules to reach beyond purely formal and express rules and arrangements often fail to avail themselves of the analytical resources Bourdieu provides. For instance, concepts such as "routines" and "compliance procedures" typically connote a mechanical and repetitive model of behavior in which "agents" become predictable, rote, and predetermined "executioners" of practice. Thus, the flexible, improvisational, and innovative dimensions of practical understanding that are the lynchpin of Bourdieu's conception of the habitus escape such models' conceptual framework. Consequently, they are not only incapable of explaining the ways in which rules and norms can generate new norms, but are also unable to illuminate the manner in

which rules, which are never fully self-interpreting, become activated and understood. Other terms, such as "decision styles," appear to be more promising (Fritz W. Scharpf, "Decision Rules, Decision Styles and Policy Choices," *Journal of Theoretical Politics* 2 [April 1989]: 149–176), but here the accent on "decisions" and explicit goals implicitly commits the analyst of institutions to a calculative and what Bourdieu calls "intellectualist" understanding of practice (Bourdieu, *Outline of a Theory of Practice*, pp. 1–2, 96–97), one in which the analyst reifies her object by displacing onto agents and practices what she wishes to do with them, namely, represent them. For discussions of some of these aspects of rules, see Ludwig Wittgenstein, *Philosophical Investigations,* trans. G.E.M. Anscombe (New York: Macmillan, 1953), pars. 185–242; and Charles Taylor, "To Follow a Rule," in *Philosophical Arguments* (Cambridge, MA: Harvard University Press, 1995), pp. 165–180.

97. Kiser and Ostrom, "The Three Worlds of Action: A Metatheoretical Synthesis of Institutional Approaches," p. 179.

98. There is now a very large, if qualitatively uneven, critical literature on Bourdieu. For a thoughtful collection of critical essays, see Calhoun, LiPuma, and Postone, eds., *Bourdieu.*

99. Bourdieu sometimes speaks, for example, of "a general theory of the economy of practices" (*The Logic of Practice*, p. 122) or "a general theory of fields."

100. Pierre Bourdieu, "*Vive la crise!* For Heterodoxy in Social Science," *Theory and Society* 17 (September 1988): 773–787.

101. Bourdieu, Chamboredon, and Passeron, *The Craft of Sociology*, p. 9.

Conclusion

1. David D. Laitin, "The Perestroikan Challenge to Social Science," *Politics and Society* 31 (March 2003): 163.

2. "An Open Letter to the APSA Leadership and Members," *PS: Political Science & Politics* 33 (December 2000): 735–737. Although plans for *Perspectives* were already underway prior to the circulation of Mr. Perestroika's e-mail, John Drysek echoes a common view when he contends that it "is taking shape mostly to respond to the perestroika critique." See John S. Dryzek, "A Pox on Perestroika, A Hex on Hegemony: Toward a Critical Political Science," paper presented at the 2002 Annual Meeting of the American Political Science Association, Boston, MA, p. 11.

3. Ibid., p. 2.

4. Parts of the following two sentences draw on Dreyzek's analysis. See ibid., pp. 2–3. For one very recent effort to provide more illuminating analysis

of contemporary methodological controversies, see Ian Shapiro, Rogers M. Smith, and Tarek E. Masoud, eds., *Problems and Methods in the Study of Politics* (New York: Cambridge University Press, 2004).

5. Rogers Smith, "Should We Make Political Science More About Science or More about Politics?" *PS: Political Science & Politics* 35 (June 2002): 200. Emphasis in original.

6. Russell Hardin, "Whither Political Science?" *PS: Political Science & Politics* 35 (June 2002): 185.

7. See Susan Hoeber Randolph, "In Defense of Diverse Forms of Knowledge," *PS: Political Science & Politics* 35 (June 2002): 193–195; and Kristen Renwick Monroe, "Interdisciplinary Work and a Search for Shared Scientific Standards," *PS: Political Science & Politics* 35 (June 2002): 203–205.

8. Robert Jervis, "Politics, Political Science, and Specialization," *PS: Political Science & Politics* 35 (June 2002): 187–189.

9. Hardin, "Whither Political Science?" p. 183. Hardin draws this analogy from John Mueller's discussion in *Capitalism, Democracy, and Ralph's Pretty Good Grocery* (Princeton, NJ: Princeton University Press, 1999), pp. 100–104. The analogy is premised on the proposition that in one important sense the state of economic understanding today closely resembles the state of medical knowledge at the start of the twentieth century. That is, just as medical science at the dawn of the past century finally advanced to the point where doctors were more likely to help rather than harm their patients, so has economic science now advanced to the point where economists' advice is "more likely to benefit than to harm national economic performance" (p. 183). John Dryzek, however, correctly observes that Hardin provides "no evidence that the good advice outweighs the bad. His argument boils down to the fact that because economists agree with each other on the desirability of laissez-faire and people listen to them, economists are important, relevant, and right." See Dryzek, "A Pox on Perestroika, A Hex on Hegemony: Toward a Critical Political Science," p. 2. Dryzek is certainly correct in his allegation that Hardin (and Mueller, whose original formulation is not addressed by Dryzek) conflates consensus among professional economists with the truth, value, or rectitude of the principles about which they agree. However, an equally worrisome issue is the very vague, confusing, and potentially misleading way in which the analogy is articulated. In proposing this analogy, Mueller emphasizes that the "substantial consensus" that exists among economists today is one that resides at the level of "broad economic principles." On issues of "nuance and detail," Mueller concedes, economists may often disagree. See Mueller *Capitalism, Democracy, and Ralph's Pretty Good Gro-*

cery, p. 101. Indeed, it is on the basis of this alleged agreement at the level of broad economic principles that Mueller proposes that "in general, economists are now substantially on top of their topic, that they are amassing knowledge in a manner that is generally progressive and cumulative, and that the advice that they render is likely—or more likely than not—to be sound" (p. 103). What is clear, however, is that whatever general agreement may be detected at the level of broad principles often disintegrates at the level of specific policy proposals, which, given Mueller's stipulation that "the 'economists' I am referring to might perhaps be better designated as 'policy economists'—people whose business it is to derive coherent and practical prescriptions from what they take to be the central notions of economic science" (p. 102), is precisely the level at which his claims of consensus and progress are framed. To take one example, in recent and enduring debates regarding tax policy one routinely finds economists editorializing both in defense of and opposition to specific proposals. These antithetical views, moreover, include both sharp disagreements about the overall wisdom of particular proposals and disputes about the likely empirical consequences of them—whether, for example, tax cuts will increase or reduce government revenues. On these issues it is clear that one's answer to the question of whether policy economists' advice is sound or unsound depends in considerable measure on which policy economists one is referring to.

It is also unfortunate that both Hardin and Mueller assert rather than demonstrate that economics is "generally progressive and cumulative," because the claim is not an uncontroversial one. Not only Nobel Prize–winning economists such as Herbert Simon and Wassily Leontief, but also distinguished philosophers of science and economics such as Alexander Rosenberg deny that such a claim can be sustained. Rosenberg, for example, rejects unequivocally the proposition that economics, conceived as either a predictive or policy science (for Rosenberg these two conceptions of science are ineluctably linked; it is, however, less clear how Hardin or Mueller would articulate the relationship between these views), has progressed over the past century. Maintaining that the present research program of economics was established over a century ago (and in its most mathematical incarnation has been in place for at least a half century), Rosenberg concludes that although economics has some predictive power, "the problem is that it does not have enough. And it never seems to acquire any more than it had at the hands of, say, Marshall in the late nineteenth century." See Rosenberg, *Economics—Mathematical Politics or Science of Diminishing Returns?* (Chicago: University of Chicago Press, 1992), p. 67. Even more sharply, Rosenberg writes: "Economics is an inexact science, but there are many such disciplines. The puzzling thing about economics is that it seems no more exact than it ever was. Methodologists have traditionally compared economics to another inexact discipline, meteorology. One thing telling about the comparison is that in our life times, meteorology has made marked improvements in exactness" (p. 112). It goes without saying that Rosenberg's own claims are highly controversial; although many would accept them as truisms, others would reject them as patently false. My aim here is not to resolve the question of whether or in what respects economics has progressed over the past century, but rather to note Hardin's and Mueller's failure to defend vigorously their own claim, which is crucial for sustaining the analogy with medical science. In fact, absent significant evidential support for the view that economics has been "generally progressive and cumulative" during the past century (albeit developing more slowly than medical science), one might propose that a more appropriate analogy would be one that took as its baseline medical science at the start of the twentieth century and economics at the start of the same century. See Mueller, *Capitalism, Democracy, and Ralph's Pretty Good Grocery,* p. 103. That is, since economists and medical researchers have had similar opportunities over the past century to exploit "the development and proliferation of a raft of probing, measuring, and analyzing methods and tools" (p. 102), one might justifiably alter the terms of the analogy and ask: Why has economics in the twentieth century failed to yield the kinds of "spectacular and historically unprecedented" (p. 101) advances that are such familiar and uncontroversial features of medical science during this same period? Why, in short, is there still lively debate about whether economics has "progressed" over the past century, but there is no parallel debate in the field of medical science?

More generally, by failing to take up these sorts of questions, Hardin and Mueller invite the suspicion that the analogy is advanced not because it is especially apt, but because it flatters economists with the promise of advances on par with those of medical science while deferring for another century all efforts to compare what up to the present are quite distinctive developmental trajectories. Moreover, in doing so they effectively evade rather than engage the difficult and important question of whether, as Roger Backhouse puts it, "the enormous homogenization within the mainstream of economic thought" over "the last quarter of the twentieth century" has been wholly beneficial, or instead has impeded understanding of a range of economic questions. See Roger E. Backhouse, *The Ordinary Business of Life: A History of Economics* (Princeton, NJ: Princeton University Press, 2002), p. 313.

10. Elinor Ostrom, "Some Thoughts about Shaking Things Up: Future Directions in Political Science," *PS: Political Science & Politics* 35 (June 2002): 191.

11. Stephen K. White, "Review of *Making Social Science Matter: Why Social Inquiry Fails and How It Can Succeed Again*," *American Political Science Review* 96 (March 2002): 179.

12. Dryzek, "A Pox on Perestroika, A Hex on Hegemony: Toward a Critical Political Science," p. 2. Although Laitin never states explicitly that the Perestroika challenge is more political than methodological in nature, his claim "that mostly we hear a desire for pluralism rather than a defense of best practices," as well his contention that the person who makes the best intellectual "case for a renewed dominance of qualitative and case study work" (Bent Flyvbjerg) is a Danish urban planner unconnected to the Perestroika movement, indicate that Laitin has little regard for the intellectual substance of Perestroikan attacks on the hegemony of formal and statistical analysis. See Laitin, "The Perestroikan Challenge to Political Science," p. 163. Finally, in claiming that "ambitions towards hegemony now seem to present themselves as more straightforwardly political—increasing the degree of one's power in departments and the discipline as a whole—and less connected with universalist ideals of science that presumably could provide some epistemological justification for hegemonic behavior," White also suggests that much of the present "methodological ferment" is at bottom political in character. See Stephen K. White, "The Very Idea of a Critical Social Science: A Pragmatic Turn," in Fred Rush, ed., *The Cambridge Companion to Critical Theory* (New York: Cambridge University Press, 2004), p. 313.

13. Ian Shapiro, "Problems, Methods, and Theories in the Study of Politics, or What's Wrong with Political Science and What to Do about It," *Political Theory* 30 (August 2002): 604. I should emphasize that in one important respect Shapiro's attack on method-driven inquiry converges with arguments advanced by Bourdieu. That is, both writers condemn a fetishization of method and data display that, as Bourdieu puts it, "wrongly identifies science with an exhibitionism of data [and, one might add, methods] and results." See Pierre Bourdieu, "For a Socio-Analysis of Intellectuals: On *Homo Academicus*," *Berkeley Journal of Sociology* 34 (1989): 4.

14. See, for example, Gregory Kasza, "Perestroika: For an Ecumenical Science of Politics," *PS: Political Science & Politics* 34 (September 2001): 597–599; John Mearsheimer, "Methodological Parochialism vs. Methodological Pluralism," paper presented at the 2001 Annual Meeting of the American Political Science Association, San Francisco, CA; Anne Norton, "Perestroika and Political Science," *Clio: Newsletter of Politics and History* 11

(Fall–Winter 2001): 1, 54; Sanford Schram, "Return to Politics: Perestroika and Postparadigmatic Political Science," *Political Theory* 31 (December 2003): 836; and Rogers Smith and David Miller (moderator),
"Colloquy Live: The Perestroika Movement in Political Science," *The
Chronicle of Higher Education,* September 19, 2001, accessed online at
http://chronicle.com/colloquylive/2001/09/perestroika.

15. Smith and Miller, "Colloquy Live: The Perestroika Movement in Political
Science"; and Mearsheimer, "Methodological Parochialism vs. Methodological Pluralism."

16. Although it is beyond the scope of this study to explore at length the
question of why opponents of the Perestroika movement have been so
reticent to scrutinize critically this central demand, it should be noted
that at least one explanation has been advanced. John Dryzek has argued
that philosophical and perhaps tactical considerations sharply limit the
ability and willingness of anti-Perestroika hegemons to undertake a
"*methodological* defense of hegemony." Rightly observing that the present
hegemony consists not of one but of two quite distinctive and not easily
reconciled modes of analysis—rational choice or, more broadly, formal
theory, and various modes of quantitative analysis—Dryzek contends that
"it is not surprising" that abstract "rhetoric on behalf of science, general-
izability of models, systematic empirical knowledge, testable hypotheses,
and the like" have substituted for real methodological argument. He goes
on to propose that "the fact that hegemony has received no methodological defense is probably a good indicator of the fact that it is indefensible." See Dryzek, "A Pox on Perestroika, a Hex on Hegemony: Toward
a Critical Political Science," pp. 3–4.

17. It is important to avoid conflating what I term "nonevaluative pluralism"
with other superficially similar views, such as "perspectivalism." Unlike
the perspectivalist, who insists on the importance of examining phenomena from a variety of different perspectives but does not ground her
view on the premise that all perspectives are equally illuminating, the nonevaluative pluralist purports simultaneously to affirm and suspend judgment on his pluralist convictions.

18. Dryzek, "A Pox on Perestroika, a Hex on Hegemony: Toward a Critical
Political Science," p. 2.

19. Ibid., p. 7.

20. Laitin, "The Perestroikan Challenge to Social Science," p. 163.

21. Ibid.

22. For a spirited response to Laitin's allegations, see Bent Flyvbjerg, "A Perestroikan Straw Man Answers Back: David Laitin and Phronetic Political
Science," *Politics and Society* 32 (September 2004): 389–416.

23. Dryzek, "A Pox on Perestroika, a Hex on Hegemony: Toward a Critical Political Science," p. 3.

24. Ibid., p. 4.

25. In saying this, I do not intend to diminish the significance of the arguments I have advanced throughout this book. Indeed, I have vigorously defended some key commitments of social scientific inquiry, such as the claim that internal understanding of actions and practices is an indispensable part of any adequate social science, and sharply criticized others, such as the covering law model of scientific explanation. My view of social and political inquiry therefore cannot remain indifferent toward rival conceptions that aim either to bypass agents' self-understandings, or to transform political inquiry into a nomological and predictive science. A defense of these commitments, however, does not imply a *comprehensive* attack on either quantitative methods or rational choice research simply because neither of these methods or modes of inquiry is as monolithic as many partisans and critics assume. For example, a number of leading rational choice theorists have themselves now abandoned the covering law model of scientific explanation in favor an approach that emphasizes, as I did in chapters 4 and 5, the identification of causal mechanisms. Thus, Jon Elster, in a statement that could just as easily have been written by Charles Taylor or Clifford Geertz, remarks that "in my view, progress in the social sciences does not lie in the construction of general theories such as historical materialism, Parsonian sociology, or the theory of economic equilibrium. The aim of such theories—to establish general and invariable propositions—is and will always remain an illusory dream." See Jon Elster, *Political Psychology* (New York: Cambridge University Press, 1993), p. 2; and idem, *Nuts and Bolts for the Social Sciences* (New York: Cambridge University Press, 1989), ch. 1. More recently, Stephen White has suggested that this may be the dominant trend among scholars working in the rational choice tradition. Thus, he remarks that "although some proponents of rational choice still seem to be wedded to the grand ideal of a universalist, predictivist social science grounded in the assumption of instrumental rationality, it appears that the center of gravity in this tradition is moving away from such pretensions, towards notions that their models may be valid only in certain restricted domains of behavior, and that other domains may be better explained by different sorts of theories." Later in the same essay, White notes that "these days, rational choice theorists typically delineate their superiority over all sorts of competitors—from those who merely seek correlations in large-N studies to Critical Theorists—with reference to the fact that their explanations are couched in terms of a causal mechanism: strategic calculations on the

part of the actor." See Stephen K. White, "The Very Idea of a Critical Social Science: A Pragmatic Turn," pp. 313, 325.

In a similar vein, it should be clear from my discussion in chapter 5 that one of the most appealing aspects of Pierre Bourdieu's work is his commitment to a form of *"methodological polytheism"* that confounds and challenges the sorts of self-annihilating dualisms that characterize so much debate about the nature of social and political inquiry. Although major studies like *The Logic of Practice, Homo Academicus,* and *The State Nobility* variously draw on and fuse key elements of phenomenology, hermeneutics, pragmatism, realism, poststructuralism, and critical theory, the full range of methods and methodologies employed by Bourdieu is even wider. As Loïc J. D. Waquant remarks in his review of *The State Nobility,* Bourdieu's work judiciously "braids the insights gained by tabular and factorial analyses of survey data, archival accounts of historical trends, nosography, discourse and documentary analysis, field interviews, and ethnographic description." See Loïc J. D. Wacquant, "Reading Bourdieu's 'Capital,' " in Derek Robbins, ed., *Pierre Bourdieu,* vol. 2 (Thousand Oaks, CA: Sage Publications, 2000), p. 235.

26. Charles Taylor, "To Follow a Rule," in Craig Calhoun, Edward LiPuma, and Moishe Postone, eds., *Bourdieu: Critical Perspectives* (Chicago: University of Chicago Press, 1993), p. 53. See also Pierre Bourdieu, *Outline of a Theory of Practice,* trans. Richard Nice (New York: Cambridge University Press, 1977).

27. John Dewey, *The Quest for Certainty: A Study of the Relation of Knowledge and Action* (New York: Perigree Books, 1980).

28. On the concept of "thick description," see Clifford Geertz's canonical essay, "Thick Description: Toward an Interpretive Theory of Culture," in *The Interpretation of Cultures: Selected Essays* (New York: Basic Books, 1973), pp. 3–30.

29. Robert D. Putnam, *Bowling Alone: The Collapse and Revival of American Community* (New York: Simon & Schuster, 2000).

30. See Alexis de Tocqueville, *Democracy in America,* trans. George Lawrence (New York: HarperPerennial, 1988), pp. 690–702. For excellent discussions of the distinctive character and dangers of administrative despotism, see Charles Taylor, "The Dangers of Soft Despotism," in Amitai Etzioni, ed., *The Essential Communitarian Reader* (Lanham, MD: Rowman & Littlefield Publishers, 1998), pp. 47–54; and Sheldon S. Wolin, *Tocqueville between Two Worlds: The Making of a Political and Theoretical Life* (Princeton, NJ: Princeton University Press, 2001).

31. Many scholars have also implicitly or explicitly challenged Tocqueville's thesis. Indeed, one might well contend that for most of the past century

Tocqueville's views have constituted a minority position among scholars of politics and particularly American politics. Not only early élite theorists such as Gaetano Mosca and Robert Michels but also influential writers such as Joseph Schumpeter denied the very possibility that modern industrialized states could simultaneously be democratic and broadly participatory. Similarly, many of the most influential democratic theorists during the decades following World War II, for example, Robert Dahl (in his earlier writings), Giovanni Sartori, and Samuel Huntington, explicitly deny any positive link between civic engagement and the health of democratic societies. Indeed, perhaps the most influential case study of American democracy in action published during the past fifty years, Dahl's *Who Governs?*, explicitly naturalizes nonparticipation, arguing that "instead of seeking to explain why citizens are not interested, concerned, and active, the task is to explain why a few citizens *are*." See Robert A. Dahl, *Who Governs? Democracy and Power in an American City* (New Haven, CT: Yale University Press, 1961), p. 279. In short, the recent scholarly interest in questions about the relationship between civil society and democracy, and Tocqueville's thesis more specifically, is just that. Only in the past few decades has it achieved great prominence within the discipline of American political science.

32. As Alan Ryan has correctly remarked, Putnam is not the only writer in recent years to express Tocquevillian anxieties about "the dissolution of American civil society and the slow erosion of American social capital." What distinguishes Putnam's book from works like Mickey Kaus's *The End of Equality* or Christopher Lasch's *The Revolt of the Elites* is not only his distinctive explanatory framework, but also the volume and variety of evidence that is deployed to document the condition he aims to diagnose. See Alan Ryan, "My Way," *New York Review of Books*, August 10, 2000, p. 47; Mickey Kaus, *The End of Equality* (New York: Basic Books, 1995); and Christopher Lasch, *The Revolt of the Elites and the Betrayal of Democracy* (New York: W. W. Norton & Company, 1995).

33. The now infamous "butterfly ballot" refers to a ballot design in which candidates' names are positioned in two staggered columns (like the wings of a butterfly) on both the left and the right sides of ballot. Next to each candidate's name is an arrow pointing to one of a series of punch holes positioned in a narrow center column, with the punch hole corresponding to each candidate, alternating between candidates whose names appear in the right and left columns. In Palm Beach County, the butterfly ballot listed George W. Bush at the top of the left column, Pat Buchanon at the top of the right column, and Al Gore directly below George W. Bush (in the left column). Along with claims that confusion over the

ballot format caused many voters to unintentionally vote twice and
thereby disqualify their ballots (19,120 PBC ballots for the presidential
race were disqualified due to "overvoting"), the primary complaint was
that voters who intended to vote for Gore saw his name directly below
Bush's and punched the second punch hole, thus inadvertently casting a
vote for Buchanan. As the authors of one article on the controversy explain, "The first valid punch hole (identified on the ballot as #3) is for
Bush, the first candidate on the left-hand side. The second valid punch
hole (identified on the ballot as #4) is for Buchanan, the first candidate
on the right-hand side. On the left, however, the second candidate listed
is Gore, and someone who scanned down the left-hand column without
looking to the right could mistakenly conclude that the first two punch
holes corresponded, respectively, to Bush and Gore. Having made such an
incorrect reading, a Bush voter would still be likely to punch the first
hole, but a Gore voter might mistakenly punch the second and vote for
Buchanan." See Jonathan N. Wand, Kenneth W. Shotts, Jasjeet S. Sekhon,
Walter R. Mebane Jr., Michael C. Herron, and Henry E. Brady, "The Butterfly Did It: The Aberrant Vote for Buchanan in Palm Beach," *American
Political Science Review* 95 (December 2001): 794.

34. Don Van Natta Jr. and Mitchell Moss, "Democratic 'War Room' Tries to
    Oversee the Battle for Florida, to Mixed Results," *New York Times,* No-
    vember 11, 2000, Internet edition. Wand et al. cite reports that Demo-
    cratic Party lawyers eventually collected 10,000 affidavits in which voters
    complained "about some aspect of their election-day experience." See
    Wand et al., "The Butterfly Did It: The Aberrant Vote for Buchanan in
    Palm Beach," p. 793.

35. Bush received 271 electoral votes, one more than the minimum number
    of electoral votes needed to win the national election. Gore received 266
    votes.

36. Robert C. Sinclair, Melvin M. Mark, Sean E. Moore, Carrie A. Lavis, and
    Alexander S. Soldat, "Psychology: An Electoral Butterfly Effect," *Nature*
    408 (December 7, 2000): 666.

37. Wand et al., "The Butterfly Did It: The Aberrant Vote for Buchanan in
    Palm Beach County, Florida," p. 804.

38. Ibid., p. 801.

39. Ibid. It should be noted that in addition to the article cited here, a
    number of other scholars conducted related analyses, many very shortly
    after the election. All that I have located estimated that 2,000–3,000 votes
    intended for Gore were miscast for other candidates, with most estimates
    tending toward the upper rather than lower end of the spectrum. See, for
    example, E. David Klonsky, "How Many Buchanan Votes Were Meant for

Gore?" accessed online at http://www.people.virginia.edu/~edk8e/floridaelection.html; Matthew Rubin, "Statistical Analysis of the Vote in Palm Beach, Florida," accessed online at http://weber.ucsd.edu/~mrubin/florida.htm; Fahim Ahmed, Saad Kamal, and Paul Sommers, "The Fuzzy Math on Butterfly Ballots and the Buchanan Vote," Middlebury College Economics Disussion Paper no. 02–05; and Burt Monroe, "Did Votes Intended for Gore Go to Buchanan? (Version 3.1)," unpublished paper.

40. Wand et al., "The Butterfly Did It: The Aberrant Vote for Buchanan in Palm Beach County," p. 793.

41. Ibid., p. 803.

42. Gabriel A. Almond and Sydney Verba, *The Civic Culture: Political Attitudes and Democracy in Five Nations* (Princeton, NJ: Princeton University Press, 1963). Not only is *The Civic Culture* widely recognized as one of the most influential works in the field of comparative politics, it is also, in the words of Carole Pateman, "perhaps the best known study of political culture." See Carole Pateman, "Political Culture, Political Structure and Political Change," *British Journal of Political Science* 1 (1973): 291.

43. Almond and Verba, *The Civic Culture*, p. vii.

44. In keeping with their empiricist commitments, Almond and Verba define "political culture" exclusively in psychological and individualistic terms, as individuals' "attitudes toward the political system and its various parts, and attitudes toward the role of the self in the system." Ibid., p. 13. The "orientations" that constitute the political culture of a society are in turn disaggregated into a threefold classification consisting of "cognitive orientation," "affective orientation," and "evaluative orientation." Ibid., p. 15.

45. Ibid., p. 474.

46. Robert D. Putnam, *Making Democracy Work: Civic Traditions in Modern Italy* (Princeton, NJ: Princeton University Press, 1993), p. 11.

47. Almond and Verba, *The Civic Culture*, p. vii.

48. Ibid., p. 15.

49. Alasdair MacIntyre, "Is a Science of Comparative Politics Possible?" in *Against the Self-Images of the Age: Essays on Ideology and Philosophy* (Notre Dame, IN: University of Notre Dame Press, 1978), p. 262.

50. Almond and Verba, *The Civic Culture*, p. 475.

51. MacIntyre, "Is a Science of Comparative Politics Possible?" p. 262.

52. Ibid. pp. 262–263.

53. Although both the authors of *The Civic Culture* and MacIntyre direct their attention to the five nations or "national cultures" that are the principal focus of the study's comparative analysis, it is worth noting that discordant conceptions of pride exist not just across cultural boundaries, but also across philosophical, religious, and other boundaries. Both Stoic and

Christian traditions, for example, view feelings and expressions of pride as a moral defect and source of great evil. In both of these traditions it might well be said that pride is nothing to be proud of. This observation suggests a further point that emerges from MacIntyre's Wittgensteinan analysis but is not explicitly taken up by him, namely, that there may be profound problems in assuming, as Almond and Verba do, that countries like the United States, Britain, and Italy have a *single* political or civic culture. As Carole Pateman has pointed out, and as I will discuss shortly, much of Almond and Verba's empirical data suggest otherwise. See Carole Pateman, "*The Civic Culture:* A Philosophic Critique," in *The Disorder of Women: Democracy, Feminism and Political Theory* (Stanford, CA: Stanford University Press, 1989), p. 156.

54. A number of critics have made precisely these sorts of allegations. See, for example, ibid., pp. 142, 149.

55. Ibid., p. 141.

56. Ibid., p. 164.

57. Almond and Verba, *The Civic Culture*, p. 257.

58. Pateman, "*The Civic Culture*: A Philosophic Critique," p. 158.

59. Ibid., p. 156.

60. Ibid.

61. Ibid., p. 158.

62. Ibid.

63. Ibid., p. 493.

64. Pateman, "*The Civic Culture:* A Philosophic Critique," p. 159.

65. See Gianfranco Pasquino, "Review of Adam Przeworski et al., *Democracy and Development: Political Institutions and Well-Being in the World, 1950–1990,*" *West European Politics* 25 (July 2002): 213, 214; Scott Mainwaring, "Review of Adam Przeworski et al., *Democracy and Development: Political Institutions and Well-Being in the World, 1950–1990,*" *Latin American Politics and Society* 43 (Fall 2001): 178; and Michael Coppedge, "Review of Adam Przeworski et al., *Democracy and Development: Political Institutions and Well-Being in the World, 1950–1990,*" *Studies in Comparative International Development* 38 (Spring 2003): 123.

66. See Scott Mainwaring, "Review of Adam Przeworski et al., *Democracy and Development: Political Institutions and Well-Being in the World, 1950–1990,*" p. 179; and Michael Coppedge, "Review of Adam Przeworski et al., *Democracy and Development: Political Institutions and Well-Being in the World, 1950–1990,*" p. 127.

67. Adam Przeworski, Michael E. Alvarez, José Antonio Cheibub, and Fernando Limongi, *Democracy and Development: Political Institutions and Well-Being in the World, 1950–1990* (New York: Cambridge University Press,

2000), p. 14. As the authors explain, all but the first chapter of the book relies on a smaller or " 'short' data base." See ibid., p. 77.

68. Ibid., p. 179.

69. Ibid., p. 13.

70. Ibid., p. 14.

71. Ibid., p. 15. Although the Przeworski et al. claim that their conception of democracy is closer to Dahl's than Schumpeter's—a difference that hinges on a distinction between contestation and competition as the essential features of democracy—their decision to define democracy exclusively in terms of electoral competition is Schumpeterian in both spirit and flesh.

72. Ibid., p. 19.

73. Ibid.

74. Ibid., p. 20.

75. Ibid., p. 27.

76. Ibid., p. 18.

77. On the value of electoral competition, see Ian Shapiro, *The State of Democratic Theory* (Princeton, NJ: Princeton University Press, 2003), pp. 57–64. Given the diversity of interests and aspirations in even the most "homogeneous" polities, as well as the well-documented history of the suppression of dissent and the manufacturing of consent among both political élites and democratic majorities, the widespread absence of political conflict must be understood prima facie as a worrisome phenomenon, one that requires investigation and explanation. This is generally the case even if one is committed to a consensus-based rather than agonistic conception of democracy. All but the most unitary conceptions of consensus-based democracy presume that moral and political conflict is an integral and ineradicable aspect of public life in democratic societies. Consensus is therefore conceived as a regulative ideal of democratic politics rather than a presupposition of such politics.

78. Shapiro, *The State of Democratic Theory*, p. 58.

79. Ibid., p. 14.

80. On this point, see Lisa Wedeen, "Concepts and Commitments in the Study of Democracy," in Ian Shapiro, Rogers Smith, and Tarek Masoud, eds., *Problems and Methods in the Study of Politics* (New York: Cambridge University Press, 2004), pp. 274–306. My discussion of Przeworski et al. draws substantially on Wedeen's analysis.

81. As Hanna Pitkin has remarked, "Operational definitions ultimately are useful only if they come close to real definition; if our operational definition of 'power' is not related to the meaning of 'power' then the results of any study we conduct with it will not yield information about power. And the attempt to redefine familiar terms to make them scientific is

subject to vicissitudes of its own." See Hanna Fenichel Pitkin, *Wittgenstein and Justice: On the Significance of Ludwig Wittgenstein for Social and Political Thought* (Berkeley and Los Angeles: University of California Press, 1972), p. 275.

82. David Held, *Models of Democracy* (Stanford, CA: Stanford University Press, 1987), p. 2.

83. Ibid. My emphasis on the enduring linkage, both historical and theoretical, of democracy with rule of the people is not meant to suggest that the meaning of democracy has remained stable since its entry into the classical Greek lexicon. To the contrary, understandings of both "people" and "rule" have varied widely, which is perhaps one reason why democracy is often held to be an essentially contested concept. For a survey of these shifting meanings, see Russell L. Hanson, "Democracy," in Terence Ball, James Farr, and Russell L. Hanson, eds., *Political Innovation and Conceptual Change* (New York: Cambridge University Press, 1989), pp. 68–89.

84. In saying this I am not denying the obvious fact that many, indeed most, democracies have been highly exclusive. Women; slaves; racial, ethnic, and religious minorities; residents; and the propertyless are just a few of the categories of persons that have been excluded from participation in classical and modern democracies. Nonetheless, what Moses Finley has said about classical Greek democracy can also be said about many modern democracies, namely, that even in those cases where " 'the many' was a minority of the population," the choice between "rule by the few" and "rule by the many" remained a "meaningful" one. This is surely one reason why for most of its history, democracy has been scorned by élites as a dangerous form of politics. See M. I. Finley, *Politics in the Ancient World* (New York: Cambridge University Press, 1983), p. 9. It should perhaps also be added that the tendency among some contemporary scholars to dismiss Athenian democracy on the basis of its exclusivity may reveal less about their commitment to highly inclusive forms of democracy than about their investment in discrediting "stronger" forms of democratic life.

85. Przeworski et al., *Democracy and Development*, pp. 34–36.

86. Ibid., p. 36.

87. Although the authors endorse their minimalist conception of democracy in part on the grounds that one should not, as more substantive conceptions of democracies allegedly do, decide by definitional fiat the meaning of democracy, the logic of their argument is not at all clear. Minimalist definitions are by virtue of their minimalism no more impartial or free of metaphysical presuppositions than other conceptions. On this issue, see Charles Taylor's classic essay, "Neutrality in Political Science," in *Philos-*

ophy and the Human Sciences: Philosophical Papers, vol. 2 (New York: Cambridge University Press, 1985), pp. 58–90.

88. Wedeen, "Concepts and Commitments in the Study of Democracy," pp. 8–9. Although Przeworski et al.'s explicit exclusion of participation from their list of defining characteristics of democracy, as well as their corollary exclusion of activities unrelated to elections from their definition of democratic action, may seem rather surprising, they are consistent with the Schumpeterian legacy that the authors invoke. Schumpeter himself was notoriously critical of "participatory" theories of democracy; indeed, he—like the authors, whose classificatory rules are conspicuously silent about the scope of the electorate in democratic elections—did not regard universal suffrage as a necessary feature of democracy. And unlike contemporary theories of democracy that emphasize the importance of civic action across a wide range of settings, Schumpeter sharply limited the scope of citizen participation, acknowledging voting as the only appropriate outlet of citizen participation. In his view, even letter-writing campaigns were inappropriate outlets of citizen activism, as they were inconsistent with the very concept of leadership.

89. As Wedeen notes, Przeworski et al. are inconsistent in their treatment of at least one of these terms, namely, accountability, claiming it is and is not "a defining feature of democracy." Ibid., p. 278.

90. Ibid., p. 277.

91. Ibid.

92. Ibid, p. 278.

93. It should be emphasized that these definitional disputes are not, in the pejorative sense of the phrase, "merely semantic." In the past few decades, writers from Theodore Lowi to Sheldon Wolin have charged that institutional arrangements in the United States, for example, subvert efforts to constitute legitimate forms of democratic power. Given a constitutional system of checks and balances that enables powerful but narrow interest groups to block even widely supported public initiatives, questions about the adequacy of conceptions of democracy that focus exclusively on questions of electoral contestation are anything but moot.

94. Mainwaring, "Review of Adam Przeworski et al., *Democracy and Development: Political Institutions and Well-Being in the World, 1950–1990,*" p. 179.

95. Wedeen, "Concepts and Commitments in the Study of Democracy," p. 279.

96. On these tendencies in Przeworski et al., see ibid., p. 279. As Wedeen remarks, "*Democracy and Development* occasionally reads as if it were an advertisement for the Anglo–American system—'the yearnings of an ide-

ology seeking repose'—to borrow from Sheldon Wolin's description of John Rawls' theory of liberalism, rather than the disinterested study it purports to be."

97. This example as well as the subsequent analysis of it draw on Joseph Heath, "Ideology, Irrationality, and Collectively Self-Defeating Behavior," *Constellations* 7 (September 2000): 363–371. The example is discussed on pp. 366–368.

98. Ibid., p. 367.

99. Ibid.

100. Ibid.

101. Ibid.

102. Ibid.

103. Charles Taylor, "Formal Theory in Social Science," *Inquiry* 23 (1980): 142.

104. Norman Schofield, "Rational Choice and Political Economy," in Jeffrey Friedman, ed., *The Rational Choice Controversy: Economic Models of Politics Reconsidered* (New Haven, CT: Yale University Press, 1996), p. 190. See also Mancur Olson, "Toward a Unified View of Economics and Other Social Sciences," in James E. Alt and Kenneth Shepsle, eds., *Perspectives on Positive Political Economy* (New York: Cambridge University Press, 1990), pp. 212–247.

105. Roxanne L. Euben, *Enemy in the Mirror: Islamic Fundamentalism and the Limits of Modern Rationalism* (Princeton, NJ: Princeton University Press, 1999), p. 32.

106. Ibid., p. 33. To see more clearly what is missing from or misguided about such accounts of fundamentalism, as well as what might be gained by examining it from a very different methodological perspective, one might consult Euben's book, which employs what she terms a "dialogic model of interpretation."

107. On the concept of the "social imaginary," see Charles Taylor, *Modern Social Imaginaries* (Durham, NC: Duke University Press, 2004). In her discussion, Euben cites more specific features of fundamentalism that lie "outside the purview of the rational actor model," namely, "the role of divine authority in all aspects of human life, the importance of emotion and intuition for religious devotion, [and] the ways in which divine omnipotence is understood *in terms of* the limits of human comprehension." See Euben, *Enemy in the Mirror*, p. 31.

108. Brian Barry, *Sociologists, Economists and Democracy* (Chicago: University of Chicago Press, 1978), p. 33.

109. For additional examples of this phenomenon, see Gordon Tullock's effort to explain why people become revolutionaries by introducing selective in-

centives in the form of an E term, that is, "entertainment value of participation"; Morris Silver's subsequent expansion of Tullock's E term to include "psychic income" and "the individual's sense of duty to class, country, democratic institutions, the law, race, humanity, the rulers, God, or a revolutionary brotherhood as well as his taste for conspiracy, violence, and adventure"; and the still further expansion of the model to include as private, selective incentives feelings of solidarity and the psychological gratification derived from conforming to group norms. See Gordon Tullock, "The Paradox of Revolution," *Public Choice* 11 (1971): 89–99; Morris Silver, "Political Revolution and Repression: An Economic Approach," *Public Choice* 17 (1974): 64–65; and Edward N. Muller and Karl-Dieter Opp, "Rational Choice and Rebellious Collective Action," *American Political Science Review* 80 (June 1986): 474.

110. Amaryta K. Sen, "Rational Fools: A Critique of the Behavioral Foundations of Economic Theory," *Philosophy and Public Affairs* 6 (Summer 1977): 317–344.

111. Ibid., p. 328. Although it is true that not all rational choice theories of politics assume that agents engage in strategies of utility maximization— some theories assume only that agents "satisfice"—they do generally assume that agents act in accordance with their preferences. One of the distinctive features of Sen's conception of counterpreferential choice is that it challenges both of these assumptions.

112. On normative reasoning and expressive rationality, see Alan Ryan, "Problems and Methods in Political Science," in Ian Shapiro, Rogers M. Smith, and Tarek Masoud, eds., *Problems and Methods in the Study of Politics* (New York: Cambridge University Press, 2004), pp. 189–192. For a discussion of altruistic, moral, and social norm guided actions, see Jon Elster, "Rationality, Morality, and Collective Action," *Ethics* 96 (October 1985): 136–155; and idem, *The Cement of Society* (New York: Cambridge University Press, 1989). On identificatory and intrinsic motivations, see Michael Taylor, "When Rationality Fails," in Jeffrey Friedman, ed., *The Rational Choice Controversy: Economic Models of Politics Reconsidered* (New Haven, CT: Yale University Press, 1996), pp. 230–231. On communication and meaning-seeking mechanisms of action, see James Johnson, "Is Talk Really Cheap? Prompting Conversation between Critical Theory and Rational Choice," *American Political Science Review* 87 (March 1993): 74–86; and White, "The Very Idea of a Critical Social Science: A Pragmatist Turn," p. 327.

113. As John Dupré, discussing the field of economics rather than political science, has remarked, "The point . . . is . . . not to discourage economists from attempting to extend their theoretical treatment of markets into . . .

more difficult areas, but rather to note that as the subject matter gets further removed from the central model of perfect competition, the relevance of basic Smithian insights becomes increasingly questionable." See John Dupré, *Human Nature and the Limits of Science* (Oxford: Oxford University Press, 2001), p. 123.

114. Edward Said, *Orientalism* (New York: Vintage Books, 1979).

115. In this respect I would argue that there is a discernable affinity between the approach I have outlined and recent work in the field of comparative political theory.

116. Ian Hacking, *The Social Construction of What?* (Cambridge: Harvard University Press, 1999), p. 105.

117. For an interesting discussion of these looping effects, see Ian Hacking, "The Looping Effects of Human Kinds," in Dan Sperber, David Premack, and Ann James Premack, eds., *Causal Cognition: A Multidisciplinary Debate* (New York: Oxford University Press, 1995), pp. 351–383.

118. Robert H. Frank, Thomas Gilovich, and Dennis T. Regan, "Does Studying Economics Inhibit Cooperation?" *Journal of Economic Perspectives* 7 (Spring 1993): 159.

119. Ibid., p. 162.

120. Ibid., pp. 159–161, 163–167.

121. Ibid., p. 169.

122. Ibid., p. 167–168.

123. Ibid., p. 170.

124. Ibid.

125. It is important to note that although "the belief that individuals pursue their self-interest" is typically characterized as "the key assumption of the rational actor theory" (Kristen Monroe, "The Theory of Rational Action: Its Origins and Usefulness for Political Sciences," in Kristen Renwick Monroe, ed., *The Economic Approach to Politics: A Critical Reassessment of the Theory of Rational Action* [New York: HarperCollins Publishers, 1991], p. 7), some rational choice theorists do include altruistic and other seemingly non-self-interested, nonegoistic motives as goals and preferences to be modeled. By definition, these "thin-rational" theories have a broader view of human motivation than "thick-rational accounts" in which "the analyst posits not only rationality but some additional description of agent preferences and beliefs" (John Ferejohn, "Rationality and Interpretation: Parliamentary Elections in Early Stuart England," in ibid., p. 282). There is, however, controversy not only among the critics of rational actor theories but also among rational actor theorists themselves regarding the status of thin-rational theories, particularly their allegedly tautological character. Perhaps more to the point, even those who defend thin-

rational theories tend to view them as second-best options to be invoked only when thick-rational accounts fail. For a discussion of the controversies surrounding thin-rational accounts, see Donald P. Green and Ian Shapiro, *Pathologies of Rational Choice Theory: A Critique of Application in Political Science* (New Haven, CT: Yale University Press, 1994), pp. 17–19.

Index

Abraham, Max, 45–46
Actual, domain of, 121–122, 128
Agency, 14, 35, 95, 125, 157, 172, 214, 229n50
Almond, Gabriel, 78, 196–198, 200, 206, 305n44
Althusser, Louis, 160
American Political Science Association, 6, 182, 244n65
Anscombe, G.E.M., 138
Anti-essentialism, 27, 58, 66
Anti-foundationalism, 15, 22, 172
Anti-naturalism, 115, 128, 135, 270n91; and language, 151, 153, 154
Antiscience, 5, 56, 115, 153–154, 155, 180, 215, 283n165
Archer, Margaret, 108
Arendt, Hannah, 15; on public speech, 173–174, 180; on power, 174; on violence, 177
Aristotle, 37, 42, 133, 173, 234n95, 243n61, 262n20
Ashcraft, Richard, 77

Barry, Brian, 211
Baudrillard, Jean, 172
Behavioralism, 63, 71, 78, 84, 126, 142, 160, 244n65, 249n87, 285n15
Beliefs, as objects of social science inquiry, 131, 268n83
Berlin, Isaiah, 88
Bernstein, Richard, 28

Bhaskar, Roy, 13, 15, 98, 108, 125, 154, 258n10, 261n19, 266n76, 267n83, 279n142, 281n147; on critical realism, 16–17, 29, 112, 114, 115, 116, 127, 131, 133–134, 143; on explanatory critique, 17, 131–132; on natural science, 30, 110, 111, 114, 128, 129, 130, 134–136, 155, 271n96; on ontology, 109, 114, 120, 121, 126–128, 130, 134, 145, 154, 263n31, 271n96, 272n103; on causality, 109, 114, 120, 122, 123, 135–138, 145, 152, 155, 267n83, 277n133; on human emancipation, 110, 113, 117, 125, 133–134, 155; and hermeneutics, 113–115, 134–155, 268n92, 270n92, 271n96, 272n104, 277n133, 280n147; on the role of philosophical reflection, 116–117; on philosophy as underlaborer, 117, 262nn21,23; appropriation of Kant's style of transcendental argument, 117–122; on transitive and intransitive objects of knowledge, 119, 125–126; on transfactual causal laws, 120, 264n45; on transdiction, 123, 143, 274n111; and qualified naturalism, 128–132, 153–154; on ontological limits of naturalism, 128–129; on epistemological limits of naturalism, 130; on relational limits of naturalism, 130–131, 266n76; criticisms of hermeneutics, 132, 134–135, 137–138, 145–147, 148, 150–152, 153–154, 262n20, 265n49, 277n133, 281n149

315